Computer Communications and Networks

Series editor
Prof. A.J. Sammes
Cyber Security Centre
Faculty of Technology
De Montfort University
Leicester, UK

The **Computer Communications and Networks** series is a range of textbooks, monographs and handbooks. It sets out to provide students, researchers, and non-specialists alike with a sure grounding in current knowledge, together with comprehensible access to the latest developments in computer communications and networking.

Emphasis is placed on clear and explanatory styles that support a tutorial approach, so that even the most complex of topics is presented in a lucid and intelligible manner.

More information about this series at http://www.springer.com/series/4198

Shao Ying Zhu • Sandra Scott-Hayward
Ludovic Jacquin • Richard Hill
Editors

Guide to Security in SDN and NFV

Challenges, Opportunities, and Applications

Springer

Editors
Shao Ying Zhu
University of Derby
Derby, UK

Sandra Scott-Hayward
Queen's University Belfast
Belfast, UK

Ludovic Jacquin
Hewlett Packard Labs
Bristol, UK

Richard Hill
University of Huddersfield
Huddersfield, UK

ISSN 1617-7975   ISSN 2197-8433   (electronic)
Computer Communications and Networks
ISBN 978-3-319-87844-7   ISBN 978-3-319-64653-4   (eBook)
DOI 10.1007/978-3-319-64653-4

Foreword

When I joined the Open Networking Foundation on its launch day in 2011, I enjoyed nearly a full year of unbridled excitement at how SDN would transform the networking industry (the promise that had (finally) convinced me to return to the networking industry) before the topic of security barged in on my reverie. I had just finished what I thought were some inspiring remarks at a conference in Germany when a reporter confronted me with the assertion that the SDN controller would be a single point of failure and an obvious target for cybercriminals. "Now they can take down the entire network by hacking one box", he contended. That same month I sat in the audience for a seminar at the RSA Conference in San Francisco on the subject of SDN security led by Roy Chua and Matt Palmer of what is now SDxCentral. Every talk related to the topic of SDN's vulnerabilities. A month later I had my first (and only) encounter with Vint Cerf (the so-called Father of the Internet for his invention of TCP/IP and now Chief Internet Advocate at Google). Vint was famous and I wanted to meet him, so I asked ONF's Board Chair Urs Hölzle of Google for an introduction. In my private one-hour meeting with Vint, the only subject he wanted to discuss was whether OpenFlow mandated out-of-band signalling (for the security of control flows). Reverie over.

Not long thereafter, Marc Woolward, then of Goldman Sachs and now with vArmour, spearheaded a working group in ONF on security that moved swiftly to require all ONF working groups to include a statement in their charter on the security impacts of their respective projects. This attempt to build in security rather than adding it on after the fact achieved only marginal success due to the inertia of the groups and the lack of expertise in security matters. We did not really get our arms around what SDN security even meant until I witnessed a presentation at the Ethernet Technology Summit by an academic researcher from Northern Ireland (of all places, I remember thinking) who depicted the landscape – in both theoretical and commercial terms – with such clarity that I believed we could systematically tackle the challenge and the controversy of SDN security. That researcher was this volume's editor Sandra Scott-Hayward, who immediately joined ONF as a research associate and led the project to develop threat models that finally enabled us to quantify the issues defining how to make sure an SDN was itself secure. The working group even built some open-source tools (called Project Delta) that went on to win awards.

I do not remember exactly when I realized that the most interesting aspect of SDN security was its ability to provide unprecedented capabilities to assure the security of networks. Consider the routing provided by OpenFlow versus that of Open Shortest Path First (OSPF). With OSPF, autonomous systems (Internet routers) exchange distributed protocols to choose a route (the shortest path) between two IP addresses. All flows – and there could be many, even between your browser and a website – between those two addresses follow the same route, regardless of their individual characteristics. At any given time it's almost impossible to predict or detect, much less control, that route. With OpenFlow, on the other hand, the SDN controller explicitly instructs the switches in its domain to set up specific, known paths from source to destination. Moreover, these paths apply to individual flows, defined by not just IP addresses but also MAC addresses, application identifiers or even user metadata. Network operators may create control programmes (path-selection algorithms) that reflect technical objectives such as minimizing congestion or latency or business objectives such as maximizing network utilization, minimizing energy consumption or guarding profit or assuring security.

When ONF launched, the pesky press in Germany suggested SDN could be a tool for evil network operators to manipulate traffic flows against the public interest. Then at the same conference in Germany I mentioned above, another journalist warned of the emerging regulations for data border control, by which some countries mandated that certain data never flow outside the borders of that country, for reasons of national security and privacy. Here, I seized upon SDN's being the only way to provide data border control. Flows of national interest (or of national residents) follow only those paths that keep them within the borders of the country. Like any tool, SDN can serve noble ends or evil ones, depending on how an operator chooses or a government regulates. Over time we have seen more and more examples of how SDN enhances network security, perhaps most commonly in its rapid isolating of distributed denial of service (DDoS) attacks. As IoT brings the dramatic proliferation of traffic sources on networks of all scales, and mobile edge computing places more computing power near traffic sources, SDN looks to me as the saviour of network security.

This book wisely includes both SDN and NFV; they are not unrelated. Yes, NFV virtualizes network functions (many of them artifacts of hardware-defined networking that will seem archaic in a few years) while SDN separates, both logically and physically, the control and data planes. NFV may operate almost self-contained in a hypervisor environment within a data centre, but in the real world, networks operate with real switching in the network access, aggregation and core sections. Both network operators and their customers (enterprises, governments, small businesses and even consumers) increasingly expect network operation to reflect policies and priorities of their choice. The only way for the control software to convey the desired behaviour to the network elements that implement it is via SDN (whose toolbox contains OpenFlow, Netconf and other communication vehicles).

As the networking industry embraces the advances of modern computing, from distributed systems (such as those that prevent the SDN controller from becoming a single point of failure with any greater likelihood than whatever server gives you your bank balance the next time you check could also fail and take your money with it) to predictive analysis and other elements of AI, we will see more and better choices on how to build and govern networks. Frameworks for orchestration and policy, based on combinations of open-source and proprietary code, will modularize what today are monolithic programmes that lock operators into rigid, single-vendor solutions with little opportunity for operator uniqueness. High-performance chips with DPI will add new granularity to the definition of what constitutes a flow and how to treat it. Microservices architectures will place appropriate computing, storage and connectivity resources at the behest of individual workloads, in a highly time-dynamic fashion.

None of this computing and networking exists to perform security. It exists to support commerce and the social fabric of life. We need security only because more and more valuable portions of our lives depend on information technologies. These technologies fail from a security standpoint because of errors we make in design or operation and because some people deliberately attack them for either profit or the morbid satisfaction of disruption.

It won't be many years before we look back and wonder how in the world we got along without Software Defined Network Function Virtualization (SDNFV). Because it will be so pervasive, we have an obligation to assure its security. This book offers an excellent purview of the challenges, solutions and remaining opportunities to both secure SDNFV and exploit it as a tool to assure network security, perhaps the best tool we have ever found.

Palo Alto Innovation Advisors, Palo Alto, CA, USA   Dan Pitt

Preface

We have been motivated to produce this book through our research work on security in and of software-defined networking (SDN) and network functions virtualization (NFV). One of the editors of the book has been directly involved with the Open Networking Foundation (ONF), acting as Vice-Chair of the Security Working Group. A second editor has been engaged with the security programme of ETSI NFV and the IRTF SDN Research Group. Our observation through this work and the academic and industry research communities is that there is a necessity to broaden awareness of the importance of security in the design, development and deployment of SDN- and NFV-based systems, as well as to understand how current security mechanisms can be applied, either directly or with modification in the SDNFV context.

Since the beginning of the SDN/NFV security discussion, there has been an obvious split between, on the one hand, consideration of security challenges introduced by the new SDN architecture and the virtualization of network functions and, on the other hand, the potential benefits to securing the network with the technologies of SDN and NFV. Over a number of years, it has become clear that these technologies will be fundamental to the evolution of future networks.

From these aspects of SDNFV security, three sections of the book have naturally emerged. Part I introduces the key concepts of security in SDNFV. Part II presents a series of SDNFV-based network security solutions, and Part III covers the application of SDNFV security in future networks.

In Part I, we begin with Hoang and Farahmandian's introduction to the security challenges of SDN, NFV and cloud computing. In this chapter, they bring together these three interlinked technologies for a survey of the security of the integrated software infrastructure and conclude with a conceptual software-defined security service architecture. In Chap. 2, Faynberg and Goeringer discuss NFV security with a detailed reflection on the work of the ETSI NFV Security Working Group and the industry view it has formulated since its foundation in 2012. This chapter presents a comprehensive, tutorial-style description of NFV security. Much work on SDNFV security targets either SDN or NFV security separately. In Chap. 3, Murillo et al. present a survey of the proposals to secure SDN/NFV platforms and the challenges for their integration. Chavers et al. present a comprehensive overview of the use of root-of-trust services to secure NFV and Lioy et al. propose a solution to evaluate trust by exploiting remote attestation. Together, the chapters of Part I cover the key concepts in SDNFV security, providing a baseline for exploring the solutions presented in subsequent chapters.

The focus of Part II is to present some specific SDNFV security solutions. In Chap. 5, Pastor and Folgueira describe the process of implementing a virtual home gateway with real residential broadband customers and the practical experience of the security design requirements to do this. Cox et al. present a security policy transition framework for SDN tackling the real issue of revoking or updating policy enforcements following a client resolution of the network policy violation. In Chap. 7, Ali et al. demonstrate the potential for the combined power of SDN and NFV to offer network-wide security in virtualized ICT environments. Their solution is an SDNFV-based DDoS detection and remediation framework. In the final chapter of Part II, Attak et al. present the work of the EU-funded SHIELD project, securing against intruders and other threats through a NFV-enabled environment. SHIELD aims at combining flexible and dynamic security monitoring with big-data analytics to detect threats at the network-wide level.

With Part III, the security implications of SDNFV in evolving and future networks are considered. The section begins with a look at Industry 4.0. Khondoker et al. investigate the use of SDN tools and technologies to protect Industry 4.0 machines and components from network-based threats. The ability to fulfil the requirements of 5G is recognized to be dependent on SDNFV technologies. In Chap. 11, Santos et al. study the security requirements for multi-operator virtualized network and service orchestration for 5G. The security perspectives of the standards organizations (ITU-T and ETSI) are described and a threat analysis is presented. The improvement of security in coalition tactical environments is the subject of Chap. 12. Mishra et al. present the Observe, Orient, Decide and Act (OODA) paradigm and how the security of OODA can be enhanced with SDN. Finally, in Chap. 13, Combe et al. propose a monitoring solution for a Named Data Networking (NDN) architecture that builds on the capabilities of SDN and NFV for more efficient security monitoring.

As previously identified, one of the main objectives of publishing this compilation is for this to be an educational tool focussing on this important aspect of network technologies. In support of this, each author has included a number of questions at the end of their chapter to test the reader's understanding of the key concepts introduced in the chapter. The layout of the book is designed with this in mind, beginning with some survey style introductions to security in SDN and NFV and leading on to future network concepts.

We believe that the reader of this book will grasp the large scope of the security challenges and potential in relation to SDNFV systems. In addition, with his/her awareness raised, the reader will be able to develop new security-related mechanisms for SDNFV systems or to design next-generation communication networks more securely, thanks to SDNFV.

Derby, UK   Shao Ying Zhu
Belfast, UK   Sandra Scott-Hayward
Bristol, UK   Ludovic Jacquin
Queensgate, UK   Richard Hill

Acknowledgement

The editors acknowledge the support of the following colleagues during the review and editing phases of this book:

Colin Allison (University of St Andrews)
Marco Anisetti (Università degli Studi di Milano)
Marta Beltran (Universidad Rey Juan Carlos)
Stéphane Betgé-Brezetz (Nokia Bell Labs)
Gergely Biczók (Univ. of Technology and Economics)
Carolina Canales-Valenzuela (Ericsson)
Augusto Ciuffoletti (Università di Pisa)
Emmanuel Dotaro (Thales)
Jordi Ferrer Riera (i2CAT)
Olivier Festor (Inria)
Georgios Gardikis (Space Hellas S.A.)
Bernat Gaston (Fundació Privada I2CAT)
Dimitrios Gkounis (NEC Laboratories Europe)
Doan Hoang (University of Technology, Sydney)
Michail Alexandros Kourtis (NCSR Demokritos)
Bryan Larish (Verizon)
Kahina Lazri (Orange Labs)
Jianxin Li (Beihang University)
Antonio Lioy (Politecnico di Torino)
Diego Lopez (Telefonica I + D)
Linas Maknavicius (NOKIA Bell Labs)
Evangelos Markakis (Technological Education Institute of Crete)
Marie-Paule Odini (Hewlett Packard Enterprise)
Abdelkader Outtagarts (Alcatel-Lucent Bell Labs)
Nicolae Paladi (RISE SICS)
Antonio Pastor (Telefonica I + D)
Dimitrios Pezaros (University of Glasgow)
Fernando Ramos (University of Lisbon)
Sachin Sharma (NEC Laboratories Europe)

Seungwon Shin (Korea Advanced Institute of Science and Technology)
Muhammad-Shuaib Siddiqui (i2CAT)
Eleni Trouva (NCSR Demokritos)
Ziming Zhao (Arizona State University)
Thomas Zinner (University of Wuerzburg)

The editors acknowledge the effort of the authors of the individual chapters without whose work this book would not have been possible.

Shao Ying Zhu, University of Derby, UK
Sandra Scott-Hayward, Queen's University Belfast, UK
Ludovic Jacquin, Hewlett Packard Labs, UK
Richard Hill, University of Huddersfield, UK

Contents

Part I   Introduction to Security in SDNFV – Key Concepts

1   Security of Software-Defined Infrastructures with SDN, NFV, and Cloud Computing Technologies 3
Doan B. Hoang and Sarah Farahmandian

2   NFV Security: Emerging Technologies and Standards 33
Igor Faynberg and Steve Goeringer

3   SDN and NFV Security: Challenges for Integrated Solutions 75
Andrés F. Murillo, Sandra Julieta Rueda, Laura Victoria Morales, and Álvaro A. Cárdenas

4   Trust in SDN/NFV Environments 103
Antonio Lioy, Tao Su, Adrian L. Shaw, Hamza Attak, Diego R. Lopez, and Antonio Pastor

Part II   SDNFV Security Challenges and Network Security Solutions

5   Practical Experience in NFV Security Field: Virtual Home Gateway 127
Antonio Pastor and Jesús Folgueira

6   A Security Policy Transition Framework for Software-Defined Networks 149
Jacob H. Cox Jr., Russell J. Clark, and Henry L. Owen III

7   SDNFV-Based DDoS Detection and Remediation in Multi-tenant, Virtualised Infrastructures 171
Abeer Ali, Richard Cziva, Simon Jouët, and Dimitrios P. Pezaros

8   **SHIELD: Securing Against Intruders and Other Threats
     Through an NFV-Enabled Environment** 197
     Hamza Attak, Marco Casassa-Mont, Cristian Dávila,
     Eleni-Constantina Davri, Carolina Fernandez, Georgios Gardikis,
     Bernat Gastón, Ludovic Jacquin, Antonio Lioy, Antonis Litke,
     Nikolaos K. Papadakis, Dimitris Papadopoulos, Jerónimo Núñez,
     and Eleni Trouva

Part III   Security Implications of SDNFV in Future Networks

9   **Addressing Industry 4.0 Security by Software-Defined
     Networking** 229
     Rahamatullah Khondoker, Pedro Larbig, Dirk Scheuermann,
     Frank Weber, and Kpatcha Bayarou

10   **Security Requirements for Multi-operator Virtualized
     Network and Service Orchestration for 5G** 253
     Mateus Augusto Silva Santos, Alireza Ranjbar, Gergely Biczók,
     Barbara Martini, and Francesco Paolucci

11   **Improving Security in Coalition Tactical Environments Using
     an SDN Approach** 273
     Vinod K. Mishra, Dinesh C. Verma, and Christopher Williams

12   **An SDN and NFV Use Case: NDN Implementation
     and Security Monitoring** 299
     Théo Combe, Wissam Mallouli, Thibault Cholez, Guillaume Doyen,
     Bertrand Mathieu, and Edgardo Montes de Oca

Index 323

Contributors

Abeer Ali School of Computing Science, University of Glasgow, Glasgow, Scotland, UK

Hamza Attak Hewlett Packard Labs, Bristol, UK

Kpatcha Bayarou Fraunhofer Institute for Secure Information Technology (Fraunhofer SIT), Darmstadt, Germany

Gergely Biczók CrySyS Lab, Department of Networked Systems and Services, Budapest University of Technology and Economics, Budapest, Hungary

Álvaro A. Cárdenas Department of Computer Science, UT Dallas, Richardson, TX, USA

Marco Casassa-Mont Hewlett Packard Labs, Bristol, UK

Jesús Folgueira Telefonica I+D, Madrid, Spain

Thibault Cholez INRIA, Rocquencourt, France

Russell J. Clark College of Computing, Georgia Institute of Technology, Atlanta, GA, USA

Théo Combe Thales Services, La Défense, France

Jacob H. Cox Jr School of Electrical and Computer Engineering, Georgia Institute of Technology, Atlanta, GA, USA

Richard Cziva School of Computing Science, University of Glasgow, Glasgow, Scotland, UK

Cristian Dávila Fundació I2CAT, Barcelona, Spain

Eleni-Constantina Davri Orion Innovations P.C., Athens, Greece

Edgardo Montes de Oca Montimage, Paris, France

Guillaume Doyen UTT, Troyes, France

Sarah Farahmandian University of Technology Sydney, Ultimo, NSW, Australia

Igor Faynberg Cable Labs, Louisville, CO, USA

Carolina Fernandez Fundació I2CAT, Barcelona, Spain

Georgios Gardikis Space Hellas S.A., Athina, Greece

Bernat Gaston Fundació I2CAT, Barcelona, Spain

Steve Goeringer Cable Labs, Louisville, CO, USA

Doan B. Hoang University of Technology Sydney, Ultimo, NSW, Australia

Ludovic Jacquin Hewlett Packard Labs, Bristol, UK

Simon Jouët School of Computing Science, University of Glasgow, Glasgow, Scotland, UK

Rahamatullah Khondoker Fraunhofer Institute for Secure Information Technology (Fraunhofer SIT), Darmstadt, Germany

Pedro Larbig Fraunhofer Institute for Secure Information Technology (Fraunhofer SIT), Darmstadt, Germany

Antonio Lioy Dipartimento di Automatica e Informatica, Politecnico di Torino, Torino, Italy

Antonis Litke Infili Technologies PC, Athens, Greece

Diego R. Lopez Telefonica I+D, Seville, Spain

Wissam Mallouli Montimage, Paris, France

Barbara Martini Consorzio Nazionale Interuniversitario per le Telecomunicazioni (CNIT), Pisa, Italy

Bertrand Mathieu Orange, Paris, France

Vinod K. Mishra U.S. Army Research Labs, Aberdeen, MD, USA

Laura Victoria Morales Systems and Computing Engineering Department, Universidad de los Andes, Colombia

Jerónimo Núñez Telefónica I+D, Madrid, Spain

Henry L. Owen III School of Electrical and Computer Engineering, Georgia Institute of Technology, Atlanta, GA, USA

Francesco Paolucci Scuola Superiore Sant'Anna, Pisa, Italy

Nikolaos K. Papadakis Infili Technologies PC, Athens, Greece

Dimitris Papadopoulos Infili Technologies PC, Athens, Greece

Antonio Pastor Telefonica I+D, Madrid, Spain

Dimitrios P. Pezaros School of Computing Science, University of Glasgow, Glasgow, Scotland, UK

Andrés Felipe Murillo Piedrahita Systems and Computing Engineering Department, Universidad de los Andes, Bogotá, Colombia

Alireza Ranjbar Ericsson Research, Finland, Finland

Sandra Julieta Rueda Systems and Computing Engineering Department, Universidad de los Andes, Bogotá, Colombia

Mateus Augusto Silva Santos Ericsson Telecomunicações S/A, Indaiatuba, Brazil

Dirk Scheuermann Fraunhofer Institute for Secure Information Technology (Fraunhofer SIT), Darmstadt, Germany

Adrian L. Shaw Hewlett Packard Enterprise, Bristol, UK

Tao Su Dipartimento di Automatica e Informatica, Politecnico di Torino, Torino, Italy

Eleni Trouva Institute of Informatics and Telecommunications NCSR "Demokritos", Agia Paraskevi, Greece

Dinesh C. Verma IBM T J Watson Research Center, Yorktown Heights, NY, USA

Frank Weber Fraunhofer Institute for Secure Information Technology (Fraunhofer SIT), Darmstadt, Germany

Christopher Williams Defence Science and Technology Laboratories, Salisbury, Wiltshire, UK

About the Editors

Dr. Shao Ying Zhu is a Senior Lecturer in Computing at the University of Derby, UK. She is the programme leader for M.Sc. Advanced Computer Networks and B.Sc. Computer Networks and Security. She has published many peer-reviewed conference and journal papers on a wide range of topics such as image processing, e-learning, computer networks and cloud security. She has edited a number of books for Springer's Computer Communications and Networks series and organised many IEEE workshops on network security subject areas. She has also served as programme committee member for many conferences and reviewer for several international journals.
Email: s.y.zhu@derby.ac.uk

Dr. Sandra Scott-Hayward, CEng, is a Lecturer (Assistant Professor) at Queen's University Belfast. She has experience in both research and industry, having worked as a Systems Engineer and Engineering Group Leader with Airbus before returning to complete her Ph.D. at Queen's University Belfast. In the Centre for Secure Information Technologies at QUB, Sandra leads research and development of network security architectures and security functions for software-defined networks (SDN). She has presented her research globally and has published a series of IEEE papers on performance and security designs for SDN. Sandra is Vice-Chair of the Open Networking Foundation (ONF) Security Working Group and has received Outstanding Technical Contributor and Outstanding Leadership awards from the ONF in 2015 and 2016, respectively.
Email: s.scott-hayward@qub.ac.uk

Dr. Ludovic Jacquin is a Senior Researcher at Hewlett Packard Labs – the research organisation of Hewlett Packard Enterprise – in Bristol, UK. He holds an M.Sc. in Applied Mathematics and Computer Science from ENSIMAG (Grenoble, France) and received his Ph.D. in Computer Science from Grenoble University (France) in 2013. His broader research interest is to develop security mechanisms for computer and network infrastructure, both at the hardware and operating system level. He joined the Security Lab of Hewlett Packard Enterprise in 2014 with a focus on trust and attestation of the network infrastructure in the new paradigm of SDN and

their application to related environments such as NFV. During his Ph.D., he mainly worked on the impact of network signalling protocols on security protocols such as IPsec.
Email: ludo@hpe.com

Professor Richard Hill is Head of the Department of Informatics and Director of the Centre for Industrial Analytics and Design Innovation at the University of Huddersfield. Richard has published widely in the areas of Big Data, predictive analytics, the Internet of Things, and Industry 4.0, and has specific interests in the use of digital technologies to create new value-creation opportunities.
Email: r.hill@hud.ac.uk

Part I

Introduction to Security in SDNFV – Key Concepts

Security of Software-Defined Infrastructures with SDN, NFV, and Cloud Computing Technologies

1

Doan B. Hoang and Sarah Farahmandian

1.1 Introduction

Software-defined networking separates the control plane from the underlying network data plane for both efficient data transport and fine-grained control of network management and services. SDN allows network virtualization and provision of virtual networks on demand. Network functions virtualization is a network architecture concept in which network functions are virtualized, implemented in software, and deployed strategically with the support of a dynamic virtual/physical infrastructure/platform to provide network services.

Cloud computing relies on its aggregation and centralization of virtual resources and their flexible provision and orchestration to provide services to its customers.

Software-defined networks, network functions virtualization platforms, and clouds have established themselves as modern IT service infrastructures. They all rely on the virtualization technology to virtualize and aggregate physical resources into pools of virtual resources (virtual machines, virtual networks, virtual storage, virtual functions, and virtual services) and provision them to users on demand. Security has been recognized as an essential and integral part in the design of systems, infrastructures, organizations, and services; yet, the current state of security research and practice is at best fragmented, local, or case specific. With modern infrastructures that support ever-increasing complex and pervasive applications, such as social networks, Internet of everything, mobile applications, cloud services, new security models, and innovative security, technologies must be invented to match the complexity of emerging applications and the sophistication of their attackers.

D.B. Hoang (✉) • S. Farahmandian
University of Technology Sydney, Ultimo, NSW, Australia
e-mail: Doan.Hoang@uts.edu.au; sarah.farahmandian@student.uts.edu.au

© Springer International Publishing AG 2017
S.Y. Zhu et al. (eds.), *Guide to Security in SDN and NFV*, Computer Communications and Networks, DOI 10.1007/978-3-319-64653-4_1

This chapter discusses the security of those software-defined infrastructures using their paradigms and their underlying technologies: virtualization of network infrastructures, virtualization of virtual machines, network functions, and security functions and services. In particular, it explores security architectures, virtual security elements, and virtual connectivity infrastructures for supporting security goals and services. The chapter is organized as follows. Section 1.2 summarizes the defining characteristics and the common virtualization technology of SDN, NFV, and cloud computing. Section 1.3 provides a summary of major security challenges specific to SDN, NFV, and cloud. Section 1.4 discusses key security challenges and solutions to SDN, NFV, and cloud including virtualization, isolation, and security of identity and access management. Section 1.5 discusses the security of OpenStack, a widely deployed platform for implementing cloud-SDN-NFV infrastructure. Section 1.6 reviews and discusses the development of the new software-defined security approach. Section 1.7 concludes the chapter with some remaining challenges.

1.2   Defining Characteristics of Software-Defined Networking, Network Functions Virtualization, and Cloud Computing

This section provides a brief description of SDN, NFV, and cloud computing and their defining characteristics. Virtualization is described as the common underlying technology, and its security is one of the key security challenges in SDI.

1.2.1   Software-Defined Networking

Software-defined networking has emerged as a networking paradigm that separates the data forwarding plane from the control plane by centralizing the network state and the decision-making capability in the control plane (SDN controller), leaving simple forwarding operation at the data plane (SDN network devices), and abstracting the underlying network infrastructure to the application plane. The separation of the control plane and the data forwarding plane is through a programming interface between the SDN network devices and the SDN controller.

The Open Networking Foundation (ONF) defines a high-level architecture for SDN [3], with three main layers as shown in Fig. 1.1: the application layer for expressing and orchestrating application and network service requirements; the control layer for network control, services provisioning, and management; and the infrastructure layer for abstraction of physical network resources. The infrastructure layer can be expanded into two planes: the physical plane and the virtual plane. The physical resources plane consists of the underlying physical infrastructure, and the virtual resources plane represents the virtual resources abstracted from the physical resources through virtualization.

SDN network devices are all placed at the infrastructure layer. The SDN network devices make a simple decision of what to do with incoming traffic (frames or packets) according to instructions programmed by their SDN controller. The SDN

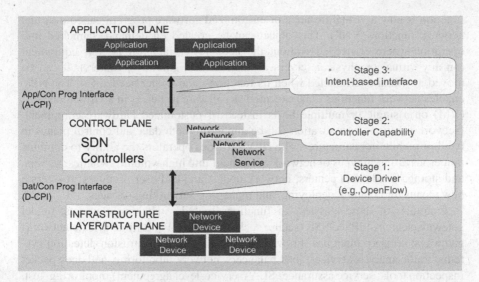

APPLICATION PLANE

Application   Application

Application   Application

Stage 3:
Intent-based interface

App/Con Prog Interface
(A-CPI)

CONTROL PLANE   Network
                        Network
SDN   Network
                            Network
Controllers   Service

Stage 2:
Controller Capability

Stage 1:
Device Driver
(e.g.,OpenFlow)

Dat/Con Prog Interface
(D-CPI)

INFRASTRUCTURE   Network
LAYER/DATA PLANE   Device

Network   Network
Device   Device

Fig. 1.1 Software-defined network architecture

controller (or group of controllers) is located in the control layer. It programs and controls the forwarding behavior of the network devices and presents an abstraction of the underlying network infrastructure to the SDN applications. Applications and network services are on the application layer. The controller allows applications to define traffic flows and paths, with the support of a comprehensive information database of all underlying network infrastructure operations, in terms of common characteristics of packets to satisfy the applications' needs and to respond to dynamic requirements by users and traffic/network conditions [11].

The SDN controller uses interfaces for communicating with other layers. To communicate with the data/infrastructure layer, a southbound interface (SBI) is used for programming and configuring network devices. To communicate with the application layer, a northbound interface (NBI) is provided for the interaction between the SDN controller and applications. The NBI is to describe the needs of the application and to pass along the commands to orchestrate the network. East/west interfaces are for information exchange between multiple or federated controllers. The OpenFlow protocol has been developed and widely adopted as one of the SBIs between SDN controllers and SDN switches. OpenFlow uses a secure channel for message transmission over the Transport Layer Security (TLS) connection.

1.2.2 Network Functions Virtualization

Network functions virtualization (NFV) is proposed aiming to virtualize an entire class of network component functions using virtualization technologies. The objective is to decouple the network functions from the network equipment. A network function is now a virtual instance of customized software program called a virtual network function (VNF). This object can be created on demand, launched into operation wherever needed without the need for installation of new equipment (on any virtual or physical servers at data centers, gateways, routers). It can be moved at will and terminated when its function is no longer needed [2]. The NFV enables network functions to be executed as software instances in a virtual machine (VM) on a single or multiple hosts instead of customized hardware equipment. Network functions virtualization can be applied to both data and control planes in fixed or mobile infrastructures. The NFV provides operators the ability to combine numerous different types of network equipment into high-volume switches, servers, and storage inside data centers, network nodes, and end user premises. It offers a new means for creating, deploying, and managing networking services.

Examples of these classless of functions include switching elements; tunnel gateway elements: IPSec/SSL (secure sockets layer), VPN (virtual private network) gateways; security functions: firewalls, virus scanner, and intrusion detection systems; traffic analysis services: load balancers, network monitoring, and deep packet inspection tools; service assurance: SLA (service-level agreement) monitoring, test, and diagnostics; mobile network elements: multifunction home router, set top boxes, base stations, and the evolved packet core (EPC) network [13].

ETSI provides an NFV reference architecture for a virtualized infrastructure and points of reference to interconnect the different components of the architecture. The NFV architecture has three key components for building a practical network service: network functions virtualization infrastructure (NFVI), VNFs, and NFV management and orchestration (MANO) [8]. Figure 1.2 shows an overall view of NFV architecture adapted from ETSI NFV model.

The NFVI includes hardware and a hypervisor that virtualizes and abstracts the underlying resources. The VNF is the software implementation of a network function which runs over the NFVI. The NFV MANO is responsible for configuring, deploying, and managing the life cycle of VNFs. An important key principle of NFV is service chaining: as each VNF provides limited functionality on its own, service chaining allows combining multiple VNFs to create useful new network functions and services.

1.2.3 Cloud Computing

Cloud computing has become an alternative IT infrastructure where users, infrastructure providers, and service providers all share and deploy resources for their business processes and applications. Business customers are shifting their services and applications to cloud computing since they do not need to invest in their own costly IT infrastructure but can delegate and deploy their services effectively to cloud vendors and service providers [37].

Cloud computing offers an effective solution for provisioning services at lower costs, on demand over the Internet by virtue of its capability of pooling and virtualizing computing resources dynamically. Clients can leverage a cloud to store

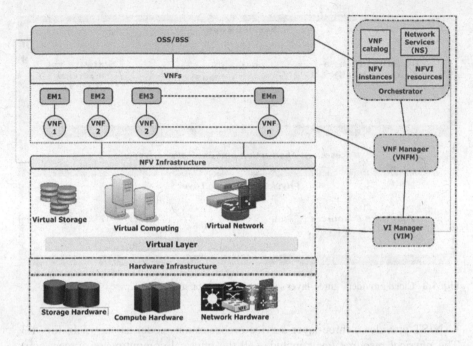

Fig. 1.2 NFV architecture

their documents online, share their information, and consume or operate their services with simple usage, fast access, and low cost on a remote server rather than physically local resources [26].

The most relevant definition is probably the one provided by the National Institute of Standards and Technology (NIST) [17]: "Cloud computing is a model for enabling ubiquitous, convenient, on-demand, network access to a shared pool of configurable computing resources (e.g., networks, servers, storage, applications, and services) that can be rapidly provisioned and released with minimal management effort or service provider interaction." This cloud model is composed of five essential characteristics, three service models, and four deployment models. The five characteristics are on-demand self-service, broad network access, resource pooling, rapid elasticity, and measured service. Software as a service (SaaS), platform as a service (PaaS), and infrastructure as a service (IaaS) constitute the three service models. SaaS directly offers cloud services such as Google Docs, Google Map, Google Health, etc., online to users. With PaaS, developers can order a required development platform, which may consist of SDK (software development kit), documentation, and test environment, to develop their own applications. IaaS is more about packaging and provisioning underlying virtual resources to customers, who then build, orchestrate, provision, and sell tailored infrastructure resources to organizations to support their own businesses.

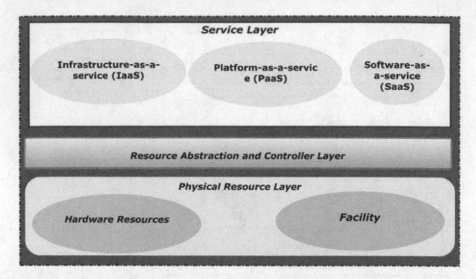

Fig. 1.3 Cloud provider—three-layer service orchestration model

NIST provides a three-layer service orchestration model as shown in Fig. 1.3. The *physical resource layer* includes all the physical computing resources: computers (CPU and memory), networks (routers, firewalls, switches, network links, and interfaces), storage components (hard disks), and other physical computing infrastructure elements. The *resource abstraction and control layer* contains the system components that cloud providers use to provide and manage access to the physical computing resources through software abstraction (virtualization layer). The resource abstraction components include software elements such as hypervisors, virtual machines, virtual data storage, and other computing resource abstractions. The control aspect of this layer refers to the software components that are responsible for resource allocation, access control, and usage monitoring. The *service layer* contains interfaces for cloud consumers to access the computing services.

1.2.4   Virtualization

Virtualization is a key technology for cloud computing, SDN, and NFV. The technology enables network functions virtualization and software-defined network the ability to create a scalable, dynamic, and automated programmable virtual network functions and virtual network infrastructures in integrated cloud platforms such as telecom clouds. Virtualization is the technology that simulates the interface to a physical object by *multiplexing*, *aggregation*, or *emulation*. It is a process that translates hardware into emulated software-based copies. The virtualization simulates the interface to a physical object by several means: with multiplexing, it creates multiple virtual objects from an instance of a physical object; with aggregation, it creates one virtual object from multiple physical objects; and with emulation, it constructs a virtual object from a different type of physical object [16].

On another level, virtualization can be defined as the logical abstraction of assets, such as the hardware platform, operating system (OS), storage devices, network, services, or programming interfaces. More commonly, virtualization is introduced as a software abstraction layer placed between an operating system and the underlying hardware (computing, network, and storage) in the form of a hypervisor. A hypervisor is a small and specialized operating system that runs on a physical server (host machine), allowing physical resources to be partitioned and provisioned as virtual resources (virtual CPU, virtual memory, virtual storage, and virtual networks). On computing resources, a hypervisor creates and manages virtual machines which are isolated instances of the application software and guest OS that run like separate computers. A virtual machine (VM) encapsulates the virtual hardware, the virtual disks, and the metadata associated with the application. In cloud data centers, since the hypervisor manages the hardware resources, multiple virtual machines each with its own operating system and applications and network services can run in parallel in a single hardware device [25]. Figure 1.4 illustrates the virtualization of virtual machines.

Virtualization allows elastic and scalable resource provisioning and sharing among multiple users. The technology allows multi-tenancy in clouds through isolation mechanism and enables each cloud tenant to perform its own services, applications, operating systems, and even network configuration in a logical environment without concerns over the same underlying physical infrastructure. Virtualization results in better server utilization and server/data center consolidation (multiple VMs run within a physical server) and workload isolation (each application on a physical server has its own separate VM).

Virtualization technology has been deployed by enterprises in data centers storage virtualization (NAS (network-attached storage), SAN (storage area network)),

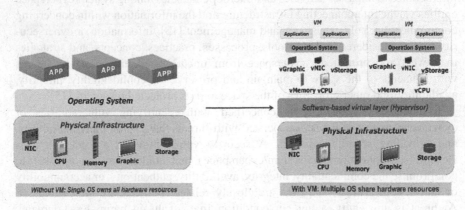

Fig. 1.4 Virtual machines virtualization

database), OS virtualization (VMware, Xen), software or application virtualization (Apache Tomcat, JBoss, Oracle App Server, Web Sphere), and network virtualization [35].

1.3   Security Challenges of NFV, SDN, and Cloud

This section summarizes concepts that are pertinent to our discussion on security issues of SDN, NFV, and cloud. It summarizes their current security challenges.

1.3.1   General Security Requirements and Definitions

For securing an entity/system, it is widely accepted that five essential security functions are required: confidentiality, integrity, availability, authenticity, and accountability (CIAAA). Confidentiality ensures that private and confidential information about data or individuals is not disclosed to unauthorized users. Integrity ensures that information and intended system operation are not tampered with inadvertently or deliberately by unauthorized users. Availability ensures that systems and services are not denied to unauthorized users. Authenticity ensures that users can be verified and trusted as who they claim they are and that inputs arriving at the system came from a trusted source. Accountability generates the requirement for actions of an entity to be traced uniquely to that entity [30].

A system, an organization, or a cyberspace consists of three key elements: *real and virtual entities*, an *interconnecting infrastructure*, and *interactions among entities through the infrastructure*. Real and virtual entities include real things of physical devices such as human beings, computers, sensors, mobile phones, electronic devices, and virtual abstraction of entities such as data/information, software, and services. Infrastructure includes networks, databases, information systems, and storage that interconnect and support entities in the system/space. Interaction encompasses activities and interdependencies among system/cyberspace entities via the interconnecting infrastructure and the information within concerning communication, policy, business, and management [15]. Information or cybersecurity can be considered systems, tools, processes, practices, concepts, and strategies to prevent and protect the cyberspace from unauthorized interaction by agents with elements of the space to maintain and preserve the confidentiality, integrity, availability, and other properties of the space and its protected resources [15].

Essentially, cybersecurity is concerned with identifying vulnerabilities of cyberspace, assessing the risk associated with threats that exploit the vulnerability, and providing security solutions. A security vulnerability is a weakness in a system (component/product/system/cyberspace) that could allow an attacker to compromise the confidentiality, integrity, availability, authenticity, or accountability of that system. Threats and risks are closely related, but they are not equivalent. A threat is any entity, action, or condition that results in harm, loss, damage, and/or a deterioration of existing conditions. The risk associated with a threat is a characteristic that embraces three components: *the impact or importance of a threat incident*, *the likelihood or potential of a future threat incident*, and *the potential loss due to a threat incident*. Evaluating the risk associated with a threat provides the impetus for going forward with security solutions and the requirements for those solutions [36].

1.3.2   NFV Security Challenges

Because network components are virtualized, NFV networks contain a level of abstraction that does not appear in traditional networks. Securing this complex and dynamic environment, that encompasses the virtual/physical resources, the controls/protocols, and the boundaries between the virtual and physical networks, is challenging for many reasons according to CSA [18]:

- *Hypervisor dependencies* Hypervisors are available from many vendors. They must address security vulnerabilities in their software. Understanding the underlying architecture, deploying appropriate types of encryption, and applying patching diligently are all critical for the security of the hypervisors.
- *Elastic network boundaries* In NFV, the network fabric accommodates multiple functions. Physical and virtual boundaries are blurred or nonexistent in NFV architecture, which makes it difficult the design of security systems.
- *Dynamic workloads* While NFV is about agility and dynamic capabilities, traditional security models are static and unable to evolve as network topology changes in response to demand.
- *Service insertion* NFV promises elastic, transparent networks since the fabric intelligently routes packets that meet configurable criteria. Traditional security controls are deployed logically and physically in-line. With NFV, there is often no simple insertion point for security services that are not already layered into the hypervisor.
- *Stateful versus stateless inspection* Security operations during the last decade have been based on the premise that stateful inspection is more advanced and superior to stateless access controls. NFV may add complexity where security controls cannot deal with the asymmetry flows created by multiple, redundant network paths and devices.
- *Scalability of available resources* Deeper inspection technologies—next-generation firewalls and Transport Layer Security decryption, for example—are resource intensive and do not always scale without offload capability.

The ETSI Security Expert Group focuses on the security of the software architecture. It identified potential security vulnerabilities of NFV and established whether they are new problems or just existing problems in different guises [32]. The identified new security concerns resulting from NFV are as shown in Table 1.1.

Table 1.1 Summary of potential areas of concern [32]

Topology validation and enforcement
Availability of management support infrastructure
Secure boot
Secure crash
Performance isolation
User/tenant authentication, authorization, and accounting
Authentication time services
Private keys within cloned images
Backdoors via virtualized test and monitoring functions
Multi-administrator isolation

1.3.3 SDN Security Challenges

SDN introduces a new networking paradigm, and its impact is in the form of a new framework, new components, structural layers, and interfaces. SDN brings with it new security challenges beyond those existed in traditional networks. As SDN decouples the control plane from the data plane, the technology brings with it new sets of components, interfaces, as well as many new security issues. Security challenges in SDN can be divided based on its three layers: *the data plane*, *the control plane*, and *the application plane*. The data plane can suffer from various security threats such as malicious OpenFlow switches, flow rule discovery, flooding attacks (e.g., switch flow table flooding), forged or faked traffic flows, credential management, and insider malicious host. The application plane inherits security challenges such as unauthorized or unauthenticated applications, fraudulent role insertion, lack of authentication methods, and lack of secure provisioning. The control plane faces several security issues related to centralized SDN controller, communication interfaces, policy enforcement, flow rule modification for modifying packets, controller-switch communication flood, system level SDN security challenges (related to lack of auditing accountability mechanisms), and lack of trust between the SDN controller and third-party applications [9]. Since the control plane in the SDN architecture acts as the heart of this virtual network infrastructure, security vulnerabilities on this layer can cause failure to the entire virtual network architecture.

Scott-Hayward et al. presented a comprehensive analysis of the security challenges of SDN [27]. Security challenges associated with the SDN framework by affected layer/interface are categorized as follows:

- *Application Layer* Unauthorized access is through the unauthenticated application. Malicious applications may introduce fraudulent rule insertion. Configuration issues arise from lack of policy enforcement.
- *Control Layer* Unauthorized access can be introduced through unauthorized controller access and unauthenticated application. Data modification is introduced in the form of flow rule modification to modify packets. Malicious applications can

introduce fraudulent rule insertion and controller hijacking. Denial of service (DoS) may occur due to controller-switch communication flood. Configuration issues may arise because of the lack of TLS (or other authentication techniques) adoption or lack of policy enforcement.

- *Data Layer* Unauthorized access may occur with unauthorized controller access. Data leakage may result from flow rule discovery (side-channel attack on input buffer) or forwarding policy discovery (packet processing timing analysis). Data modification is a result of flow rule modifications. Malicious applications may introduce controller hijacking. Denial of service may occur due to controller-switch communication flood or switch flow table flooding. Configuration issues may arise from lack of TLS (or other authentication techniques) adoption.
- *Application-Control Interface* (*NBI—Northbound Interface*) Unauthorized access may occur because of unauthenticated applications. The malicious application may introduce fraudulent rule insertion. Configuration issues may occur due to lack of policy enforcement.
- *Control-Data Interface* (*SBI—Southbound Interface*) Unauthorized access can be introduced through unauthorized controller access. Data modification is introduced in the form of flow rule modifications. Malicious applications can introduce controller hijacking. Denial of service may occur due to controller-switch communication flood. Configuration issues may arise from lack of TLS (or other authentication techniques) adoption.

1.3.4 Cloud Security Challenges

While there are many security concerns in cloud computing, Cloud Security Alliance (CSA) released twelve critical security threats specifically related to the shared, on-demand nature of cloud computing for cloud computing with the highest impact on enterprise business [5]:

1. *Data Breaches* A data breach is an incident in which sensitive, protected, or confidential information is released, viewed, stolen, or used by an individual who is not authorized to do so.
2. *Weak Identity, Credential, and Access Management* Data breaches and enabling of attacks can occur because of a lack of scalable identity access management systems, failure to use multifactor authentication, weak password use, and a lack of continuous automated rotation of cryptographic keys, passwords, and certificates.
3. *Insecure APIs (Application Programming Interface)* Provisioning, management, orchestration, and monitoring are all performed using a set of software user interfaces (UIs) or application programming interfaces. These interfaces must be designed with adequate controls to protect against both accidental and malicious attempts to circumvent policy.

4. *System and Application Vulnerabilities* System vulnerabilities are exploitable bugs in programs that attackers can use to infiltrate a computer system for stealing data, taking control of the system or disrupting service operations.
5. *Account Hijacking* This is a significant threat, and cloud users must be aware of and guard against all methods such as phishing, fraud, and exploitation of software vulnerabilities to steal credentials.
6. *Malicious Insiders* A malicious insider threat to an organization is a current or former employee, contractor, or another business partner who has authorized access to an organization's network, system, or data and intentionally misused that access in a manner that negatively affected the CIAAA of the organization's information system.
7. *Advanced Persistent Threats (APTs)* These are a parasitical form of cyber-attack that infiltrates systems to establish a foothold in the computing infrastructure of target companies from which they smuggle data and intellectual property.
8. *Data Loss* Data stored in the cloud can be lost for reasons other than malicious attacks. An accidental deletion by the cloud service provider or a physical catastrophe such as a fire or earthquake can lead to the permanent loss of customer data.
9. *Insufficient Due Diligence* An organization that rushes to adopt cloud technologies and chooses cloud service providers (CSPs) without performing due diligence exposes itself to a myriad of commercial, financial, technical, legal, and compliance risks.
10. *Abuse and Nefarious Use of Cloud Services* Poorly secured cloud service deployments, free cloud service trials, and fraudulent account sign-ups via payment instrument fraud expose cloud computing models such as IaaS, PaaS, and SaaS to malicious attacks. Malicious actors may leverage cloud computing resources to target users, organizations, or other cloud providers.
11. *Denial of Service (DoS)* Denial-of-service attacks are attacks meant to prevent users of a service from being able to access their data or their applications by forcing the targeted cloud service to consume inordinate amounts of finite system resources so that the service cannot respond to legitimate users.
12. *Shared Technology Issues* Cloud service providers deliver their services by sharing infrastructure, platforms, or applications. The infrastructure supporting cloud services deployment may not have been designed to offer strong isolation properties for a multi-tenant architecture (IaaS), re-deployable platforms (PaaS), or multi-customer applications (SaaS). This can lead to shared technology vulnerabilities that can potentially be exploited in all delivery models.

1.4 Security Challenges and Solutions for Cloud-SDN-NFV Integrated Software Infrastructure

Since virtualization, isolation, and identity and access management (IAM) are the common underlying technologies and techniques for cloud, SDN, and NFV, they are fundamental and critical in term of security to all these infrastructures. We discuss the security aspects and guidance for virtualization, isolation, and identity and access management in this section.

1.4.1 Security of Virtualization

With virtualization, the complete state of an operating system and the instances of the application software together with their associated virtual hardware, disks, and metadata are captured by the VM. This state can be saved in a file, and the file can be copied and shared. Creating a VM reduces ultimately to copying a file. VM is an essential component of the cloud, SDN, and NFV. In SDN, a virtual network is created (virtualized) from the underlying network resources, and its virtual image can be captured by a file. Within this file, VMs exist as network elements (switches, routers, and communication links) of the virtual network. In NFV, a single VM or multiple VMs capture the complete state of a VNF instance which can be recorded as a file.

In the architecture of these infrastructures, a hypervisor is a centerpiece that performs the task of virtualizing resources. Virtualization thus brings with it all the security concerns of the guest operating system, along with new virtualization-specific threats, including hypervisor attacks, inter-VM attacks, inter-virtual network attacks, and inter-virtual function attacks [4].

1.4.1.1 Fundamental Security Issues with Virtualization
This part describes a number of security issues pertaining to virtualization and virtual environments.

Software Life Cycle of Virtual Image Object The traditional assumption is that the software life cycle is sequential on a single line, so management processes progress monotonically along the sequence. However, the virtual execution object model maps to a tree structure rather than a line. At any point in time, multiple instances of the virtualized entity (e.g., VM, VNF) can be created, and then each of them can be updated, different patches installed, and so on. This problem has serious implications for security [16].

The Indefinite Attack in a Virtual Environment Some of the infected VMs, VNs (Virtual Network), and VNFs may be dormant at the system clean up time, and later, they could surface up and infect other systems. This scenario can repeat itself and guarantee that infection will perpetuate indefinitely. In the non-virtual environment, once an infection is detected, the infected systems are quarantined and then cleaned up.

Rollback VM Attack Rollback is a feature that reverts all changes made by a user to a virtual machine when the user logs off from the virtual machine. As the complete state of a VM can be recorded, the feature opens the door for a new type of vulnerability caused by events recorded in the memory of an attacker. The first scenario is that one-time passwords are transmitted in the clear and the protection is not guaranteed if an attacker can replay rolled-back versions and access past sniffed passwords. The second scenario is related to the requirement of some cryptographic protocols regarding the *freshness* of the random-number source used for session keys and nonce. When a VM is rolled back to a state in which a random number has been generated but not yet used, the door is left open for protocol hijacking [16].

Security Risks Posed by Shared Images A user of a public cloud such as Amazon Web Service (AWS) has the option to create an image (Amazon Machine Image, AMI) from a running system, from another image in the image store, or from the image of a VM and copy the contents of the file system to the bundle. Three types of security risks were identified and analyzed: (1) backdoors and leftover credentials, (2) unsolicited connections, and (3) malware. The software vulnerability audit revealed that 98% of the Windows AMIs and 58% of Linux AMIs had critical vulnerabilities [16]. Analysis of these risks is left as an exercise at the end of the chapter.

Hypervisor Security Another critical security issue in virtualized environments is hypervisor vulnerabilities. A hypervisor creates virtual resources (VMs, VNs, and VNFs) inside the SDI and has the ability to monitor each of them. This feature introduces a high security risk in terms of confidentially, integrity, availability, authenticity, and accountability. It may allow an attacker to view, inject, or modify operational state information connected with the SDI through a direct/indirect method, and as a result, the attacker is able to read/write contents of resources such as memory, storage, and other components of the SDI. Hypervisor hijacking is a type of attacks that allow an adversary to take control of a hypervisor and access all VMs created by that particular hypervisor or other less secure hypervisors in the infrastructure. In the worst case, it may even introduce misconfigurations in SDN controllers when integrated with NFV technology. Furthermore, existing errors or bugs inside a virtual function or a hypervisor may allow an attacker to compromise other virtualized network functions for more serious attacks.

1.4.1.2 Solutions and Guidance

Cloud Security Alliance (CSA Security Guidance V3.0) has produced guidance for critical areas of focus in cloud computing and offered recommendations on the following issues:

- *Virtual machine guest hardening* Proper hardening and protection of a VM instance can be delivered via software in each guest.
- *Hypervisor security* The hypervisor needs to be locked and hardened using best practices. The primary concerns should be the proper management of configuration and operation as well as physical security of the server hosting the hypervisor.
- *Inter-VM attacks and blind spots* VMs may communicate with each other over a hardware backplane, rather than a network, and as a result, standard-network-based security controls are blind to this traffic and cannot perform monitoring or in-line blocking. In-line virtual appliances help to solve this problem.

- *Migration of VMs* An attack scenario could be the migration of a malicious VM in a trusted zone, and with traditional network-based security control, its misbehavior will not be detected. Installing a full set of security tools on each individual machine is another approach to add a layer of protection.
- *Performance concerns* Installing security software for physical servers onto a virtualized server can result in severe degradation in performance. Security software needs to be virtualization-aware.
- *Operational complexity from VM sprawl* The ease at which VM's can be provisioned has led to an increase in the number of requests for VM's in typical enterprises. This creates a larger attack surface and increases the odds of misconfiguration or operator error opening a security hole. Policy-based management and use of a virtualization management framework are critical.
- *Instant-on gaps* A VM can be started and stopped with ease, and this creates a situation where threats can be introduced into the gap when a VM is turned off and when it is restarted, leaving the VM vulnerable. Best practices include network-based security and virtual patching that inspects traffic known attacks before it can get to a newly provisioned or newly started VM.
- *Virtual machine encryption* VMs are vulnerable to theft or modification when they are dormant or running. The solution to this problem is to encrypt VM images at all times, but there are performance concerns.
- *Data comingling* There is concern that different classes of data (or VM's hosting different classes of data) may be intermixed on the same physical machine. *VLAN, firewalls, and IDS/IPS* should be used to ensure VM isolation as a mechanism for supporting mixed model deployments. Data classification and policy-based management can also prevent this.
- *Virtual machine data destruction* When a VM is moved from one physical server to another, enterprises need the assurance that no bits are left behind on the disk that could be recovered by another user or when the disk is de-provisioned. Zeroing memory/storage encryption of all data are solutions to this problem. Encryption keys should be stored on a policy-based key server away from the virtual environment.
- *Virtual machine image tampering* Pre-configured virtual appliances and machine images may be misconfigured or may have been tampered with before you start them.
- *In-motion virtual machines* The unique ability to move VMs from one physical server to another creates complexity for audits and security monitoring. In many cases, VMs can be relocated to another physical server (regardless of geographical location) without creating an alert or trackable audit trail.

1.4.2   Security by Isolation

Isolation is a technique for separating or partitioning different concerns that can be used for both resource management and security purposes. For example, process isolation in the time-sharing operating system is realized with virtual address space, and network isolation in the early network operating system is realized with a firewall. In network management, system management, and service management, isolation is used to identify, detect, and isolate faults, misconfiguration, and performance issues. Security isolation has been a key approach to system and network security. Virtualization has been adopted by the systems community as the technique of choice for providing isolation.

The responsibility of the infrastructure service provider (ISP) is to provide a secure infrastructure that ensures tenant's virtual machines are isolated in a multi-tenancy environment, and the various networks within the infrastructure are isolated from one another. Virtual networks can be one or many networks over which virtual machine traffic flows. Isolation of virtual machines within this network can be enhanced with the use of virtual firewall solutions that set firewall rules at the virtual network controller. Although virtual machines are often marketed as the ultimate security isolation tool, it has been shown that many existing hypervisors contain vulnerabilities that can be exploited. In a multi-tenant environment, *traffic isolation*, *address space isolation*, *performance isolation*, and *control isolation* are often required for different purposes. Traffic isolation prevents any data packets from leaking between tenants. Address space isolation allows the tenants to isolate their network by choosing their end-host IP and media access control (MACs) addresses independently from each other. Control isolation enables the tenants to control and configure their network without affecting other tenants [23].

The design of classical security devices is unable to protect the components of virtualized environments, since the traditional security depends on physical network devices and these devices cannot see the significant security activities inside virtualized environments [12]. Isolation will become an important technique for monitoring virtual security boundaries.

1.4.2.1 Isolation Classification

In this section, we classify different types of isolations and their potential usage:

Tenant Isolation In a cloud configuration, tenants share the same underlying physical infrastructure. Without network isolation, tenants could intentionally or unintentionally consume a large part of the network, intrusively see data on the network that does not belong to them, or invoke breaches such as unauthorized connection monitoring, unmonitored application login attempts, malware propagation, and various *man-in-the-middle* attacks.

Domain Isolation In order to label packets and enforce the isolation policies, it is necessary to determine the domain for each data flow. Each domain is associated with a set of input ports of the edge switches. Since the architecture distinguishes intra-tenant, inter-tenant, and external communications, the controller needs to check to which IP range the destination IP address belongs. There is a separate database table for mapping public IP addresses to the tenants who have been allocated such addresses.

Data Isolation   Customers in fields such as banking or medical records management often have very strong data isolation requirements and may not even consider an application that does not supply each tenant with its own individual database.

VM Isolation   A hypervisor divides the host hardware resources among multiple VMs. It coordinates all accesses by VMs to the underlying hardware resources and thus provides the necessary isolation between the virtual machines. In other words, VMs can share the physical resources of a single computer and remain completely isolated from each other as if they were in separated physical machines [33].

Traffic Isolation in Hypervisor-Based Environments   Network traffic isolation is through the creation of segmented networks. In physical network isolation, network interface cards will be dedicated to a specific application or group of applications, and thus physical segmentation is provided between networks. In logical/virtual network isolation, software such as VLAN or network interface virtualization is used. Each interface is assigned a unique IP and MAC address; thus, each is logically distinct. The VLAN tagging can be defined in the host server to isolate network traffic further. Traffic for multiple applications share the same physical interfaces, but each application sees only the network traffic and resources assigned to it and cannot see traffic or resources assigned to other applications.

Traffic Isolation in Zones-Based Environments   Similar to hypervisor-based virtualization, when a zone is provisioned, one or more network interfaces are presented, and the IP stack is enabled. The IP and MAC addresses are configured on the logical interface. Routing policies and network security can be hardened in these zones when the zones are provisioned.

Network Isolation   Any isolated virtual network can be made up of workloads distributed anywhere in the data center. Workloads in the same virtual network can reside on the same or separate hypervisors. Additionally, workloads in several multiple isolated virtual networks can reside on the same hypervisor. Virtual networks are also isolated from the underlying physical infrastructure. Because traffic between hypervisors is encapsulated, physical network devices operate in an entirely different address space than the workloads connected to the virtual networks.

Network Segmentation   Network isolation is between discrete entities. Network segmentation applies to homogeneous entities, e.g., protection within a group. Traditionally, network segmentation is a function of a physical firewall or router, designed to allow or deny traffic between network segments or tiers. For example, segmenting traffic between a web tier, application tier, and database tier. In a virtual network, network services that are provisioned with a workload are programmatically created and distributed to the hypervisor vSwitch. Network services, including L3 segmentation and firewalling, are enforced at the virtual interface.

1.4.2.2 Standard Network Security Solutions by Isolation

With compliance and regulatory requirements, network isolation along with network security has become essential elements of any service infrastructure deployment. The technology used for network traffic isolation does not always cover issues with security breaches that stem from external networks, side-channel attacks, or regulatory concerns between tenants. Network security is built on top of network isolated traffic. Standard security solutions include:

* *Network Firewalls*: Firewalls are often situated at the edges of networks to filter potential security threats coming from untrusted sources. Network firewalls may be hardware devices, software such as soft switches, or a combination of both.
* *LAN Tagging*: Tagging allows multiple logically separated networks (VLANs) to use the same physical medium. Thus, two separate VLANs cannot communicate with each other. VLAN configurations are performed at the switch and define the mapping between VLANs and ports. Packets sent by a virtual network interface on a VLAN cannot be seen by virtual interfaces on other VLANs, and broadcast and multicast packets sent from a virtual network interface on a VLAN will be distributed only to the network interfaces on the same VLAN.
* *Role-Based Security*: On the client side, the user devices must have hardened user authentication. On the database server side, role-based security, or role-based access control (RBAC), needs to be employed.

1.4.3 Security of Identity and Access Management

Identity and access management (IAM) is considered as one of the most critical and challenging security concerns in both physical and virtual infrastructure. The identity and access management concentrates on authentication, authorization, and administration of identities. The major concerns in IAM are related to identity verification of each entity, granting a correct level of access to cloud resources, policy managements, and role-based access controls. IAM architectures are more complex and different in cloud infrastructure in comparison to traditional IAMs since they have to deal with virtual functions and their dynamic changes. The aim of IAM is to prevent unauthorized access to physical and virtual resources as this can jeopardize the reliability, integrity, confidentiality, and availability of user's services and data. Security challenges such as identity theft, phishing, unauthorized access, and data tampering are associated with a weak identity authentication and access control mechanisms in cloud infrastructure. Identity management authenticates identification for individual entities like tenants or services by keeping their privacy from one another. Access control deals with authorization and policies to ensure only authorized entity has permission to access services [14]. The NFV technology brings further complexity in designing IAM architectures as components are virtualized and capable of changing dynamically within the infrastructure. Providing a dynamic and on-demand IAM architecture that can protect cloud against known and unknown attacks is one of biggest security challenges.

Cloud services are accessible through various types of virtual devices and applications with different privileges and authentication methods. Each cloud application can transmit user data and credentials with different policies (encrypted or un-encrypted), and this process can expose a serious vulnerability for man-in-the-middle attack [10].

Usernames and passwords have always been used as a long-time mechanism for authentication. However, vulnerabilities such as weak password policies, nonrotational password, and shared password among different cloud users and resources can expose sensitive information to attackers. There are different types of attacks exploiting vulnerabilities of IAM mechanisms to disclosure cloud tenant's data and information such as [10]:

Phishing Attack The aim is to collect cloud customer information such as their login credentials and credit card numbers, social numbers, etc. The attackers are launching their attacks by exploiting vulnerabilities in IAM methods that have no support for user-centricity, weak password policy, and weak web application controls.

Side-Channel Attack Since multi-tenancy and virtualization enable resource sharing among tenants (trusted/untrusted), cloud infrastructure could be a target of side-channel attacks such as time and bandwidth monitoring attacks. This kind of attacks occurs as a result of weak and improper distributed and structured access control architectures. The attacker can collocate its malicious VM and perform a side-channel attack and leak sensitive information relevant to cloud service provider or hypervisor that hosting targeted VM. This type of attacks can bypass access control policies of either the hypervisor or VM's guest OS, and access through shared resources belongs to another VM in the same platform [10].

Data Tampering Attack in Cloud This type of attacks is referred as unauthorized data modification related to identification of cloud service customer in an identity data store within the cloud. The attack can target existing cloud resources and services. It happens due to loopholes and misconfiguration of access control methods inside the cloud infrastructure.

Identity Forgery/Spoofing Attack Lack of multifactor authentication and improper access control method can lead to unauthorized copying or modification of identity tokens or credentials issued from cloud providers or trusted cloud authorities. Furthermore, this kind of attacks helps attackers in committing fraud and identity theft.

To prevent those threats, IAM mechanisms must be placed in each of the following layers [14]:

- *System layer* Only users with acceptably defined policy rules can access hosts or systems in cloud environment.

- *Application layer* Accessibility to any cloud application or its functions must be governed by access control rules, and access is only permitted after confirming the identity of cloud user.
- *Network layer* Since the cloud is a multi-tenancy architecture, it is critical that tenants be unable to see any portion of the network and its underlying systems in the cloud network unless access policies allow them.
- *Process layer* The way a user can use or run functions and processes of a cloud application should be strictly defined based on access control rules and policies.

1.5   Case Study: Security of OpenStack Platform

OpenStack is known as an IaaS cloud platform based on sharing storage, compute, and network resources. OpenStack is a collection of open-source technology projects with various functional components. OpenStack is an example of an integrated software-defined infrastructure involving ETSI NFV architecture framework, SDN network infrastructure, and cloud IaaS. It provides an automated infrastructure for cloud users. The OpenStack uses SDN technology to generate automated network infrastructure, NFV to create VNFs, and cloud to orchestrate and manage services. It is an IaaS cloud solution based on the integration of numerous services that interact through a set of OpenStack APIs, which is available to all cloud users. OpenStack consists of several main components; each represents a specific task within the OpenStack infrastructure. Figure 1.5 shows an overview of OpenStack with its main components [21].

The fundamental components of OpenStack are known as compute (Nova), network (Neutron), block storage (Cinder), object storage (Swift), identification (Keystone), image (Glance), dashboard (Horizon), and orchestration (Heat).

1.5.1   Security Challenges and Threats in OpenStack

As a cloud infrastructure platform, integrated with SDN and NFV technologies, OpenStack inherits all traditional security issues for cloud as well as issues introduced by SDN and network functions virtualization discussed earlier in the chapter. In this section, we present major security challenges in OpenStack and their recommended solutions.

Hypervisor Security Nova is responsible for the management of virtual machines through a virtual layer supported by various types of hypervisors. This OpenStack multi-hypervisor is prone to security challenges related to hypervisor security. Another major hypervisor security issue in Nova is related to compatibility and trust relation between different types of hypervisors and their configuration from different vendors.

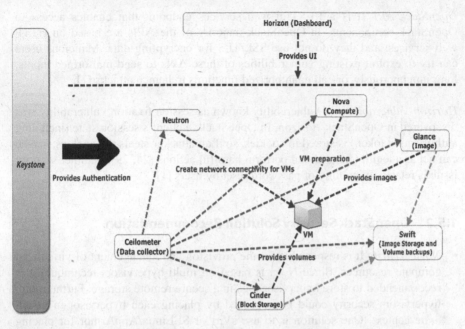

Fig. 1.5 Overall picture of OpenStack components and their relation

Neutron Vulnerability According to the CVE (*Common Vulnerabilities and Exposures*) list, one of the security issues of OpenStack Neutron is related to existing vulnerabilities of IPtables firewalls. This vulnerability enables attackers to bypass deliberate MAC- and DHCP-spoofing security mechanisms. Neutron can be a victim of denial-of-service (DoS) attack as a result of abnormal Dynamic Host Configuration Protocol (DHCP) discovery messages or non-IP traffic. The attacker can exploit software vulnerabilities within Neutron virtual machine and launch a DoS attack.

Identity Service It is one of the most critical components of the OpenStack architecture that is responsible for the authentication and authorization of users and component in OpenStack. It keeps records of policies and roles of users and tenants of the infrastructure. Keystone/identity service is known as the identity management component of OpenStack. OpenStack components will access their required information through a REST API. It also permits various access control methods such as username and password, token-based systems, and role-based methods. Keystone uses two authentication methods which are based on UUID (universally unique identifier) and standard PKI (public key infrastructure) token. Keystone can be targeted for denial of services, reply attacks, and information disclosure attacks if an attacker is able to bypass defined access control policies and gains access through user credential when sending username and password in a clear-text format or storing them in keystone logs. Since it is only based on tokens, an attacker can gain user's privilege by compromising the user token [6].

OpenStack API It is a RESTful web services endpoint that enables access to OpenStack components. In OpenStack majority of the APIs are based on HTTP web services, and they do not use SSL/TLS for encrypting data. Malicious users can try to exploit existing vulnerabilities of these APIs to send malformed inputs, long input porously, or call unauthorized functions to launch attacks [1].

Horizon Vulnerability A vulnerability known as session fixation vulnerability was discovered in OpenStack Horizon. In OpenStack, a client's session state (including authorization token) is stored in cookies, so if an attacker steals the cookies, he/she can act as a legitimate user and perform harmful actions [24, 29]. Another security issue is related to inability of password reset by users [1].

1.5.2   OpenStack Security Solution Recommendation

- *Nova security* It is responsible for the provision and management of virtualized compute resources. Since Nova is based on multi-hypervisors technique, it is recommended to store hypervisor logs in a secure remote storage. Furthermore, hypervisors security could be improved by placing each hypervisor in a separate context. One solution is to use sVirt or SELinux/AppArmor for placing hypervisors in separate security context. It is recommended to use TLS for any communication between Nova components and other Nova services like Keystone and Glance [31].
- *Neutron security (previous quantum)* This component provides virtual network connectivity and IP addresses for each VM instance within the infrastructure. It is recommended to use an SDN controller that can automate network configuration dynamically such as Juniper Contrail SDN controller or Brocade SDN Controller. To provide isolation in network structure, it is suggested to establish L2 isolation with VLAN segmentation and tunneling using GRE (Generic Routing Encapsulation) or VXLAN (Virtual Extensible LAN) or other protocols. Additionally, to avoid DoS/DDoS attacks, it is useful to apply network resource quotas for existing tenants. OpenStack network security can be achieved by using security groups and firewalls. Security groups mechanism provides traffic security between the east and west traffic (intra-VLAN traffics) and firewalls to protect OpenStack network north to south traffic (inter-VLAN traffic and edge traffic) [31].
- *Keystone security* Because of various limitations in Keystone related to password strength, expiration time, and fail attempt lock down policies, it is recommended to use password policy enforcement or deploy third-party authentication systems such as *LDAP* and *Active Directory*. Due to existing threats like identity theft, information disclosure, and spoofing, it is critical to use two-factor authentication mechanisms. Since Keystone provides token for the authentication and authorization process, it is useful to use Fernet token (based on cryptographic authentication method using symmetric key encryption) designed for *REST APIs* instead of standard and less secure tokens [31].

- *Cinder security* This component provides block-level storage to store device images used by Nova for installing a VM instance. Since all images are stored as files inside Cinder, if an attacker can access to those files, he/she can run a malicious instance inside the network. It is critical that only the user with the highest privilege (e.g., root) can have access right to Cinder configuration files [31].

1.6   Integrated Software-Defined Infrastructure Security

SDN, NFV, and cloud all share the *software-defined* concept where physical resources are virtualized into software components. In fact, they share the underlying physical infrastructure and the virtualization layer and require controllers and orchestrators to provision services. Naturally, SDN, NFV, and cloud evolve into an integrated software-defined infrastructure or software-defined system (SDS) for optimizing the use of resources, eliminating the redundancy in their structure, and providing a richer set of services on demand. The security of such an integrated software-defined infrastructure will entail more than just the security issues common to all domains, the security issues specific to each domain, the security gaps among them, and the security of the overall infrastructure. The security architecture of the infrastructure and its own security must be considered. This section elaborates on the software-defined security (SDSec), reviewing its development and describing our SDSec Service—SDS$_2$.

1.6.1   SDSec Concept

Traditional security mechanisms are not able to deal with virtualized environments. The design of classical security devices is unable to protect the components of virtualized environments, since the traditional security depends on physical network devices and these devices cannot see the significant security activities inside virtualized environments [12]. In order to combat security attacks where attackers make use of software to exploit the vulnerabilities of our infrastructures and virtualized agents to attack our infrastructures from anywhere and on multiple fronts instantaneously, we need to deploy the very tools and technologies of the attackers. SDSec is a new approach in designing, deploying, and managing security by separating the forwarding and processing plane from security control plane, similar to the way that SDN abstracts the forwarding plane from control and management plane. Such separation provides a distributed security solution, which scales as VMs by virtualizing the security functions, and provides the ability to manage it as a logical, single system [28]. In SDSec the security hardware appliances such as intrusion detection, firewalling, and others are replaced by software functions (virtual security functions in NFV). Orchestration of security components (virtual security networks and virtual network functions) into security services is the task of an orchestrator in the layer above the controller.

Several products that consider SDSec approach have been developed [7, 12]. Catbird implements a number of features and attributes that distinguish the SDSec approach from traditional security approaches. Catbird consists of two main elements: *Catbird control center* and *a set of virtual machine appliances (VMAs)* implemented as VMs. The system configures a mesh topology, where the Catbird control center is located at the center of the network as the policy enforcement point to manage and distribute the security controls across the connected VMAs. For every virtual switch, there is a Linux-based VMA (virtual memory address) implemented inside it, executing different security tasks through a hypervisor interface [19].

vArmour is another SDSec solution that exploits the benefits of virtualized environments. The architecture of vArmour is like any software-defined system architecture, where the control plane is decoupled from the forwarding plane. The vArmour Distributed Security System consists of a logically centralized controller and multiple autonomous enforcement point appliances connected by an intelligent fabric and constitutes a security (SDSec) service layer to enforce a security rule to a whole data center [20].

vShield is another solution for VMware vCloud. vShield provides the customer the ability to build policy-based groups and establish logical boundary between them. vShield integrates of several components: vShield App and Zones protects the virtual data center applications by creating segmentation between enclaves or silos of workloads. vShield Edge secures the edge of the virtual data center boundary and protects the communication between segmentations. vShield Endpoint offloads antivirus processing. vShield Manger provides a centralized control point to manage all vShield components [34].

1.6.2 Software-Defined Security Service (SDS₂) Architecture

We propose SDS_2 as a SDSec Service that uses cloud virtual resources and can be deployed by cloud provider to protect its integrated infrastructure.

SDS_2 exploits four main concepts: logically centralization of security control, virtualization of security connectivity, security functions virtualization, and orchestration of virtual resources. Applying the NFV concepts for security, virtualization technologies are used to implement virtual security functions (VSFs) on a VM or an industry-standard commodity hardware. These virtual security functions can be created on demand and moved to or instantiated in strategic locations in a software-defined dynamic virtual network environment. Applying the SDN concepts for security, network virtualization is deployed to provision virtual security networks (VSNs) connecting virtual security functions. A logically centralized SDSec controller forms a domain-wide view of the underlying network of virtual security functions. The SDSec controller is able to program, configure, and control the VSFs autonomously. Applying cloud computing concepts for security, physical storage, network, and computing resources are virtualized to accommodate virtual network functions, virtual security networks, and virtual security storage. Cloud platform is used for orchestrating the provisioned security components to provide

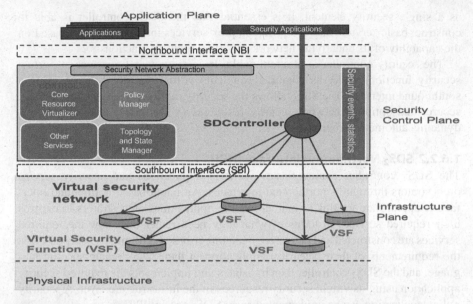

Fig. 1.6 SDS$_2$ architecture

security services for the target cloud infrastructure. The proposed SDS$_2$ architecture is shown in Fig. 1.6. It consists of three separate planes: the security application plane, the security control plane, and the security infrastructure plane or data plane. The SDSec control plane, which includes one or more SDSec controllers, provides an abstraction to build security services over virtual security elements. It is considered as a SDSec network operation system that provides basic security services via interfaces: the southbound interface (SBI) to network devices and the northbound interface (NBI) to security applications.

1.6.2.1 SDS$_2$ Controller

Like an SDN controller, SDS$_2$ controller is the brain of the whole security system, controlling its components and operations. It has a global view of its virtual security network and interconnected virtual security functions. The SDS$_2$ controller is similar to an SDN controller in that it consists of multiple components, but they deal only with security functions and security services. Security policy manager, topology and security state manager, and virtual security functions manager are its main components.

The SDS$_2$ controller has a complete topological graph of the connectivity of its virtual security functions (VSFs), allowing it to construct appropriate responses to attacks in real time. The controller will be able to construct service chaining of VSFs to create new security services to address emerging threats. Security intelligence is logically centralized in the software-based controller that maintains the global view of the security network and hence the global view of the security status of the protected system which appears to the security applications and policy engines as a single security element. It is essential that the SDS$_2$ controller is able to construct basic services and compose complex services into new services based on the capability of its underlying network of virtual security functions.

The security controller is programmable. It configures and manages all virtual security functions under its control through its virtual security network using a southbound interface. The SDS$_2$ allows the security manager to configure, manage, secure, and optimize network security resources (VSNs and VSFs) quickly via dynamic, automated programs.

1.6.2.2 SDS$_2$ Northbound Interface (NBI)
The SDS$_2$ controller communicates with its applications and security service orchestrators through its northbound interfaces. An intent-based northbound interface is appropriate for this as that allows the applications/orchestrators to express their required services in terms of what they need rather than how the required services are constructed and delivered. In an intent-based NBI model, users describe the requirements of their (security) application in their own domain-specific language, and the SDS$_2$ controller then translates and implements the required security application using its virtual security resources in the infrastructure layer. A security policy application can be implemented as an SDS$_2$ service [22].

1.6.2.3 SDS$_2$ Virtual Security Function
This is a security element or function implemented in software and deployed on a virtual resource such as a VM in a physical server (host). This is a generalization of NFV VF that abstracts a physical security appliance and deployed on a commodity server.

A VSF is created to perform a specific security function. It is a software object that can be created, instantiated, and operated on any VM. A VSF is a software entity that has a life cycle starting from the instant when it is created through its operation and then its termination. VSFs can be chained by a service chaining function to create a new security function. It can also be combined with other to create complex security functions. Typical VSFs include firewalls, virus scanners, intrusion detection systems, security gateways, and deep packet inspections. Other functions include policy/rule checkers, security metric meters, etc.

1.6.2.4 SDS$_2$ Southbound Interface (SBI)
OpenFlow and OFConfig can be used to configure SDS$_2$ VSFs, but they may be heavy for security purposes. A simple protocol may be designed to program, configure, and manage VSFs and allow them to report its operational status to the controller. It should be noted that VSFs are not switches or routers; they only perform their defined security functions and relay their data/status to their controller and other VSFs when directed such as in chaining operations.

1.6.2.5 Application of SDS$_2$ to Data Center Security
With the SDSec approach, we are able to design, implement, and modify the individual subsystems independently. A data center is an integrated cloud-SDN-NFV infrastructure whereby entities in it include physical resources (physical

servers, routers, links, storage, and their interfaces), tenants, and their virtual resources (virtual networks, virtual machines, virtual storage, virtual services, and their virtual interfaces).

A common approach to managing system complexity is to identify a set of layers with well-defined interfaces among them. Layering minimizes the interactions among the subsystems and simplifies the description of the subsystems. Security of a system is often achieved by ensuring the integrity of its subsystem and authorized access to the system (subsystems) at their interfaces. A less common approach in system security is through isolation as discussed in Sect. 1.4.2. The security isolation approach can identify not only physical but also virtual boundaries that are missing in traditional security mechanisms. Furthermore, security isolation is effective in localizing security issues and can be tailored to deal with appropriate concerns.

With this in mind, SDS_2 can be implemented and offered as a security service to protect a data center. Depending on the data center, different numbers and types of virtual security functions can be instantiated, dynamic virtual security networks can be provisioned to interconnect those VSFs, and a logically centralized SDS_2 controller can be created on demand to serve the required security service. The provisioned SDS_2 configuration can be attached/imposed on the specified data center as dictated by its policies and architecture. The SDS_2 will enable security isolation through its software-based agents located at critical locations in both physical and virtual layers within the infrastructure under the control of the controller.

1.7   Summary

This chapter discusses the security of software-defined infrastructures with cloud, SDN, NFV, and technologies. It provides a brief description of cloud, SDN, NFV, and virtualization in terms of their defining features and summarizes critical security challenges of these infrastructures. It then discusses the fundamental underlying technologies and techniques (virtualization, isolation, and identity and access management) for software-defined infrastructures, their security issues, and solution guidance. Security OpenStack platform is described as a case study. Finally, the chapter reviews efforts in software-defined security and describes a new software-defined security service solution architecture.

SDSec is a promising research approach in software-defined infrastructure; however, there remain several challenges. SDI requires virtual networks from SDN, virtual network functions from NFV, and computing, storage, and orchestration resources from cloud, but there has not been a standard integrated architecture for SDI, and this presents a huge challenge in designing a sound framework for an SDI security architecture. Cloud, SDN, and NFV each have its own hypervisor in the virtualization layer, controller in the control layer, orchestrator in the application layer, and different protocols/interfaces between layers; this complicates the task of defining virtual boundaries where one can apply security measures to protect the overall infrastructure.

1.8   Questions

Q1. The communication messages between the SDN controller and an OpenFlow switch are transmitted over a secure channel that is implemented via a Transport Layer Security (TLS) connection over TCP.

   (a) What would be security implications if TLS is not used in terms of threats and attacks?
   (b) Consider three examples from widely deployed systems: Transport Layer Security (TLS), Internet Protocol Security (IPsec), and Secure Shell (SSH). The three approaches combine integrity and encryption in three very different ways—the first encrypts the MAC, the second applies MAC to the encryption, and the third uses independent MAC and encryption. But which is right? Are they all secure? Compare and discuss these three constructions. Can TLS be replaced by SSH or IPsec?

Hints: Landwehr, C., Boneh, D., Mitchell, J. C., Bellovin, S. M., Landau, S., Lesk, M. E., "Privacy and Cybersecurity:The Next 100 Years," Proceedings of the IEEE, Vol. 100, May, 2012.

Q2. Identify and analyze the types of security risk posed by shared images. For example, a user of AWS has the option to choose among Amazon Machine Images (AMIs): an AMI created from a running system, from another AMI, or from the image of a stored VM?

Q3. Since security appliances can be virtualized and implemented as software-based (virtual) security components (VSFs) that can be placed in the same virtual machine in an infrastructure, how are these VSFs isolated from one another? Discuss possible solutions.

Q4. One of the difficulties in handling security in current systems is related to defining certain isolation boundaries in both physical and virtual resources/infrastructures. Discuss how isolation can solve security challenges related to physical and virtual boundaries within the cloud infrastructure with integrated SDN and NFV technologies?

Q5. Since software-based VSFs are dynamically created and may migrate to different parts of the infrastructure, how can cloud provider protect their VSFs throughout their life cycle? Does a virtual network of VSFs play a part in their security and how?

References

1. Albaroodi H, Manickam S, Singh P (2014) Critical review of openstack security: issues and weaknesses. J Comp Sci 10(1):23
2. Alliance ODC (2013) Open data center alliance master usage model: software-defined networking rev. 2.0
3. Berde P, Gerola M, Hart J, Higuchi Y, Kobayashi M, Koide T, Lantz B, O'Connor B, Radoslavov P, Snow W (2014) ONOS: towards an open, distributed SDN OS. In: Proceedings of the third workshop on Hot topics in software defined networking, ACM, pp 1–6

4. CSA (2011) Security guidance for critical areas of focus in cloud computing V3.0
5. CSA (2016) CLOUD SECURITY ALLIANCE The Treacherous 12 – Cloud Computing Top Threats
6. Cui B, Xi T (2015) Security analysis of openstack keystone. In: Innovative Mobile and Internet Services in Ubiquitous Computing (IMIS), 2015. In: 9th international conference on, IEEE, pp 283–288
7. Darabseh A, Al-Ayyoub M, Jararweh Y, Benkhelifa E, Vouk M, Rindos A (2015) SDSecurity: a software defined security experimental framework. In: 2015 IEEE International Conference on Communication Workshop (ICCW), 8–12 June 2015. pp 1871–1876
8. ETSI G (2014) 003,"Network Functions Virtualisation (NFV); terminology for main concepts in NFV"
9. Govindarajan K, Meng KC, Ong H A (2013) literature review on software-defined networking (SDN) research topics, challenges and solutions. In: 2013 Fifth International Conference on Advanced Computing (ICoAC), IEEE, pp 293–299
10. Habiba U, Masood R, Shibli MA, Niazi MA (2014) Cloud identity management security issues & solutions: a taxonomy. Complex Adapt Syst Model 2(1):5
11. Hoang D (2015) Software defined networking–shaping up for the next disruptive step? Aust J Telecommun Digital Econ 3(4):48–62
12. Jararweh Y, Al-Ayyoub M, Benkhelifa E, Vouk M, Rindos A (2016) Software defined cloud: survey, system and evaluation. Futur Gener Comput Syst 58:56–74
13. Jim Metzler AMA (2016) The 2016 guide to SDN and NFV – part 4: Network Functions Virtualization (NFV) a status update
14. Kecskemeti G, Kertesz A, Nemeth Z (2016) Developing interoperable and federated cloud architecture. IGI Global, Hershey, pp 1–398
15. Le N, Hoang D (2016) Can maturity models support cyber security? In: The IEEE international workshop on Communication, Computing, and Networking in Cyber Physical Systems (CCN-CPS)
16. Marinescu DC (2013) Cloud computing: theory and practice. Morgan Kaufmann, Newnes
17. Mell P, Grance T (2011) The NIST definition of cloud computing National Institute of Standards and Technology, Gaithersburg
18. Milenkoski A, Jaeger B, Raina K, Harris M, Chaudhry S, Chasiri S, David V, Liu W (2016) Security position paper network function virtualization. Cloud Security Alliance-Virtualization Working Group
19. Networks C (2014) Catbird® 6.0: private cloud security
20. Networks v (2015) vArmour distributed security system: protecting assets in the world without perimeters
21. OpenStack (2015) OpenStack-Networking Guide
22. Pham M, Hoang DB (2016) SDN applications-The intent-based Northbound Interface realisation for extended applications. In: NetSoft Conference and Workshops (NetSoft), 2016 IEEE, pp 372–377
23. Ranjbar A, Antikainen M, Aura T (2015) Domain isolation in a multi-tenant software-defined network. In: 2015 IEEE/ACM 8th international conference on Utility and Cloud Computing (UCC), IEEE, pp 16–25
24. Ristov S, Gusev M, Donevski A (2013) Openstack cloud security vulnerabilities from inside and outside. Cloud Comp :101–107
25. Sahoo J, Mohapatra S, Lath R (2010) Virtualization: a survey on concepts, taxonomy and associated security issues. In: Computer and Network Technology (ICCNT), 2010 Second international conference on, IEEE, pp 222–226
26. Schubert L, Jeffery K (2012) Advances in clouds. Report of the cloud computing expert working group, vol 1. European Commission
27. Scott-Hayward S, Natarajan S, Sezer S (2015) A survey of security in software defined networks. IEEE Commun Surv Tutorials 18(1):623–654

28. SDxCentral   (2017)   SDN   security   challenges   in   SDN   environments.
    https://www.sdxcentral.com/security/definitions/security-challenges-sdn-software-defined-
    networks/
29. Slipetskyy R (2011) Security issues in OpenStack. Master's thesis, Norwegian University of
    Science and Technology
30. Stallings W (2015) Foundations of modern networking: SDN, NFV, QoE, IoT, and cloud.
    Addison-Wesley Professional, Boston
31. Superuser O (2016) OpenStack security, piece by piece
32. Virtualization NF (2014) NFV security problem statement. ETSI NFV-SEC 1
33. Viswanathan A, Neuman B (2009) A survey of isolation techniques. University of Southern
    California, Information Sciences Institute, Los Angeles
34. VMware (2013) VMware vCloud networking and security overview
35. Xing Y, Zhan Y (2012) Virtualization and cloud computing. In: Future wireless networks and
    information systems. Springer, Dordrecht, pp 305–312
36. Young C (2016) Information security science-measuring the vulnerability to data compromises,
    1st edn. Syngress Elsevier, Cambridge, MA
37. Zhou M, Zhang R, Zeng D, Qian W (2010) Services in the cloud computing era: a survey. In:
    Universal Communication Symposium (IUCS), 2010 4th International, IEEE, pp 40–46

Dr. Doan B. Hoang is a Professor in the School of Computing and Communication, Faculty
of Engineering and Information Technology, the University of Technology Sydney (UTS). He
was the Director of iNEXT—UTS Centre for Innovation in IT Services and Applications (2007–
2016). Currently, he is the leader of VICS (Virtualized Infrastructures and Cyber Security) research
lab. He is also a Research Associate and UTS Principal Investigator at the Open Networking
Foundation (ONF). His current research projects include virtual resource optimization, software-
defined (SD) architecture for provisioning IoT applications on demand, SDSecurity services,
security metrics and maturity models for cloud, and trust assessment model for personal space
IoTs and IoTs for assistive healthcare. Professor Hoang has published over 200 research papers.
Before UTS, he was with Basser Department of Computer Science, University of Sydney. He held
various visiting positions: visiting professorships at the University of California, Berkeley; Nortel
Networks Technology Centre in Santa Clara, USA; the University of Waterloo, Canada; Carlos
III University of Madrid, Spain; Nanyang Technological University, Singapore; Lund University,
Sweden; and POSTECH University, South Korea.

Sarah Farahmandian is a Ph.D. student at the University Technology Sydney (UTS). She got her
master's degree on information security, in particular, on securing cloud computing environment
against distributed denial-of-service attacks from the University of Technology Malaysia (UTM).
Her current research focuses on isolation and security in cloud computing, SDN, and NFV. She
published several research papers in these areas.

NFV Security: Emerging Technologies and Standards

2

Igor Faynberg and Steve Goeringer

2.1 Introduction

This chapter addresses the NFV security while reflecting on the work of the ETSI NFV Security Working Group (NFV SEC WG), which has indeed been the key forum in the industry work on the subject since 2011, gathering network operators, major vendors, governments' representatives (primarily regulators and law enforcement agencies), and researchers. Hence the consensus reached in the group *is* the industry view.

The authors feel it is important to communicate this view. At the same time, the authors also state, where appropriate, their opinions and present a vision on how certain technologies have to develop in the future, and when these opinions are stated, it is made clear that these are the opinions rather than standards or established views of the industry.

A few words on the history of the NFV SEC WG. This WG was championed by Don Clarke (then the Head of Research in BT), the man who had spearheaded the NFV Industry Specification Group creation in the first place. The security group started and functioned for the first 2 years as an *expert group*, whose charter was merely exploratory. The main task of the group was to outline the security problems that were *specific* to the NFV (as opposed to generic cloud, whose security problems had been already tackled by a number of organizations—the US National Institute of Standards [NIST] and Cloud Security Alliance [CSA] among them) so as to avoid duplication of effort and thus develop sharp focus on what is specific to the

I. Faynberg (✉) • S. Goeringer
Cable Labs, Louisville, CO 80027, USA
e-mail: i.faynberg@cablelabs.com; s.goeringer@cablelabs.com

© Springer International Publishing AG 2017   33
S.Y. Zhu et al. (eds.), *Guide to Security in SDN and NFV*, Computer
Communications and Networks, DOI 10.1007/978-3-319-64653-4_2

telecommunications industry.[1] In 2015, the NFV SEC WG has become a working group with the charter to develop industry standards.

As it turned out, a set of problems identified in the NFV Security Problem Statement [2] has been comprehensive in that all but one NFV SEC WG's work item has been accepted by the SEC WG to address problems identified in that set. One exception was the study of the OpenStack security [3], which was carried to document the state of the art in the open-source development. (Overall, by the nature of its work, the SEC WG stayed away from abstract models, concentrating instead on specific use cases, available technologies, and operators' requirements.)

The rest of this chapter is as follows:

- Section 2 outlines the main differences between the "generic" cloud and NFV and discusses the security threats as well as new benefits for security provided in the NFV environment;
- Section 3 discusses the problems in the NFV Security Problem Statement and explains how the NFV SEC work items map into these problems;
- Section 4 explains how *trust* is bootstrapped from hardware and established among the execution components, the discussion culminating in the treatment of the subject of remote attestation;
- Section 5 introduces the requirements and architecture for lawful interception in the NFV environment and reports on the results of the NFV Security WG work on the architecture and security controls for sensitive component execution;
- Section 6 is dedicated to security management and monitoring;
- Section 7 introduces the NFV Security WG work on the analysis of the *OpenStack* security;
- Section 8 is the conclusion;
- Acknowledgments; and
- List of references.

2.2   Threats and Opportunities

The first question that needs an answer here is what is specific to the NFV environment in comparison to that provided by the generic cloud computing (as, for example, described in a recent monograph [4]).

In short, the NFV is a "Telco cloud" established for and used by network operators, and here lies the answer: While the generic cloud provides computing services, the NFV is about providing telecommunications services. Of course, with the convergence, the differences between the two types of services are blurring, but there are some essential characteristics that make the telecommunications services distinct.

---

[1]For the history of the initial development of the NFV Security Working Group, see [1].

For one thing, network operators are regulated. This places special requirements on reliability. Even more stringent (and, as we will see, much more challenging to implement in the virtualized environment) are the requirements related to lawful interception. Examples of other stringent regulatory requirements—which differ from country to country—are those related to data retention, personally-identifiable information sharing, and movement of data that are considered private across national or regional borders.

From here, we can see that networking plays as defining role in the NFV as virtualization does. To this end, the development of the NFV is coupled with that of the software-defined network (SDN) technology standardized by the Open Networking Foundation (ONF).

SDN and NFV are independent (but related) technologies that network operators are using to create open distributed network architectures. The transition to this new model of networking is well underway, expanding and extending on lessons learned in data centers.

One limitation of the regulated environment is that network operators have much less control of interconnection options. The consequence is that the open distributed architectures they develop must support multiple-operator interconnectivity, while the solutions must support multiple tenants (often providing infrastructure to other operators as clients). These networks might span continents. The result is a nebulous network with soft perimeters. Providing a comprehensive layered security solution in this environment is quite challenging.

As far as security is concerned, opening up new services is often at cross-purpose with the objective of limiting the threat surface. The nature of network services is such that once a capability that has value is developed, that value is only achieved by opening up access to it. Opening up to address a market or company need inevitably means accepting a risk that another party may exploit this new capability in some way. Introducing security controls necessarily limits how a service or device might be used, which also necessarily decreases its value. In other words, the value of a network is inversely proportional to how secure it is!

Hence security engineers are always seeking balance between addressing a target market with compelling capability and limiting the use of this capability sufficiently so that only reasonable risks remain. The goals, therefore, are to make exploitation expensive (not to eliminate threats altogether) and employ evolvable or upgradeable security controls and methods.

SDN and NFV, in and of themselves, are only contributing technologies to how networks are evolving. Open distributed networks also integrate ideas from development operations (DevOps), software repository and distribution technologies, various virtual infrastructure implementations integrating virtual machines, hypervisors, physical and logical hosts, physical and logical interfaces, and much more. The resulting network manages complexity through abstraction. This abstraction can create security comfort through obfuscation; however, obfuscation is never a reasonable security approach. Moreover, abstraction itself presents significant security challenges. Do security operations have visibility to all the physical and logical elements that must be secured? Can security professionals see all the flows that occur in their network and see far enough up through the layers of abstraction encoded in APIs and interfaces to have context? Is the architecture consistent enough to allow correlation of events and to chain dependencies so the security engineer can identify and isolate compromised devices?

Another complexity of SDN and NFV technologies is in the way they actually distribute network state. Ultimately the purpose of an SDN controller is to maintain network state by distributing the flow table entries across multiple network elements, enabling programmatic implementation of end-to-end connectivity. Similarly, NFV orchestrates the deployment of dynamic infrastructure, creating chains of service elements that run their own interdependent state machines to provide capabilities. Consequently, this creates a new, target rich environment for adversaries to do new types of denial of service attacks, different methods of pivoting to gain access and manipulate network behavior, and more.

Moreover, the consequence of failure can be much higher. Once an adversary gains access to a virtualized infrastructure, the adversary may have the opportunity to penetrate hundreds or thousands of other physical or virtual devices. Thus entire infrastructures are likely to be compromised, deeply and widely, and nearly simultaneously at that. The notions of security in-depth and threat management through kill-chain modeling are critical for open distributed networks.

Fundamentally, open distributed architectures introduce risks by two key factors. First, the new infrastructure transitions from a hardware-centric orientation to one focused on software, and so networks become vulnerable in ways traditionally associated with software-based solutions. Second, the decomposition of network elements that separate the data plane, control plane, and management plane dramatically increases the attack surface that adversaries can address. There are simply more interfaces and elements (physical and virtual) to exploit. Moreover, concurrent changes in other IT technologies (such as DevOps) introduce further emphasis on software as the actual infrastructure and really create a virtual supply chain for service delivery and deployment. Thus vulnerabilities in software development processes now become operational vulnerabilities in the nature of how networks are managed and maintained.

We refer a reader to the latest results in SDN development. The ONF summarizes threats to SDN in its Technical Report TR-530 [5]. It must be noted that the security mechanisms outlined by ONF are optimized for an environment specified in [6]. Developing specifications and concepts as outlined by the ONF view of the SDN evolution in TR-535 [7] introduce entirely new network control and flow management practices which remain to be assessed fully.

NFV has a similar, if not greater, impact on increasing the attack surface: NFV introduces a new model for management and orchestration with new interfaces, which an attacker may attempt to exploit. Most are implemented as software with inherent software vulnerabilities.[2]

---

[2]The fact that security problems are introduced by sloppy programming is well known, although it is often overlooked because it is rarely mentioned. As Dijkstra famously noted in [8], "The required techniques of effective reasoning are pretty formal, but as long as programming is done

With the newly abstracted nature of NFV elements, isolation of failures may be more difficult, affecting an often forgotten security factor—availability. Even aside from that, threat-correlating network security data so that compromises can be identified and isolated to specific physical or logical elements might be more complex.

NFV also includes the notion of service chaining—the ability for an orchestrator to provision multiple network functions in series or even in parallel to provide a composite service. This creates a level of cascading complexity which can dynamically increase the attack surface as services are dynamically and automatically created and provisioned.

A plethora of potential problems (and, as we will see soon, benefits) stems from the hypervisor administrator's capability for introspection—that is the full access to the memory of any virtual machine at run time. If the respective API falls into the wrong hands, no secrets can be kept. As a result, a virtual machine effectively escrows all cryptographic keys with the administrator as well as with any other entity that has access to the introspection API.

On the other hand, introspection is quite useful in that it allows, for example, to detect root kits and otherwise enable security monitoring services. To this end, NIST [9] encourages cloud operators to "Consider using introspection capabilities to monitor the security of activities occurring among guest O[perating] S[ystem]s." (For more information on the services that a hypervisor can provide and known attacks on the virtualization infrastructure, see [4].)

But as far as lawful interception (LI) is concerned, the hypervisor introspection presents a big problem. One critical LI requirement is that the very act of surveillance must remain undetected by the persons who don't have a need to know. The hypervisor administrator (a human or a software agent with the access to the hypervisor API) might not necessarily have such a need, but the administrator has full access to the infrastructure within an individual host. This is a major challenge in implementing reasonable support for LI on NFV infrastructure.

---

by people that don't master them, the software crisis will remain with us and will be considered an incurable disease. And you know what incurable diseases do: they invite the quacks and charlatans in, who in this case take the form of Software Engineering gurus." In the same page is a quote from an early 1984 EWD: "Machine capacities now give us room galore for making a mess of it. Opportunities unlimited for fouling things up! Developing the austere intellectual discipline of keeping things sufficiently simple is in this environment a formidable challenge, both technically and educationally." As unfortunate as it is, the "software crisis" must be a primary factor in security assessment.

The summary of the security challenges introduced by virtualization is thus as follows:

- Reliance on additional software (that is, hypervisors and modules for management and orchestration) and hence a longer chain of trust
- Reduced isolation of network functions
- Fate-sharing due to resource pooling and multi-tenancy
- Effective key escrow for hosted network functions
- Complexity of implementing LI

The good news is that there are mechanisms and tools to deal with these challenges. Furthermore, there are unique opportunities in NFV when it comes to security.

First, NFV helps streamline security operations. In a cloud environment, multi-tenancy drives the need for logical separation of virtual resources among tenants. Through orchestration, certain virtual network functions (VNF) can be deployed on separate compute nodes, and they can be further segregated by using separate networks. In addition, the use of security zones allows VNFs to be deployed on— or migrated to—hosts that satisfy security-pertinent criteria such as location and level of hardening. Centralized security management allows network functions to be configured and protected effectively according to a common policy as opposed to a collection of per-NF security procedures that may not always be consistent or up to date.

Second, NFV can ease the operational impact of deploying security updates. An upgraded instance of the VNF can be launched and tested while the previous instance remains active. Services and customers can then be migrated to the upgraded instance over a period of time (shorter or longer as dictated by operational needs). The older instance with the un-patched security flaw can be retired once this is complete.

Third, by using hypervisor introspection, root kits can be detected and, consequently, eliminated. Overall, the run-time memory analysis can improve the security posture of a VNF, a process that was very difficult on network appliances or stand-alone services used for legacy telecommunications infrastructure.

Fourth, NFV opens up new possibilities in incident response owing to the inherent flexibility it introduces. For example, automated incident response could include rapid and flexible reconfiguration of virtual resources. Another characteristic of network function virtualization that leads to improved incident response is the relative ease of decommissioning and recommissioning VNFs. If a VNF is suspected of having been compromised (for example, through unauthorized access via a backdoor), an uncompromised version can be instantiated to replace it, and the compromised version can be decommissioned and a copy of it made for forensic analysis.

Fifth, one well-recognized benefit of the cloud environment is that it stimulates the use of analytics. This, of course, immediately applies to security in more than one way: analyzing the running code for viruses (and possible anomalies) as well as

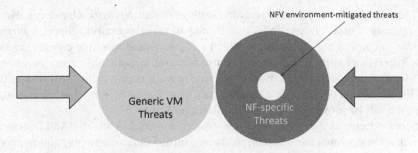

Fig. 2.1 VNF threat classification

analyzing traffic both for early detection of distributed denial of service attacks and distribution of malware. Again, the relatively central nature of the NFV enforces systematic use of analytics to develop a "big picture" of the state of a data center and the whole operator's network.

Now, we are ready to classify the threats discussed so far and consider which of them are specific to the NFV environment. Figure 2.1 illustrates this point.

In the simplest case, a VNF is an instance of a network function running on a virtual machine (VM). The overall set of security threats to a given VNF can be, at the first approximation, viewed as a combination of all generic virtualization threats (a circle on the left) and those threats specific to the network function software (a circle on the right).

As we discussed earlier, the latter set has a subset comprising the threats that can mitigated by the new mechanisms—such as hypervisor introspection and centralized security management. For this reason, we "carve out" this subset, thus reducing the threat landscape.

Now, the Cartesian product of these sets (i.e., a set of pairs of virtualization threats and unmitigated network-function threats acting simultaneously) provides the full landscape of the NFV-specific threats. The potential problems that stem from the most pertinent threats in this space are the subject of the next section.

2.3   The Problems Identified in the ETSI NFV Security Problem Statement

To understand the actual risks of the threat landscape described above, it is essential to consider the deployment models envisioned in the NFV. This is exactly what [2] does.

The simplest is what [2] calls a *Monolithic Operator.* Effectively, this is an operator's private cloud. Only operator's own network functions are represented there, and thus, most security concerns that deal with hosting are absent here. (The reason we consider such deployment unlikely is that in its pure form, it excludes even hosting of content delivery servers.)

The next model is called *Operator Hosting Virtual Network Operators*. Here, the operator's cloud hosts VNFs that belong to other operators. Since, a *virtual machine escape* (i.e., a situation in which a rogue virtual machine can get control of a hypervisor) is not unheard of and also because of potential "noisy neighbor" problems, the expectation is that an operator in such deployments will isolate the VNFs of a hosted operator on a separate hardware platform. With that, each hosted operator will be provided a separate hardware platform.

More extreme is the *Hosted Network Operator* model in which "An IT services organization operates the *compute* hardware, infrastructure network, and hypervisors on which a separate network operator runs virtualized network functions. The premises including cable chambers, patch panels, etc. are physically secured by the IT services organization." In this model, of course, the security of such operator's practice depends entirely on that of the IT service organization.

The *Hosted Communications Provider* model is a hybrid of the two previous models. Here, the IT service organization hosts either more than one communication services provider (CSP) or even a more than one wholesale network operator. In the latter case, the IT service organization sells the rights to each network that provides to run VNFs for the wholesaler. The wholesaler then resells these rights to the retailers. (We can note the necessity of a well-developed identity management framework for this case.)

The *Hosted Communications and Application Providers* model takes the next step by permitting the IT service organization to offer full-blown public cloud services, while the same facilities that are used in that offer are supporting the network operators and communication service providers.

In the *Managed Network Service on Customer Premises* model, a network operator runs VNFs on its own hardware located on a customer's premises and physically secured by the customer.[3] This model can be deployed for an enterprise or even a home network.

When the hardware belongs to and is operated by the customer, the above model becomes that of *Managed Network Service on Customer Premises Equipment*. For instance, the customer may allocate a host to the network operator where all the network operator's VNFs are to run. This specific deployment model excludes sharing the host (and hypervisor) between the network operator and a customer, although the model in which this is done is valid, too.

To determine the security implications of a deployment scenario, one needs to consider all parties at the level each of them operates (e.g., host hardware, hypervisor, or guest VNF). Then a decision has to be made as to which use rights each party may have over its resources. The fundamental security engineering design factor here is to provide a basis for trust suitable for all parties. See [2] for more discussion of how this can be effected.

Next, the NFV Security Problem Statement considers the potential attackers, traditionally classified by their respective means, motives, and opportunities. The

---

[3]Over the years, the NFV ISG has considered a number of such use cases.

introduction of NFV does alter the means and opportunity to exploit a vulnerability. How far this can go depends on the technical and contractual position of an organization in relation to others in the supply chain of NFV. To this end, the following hierarchy is considered:

- End-customers of retail network operators
- Retail network operators
- Wholesale network operators
- Hypervisor operators
- Infrastructure (i.e., hosts, storage, and infrastructure network) operators
- Facilities managers (who are responsible for the physical security of buildings and equipment)

A hosted service implies that a party at a given level contracts with (and thus places a degree of trust in) the parties operating lower levels.

The attacks are likely to occur from either a higher level, or at the same level (as in the case where a hosted network operator might spy on is competitor sharing the same facilities), or from inside (by disgruntled or unfaithful employees).

A hosting operator might mount willingly an attack on a guest (such as stealing confidential information that can be sold) as long as the attack does not degrade performance or otherwise affect the operator's reputation. Among existing threats are those related to intellectual property (i.e., proprietary algorithms, configuration files). Reverse engineering and side-channel attacks are specifically mentioned in [2] as the ones that need to be mitigated to protect the intellectual property of vendors from (1) one another, if they are running on the same platform and (2) from the platform operator. This can be achieved with the technologies for execution of sensitive components, discussed in Sect. 6. Of course, the full protection here is limited as it is infeasible for all of a guest's computing functions to be concealed from the host. One alternative technology applicable here, noted in [2] is homomorphic cryptography, which is becoming practical for certain very specific functions without too much overhead.

The rest of this section describes specific problems that the ETSI NFV Security Group has identified in [2]. These problems are:

1. Topology validation and enforcement
2. Availability of management support infrastructure
3. Secured Boot[4]

---

[4]This term has been subsequently changed to "Trustworthy Boot," defined in [11] as the means to encompass "the technologies and methods for validation and assurance of boot integrity." This subject will be addressed in the next section, but, in a nutshell, the same result can be accomplished with different alternative technologies based on different standards. Since the NFV Security Problem Statement has not changed, we keep the old term throughout this section. (As pedantic as it may sound, the term "Secured Boot" was created for a similar reason: to refer to a generic set of mechanisms vs. the UEFI *Secure Boot*.)

4. Secure crash
5. Performance isolation
6. User/Tenant Authentication, Authorization, and Accounting
7. Authenticated Time Service
8. Private Keys within Cloned Images
9. Backdoors via Virtualized Test and Monitoring Functions
10. Multi-Administrator Isolation

2.3.1 Topology Validation and Enforcement

An essential requirement for a network provider is that customers' networks and
the provider's own network are partitioned so as to be isolated from one another.[5]
This creates separate trust domains. In any pre-NFV environment, this is effected
by a set of firewalls (containing network address translators), which are properly
provisioned by the operations and management systems according to a provider's
policy.

Virtualization changes the demarcation between customers' and providers' trust
domains. As Fig. 2.2 illustrates, a virtualized forwarding function may interconnect
partitioned networks even in the simplest (i.e., virtual LAN-based) cloud environment. Overall, while the inter-host paths can be controlled in the pre-NFV ways,
the intra-host paths fall under control of virtualized forwarding functions and,
ultimately, hypervisors. Thus, this is a classic example of the generic case mentioned
earlier in which the environment is exposed to a pair of a threats, one inherent to
physical networking and another threat introduced by virtualization.

Therefore a network operator needs to be able to ensure that the connectivity of
the whole network meets the security policy. Furthermore, it is necessary to prevent
the establishment of an unauthorized connection.

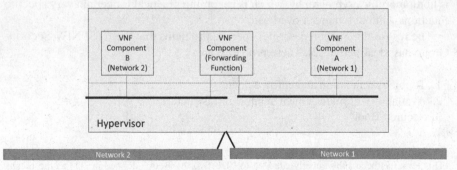

Fig. 2.2 Interconnection of partitioned network by a virtualized forwarding function

---

[5]A storage network also needs to be isolated, as does the operations-and-management network.
This issue will be addressed later in this section.

Various examples of establishing and validating service chains are presented in [2], which also recommends approaching the problem at different connection levels: the physical cabling, ports of each forwarding function, internal configuration of the forwarding function (as it relates to the assigned place in the service chain, etc.).

This is a challenging problem, which is further complicated by the possibility of introducing loops into service chains, which can be exploited to amplify a denial-of-service attack traffic. Potential mitigation steps here involve loop detection during the topology validation stage.

As may be expected when discussing networking, the subject of SDN is brought up in [2] because "SDN is considered highly complementary to NFV in certain scenarios (e.g., data centers)."[6] SDN connectivity can be defined programmatically, resulting in dynamic and flexible network configurations. Consequently, validating and constraining topologies is more difficult than in the "traditional" case. To address this complexity, [2] suggests an approach in which a network is partitioned into *security zones*, each zone defined by a distinct set of security policies. It is important to list here several reasons for such partitioning, as these reasons are specific to the managed networks and therefore are defining as far as NFV is concerned. These reasons include legislative or jurisdictional control, customer-type (e.g., government, enterprise, or residential), transferred content (as it may require rights protection or confidentiality), and multi-tenant controls, where network functions of competing network operators are hosted.

The SDN topologies are likely to be hierarchical—arranged in several layers. The simplest case is presented by one-layer, single-controller network, in which the controller will push rule sets into the switches. In more complex schemes, lower-level components request routing decisions from higher-layer components. In all cases, there is a need for a mutual authentication for every pair of interlocutors to prevent injection of malicious commands (by an entity masquerading an upper-layer component) or, divulging the network topology (by switches). Different layers may be implemented by different network operators, so trust management and network partitioning again become critical design considerations.

Network performance and security are often at cross-purposes when one tries to find the right place in the hierarchy for making forwarding decisions. Consider two extreme polar cases. Making forwarding decisions for every packet by the lowest controller in the hierarchy may provide the best security in terms of correlating and isolating distributed denial of service (DDoS) attack traffic. However, this may be impractical because of scaling and performance concerns. In contrast, making all the forwarding decisions in a switch may provide excellent performance but may also result in never detecting problems that would have been obvious had there been a possibility of correlating the traffic visible only to the higher-level entities.

---

[6]It is noted, however, that the SDN is still an emerging technology, in which (as of 2014) the full set of controls has not been standardized.

One possible solution here is for a switch to monitor the traffic and then send periodic updates to the SDN controller hierarchy. This has to be designed carefully to avoid making a controller a possible target of a denial-of-service attack, which would likely destabilize the whole network.

Another complication standing in the way of consistent topology validation process is that operators[7] can program the behavior of the switches via the operations and management interfaces independently of the controller. To avoid inconsistency, a capability to report any such change to controller must be built into the protocol. (Note that the NFV Security Problem Statement mentions *attestation* (discussed further in this chapter) as the mitigation means to ensure that the configurations and other essential operational data have not been changed since the last time they were modified legally.)

A more complex feature interaction problem may occur because the virtualized forwarding function may change the routing of packets in application-specific ways. With that some functions may take their instructions from the SDN control hierarchy (via *OpenFlow*™ interfaces), but, as [2] explains, it is one of the purposes of NFV "to enable deployment of application-specific Forwarding Functions, that will not, in general, be amenable to description by a deliberately constrained protocol such as *OpenFlow*."

Having touched on the SDN-related matters, we refer a reader to [2] for the discussion of the much better understood topology validation issues specific to the use of the traditional distributed routing protocols.

Finally, [2] stresses the necessity of keeping the overall "out-of-band" management system always alive. This can be helped by ensuring that the management ports of processing blades, switches, and storage controllers have both the physically independent connectivity to the management and orchestration system and locally accessible caching mechanisms for storing configuration state and logging events.

2.3.2 Availability of Management Support Infrastructure

The single most important requirement here is that the management infrastructure be available even when the infrastructure that it manages is out. In a way, that requirement has been spelled out already when we discussed the SDN. To quote [2]: "Ideally the management ports of processing blades, switches and storage controllers ought to have physically independent connectivity to their configuration state in the management and orchestration system, as well as locally accessible storage/caching for configuration state and the necessary access controls to these rudimentary but critical resources." The goal, or necessary practice here, is to make the operations network inaccessible from customers' networks.

---

[7] And thus an inside attacker.

The problem with fulfilling this requirement is the costs associated with providing a separate (physical) network for operations and management. It is quite possible to do so in a data center (and *OpenStack* supports that as demonstrated in [4]), but for an operator's network that spans multiple data centers spread over a sizable geographic area, the solution has been to dedicate a virtual private network for these purposes.

There are several aspects to this arrangement. First, the management network must be robust. To ensure availability, [2] recommends path diversity (including cellular network backup) whenever it is economically feasible. Second, access control to the management network also needs to be more stringent than access to the supported networks. An example of a specific challenge introduced by the NFV is booting of a hypervisor. This procedure may require network access to obtain its own configuration, software licenses, cryptographic keys, etc. For that, a hypervisor does need a "purely physical" access to the management network, which must be physically isolated from others. A similar problem arises on the start-up of a virtualized forwarding function. It may rely on accessing the network through another forwarding function in the chain only as the latter does not rely (circularly) on the very function that is being started up. One solution proposed by [2] is never to allow the management network to use a virtualized function on any forwarding path. Perhaps over time, the industry could develop a provable recursive solution though.

2.3.3   Secured Boot

Here we address the fundamental problem of establishing the chain of *trust*, on which we further expand in the next section. In a nutshell, an application's users trust both the application software and the operating system on which the software runs. An operating system, in turn, trusts the hardware on which it executes. In the cloud, a hypervisor is largely replacing the hardware as a trusted entity (by operating systems), but a hypervisor still has to trust the hardware. Finally, the cloud operator must have a basis to trust the hypervisor, the hardware, and the various software installed on it.

Overall in the NFV environment, a hosted network operator has to trust its hosting provider's virtualization platform sufficiently to run virtual network functions on it; conversely, the NFV operator must trust each VNF (which means being able to ascertain that each VNF comes intact from an accepted vendor, performs to its specifications, and is not being modified in the process). Each VNF can, in turn, be composed of multiple workloads (VMs in traditional virtualized infrastructure), and so trust chaining can become quite complex.

To bootstrap the process of building trust, we provide mechanisms and processes to base trust in the hardware (in that it has no malicious modules and otherwise acts according to its specifications). The next step is to ascertain that the booted software belongs to the trusted vendor. This is precisely the problem addressed here.

Secured boot encompasses the technologies and methods for validation and assurance of *boot integrity* validation. The secured boot process actually can do a bit more than just checking software—in addition to checking the hypervisor and OS image, it can also validate add-on hardware modules (such as acceleration hardware) and firmware.

Furthermore, the established trust base is further used to ensure that the software loaded into the VNF execution environment is authentic and has not been tampered with. This is achieved by checking cryptographic signatures of the respective modules. (Unless specifically stated otherwise, we always assume asymmetric cryptography.)

In the NFV environment, there is a need to incorporate software from multiple software vendors. As [2] notes, "to minimize certificate management complexity in such cases it may be desirable to have a single certification authority for VNFs."[8]

The relevant secured boot technology (often under different names—such as "secure boot" or "trusted boot"—and in somewhat different contexts) has been addressed in various fora. For example, the architecture and mechanisms for verifying signed firmware and software images are specified by the *Unified Extensible Firmware Interface* (UEFI) Forum (www.uefi.org). UEFI enables one to ascertain that host is booted into a known configuration based on hardware-rooted trust. Although supported on servers, the technology is not yet in use widely.

The *UEFI secure boot* involves checking the signatures of all UEFI modules as they are being loaded. If the signature check fails, the boot stops. This process leverages a public key infrastructure, in which the public keys of vendors are stored in a database, augmented with the revocation list. There is also an option for an administrator to approve a boot signature manually at the console.

Another, more general technology to achieve this—and wider—purpose is called *trusted computing* and standardized by the Trusted Computing Group (TCG) (www.trustedcomputinggroup.org). The new and essential implement here is the *Trusted Platform Module* (*TPM*), a tamper-resistant hardware "box,"[9] which stores the private endorsement key and also performs a variety of computing operations. Neither the host CPU nor, for that matter, any other hardware module may look inside the TPM arbitrarily. The TPM communicates with the outside world via a well-defined interface. The ultimate goal is to establish the *chain of trust* that encompasses all pieces of firmware and software.

Recognizing that the TPM technology can be implemented using various hardware standards, the ETSI NFV Security Group came up with a general term, *hardware-based root of trust (HBRT)* (defined in [17]), to refer to the anchoring function presented in a hardware-based TPM. There have been claims that a similar

---

[8]Indeed, there has been a long-standing work item in the NFV Security Working Group on this subject.

[9]Implemented as a dedicated ASIC or a subcomponent of another processor. The chip would provide external mechanisms to prevent or make difficult tampering or inspection and also provide mechanisms to destroy stored secrets if tampering is detected.

function can be developed by a *hardware security module (HSM)* (see [4] for a review of the HSM technology).

The trust chain is maintained through the execution of secure transactions, which (1) isolate memory (for example, for storing derived keys), (2) bind storage to specific configurations of hardware and software, and (3) provide *remote attestation* (alarming a specified party to all environment changes).

Among other functions that TPM provides are those to generate the cryptographic keys (bound to the endorsement key) and to store the *measurement* of the respective boot components. TPM has been implemented in hardware, but there has been an effort to virtualize it [10].

Given the definitions provided above, a clarification of terminology is necessary. Booting with TPM is called *trusted boot* to differentiate it from the UEFI *secure boot*.[10]

The outstanding question that [2] poses is whether these technologies have proven to be feasible to operate at network operator scale. We return to this in the next section.

2.3.4 Secure Crash

It is a common place that programs must not crash. About any crash leaves the program memory and other resources in an unknown state, and this results, among other problems, in a significant potential vulnerability. With that, a crash of an application is different in its consequence from a crash of an operating system because the latter naturally exposes the resources of all its applications. Ultimately, a crash of the host's hypervisor exposes the resources of all virtual machines; however, [2] concludes that the "Cloud technology already has a strong track-record of robust design against crash-related vulnerabilities. Therefore it would seem that NFV adds no new concerns here." The NFV-specific problem is that NFV magnifies the consequence of a successful attack.

Within the NFV framework, the key components that are at risk in this context are the hypervisors and virtual network function component instances. In the latter case, the role of the hypervisor is to ensure that all file references, hardware pass-through devices, and memory are safe from being accessed by unauthorized entities.

But not all problems are confined to the host itself. An example of a "remote" problem is the references to a crashed virtual network function component stored on remote devices. As [2] notes, the devices often use such references as the means to "authenticate" a machine. There is a need to purge those references from the devices, but this can, of course, be achieved only when they are known. An easier objective to achieve is to ensure that it is not possible for a newly executing VNF component instance to adopt identifiers (e.g., MAC or IP addresses) that were recently used by a crashed instance, lest this instance impersonate the crashed one.

---

[10] As we will see later, the industry has introduced a new, generic term, "trustworthy boot."

A similar problem is related to storage (both local and remote) resources attached to the crashed virtual network function component instances. Since the hypervisor cannot know what storage resources need to be wiped in the event of a crash, it is likely to be the job of the VNF manager to wipe them.

Naturally a crash of a virtual network function component affects the availability of a service. In this case, [2] suggests that the VNF manager needs to identify the likely cause of the problem and work with the NFV infrastructure (via the virtualization infrastructure manager) to work around it. The remedy may be the creation of a new component instance (or set of instances), rerouting of packets passing through the crashed component, or the creation of new routes among the dependent entities. This places requirements on the virtual network function descriptor to store the information to be used by the VNF manager in the case of crash.

2.3.5 Performance Isolation

The generic problem here is that a virtual machine may (more often than not because of one or another software fault in a hypervisor) affect performance of other virtual machines on the same host. In an extreme case, a machine can "escape," that is take control of the hypervisor thus control all other virtual machines. Even when done passively, this amounts to learning all cryptographic secrets of other machines and unlimited monitoring of all communications. In milder cases, without "escaping," a misbehaving machine may consume more resources (such as memory, CPU cycles, or bandwidth) than it is supposed to do, thus degrading the performance of other machines. We refer a reader to [4], which describes this problem—and some ways of dealing with it—at length.

As with the previous problem, the consequences of isolation failure in the NFV environment may be catastrophic (especially in view of the lawful interception requirements). Hence [2] is considering a range of isolation approaches, of which the most effective is static hardware segregation (hard partitioning of resources such that memory and storage at not shared at run time).

Others include ensuring proper configuration of the hypervisor so as to constrain the ability of a VNF component to acquire memory, processing cores, CPU quanta, and so on. These techniques, however, may prove inefficient when the granularity at which the resource can be allocated is too coarse or when it is impossible to predict the correct usage of resources by a given VNF. Moreover, some of these techniques significantly reduce the potential cost benefits of NFV that drives operator investment in virtualization. In fact, [2] warns that "network and I/O partitioning of ... [one guest] is hard to isolate from that of other guests, because it can range widely over different distributed network resources and it can be highly variable at any point, making any partitioning very inefficient."

Another factor that stands in the way of performance isolation is the recurrent need to optimize the performance of a hypervisor. To increase I/O throughput, for example, hypervisors may allow direct pass-through, thus allowing guests access to

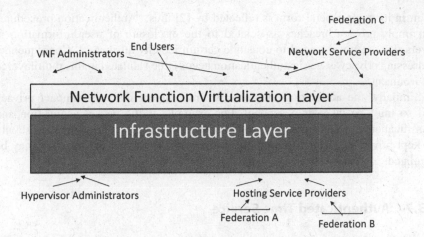

Fig. 2.3 Identities in NFV

the common physical memory. To counter this, [2] recommends using I/O memory management units.

And yet another group of attacks are those on the resources of the virtualization infrastructure. As [2] notes, "Even when isolation is in place, whether for storage I/O, network, memory or CPU, there is a class of attacks on the resources used by the hypervisor platform itself, which may vary in ease of execution and efficacy depending on the failure modes of the underlying hypervisor and the hardware architecture."

One essential security capability recommended by [2] is proactive monitoring, which can enable mitigation. Monitoring is prescribed at two levels: the infrastructure level and, independently, at each VNF. Detecting anomalous traffic behavior, degraded performance, unusual spikes in I/O processing, and other irregularities and then leveraging the management and orchestration system to bring these data into a central place where they can be analyzed so as to find a proper response is an essential technique recommended for the NFV.

2.3.6 User/Tenant Authentication, Authorization, and Accounting (AAA)

In the NFV, the identities of various actors are used in (at least) two layers: at the network and virtualization infrastructure and at the network function layer, as depicted in Fig. 2.3.

Federations of actors result in compound identities, and so identity sets develop both horizontally and vertically. What the figure does not show, but what has been implied, is the law enforcement actors who may have access to some identities but not to others (and whose very presence must remain a secret from most actors). This point in its more general form is reflected by [2] thus: "Authentication procedures can imply privacy breaches associated to the disclosure of user information at layers that are not intended to consume certain identity attributes." Consequently, addressing privacy issues in authentication needs to be validated in this multilayered environment.

Similarly, the accounting in the NFV environment may also impact privacy and so must be taken into account. For example, traffic packet acquisition and classification as well as the policy enforcement blocks on a per-actor basis should be kept private between customers, and operator use on such information may be regulated.

2.3.7   Authenticated Time Service

The correct function of many cryptographic protocols depends on knowing the correct time of the day, which is, for example, used in timestamps or to check certificate expiration. Tampering with time is an attack that can interfere cryptographic and security protocols as transport-level security (TLS), Kerberos, DNS security (DNSSEC), and time-limited access controls. Moreover, time accurate event logging and reporting time can be critical for performance and fault isolation procedures and event identification and management for identifying security compromise. Beyond just interfering with the security protocols, tempering with time poses a plethora of additional security problems—especially in network functions—because operations on various communications caches (such as that used in DNS) depend on correct time as does operation of routing protocols such as Border Gateway Protocol (BGP).

While there are authenticated time servers that render a variety of man-in-the-middle attacks on the Network Time Protocol (NTP) difficult, in the virtualized environment, the hypervisor is a trusted man-in-the-middle, and so a compromised hypervisor can easily tamper with timing queries.

2.3.8   Private Keys within Cloned Images

The potential problem is that images from which VNFs are booted may contain private keys or other sensitive data. The recommendation in [2] is that such keys have to be supplied at boot time.

The use of Trusted Platform Modules or hardware security modules can reduce the need for key provisioning, and the work in the NFV Security Group on the architecture for sensitive component execution has addressed this.

2.3.9   Backdoors via Virtualized Test and Monitoring Functions

This problem deals with the current dubious practice of certain vendors in which they develop "hidden" (unofficial) interfaces for run-time access to their code for debugging purposes. As such, the problem is not exactly NFV-specific except for the hope expressed in [2] that virtualization technology could be used to create a more structured approach for authorizing whether testing and monitoring can be conducted, which diagnostic functions are allowed, and who is allowed to run them. A good practice would be to require all test and monitoring functions to be cryptographically authenticated just as for any management access to infrastructure or virtual components.

2.3.10 Multi-administrator Isolation

The defining use case here was dictated by needs of lawful interception as communicated by the members of the ETSI Technical Committee on Lawful Interception (TC LI). The problem here (already mentioned in the discussion of multilayered administration environment of the NFV) is that administrators of the virtualization infrastructure naturally have higher privileges than those of administrators of the virtualized functions executing on the system. For instance, a host administrator already has access to all virtual machines on the host through introspection capabilities, while an administrator of an orchestrator has access to all infrastructure controlled by the orchestrator.

This gets in the way of lawful interception—inasmuch as it occurs at the virtualization layer—because the infrastructure administrators do not necessarily have the need to know even that the lawful interception occurs, let alone be able to learn every detail of it.

In fact, the problem here is more general than that of lawful interception. Hosted operator environments are just as vulnerable to potential confidentiality violations—and exactly for the same reason. Hence the work undertaken by the NFV Security Group has been centered on solving the larger, more general problem. In effect, this solution must eventually be an evolution of role-based access control which assures administrators are able to see and do only the activities and data they should.

In conclusion, Table 2.1 demonstrates how certain work items undertaken in the group relate to the above problem set. (It should be noted that not all work items were driven by the problem statement. Some work items, such as *Report on Security Aspects and Regulatory Concerns* or *Report on Retained Data problem statement and requirements*, are of more general nature, while others—notably *Security Specification for MANO Components and Reference points*—are specific to the detail of the NFV architecture.)

2.4 Establishing and Maintaining Trust

Before we start with the formal approach, let us consider an intuitive one. We can envision the "bootstrapping" of security of three planes of the NFV as depicted in Fig. 2.4. We start at the lowest plane—the physical infrastructure. Assuming that we can trust the hardware, we can use it to boot all hypervisors securely, using the

Table 2.1 Relation of certain ETSI NFV Security WG work items to the problems in the security problem statement

	Topology validation & enforcement	Availability of management support infrastructure	Secured boot	Performance isolation	User/tenant AAA	Private keys within cloned images	Back-doors via virtualized test & monitoring functions	Multi-administrator isolation
Cataloguing security features in management software		*			*	*		*
Report on lawful interception implications			*	*	*			*
Report on certificate management					*	*		
Report on attestation technologies and practices for secure deployments	*		*					*
Report on use cases and technical approaches for multi-layer host administration			*	*				*
Security report on NFV LI architecture	*		*	*				*
System architecture specification for execution of sensitive NFV components			*					*
Security management and monitoring specification	*						*	*

* The asterisk indicates that the problem in the given column is addressed in the specification in the given row.

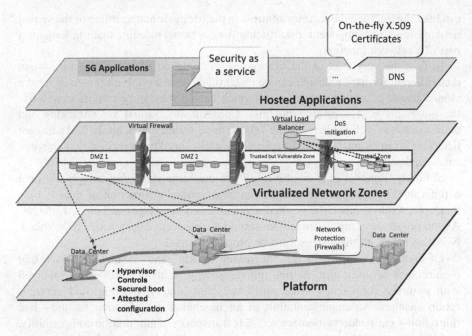

Fig. 2.4 Bootstrapping trust

HBRT. Once booted, we can maintain the same level of security by applying all software patches and otherwise following the best industry practices for security hardening.

At the same time, we have to ensure that the physical network inside the data centers is secure and that access to it is adequately protected. The word "adequately" implies adherence to the operator's security policy.

As the hypervisors start building their own local area networks, we must ensure that the respective configurations adhere to the appropriate security policies and, once deployed, remain unchanged (except for controlled changes sanctioned and performed by the operator). This can be achieved by employing remote attestation.

At this point, we can extend the trust chain to the next plane, in which we place virtual network appliances—firewalls, SDN controllers, load balancers, and so on—and develop trust zoning in the virtualized environment. This also includes hosted environments, and so various networks can coexist now founded on the trust within the platform.

Subsequently, this chain will extend toward the applications (such as fifth-generation mobile applications) of the upper plane. Incidentally, the security services deployed at the upper plane (for example, identity management services) can be used now further to strengthen the security of the physical plane—this recursive nature of developing and chaining trust should be fully leveraged.

Having developed the intuitive view, we can take a look at the standards work in this area. The first document [11] gives a high level but systematic review of establishing trust and the security controls in the life cycle management of the virtual network function component instantiation (i.e., a virtual machine that implements a part of a network function).

In fact, the very start of the life cycle—the creation of such a machine—can take different forms; a machine can be instantiated from a pre-built image or from a cloned image of another machine (in which case it may carry into its new a life the old baggage of security problems). Consequently, virtual asset tracking and audit records as well the networking-related data, security credentials, and software licensing information—just to list a few examples—need to be verified and, in some cases, updated.

Similarly, removal of a machine follows the same steps, but here, additional actions may be required for secure wipe and verified destruction of data.[11] Furthermore, removal has to be verified across backed-up images and cloned images. As the private keys are destroyed, so should the respective certificates be revoked. Needless to say, all these steps must be properly logged.

Of course, it is not only the "beginning of life" and "death" processes that require such scrutiny; the lifetime maintenance is actually much more involved with ensuring consistent (across hosts and data centers) patching and configuration changes. An implementation of an ingenious virtualization feature—live migration—must address memory reuse, feature parity, configuration compatibility, and service availability.

But what is *trust* after all? It is defined in [11] as "confidence in the integrity of an entity for reliance on that entity to fulfil specific responsibilities." Typically, trust is expressed through an *assurance level* based on specific measures, but it may be expressed merely through a relation (as is in *A* trusts *B* more than *C*).

With that, trust is temporary. (For instance, once booted, a hypervisor may be trusted for no longer than it is running; the trust has to be reestablished at the next boot.) The other constraining characteristic of trust is the context. *A* may trust *B* to know a parameter's value but not to change it. The trust may also be delegated.[12]

Some examples of parameters for measuring trust in NFV presented in [11] are software integrity, geographical location, hardware capabilities, and time elapsed since last audit.

Among well-known examples of trust relation is that established by a party with a certification authority (CA) in public key infrastructure. From that, a *chain of trust* is formed to the entities that are issued certificates by this CA. Specific to NFV, as we saw in the Security Problem Statement, is a matter of provisioning and storing the private keys. The techniques mentioned in [11] include the *injection* of

---

[11] An important point to remember is that certain data may need to be retained, for regulatory reasons (such as lawful interception). For detail, see [12].

[12] Trust delegation is typically established for the purposes of authorization. An example: when a person wants to use a printing service to print photos available on a social site, this person delegates the authority to do so to the printing service. We will see a detailed example when reviewing the *OpenStack* security below.

the private key by a hypervisor as well as the reliance on the HBRT.[13] In view of the "private key in images" problem discussed earlier, the hypervisor injection is a solution to it. Incidentally, the hypervisor trust is implicit in virtualization, and therefore, validating the hypervisor is the first and most essential step in the grand scheme of the NFV trust establishment.

Developing of a trust chain starts with the *trustworthy boot*, which, according to [11], "encompasses the technologies and methods for validation and assurance of boot integrity."

This term was defined to differentiate from earlier industry terms: the *secure boot* and *measured boot*. With secure boot, the integrity checks are based on the known hardware-based *roots of trust*. The booting process stops when integrity check fails. With measured boot, the integrity state is merely recorded without affecting the boot process. This state is checked by a *verifier* after the boot is complete, and it is up to the verifier to validate it and assign the appropriate level of trust.

The trustworthy boot process can use any of the existing boot types either alone or in combination. One overarching requirement here is that the virtual network function manager is assured that the boot process of the VNF component instance has completed.

The interpretation of the results of the process is not simply "black or white," as in the case of secure boot. Booting can still be allowed, but with reduced privileges and restricted access to certain hardware. Handling of failed integrity checks is subject to respective policies.

As a hypervisor is aided by the on-the-chip TPM, which cannot be directly used by the operating systems of the virtual machines, virtual TPMs can be created— under control of the hypervisor. There is a certain amount of controversy in the industry whether a virtual TPM can be trusted, and [11] neither prescribes nor proscribes its use.

Now we can delve into what should constitute the trust measurements in the NFV environment and how the remote attestation of this environment is performed. Here we report on the research results rather than a standard as, at the moment of this writing, the respective work in the NFV SEC Working Group is still in a progress, and so the resulting specification [13] is still in its draft form.

Attestation is formally defined in [13] as "the process through which a remote challenger can retrieve verifiable information regarding a platform's integrity state [TCG PCSISCB]." The term *remote attestation* is often used in the industry to point out that the attestation process is to be observed by a geographically remote party (a *challenger*)—not only by someone at the console of a host. Thus, even though there is no suggested central use of attestation at the moment, the notion lends itself naturally to an operations and management environment in which the whole of a provider infrastructure can be measured and attested to.

The platform's integrity information is delivered to a challenger in the form of a measurements log. One immediate difficulty here is that such a measurement log is generated by the software that is being measured. Since the challenger is trying

---

[13]The detail of this is not elaborated on and "left for further study."

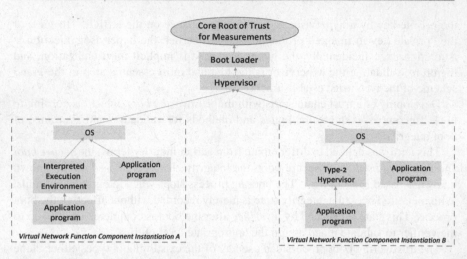

Fig. 2.5 Establishing chains of trust

to ascertain whether this software can be trusted, it is follows that it is necessary to establish a chain of trust first and then maintain the evidence that the measurement log has not been tampered with.

The chain of trust is developed recursively, as shown in Fig. 2.5.

The process starts with establishing the *Root of Trust for Measurement (RTM)*. The boot loader is measured using the *Core Root of Trust for Measurement (CRTM)* whom everyone and everything trusts. When the boot loader is executed (after having been measured and approved for execution), it inherits from the CRTM transitive trust and thus becomes the first node in a trust tree. Every path in this tree—traversed from a leaf to the root—forms a trust chain. At this point a hypervisor or an operating system (in the case of non-virtualized environments where containers are run instead of virtual machines) is similarly measured and then booted, joining the trust chain. Similarly, once the operating system runs, an interpreted execution environment (such as *Java execution* environment) or a type-2 hypervisor can in turn be measured and approved for becoming a link in the trust chain, thus being able to measure the application, which could in turn measure its software components.

As we have already mentioned, the hardware and network configuration of the platform must be measured and verified to provide the holistic view of the platform security.

At the moment, the industry proposes six *levels of assurance* (LOAs) for the NFV [13]. In the first five LOAs, each subsequent level contains all the checks performed for the previous levels and then the additional ones that go deeper in checking the corresponding link in the chain. The sixth level checks the infrastructure network.

In relation to the last point, [13] provides an example of how a TPM can be used to verify SDN and otherwise extend the network function's attestation features to report on the current SDN configuration.

To effect that, the SDN verifier retrieves from the SDN controller the configuration of the attested network element, measures it, and then compares it with the attestation result.

The last example is a special type of *run-time attestation*, which is the attestation performed on a running program. It is fairly easy because what is measured here is a specific data segment of a program, which is not supposed to be modified. With the general programs, the problem is much harder and remains a topic of active research. (See [14] for the problem description, bibliography, and a description of a prototype implementing a partial solution.)

2.5   Lawful Interception and the Environment for the Execution of Sensitive Components

Lawful interception (LI) concerns two aspects of communications: the *intercept-related information* (IRI) (which can be anything but the actual content—that is signaling, call information, log record information, etc.) and the actual *content of communication* (CC) in the form of streaming traffic.

The related data are acquired through the *point of interception* (POI) in the operator's network, whose precise location must be handed by the network operator along with the above data.

An operator is expected to support three interfaces called HI1, HI2, and HI3, which are, respectively, used for administration, IRI, and CC.

LI can take place only when requested by an authorized law enforcement agency (LEA). With that the POI must be physically present in the jurisdiction in which the law enforcement has authority, and it is a requirement that the network operator must ensure this. This requirement has an implication for the NFV—specifically for the NFV orchestration and management system—in that the function component that implements POI must always be deployed on the hardware located within the appropriate jurisdiction.[14]

The next major LI requirement that constrains NFV is that of LI being undetectable. All the LI data—and the very fact that the LI takes place—must be contained within the jurisdictional borders and protected from exposure to anyone except those authorized to have access to it by both the law enforcement agency and the network operator.

To summarize, the high-level LI requirements are as follows:

- The LI service capability must always be available.
- The LI service must be activated upon issuing a valid interception order from law enforcement.

---

[14]We can see now how remote attestation of geographic attributes can be useful in meeting this requirement.

- The LI service must be deactivated when the interception warrant expires (or earlier, if requested).
- The LI service must be invoked on any communication authorized for interception from or to the target visible to the network.
- Interrogation (in the form of operations and management queries) can be admitted only by an LI interface administrator authorized by both the network operator and the law enforcement agency.
- An authorized user for the purposes of interrogation is one who is allowed and authorized by both LEA and the CSP to administer the LI interface.
- LI must not visibly interact with other services (in order to ensure that it is only visible to authorized entities).

For the detail of handling encryption, identities of potential and actual interlocutors, triggers for sending the IRI, and parameters to be enclosed, see [15].

As we noted earlier, the "interrogation" requirement poses a problem in the virtualized environment because of the administrative access to the hypervisor introspection capabilities. As [15] states: "It is very unlikely that the administrator of a conventional hypervisor or orchestrator will be authorized as an interrogator who should be allowed to know that the LI function is activated, and against whom, as information that has to be strictly controlled." The problem is further amplified by the potential capabilities of the analytics software to infer the presence of LI.

The actual LI architecture for virtualized environment is being specified in [16], and the current consensus[15] of the NFV Security Working Group is summarized in Fig. 2.6.

The *LI virtual machine* (LI VM) is to be placed at the optimal POI in the CSP infrastructure to intercept the target traffic. The LI VM then passes the intercepted traffic to the *LI Mediation Function* (MF)/*Delivery Function* (DF), which, in turn, frames the traffic in the standard format and then forwards it to the *Law Enforcement Monitoring Facility (LEMF)* in LEA. There is a range of present implementations of the MF/DFs: from a single MF/DF per POI to an MF/DF being a large concentration point serving multiple POIs.

This is as much as we can say here about handling the LI data. But what about management and control?

The first element here is the *Administrative Function* (ADMF), imported from the legacy environment, which is responsible for administering target warrants and instructing the POI and MF/DFs to take the actions necessary to capture communications of a given target. To perform this function, the ADMF must keep the database of all POIs and MF/DFs under its control. This database is effectively built by the *LI Controller* (LI CTRL), another entity exported from legacy environment, which is responsible for the activation, configuration, and audit of the POIs, as well as for notifying the ADMF that a POI is ready for interception. In the NFV environment, the ADMF has to adapt dynamically to the

---

[15] As of December 2016.

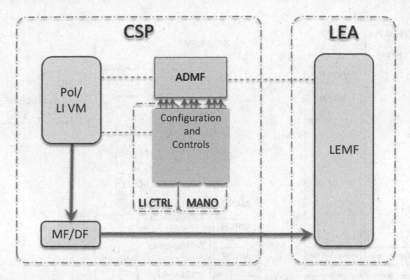

Fig. 2.6 (Draft) LI architecture in virtualized environment (a simplified version of Fig. 6-2-2 of [16])

newly instantiated (or migrated) POIs and MFs. This can be achieved only through some form of cooperation with the NFV management and orchestration.[16]

In the NFV environment, as [16] observes, "it may be desirable for security reasons to place the MFs outside of the NFV platform in which the LI POIs are implemented. However as the LI POIs move and change in scale, this may make the routing complexity required to backhaul traffic from the LI POIs to the MF/DFs unacceptable. It would potentially be difficult to adequately hide the routing/traffic flows in an SDN connectivity environment." This backhaul problem (known as "trombone effect") is essential for understanding the complexity of the SDN and NFV interactions. This is an open problem. Even though it has first manifested itself during the LI case study, it is likely to arise in other use cases.

In terms of the infrastructure development, [16] suggests that either LEMF be moved into the CSP or a trusted third-party proxy be used to represent the LEMF in the CSP. One problem with implementing this is that national security requirements, which differ across the LEAs, might make this difficult to achieve.

The consensus on the nature of the ADMF is clear. As the ADMF is the root of trust and central point of control, [16] recommends that it be implemented "as standalone hardware which is fully separated from the NFV platform hosting the VNF POIs."

Finally, as far as the respective interfaces (or, *reference points*, in the standards parlance) are concerned, Fig. 2.7 should give a reader a good idea of the current consensus on the subject.

---

[16]Several such scenarios are discussed in [16].

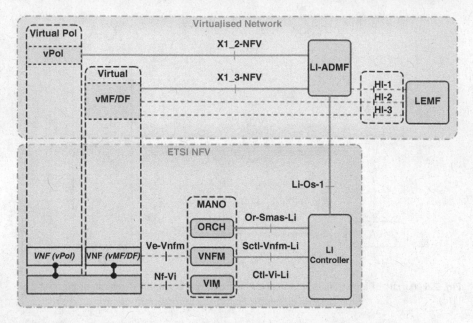

Fig. 2.7 LI reference points (Fig. 6.5-1 of [16], Draft)

· Unfortunately, the space limit of this chapter does not allow us to go into detail of various deployment scenarios (and their respective vulnerabilities and controls). We refer a reader to [16].

We note one particular scenario—the one called the "POI VNF Embedded," in which the POI is part of a VNF. This, of course, is the ultimate NFV-based use case. [16] notes that this scenario, when implemented in conjunction with the security mechanisms for the execution of sensitive components, "most closely provides an equivalent level of LI capability and security to that of an 'on-switch' legacy hardware implementation . . . [which] should address most national security requirements."

This naturally brings us to the subject of the implementation. As should be obvious to a reader now, in order to meet the most basic requirements of LI, the platform must provide both specialized hardware and the capabilities for implementing special security controls.

These have been addressed in [17] in terms of the overall platform hardware and software requirements as well as the life cycle maintenance requirements, system-hardening mechanisms, and identity management controls.

The major requirement is the presence of the HBRT, which is tamper-resistant and tamper-evident and whose interfaces to other hardware components are protected—to a level established by a certification process—from eavesdropping, manipulation, and replay attacks.

With that, a control must be present to restrict (e.g., halt) booting "if assistance from the HBRT is not available or the HBRT currently does not contain valid cryptographic material."

As the HBRT is first and foremost serves as the identification of the platform, it is essential that it be an irremovable part of the host hardware. Any attempt to tamper with the HRBT itself or separate it from the host, must be detected and reported.

An essential task of the HBRT module is key management, which includes creation and deletion of cryptographic keys. HBRT must store the cryptographic material in a "shielded" (i.e., physically protected from an unauthorized access) location. Based on these capabilities, the overall key management system, which also includes access right management, is developed. An essential requirement in terms of services based on HBRT is that the "host system shall provide cryptographically separated secure environments to different applications."

The core software requirements presented in [17] are based on the premise that the HBRT, with the valid cryptographic material be present and its services available. Otherwise, the booting procedure must prevent running of workloads.

With HBRT firmly present, the hardware and software of the system can be molded into the foundation called the *trusted computing base (TCB)*. A number of requirements in [17] concern the life cycle of the operation in the presence of the TCB. One of these requirements is that the host system strictly authorize the use of potentially dangerous capabilities (such as memory sharing among virtual machines), with the established default that none such capabilities be available.

The run-time techniques are prescribed to ascertain the level of integrity such of running machines and their respective file systems. This is performed by specialized agents, but those can be also compromised, and so the external behavioral monitoring is also recommended. To run software in a stealth mode, [17] suggests the use of hardware-mediated execution enclaves.[17]

As far as cryptographic algorithms are concerned, [17] has both prescribed and proscribed a number of them, referencing the ISO/IEC standards and the NIST specifications. For communications security, the latest stable versions of the application and network protocols are prescribed.

Further to life cycle-related requirements, [17] refers to a set of prescribed system-hardening and logging techniques, including the operating system-level access and confinement controls as well as physical controls and alarms. The attribute-based access control defined by NIST is declared mandatory. In addition, logging controls are recommended. At the end of the workload life cycle, secure wipe of the relevant storage should be performed. Making provisions for a rainy day, [17] specifies a set of requirements for dealing with the failure conditions.

---

[17]This term is rather loosely defined in the NFV, but the authors have ascertained two firm implementation examples: (1) that of the Intel's Software Guard Extensions (SGX) (https://software.intel.com/en-us/sgx) and (2) a joint proprietary implementation developed by ARM and Apple (https://www.quora.com/What-is-Apple%E2%80%99s-new-Secure-Enclave-and-why-is-it-important).

While the requirements for the execution of sensitive components naturally apply to the hosts, there is a natural dependency on the operations and management systems (e.g., Management and Orchestration [MANO], attestation authority, certificate authority, or logging systems) to act in concert supporting and enforcing the NFV provider-wide compliance with the requirements.

2.6   Security Management and Monitoring

The draft specification [18] is still under development at the time of this writing. A number of factors have been shaping it, and the authors feel that explaining these factors (and also providing some history) will help with understanding the resulting standard.

The work on the subject, or rather the monitoring part of it, started in 2014[18]. The initial objective was to define a security monitoring framework that would provide sufficient material to which analytics could be applied to detect attacks.

The first plan was concrete: to consider specific use cases (such as the *IP Multimedia Subsystem (IMS)* and the *Evolved Packet Core (EPC)* environment) that were of immediate concern to network operators, develop the monitoring solutions for those use cases, and then derive the generic architecture that would support security monitoring for all of these use cases.

But in the beginning of 2015, a proposal for the work on developing an active security management (as opposed to just monitoring) framework came. There was unanimous agreement that the work should proceed, but specifying active controls separately from the mechanisms that trigger them did not make much sense and so the scope of the monitoring work item. As a result, the new work item[19] was created, resulting in a numbering gap, but this was the least controversy.

Over the 2 years of the development of this work (which is expected to be completed in 2017), significant questions were raised as to what should be visible to the monitoring software and what actions it may take. As a reader has probably inferred from the previous section, lawful interception requirements pose a major problem. For one thing, the copied stream would be perceived as anomaly (perhaps even an attack) by a monitoring system, and so all the attributes of an operation that is supposed to be secret would be divulged. Even worse, any action to stop this "attack" would interfere with the lawful interception traffic.

Hence the overarching principle that security management should be confined within a *trust domain*. The latter has been defined in [18] as "a collection of entities that share a set of security policies." Actually, lawful interception is not the only case where trust domain separation—and the confinement of security management to its own a trust domain—is required. Another such case is when a provider of

---

[18]As part of now extinct work item 8 (https://portal.etsi.org/webapp/workProgram/Report_WorkItem.asp?wki_id=45992).

[19]Work item 12.

the NFV infrastructure hosts a network operator. Naturally, the NFV infrastructure provider's concern is the security of the infrastructure, and so the job of the security management software is to enforce *these* policies rather than secure the operations of the hosted operator. The hosted domain operates under a different set of policies. It may require its own security management operation to enforce those. Alternatively, the infrastructure provider may deliver security management as a service, but in this case, its operation will be distinct from that of the security management of the infrastructure.

There is a detailed discussion in [18] of the use case in which the IMS is deployed on the infrastructure that belongs to a single operator but consists of multiple trust domains.

The life cycle of security management, according to [18], is recursive in that it employs three processes (called phases), which run concurrently and influence one another. The operation starts with the *security planning phase*, in which the security policies are specified for the respective trusted domain. Then, in the *security enforcement* phase, the policies are deployed, at which point the *security monitoring* phase kicks off. The latter observes whether the policies are followed and reports violations to the security enforcement phase, which sends back the updates. Security monitoring may also pass to the security planning phase the request for changes in policies (as, for example, may be required in order to optimize security operations).

We introduce the security management framework, the following discussion accompanied by Fig. 2.8, with the warning to a reader that this is still a work in progress. Some nuances, which will point out in due time, remain to be worked out before the standard is published.

Following the MANO model, [18] defines the VNF layer security function (VSF) for security management of a specific function, a (subordinate) VNF instance security function (ISF) and—to take into account the remaining un-virtualized physical network functions in legacy operations—the physical security function (PSF).

Lest these definitions sound too abstract, [18] provides examples of the VSF, of which we list two: (1) a firewall and (2) a tap for monitoring. The two examples of the ISF are an appliance provided directly by a hypervisor and a hardware box (an HSM, or TPM, or a crypto accelerator).

As far as the management is concerned, there are three blocks. First is the block of traditional security element managers, which enable the NFV security management functional block (NSM-FB)—depicted at the top of the figure. The NSM-FB is in charge of the overall security management. The three phases described earlier are exactly the processes it manages. The NFVI security management functional block (ISM-FB), depicted as part of the MANO virtual infrastructure manager,[20] is responsible for the horizontal management of the virtualization layer. There is a set of requirements specified in [18] that govern the operation of these entities.

---

[20]This depiction is likely to change as some participants in the NFV Security Working Group share the opinion that security management should not be performed by MANO.

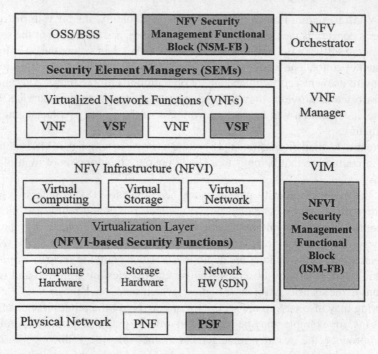

Fig. 2.8 (After Fig. 6.3-1 of [18]): Security management framework

Without going into the detail, we conclude this section with the note that [18] also defines a separate functional architecture for monitoring. Within this architecture a set of services and a protocol are specified for bootstrapping the trust for the whole infrastructure assuming the existence of the trust chain extending to virtual network functions.

2.7   Analysis of the *OpenStack* Security

The work on analyzing the *OpenStack* security was set up at the ETSI NFV Security Group at a very early stage, as the second work item after the NFV Security Problem Statement.[21] The work resulted in the publication of [19]; its findings communicated to *OpenStack* whose contributors were actively involved in writing this document.

Before introducing the findings of [19] (which assumes familiarity with the *OpenStack* architecture), the authors feel that an introduction to the architecture

---

[21]In fact, for the first 2 year of its existence, the group was an *expert* group (rather than a working group—the status achieved in 2015). As an expert group, the security group was not expected to produce its own documents except for the Problem Statement. Yet, the founders felt that a bottom-up study was necessary both to develop a sound standard and to influence *OpenStack*.

is in order. The *OpenStack* documentation, available at http://www.openstack.org/, is somewhat overwhelming as a first reading because of the sheer amount of detail. This is distilled to a more basic form in [4], to which we refer a reader. Here, we briefly list the most essential facts.

The foundation software components of the OpenStack deal with compute (i.e., host administration), networking, and storage. These are governed by the management functions, which include those of orchestration and identity and access management (to be addressed in the last section of this chapter).

The part of a component that implements an HTTP server (and is thus accessed via a API) is referred to by the OpenStack documentation as a *service*.

Each component is associated with a separate project in charge of its software development. The names of components and their associated projects are used interchangeably in the OpenStack documentation.

The compute component (developed in the project called *Nova*) contains functions that govern the life cycles of all virtual machines. Within the compute, the controller processes—the cloud controller, volume controller, and network controller—take care of the compute resources, block-level storage resources, and network resources, respectively.

The networking component (developed in the *Neutron* project) is concerned with enabling network connectivity for all other components. The services provided by this component support network connectivity and addressing. The native Neutron software presently supports configuring the TLS support for all API and implements Load-Balancer-as-a-Service (LBaaS) and Firewall-as-a-Service (FWaaS).

Neutron also allows to create routers, which are gateways for virtual machines deployed on the nodes that run the Neutron L3 agent software. Among other things, the routers perform NAT translation for the floating IP address—the public IP address that belongs to the cloud provider. It is a unique feature of the Neutron design that this address is not assigned through Dynamic Host Configuration Protocol or set statically. In fact, the guest operating system is unaware of it as the packet delivery to the floating IP address is handled exclusively by the Neutron L3 agent. That arrangement provides much flexibility as the floating (public) and private IP addresses can be used at the same time on any network interface.

To deal with detailed network management, Neutron supports plug-ins—among them that for SDN software. The plug-ins run in the back end. The front-end REST API allows, among other things, to create and update tenants' networks as well as specific virtual routers.

As far as storage is concerned, there are two projects in the OpenStack: Swift and Cinder. The former deals with unstructured data objects, while the latter provides access to the persistent block storage (here again, there is room for plugging in other block storage software).

Also related to storage—of a rather specialized type—is the service component (developed in the Glance project). True to its name, the service deals with storing and retrieving the registry of the virtual machine images. The state of the image database is maintained in Glance Registry, while the services are invoked through Glance API.

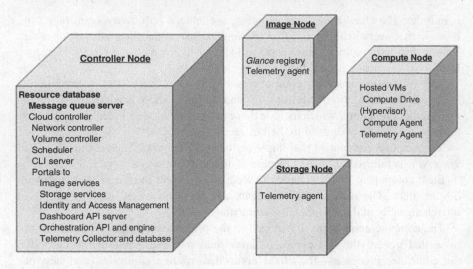

Fig. 2.9 Deployment example

The authentication and access authorization component is worked in the Open-Stack *Keystone* project, which governs the identity and access management. Needless to say, this function was a centerpiece of the security-related study.

Finally, there are three management and orchestration components. The user interface is available both in the "old" CLI form and through the web-based portal, the OpenStack Dashboard, developed as part of the OpenStack Horizon project. Two other components are (1) telemetry, developed in the OpenStack *Ceilometer* project, which is in charge of metering (achieved through monitoring) and (2) service orchestration, developed in the OpenStack *Heat* project.

To give a reader the feel for how these components may be deployed on physical architecture, Fig. 2.9 introduces a four-node deployment example.

The *compute node* is the workhorse of a data center—this is where the virtual workload is deployed. A compute node also runs various applications that belong to the management infrastructure. Some of these applications—called *agents*—initiate interactions with other components (and so act as *clients*); others respond to communications initiated elsewhere (and so act as *servers*). An agent can also be both a client and a server.

The *compute agent* creates and deploys virtual machines. It acts as a server to the *scheduler* (located at the *controller node*), but it acts as a client when dealing with the central resource database, *image node* and *storage node*, which, respectively, maintain the *Glance* image registry and either type (block or object) of storage.

The t*elemetry agents*, present in all three nodes, collect the performance data used in orchestration.

Finally, the *controller node* is in charge of cloud management. To begin with, it contains the global resource *database*. This database is replicated in all practical

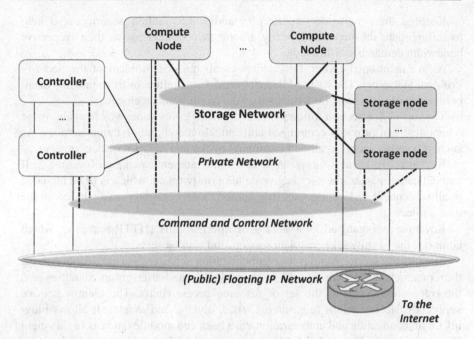

Fig. 2.10 Physical network isolation in *OpenStack*

deployments—for scaling reasons, and thus it needs a front-end (called *Nova conductor*), which handles the *compute agent* interface.

The *scheduler* is in charge of the placement function. It makes the decision on where (i.e., on which compute node) a new virtual machine is to be created and on which storage node a new block storage volume is to be allocated. For scheduling, the *Nova scheduler* is employed and for storage, the *Cinder scheduler.*

The *Message Queue Server* is the communications center for the messaging among the *OpenStack* API servers representing its components.

The practical deployments follow the principles of isolation outlined in the NFV Security Problem Statement. A typical deployment in a cloud data center is depicted in Fig. 2.10.

There, four networks are completely separate from one another:

- The storage network, which is intended only for accessing storage (and thus interconnects only the compute nodes and storage nodes)
- The private network, which exists only for communications among the hosted virtual machines
- The command-and-control network, which supports orchestration and management
- The public network, which allows connection to the Internet and which, for this reason, employs floating IP addresses

Keeping these networks separate, in addition to aiding security, also help to differentiate the network capacity among the components as their respective bandwidth demands are different.

As we mentioned earlier, [19] addresses all but one problem of the Security Problem Statement. The space of this chapter does not allow us to go into any detail here, except for the most important part—the identity management.

The rest of this section follows [19] in describing Keystone, which, again, is the component that provides centralized authentication and authorization services. As such, it controls access to all API consumed by the rest of OpenStack components.

Keystone works as follows. A user is first authenticated by Keystone.[22] If authentication passes, the user is given a temporary token, which is to be included in all subsequent service requests. The authorization decision is made based on the user's role.

Keystone is organized as a library of internal calls (HTTP requests), which comprise the identity service, token service, and catalog service.

The identity service handles user authentication and user-data validation. Among the constructs used here are the user, project,[23] and user-group identities and the role, whose value is the set of resource access rights. The identity service supports basic operations (e.g., *create*, *read*, *update*, and *delete*). It allows plug-ins for authentication and authorization via a back end module (such as Lightweight Directory Access Protocol (LDAP) servers or an SQL database server, the latter being the default).

The token service supports token management and validation. It relies on a database to store tokens and the token-management data, such as token revocation lists, token lifespan, and token scope—the set of projects and roles associated with the user. Initially, at the authentication time, the token is *unscoped* as no scope is yet defined. The scope of a token is determined by a combination of projects and roles associated with the user. An unscoped token may be issued during the initial authentication of the user, which can then use the token to discover accessible projects and then exchange it for a scoped token.

The token service ensures that tokens be protected from unauthorized access or alteration. Several types of tokens are supported, including public key infrastructure (PKI) (that assume the existence of PKI infrastructure) and the universally unique identifier (UUID), the latter type—defined by the IETF in [20]—being the default. The PKI-type tokens are verified based on the RSA signatures; the UUID tokens are merely random strings. We will discuss both types in more detail in a moment. It is important to note right away that both types of tokens are *bearer tokens*; in other words, a token is a magic wand—whoever possesses it has all the rights associated with it. It follows that it is essential to safeguard a token, for which OpenStack makes special provisions.

---

[22] Keystone provides the flexibility of employing an external authentication system.

[23] A *project* is defined as a specific set of OpenStack resources.

The catalog service manages the registry of all OpenStack services, supporting the service discovery—including the discovery of addresses of the respective servers. The region is where a server is located, and the characteristic of a server (i.e., public, internal, or administrative) is an attribute that can be defined here, and it is also possible to specify tenant-specific endpoints. As a reader may recall, this feature is essential for meeting the separation requirements for multi-administrative domains.

An important feature of OpenStack is that access permissions can be delegated. See [4] for the explanation and use cases. The construct for delegation is called a *trust*. The trust is implemented as an augmented token, where the delegation-specific information is added. It is created by the delegating party, called a *trustor*, and issued to the *trustee*. The trustor can revoke a trust that it had created.

The scope of the trust is limited to the set of rights that are being delegated. Once created, a trust cannot be changed. Unlike the tokens, the trusts may have unlimited lifetime. This feature is important since it is often unknown when a delegated operation needs to take place. If the lifetime is specified as *infinite*, the trust is valid until it is revoked. The original trustor can allow re-delegation, in which case the trustee may, in turn, become a trustor and delegate the rights it acquired as a trustee to another trustee.

Let us illustrate the use of the UUID and PKI tokens with a (simplified) workflow for provisioning a virtual machine.

We consider the UUID case fist. The workflow starts with the user agent, say *Horizon*, being authenticated by Keystone and, as a result, issued a token in the form of a unique string. (Keystone, which is the only entity that can validate the token, keeps a database, in which the string is associated with the user information.) To create a virtual machine, Horizon sends a request to Nova, enclosing its token. To understand whether the request is valid, Nova has to send it back to Keystone (enclosing its own token so as to allow Keystone to authenticate the transaction). Now Keystone has to look up the date associated with both tokens, first to ensure that the validation request actually came from Nova and, second, to validate that the token passed to it indeed belongs to Horizon and that Horizon has the right to create a virtual machine of the requested type. If all is well, Keystone will respond to Nova positively. We can see that for this transaction, Keystone had to perform two database look-ups. In reality (see [4] for the actual example of what is involved in the actual process of creating a virtual machine), Keystone needs also to talk to Glance and Swift. A reader can see that always going through Keystone make create a performance bottleneck. Again, this is because, UUID tokens can be validated only by Keystone.

In contrast, a PKI token is self-contained. Its structure is depicted in Fig. 2.11.

In this structure, the roles in the domain *SuperTel* are specified as well as the authentication method. The token is protected by the Keystone signature, which can be verified using its certificate. Thus the token can be validated by the receiver without going to Keystone, which eliminates the potential bottleneck and fixing the problem caused by the UUID tokens.

```
         "expires_at": "2017-07-27T22:52:58.852167Z",
         "issued_at": "2016-11-27T21:52:58.852167Z",
         "methods": ["password"],
         "domain": {
                 "id": "3b7650cecd974bf08041328b53a62458",
                 "name": "SuperTelNFV"
             },
         "roles": [{
                 "id": "7ae2ff9ee4384b1894a90878d3e92bab",
                 "name": "admin"
                 }
                 ],
         "user": {
             "domain": {
                 "id": "3b7650cecd974bf08041328b53a62458",
                 "name": "SuperTelNFV"
                 },
             "id": "3ec3164f750146be97f21559ee4d9c51",
             "name": "EntitledUser"
         }
     }
 }
```

Fig. 2.11 A PKI token structure

Unfortunately, nothing is simple. The problem is that the size of a PKI token can grow beyond the limit allowed in the HTTP header. This constrains the use of PKI tokens, and OpenStack, after temporarily making this type of a token a default, reverting the default back to the UUID format.

2.8   Conclusion

This chapter addresses the network function virtualization (NFV) security while reflecting on the work of the ETSI NFV Security Working Group (NFV SEC WG), and the industry view it has formulated in the past 4 years. The chapter has explained the differences between the "generic" cloud and NFV and discusses the security threats as well as new benefits for security provided in the NFV environment. The chapter further explained how *trust* is bootstrapped from hardware and established among the execution components and introduced the current work on the remote attestation. The requirements and architecture for lawful interception (LI) in the NFV environment, as well as the security monitoring and management in the NFV environment, are treated in much detail. Finally, a separate section is dedicated to the analysis of the *OpenStack* security. There is substantial bibliography offered to a reader who wishes to understand the background and minute detail of the subject.

2.9 Review Questions

1. Explain how the NFV environment differs from the generic cloud environment and list as many NFV security challenges and benefits as you can.
2. Explain how the NFV and SDN rely on each other's features in delivering network services and explain the security problems related to service chaining.
3. Explain why hypervisor introspection presents a problem for LI. What is being done to deal with this problem (name specific hardware components)? How can the proposed solution be applied to solving other (non-LI-related) problems?
4. Explain the differences between the TPM and HSM, and give one example for a typical use of each of these two modules.
5. Explain why remote attestation is needed and outline its steps.
6. Outline the architecture for the delivery of security management and monitoring services and explain its interfaces.
7. Explain how *OpenStack Keystone* uses *trusts* for tokens and outline potential security attacks when *bearer tokens* are used. How can tokens be changed to eliminate the security threats you described?

Acknowledgments The authors thank all participants of the ETSI NFV Security Working Group for the continuous discussion and development of the very subject of this chapter. In particular, thanks go to the Rapporteurs—who have been leading the work on the group's work items as follows:

Problem Statement (work item 1)—Bob Briscoe;
Cataloguing security features in management software (work item 2)—Hui-Lan Lu;
Security and Trust Guidance (work item 3)—Mike Bursell, Kurt Roemer, and Mihai Serb;
Report on Lawful Interception Implications (work item 4)—Scott Cadzow
Report on Certificate Management (work item 5)—Markus Wong;
Report on Security Aspects and Regulatory Concerns (work item 6)—Scott Cadzow;
Report on Attestation Technologies and Practices for Secure Deployments (work item 7)—Diego Lopez and Mihai Serb;
Report on use cases and technical approaches for multi-layer host administration (work item 9[24])—Mike Bursell and Anne-Marie Praden;
Report on Retained Data problem statement and requirements (work item 10)—Mark Shepherd;
Security Report on NFV LI Architecture (work item 11)—Alex Leadbeater;
Security Management and Monitoring specification (work item 12)—Ashutosh Dutta, Wei Lu, and Kapil Sood;
Security Specification for MANO Components and Reference points (work item 13) and *Security Specification for other MANO reference points* (work item 14)—Pradheepkumar Singaravelu.

We are very grateful to Michael Bilca whose LI architecture figures we re-used. Special thanks go to Don Clarke, whose leadership in the NFV ISG ensured that the work on security got the attention, support, and resources needed to produce the results partially described here.

---

[24]There is the gap in numbering because of renaming a former work item 8, as explained in Sect. 6.

References

1. Amzallag David (2014) "NFV Insights: The making of NFV Security—from Vision to Reality. Published by TNT at http://blog.tmcnet.com/next-generation-communications/2014/06/nfv-insights-the-making-of-nfv-security---from-vision-to-reality.html. Retrieved on December 14, 2016
2. ETSI Group Specification (2015) ETSI GS NFV-SEC 001 V1.1.1 (2014–10): Network Function Virtualization; NFV Security; Problem Statement
3. ETSI Group Specification (2015) ETSI GS NFV-SEC 002 V1.1.1 (2015-08): Network Functions Virtualization; NFV Security; Cataloguing security features in management software. Sophia Antipolis, France
4. Faynberg I, Lu H, Skuler D (2016) Cloud computing: business trends and technologies. Wiley, LTF, Chichester
5. Open Network Foundation (2016) TR-530, Threat analysis for the SDN Architecture Version 1.0" (https://www.opennetworking.org/images/stories/downloads/sdn-resources/technical-reports/Threat_Analysis_for_the_SDN_Architecture.pdf. Retrieved on December 19, 2016
6. Open Network Foundation (2014) OpenFlow switch specification version 1.3.4 (Protocol version 0x04). https://www.opennetworking.org/images/stories/downloads/sdn-resources/onf-specifications/openflow/openflow-switch-v1.3.4.pdf. Retrieved on December 19, 2016
7. Open Network Foundation (2016) TR-535 "ONF SDN Evolution Version 1.0 ONF." Retrieved on December 19, 2016
8. Edsger W. Dijkstra, EWD 1305. https://www.cs.utexas.edu/ EWD/transcriptions/EWD13xx/EWD1305.html. Retrieved on December 19, 2016
9. Scarfone K, Souppaya M, Hoffman P (2011) Guide to security for full virtualization technologies. Special Publication 800-125. National Institute of Standards and Technology. US Department of Commerce
10. Trusted Computing Group (2011) Virtualized trusted platform architecture specification. http://www.trustedcomputinggroup.org/virtualized-trusted-platform-architecture-specification/. Retrieved in December 2016
11. ETSI Group Specification (2016) GS NFV-SEC 003 V1.2.1. Network Functions Virtualization (NFV); NFV Security; Security and Trust Guidance
12. ETSI Group Specification (2016) GS NFV-SEC 010 V1.1.1. Network Functions Virtualization (NFV); NFV Security; Report on Retained Data problem statement and requirements
13. Draft ETSI Group Specification ETSI GS NFV SEC 007 Network Functions Virtualization (NFV); NFV Security; Trust; Report on Attestation Technologies and Practices for Secure Deployments. Work in progress. https://portal.etsi.org/webapp/WorkProgram/Report_WorkItem.asp?WKI_ID=44578. Retrieved on December 5, 2016
14. Simpson AK, Schear N, Moyer T (2016) Runtime integrity measurement and enforcement with automated whitelist generation. In: Proceedings of annual computer security applications conference (ACSAC). Available at https://homes.cs.washington.edu/ aksimpso/publications/ACSAC2014Abstract.pdf. Retrieved on December 5, 2016
15. ETSI Group Specification NFV-SEC 004 V1.1.1 (2015) Network Functions Virtualisation (NFV); NFV Security; Privacy and Regulation; Report on Lawful Interception Implications
16. Draft ETSI Group Specification NFV SEC 11 V0.0.6 (2016–05) Network Functions Virtualization (NFV); NFV Security; Trust; Report on Report on NFV LI Architecture. Work in progress. https://portal.etsi.org/webapp/WorkProgram/Report_WorkItem.asp?WKI_ID=47603. Retrieved on December 12, 2016
17. Draft ETSI Group Specification NFV-SEC 012 V0.0.13 (2016) Network Functions Virtualisation (NFV); Security; System architecture specification for execution of sensitive NFV components. Work in progress. https://portal.etsi.org/webapp/WorkProgram/Report_WorkItem.asp?WKI_ID=47619. Retrieved on December 15, 2016

18. Draft ETSI Group Specification NFV-SEC 013 V0.0.6 (2016) Network Functions Virtualisation (NFV); Security Report; Security Management and Monitoring for NFV [Release 2]. Work
in progress. https://portal.etsi.org//tb.aspx?tbid=799&SubTB=799. Retrieved on December 21,
2016
19. ETSI Group Specification NFV-SEC 002 V1.1.1 (2015–08) Network Functions Virtualisation
(NFV); NFV Security; Cataloguing security features in management software
20. Leach P, Mealling M, Salz R (2005) RFC 1422, A Universally Unique IDentifier (UUID) URN
Namespace. (https://tools.ietf.org/html/rfc4122)

Igor Faynberg a 2011 Bell Labs Fellow, is an industry consultant and an Adjunct Professor of
Computer Science in Stevens Institute of Technology. He represents Cable Television Laboratories
in the ETSI NFV ISG, where he has been chairing the Security Working Group for the past 4 years.

Prior to founding the Stargazers Consulting LLC in 2015, Dr. Faynberg had had various staff
and management positions in Bell Labs and Alcatel-Lucent business units where he had contributed
to a range R&D projects, starting from the development of variants of Karmarkar algorithm for
supercomputers, Intelligent Network, and its interworking with the Internet to cloud computing
and network functions virtualization. Most recently, he directed a group that researched solutions
for security and identity management problems and led their standardization in the ATIS, IETF,
ITU-T, ISO/IEC, ETSI, and INCITS Cyber Security Committee.

Prior to joining Bell Labs in 1986, Dr. Faynberg had contributed to design and development
of operating systems and a hypervisor as well as a network management suite for the Sperry
Distributed Communications Architecture and designed the Local Area Networking architecture
and protocols for the Burroughs Network Architecture.

Dr. Faynberg holds over 50 US and international patents for inventions relevant to converged
services, data communications, and security, and he has over 30 refereed publications in the area
of application of computer science to communications and network security. He has co-authored
three books entitled, respectively, Intelligent Network Standards, Their Applications to Services
(McGraw-Hill, 1997), Converged Networks and Services: Internetworking IP With PSTN (John
Wiley & Sons, 2000), and Cloud Computing—Business, Trends, and Technologies (John Wiley &
Sons, 2016).

He holds an M.A. in mathematics from Kharkov University, Ukraine, and M.S. and Ph.D.
degrees in Computer and Information Science from the University of Pennsylvania, Philadelphia.

Steve Goeringer is a principal security architect at CableLabs working on emerging technologies
and innovation projects. He has recently worked on security of network functions virtualization
(NFV), software-defined networking (SDN), medical devices, and cable modems architecture.
He has also been investigating innovations in integrating cryptography into cameras, block chain
solutions for the cable industry, and new approaches to securing home networks. He is currently
supporting the Center for Medical Interoperability as the chairperson of the security working group.

Prior to working at CableLabs, Steve had worked as a consultant for Polar Star Consulting,
LLC, providing technology leadership to government agencies. In this role, he researched WAN
acceleration solutions, investigated Ethernet security, and performed engineering and technical
selection of nationwide optical networks. Before that, he fulfilled several engineering roles at
Qwest, including Technical Director of the Access and Transport Networks team.

Steve spent 12 years at the National Security Agency where he was a Master Intelligence
Analyst. He started his career in the US Army as a Communications Station Technical Controller.
Steve has a Bachelor of Science degree in computer and information science.

SDN and NFV Security: Challenges for Integrated Solutions

3

Andrés F. Murillo, Sandra Julieta Rueda, Laura Victoria Morales, and Álvaro A. Cárdenas

3.1 Introduction

Telecommunication networks do far more than only forwarding packets; they process traffic through different network functions like proxies, firewalls, intrusion protection systems, and so on. These functions have traditionally been implemented through middleboxes, which are dedicated hardware devices inspecting, filtering, or manipulating network traffic. These middleboxes have to be physically connected between each other, and this physical connection creates a *service chain*. This paradigm has serious disadvantages such as high capital cost due to costly middleboxes, difficulty and long periods of deployment of new services because of the difficulty in reprogramming or reconnecting these middleboxes, and the inability to adapt the capacities of those services to the current demand, which inevitably causes over- or under-provision of resources.

Network functions virtualization (NFV) is a new telecommunication paradigm that enables the implementation of these network functions using software and general computing equipment, rather than dedicated hardware. In an NFV platform, a virtualization layer enables the deployment of virtual machines offering these network functions. Virtualization provides various advantages to the deployment of network functions and their management. First, commercial off-the-shelf (COTS) generic servers can be used to host these virtual machines, which avoids the use of

A.F. Murillo (✉) • S.J. Rueda • L.V. Morales
Systems and Computing Engineering Department, Universidad de los Andes, Cra. 1 #18a-12, 111711, Bogotá, Colombia
e-mail: af.murillo225@uniandes.edu.co; sarueda@uniandes.edu.co; l.morales825@uniandes.edu.co

Á.A. Cárdenas
Department of Computer Science, UT Dallas, Richardson, TX, USA
e-mail: alvaro.cardenas@utdallas.edu

© Springer International Publishing AG 2017
S.Y. Zhu et al. (eds.), *Guide to Security in SDN and NFV*, Computer Communications and Networks, DOI 10.1007/978-3-319-64653-4_3

expensive and dedicated hardware [35], lowering the capital costs of deploying and managing a network. Second, to deploy new services, we do not require buying additional equipment, only new software. Finally, virtualization can help scale up and down these network services, depending on the demand, and offer new services. For example, virtualization allows network operators to offer their physical infrastructure to multiple network services, in the same way that cloud computing providers offer their infrastructure to multiple clients. Network services may be offered to different departments in the same company or even to external customers in some cases. Such flexibility in the deployment and management of new services is the main driver behind NFV.

The deployment and management of NFV are facilitated by the use of software-defined networking (SDN). Using SDN, network traffic is steered between the network functions [38], and adding or modifying the service chain is a matter of simply creating instances of additional virtual machines and using SDN to update the forwarding decisions for such traffic. SDN also facilitates having different forwarding rules for different traffic subsets; in the traditional approach, an administrator would need to include a proxy to split traffic and forward it to different paths or use IP/MPLS labels to identify particular subsets of traffic, while by using SDN/NFV, we only need to add a proxy virtual network function (VNF) and update the forwarding rules.

The flexibility of modifying the operation of an SDN/NFV network, including new parties in the management of the network infrastructure, and the issue of sharing the infrastructure with other tenants brings new security challenges, as we need to guarantee that each network service meets its goals even when other (potentially untrusted) parties are also using the same network infrastructure. To maintain separation between different network services, we need to provide fine-grained access control. Research on improving SDN security with access control is a growing area of interest [47, 48, 64, 65]; however, previous efforts have focused solely on SDN and have not considered the new challenges of an integrated SDN/NFV network. In addition, NFV introduces the concept of service orchestration, which enables the creation of network applications through the composition of network functions using a predefined recipe. We consider that service orchestration is an important aspect of NFV that brings new security challenges for access control. These security challenges arise because service orchestration uses high-level recipes to build new network applications. In this sense, access control policies should have the same level of abstraction as these recipes. Nevertheless, it is expected that network applications built in SDN/NFV are composed of heterogeneous resources, given the diversity of network functions, possibly running on top of different implementation technologies. For this reason, different enforcement mechanisms must enforce the high-level security policies defined during orchestration.

In this book chapter, we present a survey in the main security challenges of SDN/NFV integration and discuss the definition of a secure access control system for SDN/NFV. To do so, in Sect. 3.2, we propose an integrated architecture of an SDN/NFV. In the same section, we discuss the main proposals in service orchestration and management for SDN/NFV. In Sect. 3.3, we discuss the main proposals aimed to secure the SDN/NFV platform; we also present a taxonomy of those proposals and discuss their limitations in the scope of SDN/NFV. In that analysis, we focus on the proposals offering access control for SDN and NFV. Finally, in Sect. 3.4, we consider the similarities of SDN/NFV environments with secure operating systems. Inspired by some of the best practices and lessons learned in the design of reference monitors, mandatory access control, and policy verification, we show how previous work on secure operating principles can facilitate the analysis and design of secure SDN/NFV infrastructures.

Our contributions include (i) presenting an integrated architecture that enables the discussion of a reference monitor and a mandatory access control system for SDN/NFV; (ii) discussing the new security challenges in SDN/NFV; (iii) presenting the largest (as far as we are aware) survey and taxonomy of SDN/NFV management, orchestration, and security; (iv) identifying how secure operating systems can guide our reference monitor design for SDN/NFV; and (v), based on this analysis, proposing an extended architecture for an SDN/NFV secure network operating system.

3.2   SDN and NFV Integration

A malicious or compromised network application can exploit the programmability of SDN/NFV networks to interrupt different network services, compromise the confidentiality of information, and affect network behavior in several ways. To prevent abuse of resources available in SDN/NFV environments, it is important to control how each application interacts with the infrastructure. The following use cases highlight the relevance of this control.

Service Orchestration: Service orchestration is a process that performs different steps: (i) receives a request for a specific network application; (ii) selects the appropriated VNFs to be included and chained in the application and according to the service request chains them in a specific order; (iii) creates virtual machine instances running each of the required VNFs (this step involves looking for an optimal, or near-optimal, placement of VNFs to minimize used resources, power consumption, etc.); (iv) interconnects the VNFs, deploying switches and routers to steer the traffic from one VNF to the next; and (v) monitors resource demands to detect whether it is necessary to scale assigned resources up or down. During the service orchestration process, it is very likely that multiple network functions will perform flow operations on the same flow resource, and it is important to enforce the privileges that these network functions have in order to prevent abusive behavior. The flow ownership and priority override proposed by FortNOX [47] for access control in SDN (where each application is the owner of a flow) make service orchestration difficult because allowing multiple applications to operate on the same flow would require careful planning of the application priority. Access control for SDN/NFV requires more flexible and fine-grained access control mechanisms to enable multiple applications to cooperate in the management of a flow without creating action conflicts. Nevertheless, access control for SDN/NFV also requires to offer a generic policy language that enables the definition of high-level access control policies to be enforced in the network applications.

Virtual Network Function Privileges: Service orchestration enables the development of new network services by interconnecting virtual network functions. Service orchestration is inspired by best practices in software development, which decouple each module of software in order to improve life cycle management and enable software reuse. In this way, network services are not expected to be monolithic but rather a collection of multiple VNFs, each of them performing a specific operation toward the service objective. In a future ecosystem where VNFs will be create and maintained by a large set of providers, maintaining the integrity of their software will be a challenge. A compromised or malicious VNF can perform additional functions (other than those specified) on the flows, processing; for example, a firewall VNF that only forwards or drops packets should not be allowed to modify the values of the packet headers. Static mechanisms of VNF validation and authentication are not sufficient to avoid this type of attacks, because even after a VNF is authorized to participate in a service chain, it can be compromised and affect the whole service chain. For this reason, an access control mechanism must dynamically control the operations that applications can perform over available resources.

Service Chaining using Third Party VNF: In a service chain, some virtual network functions might be offered by third parties—i.e., parties outside of the network operator domain. Third parties can offer a VNF via a virtual machine image in an offline mode or by offering virtual machine instances ready to interconnect in the chain. In each case, network operators must ensure that only the authorized network function participates in the service chain in the way agreed by all parties. This case requires the identification of the source of the resources and a policy manager capable of specifying and enforcing constraints over the way in which resources may be included as part of a service.

3.2.1 An Integrated Architecture

Industry and academia have proposed reference architectures to integrate SDN and NFV. The Open Networking Foundation (ONF)—the organization standardizing OpenFlow and advocating SDN—proposes a context where an SDN controller sees NFV as a network resource provider [38]. Similarly, the European Telecommunications Standards Institute (ETSI) describes the advantages of SDN/NFV integration; however, their architecture only considers NFV [15]. The Open Platform for NFV (OPNFV) [40] expands the ETSI architecture by adding OpenStack [61] to the virtualization control module at the NFVI layer. Other papers have also discussed the relationship between NFV, SDN and cloud computing [35]. While several organizations and academics have discussed various aspects of NFV and SDN integration, they have not defined a security architecture for SDN/NFV. Without the

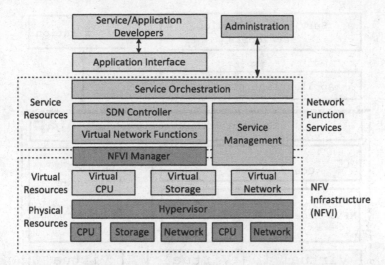

Fig. 3.1 Extended SDN/NFV architecture with three main layers: (i) NFV infrastructure, (ii) network function services, and (iii) application layer. The NFVI manager is the core of the *bottom layer*; it handles the NFVI and offers a virtual machine pool to deploy virtual network functions. The *middle layer* groups the available virtual network functions in the platform and offers tools for the orchestration of complete network applications and its management. The *top layer* groups applications that use the application interface to orchestrate and deploy services in the platform

explicit identification of trust boundaries and threat models, we cannot discuss the security issues that SDN/NFV deployments face and the security architectures that can mitigate or prevent these issues. To address this problem in the next subsection, we propose an architecture that integrates SDN/NFV elements enabling service orchestration and resource access control.

Figure 3.1 shows our integrated architecture. It extends previous proposals [15, 35, 38, 40] by adding SDN/NFV components missing by ETSI [15], ONF [38], and OPNFV [40], like the SDN controllers and the application interface and by explicitly identifying how these SDN and NFV components interact. In our architecture, a *developer* interacts with the platform through the *application interface* shown at the top of Fig. 3.1 (in yellow). This API provides the interface to the *service orchestration* module (in blue), which translates the service creation request sent by the developer and builds a network service recipe. A recipe contains the virtual network functions required to create the service, a topology description, and other qualities of service parameters that the service must meet. Using this information, the *service orchestration* module tells the *NFVI manager* (in red) to create the required number of virtual machine instances running the desired VNFs. After the VNFs are allocated, the *service orchestration* module uses the *SDN controller* to interconnect the VNFs according to the topology specified in the service recipe. Finally, after the service is deployed, the *service management* module collects metrics about the application performance and performs corrective actions (e.g., scaling up or down services or sending alerts).

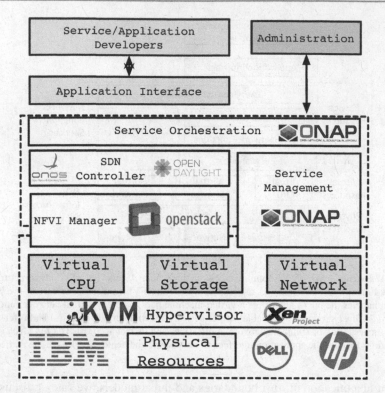

Fig. 3.2 Technologies that can support an SDN/NFV architecture. Several options are compliant with the ETSI MANO requirements for SDN/NFV, like OpenStack as NFVI manager and ONAP as the MANO module

Currently available technologies that support the proposed architecture and offer an initial set of capabilities for SDN/NFV include AT&T ECOMP [2], ONAP [60] (Open Network Automation Platform), and E2 [44] for service management and orchestration modules, SDN controllers ONOS [8] and OpenDayLight [22], and the Open Platform for NFV (OPNFV) [49] as an NFVI manager. OPNFV is based on OpenStack [61] and can be used with the KVM hypervisor. Figure 3.2 shows an example of how these technologies can support an SDN/NFV architecture.

3.2.2   Orchestration and Management in SDN/NFV

As we have seen, the orchestration and management modules control most of the resources in SDN/NFV networks, and as such, they require special attention for security purposes. In this section, we survey previous work on orchestration and management and organize them according to the following features: architecture, orchestration, configuration, and evaluation. Table 3.1 shows the classification of the proposals based on these aspects.

Table 3.1 Classification of proposals to orchestrate and manage SDN/NFV environments

	[46] OpenADN	[32] VIS	[31] ENCP	[24] Monitoring VNF	[18] Network abstraction	[27] APPLE	[44] E2	[2, 60] ECOMP	[17] Multi-domain survey	[4] OpenStack Congress	[42] OpenDayLight GBP	[6] Orchestrating VNF	[7] EnforSDN	[70] Vertex
Architecture														
Extends ETSI architecture	–	–	●	●	–	●	–	●	–	◐	◐	◐	◐	–
Extends ETSI component	–	–	●	●	–	–	–	●	–	–	–	–	–	–
Adds external component	●	●	–	–	●	–	–	–	◐	–	–	–	–	●
Integrates SDN	–	–	–	–	●	●	●	●	–	–	●	–	●	–
Orchestration														
Resource management	–	–	●	●	●	●	●	●	●	●	–	●	–	–
Traffic management	●	●	–	–	–	●	●	–	–	–	●	–	●	●
Configuration														
Physical and virtual resources	–	●	–	●	–	–	–	–	●	●	◐	–	◐	●
Virtual resources only	●	–	●	–	●	●	●	●	–	–	–	●	–	–
Single tenant	–	–	●	●	–	–	–	●	●	●	●	●	●	●
Multi-tenant	●	–	–	–	●	●	–	–	●	–	–	–	–	–
Single domain	–	●	●	–	●	●	●	–	●	●	●	●	●	–
Multi-domain	●	–	–	●	◐	–	–	–	●	–	–	–	–	●
Validation														
Simulation	●	–	–	–	–	●	●	–	–	–	–	●	●	●
Test bed	–	●	●	–	●	–	–	●	–	●	●	–	–	–

Legend: ●, feature considered by authors; ◐, feature not explicitly stated or that exhibits ambiguity

Architecture. This aspect considers if a service orchestration and management proposal fits within the ETSI management and orchestration (MANO) architecture or not. A proposal may extend the ETSI architecture by adding new components within the ETSI boundaries, may extend an ETSI component by adding functionality to it, or it may add an external component. This category also explores the integration of an SDN controller. Most of the proposals we found extend the ETSI architecture [2, 4, 6, 7, 24, 27, 31, 42, 60]. Three of these solutions build on the ETSI MANO module and extend it with more functions [2, 24, 31]. Other solutions [17,18,32,46,70] propose their own orchestration module outside the NFV architecture; they argue that it is easier to have a global view of the infrastructure from outside of the NFV architecture.

Several of the proposed solutions use SDN because it enables the construction of a global view and management of the network [2, 7, 18, 27, 42, 44, 60]; this feature can be used to orchestrate network resources and control traffic flowing through the infrastructure.

Orchestration. This aspect classifies a proposal according to the resources it handles. Approximately, 65% of the proposed solutions [2, 4, 6, 17, 18, 24, 27, 31, 44, 60] manage storage, computational, and network resources. Half of the articles address traffic management orchestration [7, 27, 32, 42, 44, 46, 70]. Two projects [27, 44] address management in both categories, resources and traffic, and both solutions use SDN.

Configuration. This aspect indicates whether a proposal handles hybrid environments (i.e., environments with physical and virtual resources) or virtual resources only. We also check if the solutions are single tenant or multi-tenant, and finally, we check if the solutions address single-domain or multi-domain environments. In the table, we can see that half of the previous work focuses on a hybrid configuration [4, 7, 17, 24, 32, 42, 70], and the other half focus on virtual configurations [2, 6, 18, 27, 31, 44, 46]. Regarding tenancy and domain, most of the proposals [2,4,6,7,31,42] were designed for a single-tenant, single-domain scenario.

Validation. This aspect classifies the proposals according to their validation methods, and they help us identify the maturity of the technology proposed. In particular we look if the technology was implemented in an emulation such as Mininet or if they used a test bed. We can see in the table that there is an equal split in the ways the service management and orchestration technologies were validated.

Security. Most of the proposals in Table 3.1 focus on tasks related to orchestration and management, but they do not consider security requirements. Nevertheless, in multi-tenant or multi-domain environments, several security issues emerge as multiple applications have access to the same resources, applications may affect the behavior of other applications, and various developers offer VNFs. Even in the single-tenant single-domain case, some security issues emerge as they also run VNFs that may come from untrusted developers and compete for shared resources.

The only two proposals in Table 3.1 discussing security are Congress [4] and GBP [42]. In particular, they propose to define and enforce rules to control network services. Congress supports the definition of a security policy to rule data services (conditions to expose data, resource owners, etc.) and also checks compliance of configurations with rules, while GBP allows users to define rules that mediate traffic between participants. Although these works address security issues, their scope is limited. Congress mentions an access control policy, but it does not support this kind of policy yet (it has not identified standard resources, operations, or defined access control rules, all steps which are necessary for access control). Similarly, GBP does not allow users to express access control rules and does not offer enough capabilities in the match/action pair to determine who is allowed to perform certain operations.

3.3   A Survey of Proposals to Secure SDN/NFV Platforms

Having defined the general architecture of SDN/NFV networks and summarized previous work on the orchestration and management of this architecture, we focus on *security* for SDN and NFV platforms. First, we identify SDN/NFV parties that may be malicious or could be compromised. We also analyze previous works and classify them according to the type of architecture (SDN, NFV, SDN/NFV) and features that may affect platform security. Finally, we analyze the scope of the proposals and their limitations.

3.3.1   Taxonomy

We grouped previous work based on (1) the type of deployment considered, (2) compromised components, (3) security goals, and (4) enforcement points. Table 3.2 summarizes previous work according to our taxonomy. In addition, we separate previous work by columns, depending on whether the authors considered SDN architectures, combined SDN/NFV architectures, or solely NFV architectures.

Type of Network. Our possible types of networks are SDN, NFV, and SDN/NFV (the columns in Table 3.2). As we can see, most of the previous work focusing on security has considered mostly SDN in isolation. Works to secure SDN include policy enforcement and analysis of applications as these are key aspects to secure SDN platforms [1,3,5,10,12,16,21,23,26,29,30,39,47,48,50,53,56–59,64–66].

SDN is more mature than NFV; SDN was proposed in 2010 [33], and some of its principles were stated in 2007 with Ethane [13], while NFV was proposed in 2012 [14]. As a consequence, the number of proposals to enhance SDN security is larger than NFV.

We did not include in our table SDN works that provide "security as a service" because their goal is not to secure the platform but to enable clients to build their own security services, like DoS attack detection and reaction [11,36,37,62,67] or enhancement of HoneyNet capabilities [19,45].

We grouped the NFV works that explicitly use an SDN controller as the component to control network configuration [9,43,51,68] in the second column of Table 3.2. Finally, although it is expected that most NFV deployments will integrate SDN in the future [2,28,41], there are some use cases for NFV security that can be studied isolated from SDN. We grouped them in the last column of Table 3.2.

Deployment. SDN/NFV architectures may be deployed with different configurations changing the trust boundaries of the system and the corresponding access control requirements. There are two parameters that affect trust: (i) tenancy, the number of different parties using physical or virtual resources available in the infrastructure, and (ii) domains, understood as the number of network administrative domains that are involved in the deployment offered to the final customer. Considering these parameters, we have four possible SDN/NFV deployments: *single*

Table 3.2 Classification of proposals to secure SDN/NFV environments

Proposal	Applicable in SDN/NFV	Single domain single tenant	Single domain multi-tenant	Multi-domain single tenant	Multi-domain multi-tenant	VNF	SDN application	SDN controller	Hypervisor	Manager	Confidentiality	Availability
[39] ONOS security	SDN	–	●	–	–	–	●	–	–	–	–	–
[65] SDNShield	SDN	–	●	–	–	–	●	●	–	–	–	–
[16] AuthFlow		–	●	–	–	●	–	–	–	–	–	–
[1] FlowChecker		–	●	–	–	–	●	–	–	–	–	●
[30] Kuai		●	–	–	–	–	●	–	–	–	–	●
[12] NICE		●	–	–	–	–	●	–	–	–	–	●
[53] Black box troubleshoot		●	–	–	–	–	●	–	–	–	–	●
[29] Anteater		●	–	–	–	●	–	–	–	–	–	●
[21] Header space analysis		●	–	–	–	–	●	–	–	–	–	●
[59] Flover		●	–	–	–	–	●	–	–	–	●	●
[66] ORewind		●	●	–	–	●	●	●	–	–	–	–
[5] PolicyCop		–	●	–	–	●	●	–	–	–	–	–
[26] SHIELD		●	–	–	–	●	●	●	–	–	●	●
[3] VeriCon		●	–	–	–	–	●	●	–	–	–	–
[57] Verificare		●	–	–	–	–	●	●	–	–	–	–
[58] Verifiable		●	–	–	–	–	●	●	–	–	–	–
[23] VeriFlow		●	●	–	–	–	●	●	–	–	–	–
[48] Se-Floodlight		–	●	–	–	–	●	●	–	–	–	–
[50] SDN Rootkits		●	–	–	–	–	●	●	–	–	–	●
[47] FortNOX		–	●	–	–	–	●	–	–	–	–	●
[56] Rosemary		–	●	–	–	–	●	–	–	–	–	●
[64] PermOF		–	●	–	–	–	●	–	–	–	–	●
[10] ToCP		–	●	–	–	●	●	●	●	–	–	●
[43] Policy checker	SDN/NFV	–	●	–	–	–	–	●	–	–	–	●
[68] Trust Framework NFV	SDN/NFV	–	–	●	–	–	●	–	–	–	●	●
[51] Network OS security	SDN/NFV	–	●	–	–	–	●	●	–	–	–	●
[9] SN-SECA	SDN/NFV	●	–	–	–	–	●	●	–	–	–	●
[34] NFV private processing	NFV	–	–	–	●	–	–	–	●	●	●	–
[55] S-NFV GX	NFV	–	●	–	●	–	–	–	●	–	●	●
[20] OPNFV Moon	NFV	–	●	–	–	●	●	●	–	–	–	–

Integrity

Access control

Accountability

Enforcement

Online enforcement point

SDN controller

Hypervisor

Platform management

Network orchestrator

VNF

Outsourced NFV

Offline evaluation

Validation

Simulation

Emulation

Test bed

Legend: ●, feature considered by authors; ⊛, enforcement is applied in physical infrastructure (server physical processor) *domain single tenant*, where the owner of the infrastructure and the user of VNFs are the same; *single domain multi-tenant*, which is analogous to a classic cloud computing example where cloud users wanted to ensure that (i) cloud providers are trustworthy and that (ii) other tenants cannot interfere with their security goals; *multi-domain single tenant*, where multiple telecommunication providers have an agreement to offer a service and where domains should interact only in ways explicitly established by an agreement between operators; and *multi-domain multi-tenant*, where a provider participates in services orchestrated among different network users to offer global or national network services.

Compromised Components. SDN/NFV domains have different actors, such as software providers, infrastructure owners, and orchestration managers. A malicious or compromised actor can have different effects on the system. For example, a compromised software vendor can offer a malicious VNF which could compromise a whole service chain. A compromised hypervisor could affect the behavior of all VNFs running on the physical machine. Finally, a compromised MANO component could harm the whole domain. Figure 3.3 illustrates the possible adversaries. To identify the adversaries, we analyzed the main articles in the area. Sometimes, the attacker model was explicit, or it was clearly mentioned what the security objective was. For other cases, these characteristics were not very clear, and we had to infer them based on certain phrases or key ideas that the author presented.

In our taxonomy, we consider five elements as potentially compromised: VNF applications, SDN applications, SDN controllers, hypervisors, and managers. From a logical perspective, SDN switches perform the same tasks that network functions offering a forwarding function. In addition, there exist multiple software implementations of SDN switches. For these reasons and to simplify our taxonomy analysis, we consider SDN switches as VNFs. A malicious manager can be either a malicious ETSI MANO component or a malicious administrator trying to affect the behavior of its company VNFs or third-party VNFs.

Security Goals. We define integrity, confidentiality, and availability at service level rather than at a packet level. Integrity ensures that commands sent by controlling applications are not adulterated and the corresponding actors implement the intended control action. Examples of integrity violations include a malicious SDN switch that affects the behavior of an SDN application by not applying a command the SDN controller issued or an unauthorized party altering the flow table of an SDN switch. Confidentiality guarantees that an application cannot observe data or behavior of other applications. An example of a confidentiality violation in a multi-tenant environment would be that one party gets unauthorized access to the policies being applied by another party to their VNFs. Availability guarantees that offered services keep running with acceptable levels of quality.

Access control guarantees that only authorized parties can perform certain operations on a set of resources. In the SDN scenario, these resources are represented by flow tables on the controllers and switches. In NFV the resources are more diverse and could be virtual machine instances, software repositories, etc.

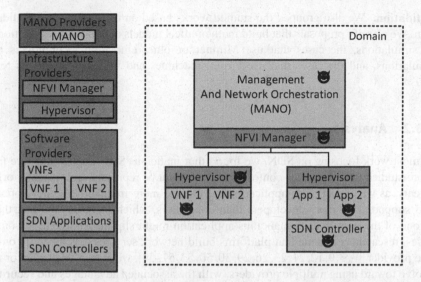

Fig. 3.3 Potential adversaries in SDN/NFV domains. Software providers offer components to create complete network services using service chaining. A malicious or compromised entity in the chain can compromise the whole chain. Software runs on top of virtual machines hosted by hypervisors. A compromised hypervisor could affect the behavior of all VMs running on the same physical machine. SDN/NFV domains also have management and orchestration (MANO) tools to build and manage network services. A compromised MANO component could harm the entire domain

Accountability is the capacity of establishing the entities that participated in a particular operation, including entities that made decisions as well as the ones that performed particular actions.

Enforcement. We identified two main mechanisms to improve SDN/NFV security: online enforcement and offline evaluation. The former includes mechanisms that enforce security policies at run time; the latter refers to static analysis or dynamic analysis in a controlled scenario, not in a production environment. Based on the architecture presented in Fig. 3.3, we identified the following online enforcement points: SDN controller, hypervisor, platform manager, and network orchestrator; the last two are MANO modules. An enforcement point at the controller mitigates faulty or malicious code in controller modules and SDN applications. Enforcement at the hypervisor mitigates the impact of compromised virtual resources, like network functions, SDN switches and routers, and even SDN controllers if they are virtualized. Enforcement at the platform manager allows having control over network resources and virtual machine instances deployed in the platform. Enforcement at the network orchestrator focuses on managing the SDN devices and applications present in the platform.

Validation. We also grouped the studied works based on their methods of validation. We classify proposals that build mathematical models or computer simulations as simulations, the cases that use Mininet or other emulation technologies as emulations, and the cases that use virtual machines and virtual networks as test beds.

3.3.2 Analysis

In most work focusing on SDN, we found that malicious SDN applications are far more studied than malicious controllers. This might be representative of real-world threats, as we expect SDN applications to change more frequently, be developed, and supported by more developers than controllers, which increases the risk that in one of these changes, a malicious application might slip in. Although, in some cases, researchers assume that platforms build network services developed by only one provider [3, 3, 9, 12, 21, 23, 26, 29, 30, 50, 53, 57–59], we expect this behavior to evolve toward using multiple providers, with the associated advantages and security problems.

Malicious or misconfigured switches have been considered in various works [5, 10, 16, 26, 29, 43, 51, 66, 68], and their impact is limited to the network service that uses the malicious switch, while malicious or misconfigured SDN applications [1, 3, 3, 9, 10, 12, 21, 23, 26, 30, 47, 50, 53, 56–59, 64, 66] may have a bigger impact, because SDN applications can affect the behavior of the SDN controller and other resources, including other switches.

Malicious VNFs. The most common type of deployment in works that consider malicious VNFs or malicious switches is single domain, including both single-tenant and multi-tenant variations.

Works that propose mechanisms to control malicious VNFs in single-domain multi-tenant deployments use two different points to implement enforcement, the SDN controller [10, 43, 64] or the hypervisor [68]. An enforcement point in the SDN controller is appropriate for this type of deployment because the controller has control over VNFs, so it can monitor, handle, and interconnect individual VNFs. Nevertheless, [50] argues that a VNF may craft a malicious packet that could be able to install a rootkit at the SDN controller, thus the need to add enforcement points in the hypervisor. A controller may check different variables at the enforcement point; AuthFlow [16], for instance, checks if an application that requests an operation has been previously authenticated and admitted in the platform. Rosemary also controls operations, but it uses sandboxing to allow only authorized actions generated by platform components [56].

Mechanisms to control malicious VNFs in single-domain single-tenant deployments mainly use offline evaluation and enforcement at the controller and the management module. Offline evaluation can detect misconfigurations, suspicious instructions, and dangerous API calls [26, 58]. For multi-tenant scenarios, enforcement at the controller includes actions like mediating all requests from SDN applications to SDN switches [64]. Enforcement at the management module involves monitoring resources and collecting statistics to detect suspicious behavior [5]. Malware and misconfiguration detection is important in multi-tenant scenarios because one party could intentionally try to affect other parties.

Malicious SDN Applications. The most common type of deployment in this case is single domain multi-tenant. Adversarial SDN applications are common in this kind of deployment because multiple applications can coexist attached to the same SDN controller and they can be developed by different parties.

Mechanisms to control malicious SDN applications use both offline and online evaluation and enforcement at the SDN controller. Offline mechanisms try to detect malware or misconfiguration that can compromise a network service [3, 12, 21, 30, 57]. The goal of enforcement at the SDN controller [23, 39, 47, 56, 64, 65] is to mitigate the impact of a compromised SDN application on a network service. Similarly, the goal of extensions to the controller or the management module to check new policies generated by SDN applications is to guarantee that new rules do not create configuration errors like loops or black holes [23].

Malicious SDN Controllers. A malicious or compromised SDN controller [9, 10, 12, 26, 39, 43, 48, 50, 51, 65, 66, 68] can have a great impact on network services. The most common type of deployment in this case is single domain multi-tenant; this may be explained because an SDN controller runs multiple SDN applications that can potentially be developed and deployed by multiple parties. Works that propose mechanisms to control malicious SDN controllers use enforcement at the controller itself. The assumption is that it is not the controller that is malicious, but the modules that have been added to add functionality. For example, [51] argues that not only the SDN applications should be sandboxed, but also some modules of the SDN controller; this prevents an entire network operating system from crashing. Another approach to contain malicious SDN controllers is to use a trust and reputation service [10]. This service requires several SDN controllers that share coordinating tasks and a protocol to select a trusted configuration out of all their different configurations.

Malicious Hypervisors and Managers. Finally, some proposals consider that hypervisors and managers may also be compromised [10, 34, 55]. This type of adversary can compromise the whole operation of an SDN/NFV platform.

The most common deployment for this adversary is multi-tenant, both single domain and multi-domain. This is the only case that considers a multi-tenant multi-domain deployment; we argue that this happens because this kind of deployment provides the only scenario where malicious hypervisors and managers may appear, as there are several infrastructure and NFV providers, as well as various network service clients. In other kind of deployments, it is expected that clients will trust domain management tools and the underlying infrastructure.

The works in [34, 55] consider scenarios where hypervisors try to break the confidentiality of VNFs running in the same machine they control. The work in [34] considers a hypervisor or NFVI that tries to gain access to the policies being used by the VNFs in the infrastructure. They address this problem using cryptography to protect the privacy of outsourced network function policies from the cloud, other tenants, and third parties. Another approach [68] argues that the NFVI manager and the MANO module should form a trusted computing base (TCB): the NFVI Trust Platform (NFVI-TP). The NFVI-TP would also guarantee trustworthiness of virtualized functions that offer critical security operations like key generation, key storage and ciphering. The work in [55] assumes the same kind of malicious hypervisor and proposes the use of specialized hardware to create protected memory pages that VNFs may use to securely store sensitive information.

We also found that the most considered security goal is availability; it is reasonable as one of the key tasks of SDN/NFV platforms is to ensure connectivity of all flows going throughout the platform and availability of supported services.

Integrity, confidentiality, and availability are partially supported by access control, and this is the second most considered security goal. Access control in SDN is approached by works like FortNOX [47] and SE-Floodlight [48]. Both approaches extend the SDN controller to mediate requests sent by SDN applications and allow or reject those requests according to a previously defined policy. Both proposals use similar characteristics: (1) they both use the controller as a policy enforcer, (2) policies are based on a role hierarchy, and (3) administrators assign roles to SDN applications. SDNShield [65] propose a policy language, compiler, and reference monitor to enforce permissions on SDN applications, inspired by Android manifests with Android applications.

Access control for SDN has also been studied in other proposals; for example, Wan et al. [64] identify operations that should be controlled via permissions to be able to implement the *minimum privilege* principle, and Ropke et al. [51] mediate critical operations with a function that checks whether a caller is authorized to access a critical operation or not. This enables the creation of access control policies for network operating system (NOS) components and for SDN applications, increasing the resilience of the NOS in case of failures or compromised parties. In this type of proposals, the enforcement point is not located at the SDN controller, but on the hypervisor or the element that is in charge of hosting/managing the SDN controller.

More importantly, access control in NFV and SDN/NFV has not been explicitly addressed, except for brief mentions in Congress [4] and Moon [20]. Congress considers access control policies, but the subjects of these policies have not been defined yet. Moon aims to build a security management layer for OpenStack and the OPNFV platform. Moon allows users to create security modules to protect different tenants in OpenStack. These projects include security policies that are enforced by several OpenStack modules (Nova, Swift, and Keystone). One advantage of Moon is that it enables the creation of a centralized security policy and it enforces it across the OpenStack platform. Nevertheless, Moon does not address security properties specific to VNFs yet.

Finally, we analyze related work in security for cloud computing. We consider that NFV and cloud computing share certain elements. First, services are offered by software running on top of virtual machines. Thus, the physical substrate is shared

among instances, which arises access control, integrity, and confidentiality issues
that need to be addressed. Second, the owner of the application hosts its business
logic in an infrastructure that belongs to another entity, creating trust challenges
between the parties involved.

Authors in [69] propose key-policy attribute-based encryption to protect user
information stored in a cloud. In the proposal, system attributes are associated to
a file for encryption and decryption. In a similar way, Excalibur [52] ciphers the
data using system attributes which can only be deciphered if the platform trying to
read the data has the same set of attributes. A Trusted Platform Module (TPM) seals
the information using the platform software stack. Although these proposals enable
access control for the files of different users, they only protect the confidentiality of
the data. We consider that in NFV access control for the operations needs also to be
enforced.

Distributed information flow control (DIFC) is used in [69] to increase the
privacy level in multi-tenant environments. Data flow control uses labels to represent
a privacy or integrity attribute. Using these labels, policies ensuring certain level of
privacy or integrity are enforced. Although DIFC can offer total mediation and a
framework to define security policies, its objective is to protect the data integrity or
security. We consider that protection is needed in the set of operations a determined
NFV can perform.

In [25] different architectures to achieve multi-tenancy in a storage cloud
service are presented. The architectures are based on virtual machines at hypervisor
level and use mandatory access control checks in one shared operating system
kernel. Nevertheless, we consider that NFV access control should address the
operations that VNFs can perform on resources. These operations are not limited
to read/write operations; instead, they could affect the network state or create
new instances of virtual machines. This is the main difference between network
functions virtualization and cloud computing. Instances in cloud computing mostly
offer computing services to tenants, while in NFV these instances offer networking
services to create network applications.

3.3.3   Limitations

While some of the discussed proposals address access control, they only consider
SDN and do not consider specific characteristics of SDN/NFV. Contrary to SDN,
SDN/NFV platforms have heterogeneous resources. While in SDN it is enough
to control access to operations over the flows, SDN/NFV platforms also need to
control operations on virtual machines and VNFs. Some proposals provide an initial
approach to virtual machines operations [20]. Nevertheless, none of the studied
works addresses issues related to VNF operations. In addition, the granularity of
the proposals may not be enough. For example, for one of the previously defined
use cases, virtual network function privileges (Sect. 3.2), FortNOX cannot handle
service chaining because it does not allow multiple VNFs to perform a set of
operations on the same resource (a determined flow). SDNShield is a proposal

that could handle service chaining if it were adapted to the NFV environment. Nevertheless, we consider that their approach is not sufficient to protect SDN/NFV infrastructures. First, we consider that their syntax is complex and does not consider the heterogeneity of resources and operations that may be performed in these architectures. The definition of flow filters, action filters, statistics, and topology filters does not include other types of resources like virtual machines and instances deployed; these resources also need to be controlled. In addition, due to distributed nature of SDN/NFV environments, multiple enforcement locations are necessary. For these reasons, we consider that a mandatory access control framework for SDN/NFV must provide a two complementary properties: (i) a general policy language that allows to describe the diverse resources and operations present in SDN/NFV and (ii) a compiler that translates these policies into security rules enforced across the platform, at different levels, and using different vendor technologies.

The rules that integrate the policy that governs platform behavior are not static; rules change as administrators add new resources and change or remove old ones. A policy manager must be consistent with this characteristic of the platform: this requires a language to express changes, a module to translate new rules to platform representation and back, and a mechanism to install new rules so they can be enforced. Some works provide policy management for NFV orchestration and management, but they do not provide management of security policies.

Besides, a particular VNF may be used to build different services for two different clients, and while it may be allowed to participate in one, the owner of the other one may decide that the VNF's provider is not trustworthy. Thus, SDN/NFV needs a component to consistently handle these types of policies when services are being built. While some works already address trust management both in SDN and NFV, we want to extend their approaches by enabling clients to define service constraints based on trust, i.e., the providers that are allowed to participate in a service.

All the identified requirements should be addressed by a single entity, although its decisions may be executed by other components subordinated to it. Some approaches to secure SDN/NFV platforms like Moon [20] follow this principle. We consider that this is in the correct direction; to enable administrators to define policies in a single place and that the platform translates those policies and sends them to the appropriate enforcement mechanisms. Operating systems approach similar problems in a principled and coordinated way, and these principles may be used to guide a security architecture for SDN/NFV platforms.

3.4 New Directions in Mandatory Access Control Systems for SDN/NFV

We envision that access control for SDN/NFV must integrate components at several layers, with a main coordinator, running as part of the service management and orchestration (MANO) module, making decisions, and delegating tasks.

The mechanism should support several tasks: it must enable trusted parties (domain administrators) to define policies to control the set of actions that any software deployed on the platform (SDN and NFV applications) is allowed to perform. These policies must be translated into proper security mechanisms enforced at the required levels in the platform.

This access control mechanism should meet the following characteristics:

- Provide a language that allows administrators to create policies representing the diversity of resources, operations, and users present in the SDN/NFV environment,
- Policies should be created using high-level definitions. That is, rules that integrate a policy should express what is allowed rather than how it will be enforced,
- Provide tools to map high-level policies to appropriate enforcement points and strategies,
- The access control mechanism should be mandatory and have complete mediation in the SDN/NFV infrastructure over the critical operations and resources.

Operating systems share certain similarities with SDN/NFV platforms, especially considering multi-tenant deployments. In both cases, the infrastructure owner is not the same that deploys software in the platform, also the software is developed and managed by multiple parties, and this software must perform operations that could be considered critical or that have a wide impact on the platform. Considering the similarities between SDN/NFV and operating systems, we argue that secure SDN/NFV environments can obtain valuable insights from access control fundamentals developed by secure modern operating systems. An SDN/NFV architecture enables a variety of network services that must be supported and controlled through an access control mechanism; not all applications running on an instance of this architecture must have access to all provided services. Considering this, we propose a mandatory access control framework for SDN/NFV. In the following, we extend this definition and explain its components.

In secure operating systems, the general authorization procedure works as follows [63]: A process tries to perform an operation on a specific object. The kernel mediates the request, looks for the labels of the process and the object, and queries a previously defined mandatory access control (MAC) policy to check if it allows the operation for a process and an object with the found labels. If the policy allows the operation, then it is performed; otherwise, the operation is rejected. We envision a similar procedure for SDN/NFV environments. To accomplish this, we propose an architecture that implements a reference monitor that should mediate all requests from applications to access resources of the NFV infrastructure (NFVI). Figure 3.4a, b illustrates similarities between secure operating systems and the proposed secure SDN/NFV architecture. Figure 3.4a shows how secure operating systems deploy mandatory access control and reference monitors. The reference monitor and the MAC are part of the operating system kernel. The reference monitor intercepts all operations identified as critical using hooks installed in the interfaces that grant access to critical services. The monitor queries the policy store and the MAC to

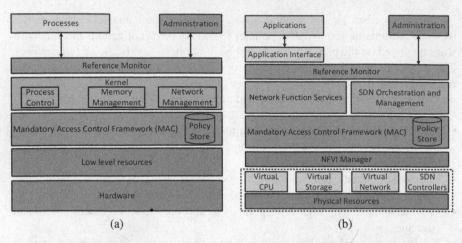

Fig. 3.4 Architecture of a secure operating system and proposed architecture for a secure
network operating system. (a) Operating system security architecture (SELinux). Processes request
operations, and the reference monitor mediates all requests, using a mandatory access control
framework [63]. (b) SDN/NFV secure architecture. The reference monitor controls the operations
that applications can perform on the SDN/NFV resources. The reference monitor queries the MAC
to check application permissions on objects

determine if the operation request should be accepted and answers depending on the
access control rule in the policy store. We envision that a similar approach should
be followed for SDN/NFV. Nevertheless, this system should have differences with
the traditional approach of operating systems due to the diversity and distributed
nature of SDN/NFV platforms. First, the tools and language to define access control
policies should be offered by the MANO component. Depending on the type of
operation, user, and resource being related in the access control rule, appropriate
hooks and enforcement mechanisms should be deployed in the correspondent layer
or module handling that entity.

3.4.1 Access Control

In a multiuser environment, it is important to authenticate each user and authorize
each request to access resources. The MAC concept introduced in our architecture
makes it possible to have authentication and authorization by assigning permissions
to specific authenticated users and applications running on their behalf.

As an example, suppose an administrator installs an application to monitor web
traffic in a specific network. This application would run on top of several virtual
machines across the platform. These virtual machines would have two interfaces:
one would be connected to the internal network the application is monitoring,
and the other one would be connected to an external domain, for administrative

Fig. 3.5 Policy compiler and high-level policies. The policy compiler takes high-level policies and translated them to lower-level rules, according to the underlying technology

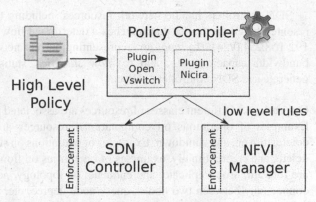

purposes. Although the expected behavior for this application is to only monitor web traffic, an application could also execute other instructions, like creating additional network flows.

To control application behavior, a network administrator would need to define policies and have an enforcement system. An example of policy is that the application only is allowed to receive statistics about web traffic in a particular network. Another policy would constrain management connections to an application by only allowing connections from a specific IP address to a specific port in the server that runs the application.

An administrator would define this kind of high-level policies, and a policy compiler must translate them into several lower-level rules that would be sent to the enforcement points like SDN controllers and NFVI managers. In the example, while the first policy will be translated to a rule to be deployed at the SDN controller in order to restrict access to the flow space, the second policy will be translated to a rule to be deployed at the NFVI manager in order to restrict connections from external domains. After installing the lower-level policies in the controllers and managers, new instances of the application will be secured (their behavior will be ruled by the policies). If the same application were deployed on an infrastructure with different SDN controllers or NFVI managers, the high-level policies would not change; the compiler translates high-level policies to lower-level rules according to underlying technology. Figure 3.5 illustrates this behavior. Secure operating systems use access control policies that combine resources, operations and users to rule behavior of different agents, like the ones present in SDN/NFV. In the following, we identify the resources, operations, and users for SDN/NFV environments.

Resources. In SDN/NFV, there are three classes of resources: (i) computational resources, (ii) storage resources, and (iii) network resources. NFVI managers handle computational resources (virtual machines with various CPU-RAM-disk configurations) and storage resources (virtual machine image repositories).

SDN controllers handle network resources including (a) *flowspaces*, [54] represented by all the traffic that matches a determined flow descriptor (like network 192.168.254.0/24); (b) *topology*, representing current network state (state of links, bandwidth capacity, etc.); and (c) *flow statistics*, statistics that SDN switches generate and SDN controllers collect.

Operations. Different classes of resources are associated with different operations. Examples of operations on computational resources are create, clone, modify, delete, turn on, and shutdown. Examples of operations on storage resources are copy, delete, and create. Finally, examples of operations on flowspace network resources are forward, drop, replicate, and enqueue; on topology, network resources are poll connectivity between two nodes, query node degree, etc. and on flow statistics are subscribe and unsubscribe. The policy compiler is in charge of translating high-level policies to lower-level rules that only include operations that correspond to the involved resources.

Users. Users are applications communicating with the SDN/NFV environment through the application interface. Each application is assigned a policy that ultimately defines the operations that are allowed on specific resources. SDN/NFV administrators define a policy per application at install time. An SDN/NFV security architecture must also provide a mechanism for administrators to update policies as needed.

Authorization. The proposed security architecture coordinates a set of enforcement points to make authorization decisions according to defined policies.

Considering the example application, an administrator would create the following kind of high-level policies:

For application A: *allow read traffic_statistics on network web_network*
For application A: *allow ingress from mgmt_endpoint*

where
web_network is { network 192.168.254.0/24 dst_port 80 }
mgmt_endpoint is { network_src 10.176.150.110 dst_port 23578 }

3.5 Conclusions and Future Challenges

SDN/NFV environments resemble operating system environments, where multiple applications make use of shared resources to achieve their goals. We discussed these similarities and analyzed the security challenges that SDN/NFV have in this area. We presented an extended SDN/NFV architecture that implements a reference monitor and a mandatory access control framework. These components enable applications to run on a shared resource platform, ensuring that access to the resources follows the policies defined by the administrators.

Further work is required to propose algorithms that can properly resolve conflicts among policies from different applications. The mechanisms used to limit resource distribution among applications and prioritizing certain applications when resources are scarce will also be developed as future work. The current proposal regarding authorization does not consider *information-flow*-based policies, like Biba or MLS. While `allow` rules enable administrators to assign permissions, on SDN/NFV resources, to applications, they are not enough to forbid flows that are contrary to defined flows, like Biba or MLS policies do because these types of policies require the identification of all possible information flows created by all types of operations allowed in the system, and to detect and deny any possible flow in conflict with policies. A future challenge is how to extended our architecture to offer enforcement for these types of policies.

Questions

1. What is service orchestration and what benefits does it bring to building network applications?
2. What issues emerge because of sharing resources in SDN/NFV architectures?
3. What is access control and how can it address these issues?
4. What are the differences in access control requirements for single-tenant and multi-tenant deployments?
5. Why is it possible to have malicious VNFs and SDN applications running in SDN/NFV platforms, and what kind of actions may they request?
6. What is policy enforcement and where can it be implemented in an SDN/NFV platform?

Acknowledgements This work is partially supported by the Department of Commerce by NIST Award 70NANB16H019 and by the Colombian Administrative Department of Science, Technology, and Innovation (Colciencias).

References

1. Al-Shaer E, Al-Haj S (2010) FlowChecker: configuration analysis and verification of federated openflow infrastructures. In: Proceedings of the 3rd ACM workshop on assurable and usable security configuration, SafeConfig'10. ACM, New York, pp 37–44
2. AT&T: ECOMP (Enhanced control, orchestration, management & policy) architecture white paper. http://about.att.com/content/dam/snrdocs/ecomp.pdf
3. Ball T, Bjørner N, Gember A, Itzhaky S, Karbyshev A, Sagiv M, Schapira M, Valadarsky A (2014) VeriCon: towards verifying controller programs in software-defined networks. In: Proceedings of the 35th ACM SIGPLAN conference on programming language design and implementation, PLDI'14. ACM, New York, pp 282–293
4. Balland P, Hinrichs T (2014) Congress a system for declaring, auditing, and enforcing policy in heterogeneous cloud environments. In: OpenStack Summit
5. Bari MF, Chowdhury SR, Ahmed R, Boutaba R (2013) PolicyCop: an autonomic QoS policy enforcement framework for software defined networks. In: 2013 IEEE SDN for future networks and services (SDN4FNS), pp 1–7

6. Bari MF, Chowdhury SR, Ahmed R, Boutaba R, Duarte OCMB (2016) Orchestrating Virtualized Network Functions. IEEE Trans Netw Serv Manag 99:1–1
7. Ben-Itzhak Y, Barabash K, Cohen R, Levin A, Raichstein E (2015) EnforSDN: network policies enforcement with SDN. In: 2015 IFIP/IEEE international symposium on integrated network management (IM), pp 80–88
8. Berde P, Gerola M, Hart J, Higuchi Y, Kobayashi M, Koide T, Lantz B, O'Connor B, Radoslavov P, Snow W, Parulkar G (2014) ONOS: towards an open, distributed SDN OS. In: Proceedings of the third workshop on hot topics in software defined networking, HotSDN'14. ACM, New York, pp 1–6
9. Bernardo DV, Chua BB (2015) Introduction and analysis of SDN and NFV security architecture (SN-SECA). In: 2015 IEEE 29th international conference on advanced information networking and applications, pp 796–801
10. Betgé-Brezetz S, Kamga GB, Tazi M (2015) Trust support for SDN controllers and virtualized network applications. In: 2015 1st IEEE Conference on Network Softwarization (NetSoft), pp 1–5
11. Braga R, Mota E, Passito A (2010) Lightweight DDoS flooding attack detection using NOX/OpenFlow. In: IEEE 35th conference on local computer networks (LCN), Denver, pp 408–415
12. Canini M, Venzano D, Perešíni P, Kostić D, Rexford J (2012) A NICE way to test openflow applications. In: Proceedings of the 9th USENIX conference on networked systems design and implementation, NSDI'12. USENIX Association, Berkeley, pp 10–10
13. Casado M, Freedman MJ, Pettit J, Luo J, McKeown N, Shenker S (2007) Ethane: taking control of the enterprise. In: Proceedings of the 2007 conference on applications, technologies, architectures, and protocols for computer communications, SIGCOMM'07, New York, pp 1–12
14. Chiosi M, Clarke D, Wilis P, Reid A, Feger J, Bugenhagen M, Khan W, Fargano M, Chunfeng C, Hui D, Benitez J, Michel U, Damker H, Ogaki KTM, Fukui M, Shimano K, Delisle D, Loudier Q, Kolias C, Guardini I, Demaria E, Minerva R, Manzalini A, López D, Salguero F, Ruhl F, Sen P (2012) Network functions virtualisation. In: Proceedings of the 2012 SDN and openflow world congress
15. European Telecommunications Standard Institute (ETSI). Network functions virtualisation (NFV); Architectural framework. http://www.etsi.org/deliver/etsi_gs/nfv/001_099/002/01.01.01_60/gs_nfv002v010101p.pdf. Accessed Aug 2017
16. Mattos DMF, Duarte OCMB (2016) AuthFlow: authentication and access control mechanism for software defined networking. Ann Telecommun 71(11):607–615. ISSN:0003–4347. doi:10.1007/s12243-016-0505-z. Springer
17. Guerzoni R, Vaishnavi I, Perez Caparros D, Galis A, Tusa F, Monti P, Sganbelluri A, Biczók G, Sonkoly B, Toka L, Ramos A, Melián J, Dugeon O, Cugini F, Martini B, Iovanna P, Giuliani G, Figueiredo R, Contreras-Murillo LM, Bernardos CJ, Santana C, Szabo R (2016) Analysis of end-to-end multi-domain management and orchestration frameworks for software defined infrastructures: an architectural survey. Trans Emerg Telecommun Technol 28(4). Published online
18. Haleplidis E, Hadi Salim J, Denazis S, Koufopavlou O (2015) Towards a network abstraction model for SDN. J Netw Syst Manag 23(2):309–327
19. Han W, Zhao Z, Doupé A, Ahn GJ (2016) HoneyMix: toward SDN-based Intelligent Honeynet. In: Proceedings of the 2016 ACM international workshop on security in software defined networks & network function virtualization, SDN-NFV security'16. ACM, New York, pp 1–6
20. He R, Chawki J, Duval T, Ba A, Compastie M, Lagadec L, Dutta A, Winandy M, Yegani P (2016) Moon project. Technical report. https://wiki.opnfv.org/display/moon/Moon. Accessed in Apr 2017
21. Kazemian P, Chang M, Zeng H, Varghese G, McKeown N, Whyte S (2013) Real time network policy checking using header space analysis. In: Presented as part of the 10th USENIX symposium on networked systems design and implementation (NSDI 13). USENIX, Lombard, pp 99–111

22. Khattak ZK, Awais M, Iqbal A (2014) Performance evaluation of opendaylight SDN controller. In: 2014 20th IEEE international conference on parallel and distributed systems (ICPADS), pp 671–676
23. Khurshid A, Zhou W, Caesar M, Godfrey PB (2012) VeriFlow: verifying network-wide invariants in real time. In: Proceedings of the first workshop on hot topics in software defined networks, HotSDN'12. ACM, New York, pp 49–54
24. Kim H, Yoon S, Jeon H, Lee W, Kang S (2016) Service platform and monitoring architecture for network function virtualization (NFV). Clust Comput 19(4):1835–1841. Springer
25. Kurmus A, Gupta M, Pletka R, Cachin C, Haas R (2011) A comparison of secure multi-tenancy architectures for filesystem storage clouds. In: Proceedings of the 12th ACM/IFIP/USENIX international conference on middleware, Middleware'11, pp 471–490
26. Lee C, Shin S (2016) SHIELD: an automated framework for static analysis of SDN applications. In: Proceedings of the 2016 ACM international workshop on security in software defined networks & network function virtualization, SDN-NFV security'16. ACM, New York, pp 29–34
27. Li X, Qian C (2016) An NFV orchestration framework for interference-free policy enforcement. In: 2016 IEEE 36th international conference on distributed computing systems (ICDCS), pp 649–658
28. Lucent A (2014) White paper: the right SDN is right for NFV. Technical report, Alcatel Lucent. https://resources.alcatel-lucent.com/asset/180618. Accessed Apr 2017
29. Mai H, Khurshid A, Agarwal R, Caesar M, Godfrey PB, King ST (2011) Debugging the data plane with anteater. In: Proceedings of the ACM SIGCOMM 2011 conference, SIGCOMM'11. ACM, New York, pp 290–301
30. Majumdar R, Tetali SD, Wang Z (2014) Kuai: a model checker for software-defined networks. In: Proceedings of the 14th conference on formal methods in computer-aided design, FMCAD'14. FMCAD Inc, Austin, pp 27:163–27:170
31. Makaya C, Freimuth D, Wood D, Calo S (2015) Policy-based NFV management and orchestration. In: 2015 IEEE conference on network function virtualization and software defined network (NFV-SDN), pp 128–134
32. Mamatas L, Clayman S, Galis A (2016) A flexible information service for management of virtualized software-defined infrastructures. Int J Netw Manag 26(5):396–418
33. McKeown N, Anderson T, Balakrishnan H, Parulkar G, Peterson L, Rexford J, Shenker S, Turner J (2008) OpenFlow: enabling innovation in campus networks. SIGCOMM Comput. Commun. Rev. 38(2):69–74
34. Melis L, Asghar HJ, De Cristofaro E, Kaafar MA (2016) Private processing of outsourced network functions: feasibility and constructions. In: Proceedings of the 2016 ACM international workshop on security in software defined networks & network function virtualization, SDN-NFV security'16. ACM, New York, pp 39–44
35. Mijumbi R, Serrat J, Gorricho J, Bouten N, De Turck F, Boutaba R (2016) Network function virtualization: state-of-the-art and research challenges. IEEE Commun Surv Tutorials 18(1):236–262
36. Morales LV, Murillo AF, Rueda SJ (2015) Extending the floodlight controller. In: 2015 IEEE 14th international symposium on network computing and applications (NCA), pp 126–133
37. Murillo Piedrahita AF, Mattos DMF, Duarte OCMB, Rueda Rodriguez S (2015) FlowFence: a denial of service defense system for software defined networking. In: Proceedings IEEE global information infrastructure and networking symposium 2015
38. ONF (2015) Relationship of SDN and NFV, Technical report, Open Networking Foundation
39. ON.LAB (2017) Security-Mode ONOS, Technical report, https://wiki.onosproject.org/display/ONOS/Security-Mode+ONOS. Accessed in Apr 2017
40. Open Network Function Virtualization, ARNO – technical overview. https://www.opnfv.org/software/technical-overview. Accessed Apr 2017
41. Open Networking Foundation, OpenFlow-enabled SDN and network functions virtualisation. https://www.opennetworking.org/images/stories/downloads/sdn-resources/solution-briefs/sb-sdn-nvf-solution.pdf. Accessed in Apr 2017

42. OpenDayLight, Group based policy (GBP), https://wiki.opendaylight.org/view/Group_Based_Policy_(GBP). Accessed in Apr 2017
43. Paladi N (2015) Towards secure SDN policy management, In: 2015 IEEE/ACM 8th international conference on utility and cloud computing (UCC), pp 607–611
44. Palkar S, Lan C, Han S, Jang K, Panda A, Ratnasamy S, Rizzo L, Shenker S (2015) E2: a framework for NFV applications. In: Proceedings of the 25th symposium on operating systems principles, SOSP'15. ACM, New York, pp 121–136
45. Pan X, Yegneswaran V, Chen Y, Porras P, Shin S (2016) HogMap: using SDNs to incentivize collaborative security monitoring. In: Proceedings of the 2016 ACM international workshop on security in software defined networks & network function virtualization, SDN-NFV security'16, New York, pp 7–12
46. Paul S, Jain R, Samaka M, Erbad A (2015) Service chaining for NFV and delivery of other applications in a global multi-cloud environment. In: 2015 international conference on advanced computing and communications (ADCOM), pp 61–66
47. Porras P, Shin S, Yegneswaran V, Fong M, Tyson M, Gu G (2012) A security enforcement kernel for openflow networks. In: Proceedings of the first workshop on hot topics in software defined networks. ACM, New York, pp 121–126
48. Porras PA, Cheung S, Fong MW, Skinner K, Yegneswaran V (2015) Securing the software defined network control layer. In: Proceedings of the network and distributed system security (NDSS) symposium
49. Price C, Rivera S, Peled A, Wolping M, Brockners F, Chinnakannan P, Sardella A, Hou P, Young M, Mehta P, Nguyenphu T, Neary D. An open platform to accelerate NFV. Linux Foundation. Published online: https://networkbuilders.intel.com/docs/OPNFV_WhitePaper_Final.pdf. Accessed Aug 2017
50. Röpke C, Holz T (2015) SDN rootkits: subverting network operating systems of software-defined networks. In: Research in attacks, intrusions, and defenses. Springer, Cham, pp 339–356
51. Röpke C, Holz T (2016) On network operating system security. Int J Netw Manag 26(1):6–24
52. Santos N, Rodrigues R, Gummadi KP, Saroiu S (2012) Policy-sealed data: a new abstraction for building trusted cloud services. In: Presented as part of the 21st USENIX security symposium (USENIX Security 12), Bellevue, pp 175–188
53. Scott C, Wundsam A, Raghavan B, Panda A, Or A, Lai J, Huang E, Liu Z, El-Hassany A, Whitlock S, Acharya H, Zarifis K, Shenker S (2014) Troubleshooting blackbox SDN control software with minimal causal sequences. SIGCOMM Comput Commun Rev 44(4):395–406
54. Sherwood R, Gibb G, Yap KK, Appenzeller G, Casado M, McKeown N, Parulkar G (2010) Can the production network be the testbed? In: Proceedings of the 9th USENIX conference on operating systems design and implementation. USENIX Association, pp 1–6
55. Shih MW, Kumar M, Kim T, Gavrilovska A (2016) S-NFV: securing NFV states by using SGX. In: Proceedings of the 2016 ACM international workshop on security in software defined networks & network function virtualization, SDN-NFV security'16. ACM, New York, pp 45–48
56. Shin S, Song Y, Lee T, Lee S, Chung J, Porras P, Yegneswaran V, Noh J, Kang BB (2014) Rosemary: a robust, secure, and high-performance network operating system. In: Proceedings of the 2014 ACM SIGSAC conference on computer and communications security, CCS'14. ACM, New York, pp 78–89
57. Skowyra R, Lapets A, Bestavros A, Kfoury A (2014) A verification platform for SDN-enabled applications. In: 2014 IEEE international conference on cloud engineering (IC2E), pp 337–342
58. Skowyra RW, Lapets A, Bestavros A, Kfoury A (2013) Verifiably-safe software-defined networks for CPS. In: Proceedings of the 2nd ACM international conference on high confidence networked systems, HiCoNS'13, New York, pp 101–110
59. Son S, Shin S, Yegneswaran V, Porras P, Gu G (2013) Model checking invariant security properties in openflow. In: 2013 IEEE international conference on communications (ICC), pp 1974–1979

60. The Linux Foundation (2017) Open network automation platform (ONAP) project releases code, expands membership and announces board positions. Technical report. https://www. onap.org/. Accessed in Apr 2017
61. Tkachova O, Salim MJ, Yahya AR (2015) An analysis of SDN-OpenStack integration. In: Problems of Infocommunications Science and Technology (PIC S T), 2015 Second International Scientific-Practical Conference, pp 60–62
62. Wang R, Jia Z, Ju L (2015) An entropy-based distributed DDoS detection mechanism in software-defined networking. In: Trustcom/BigDataSE/ISPA, 2015, vol 1. IEEE, pp 310–317
63. Watson RNM (2013) A decade of OS access-control extensibility. Commun ACM 56(2):52–63
64. Wen X, Chen Y, Hu C, Shi C, Wang Y (2013) Towards a secure controller platform for openflow applications. In: Proceedings of the second ACM SIGCOMM workshop on hot topics in software defined networking, HotSDN'13. ACM, New York, pp 171–172
65. Wen X, Yang B, Chen Y, Hu C, Wang Y, Liu B, Chen X (2016) Sdnshield: reconciliating configurable application permissions for sdn app markets. In: 2016 46th annual IEEE/IFIP international conference on dependable systems and networks (DSN), pp 121–132
66. Wundsam A, Levin D, Seetharaman S, Feldmann A (2011) OFRewind: enabling record and replay troubleshooting for networks. In: Proceedings of the 2011 USENIX conference on USENIX annual technical conference, USENIXATC'11. USENIX Association, Berkeley, pp 29–29
67. Yan Q, Yu F (2015) Distributed denial of service attacks in software-defined networking with cloud computing. IEEE Commun. Mag. 53(4):52–59
68. Yan Z, Zhang P, Vasilakos AV (2016) A security and trust framework for virtualized networks and software-defined networking. Security Commun. Netw. 9(16):3059–3069
69. Yu S, Wang C, Ren K, Lou W (2010) Achieving secure, scalable, and fine-grained data access control in cloud computing. In: 2010 proceedings IEEE INFOCOM, pp 1–9
70. Zhang Q, Wang X, Kim I, Palacharla P, Ikeuchi T (2016) Vertex-centric computation of service function chains in multi-domain networks. In: 2016 IEEE netsoft conference and workshops (NetSoft), pp 211–218

Andrés F. Murillo is a doctorate student at Los Andes University, Bogotá, Colombia. He holds an M. Sc. from Universidade Federal do Rio de Janeiro (UFRJ), Brazil. His research interests are network security, software-defined networking, and network function virtualization.

Sandra Julieta Rueda is an assistant professor at Los Andes University, Bogotá, Colombia. She holds an M.S. degree from Los Andes University and a Ph.D. from the Pennsylvania State University, Pennsylvania. Her research interests are security of software systems, access control, policy analysis, and policy generation.

Laura Victoria Morales is a doctorate student at Los Andes University, Bogotá, Colombia. She holds a master's degree on security information from Los Andes University. Her research interests are network security, software-defined networks, and the Internet of things.

Álvaro A. Cárdenas is an assistant professor at the Department of Computer Science at the University of Texas at Dallas. He holds M.S. and Ph.D. degrees from the University of Maryland, College Park. Before joining UT Dallas, he was a postdoctoral scholar at the University of California, Berkeley, and a research staff at Fujitsu Laboratories of America in Sunnyvale, California. His research interests focus on computer security, cyber-physical systems, and network intrusion detection. He is the recipient of the NSF CAREER award and best paper awards from the IEEE Smart Grid Communications Conference and the US Army Research Conference.

Trust in SDN/NFV Environments

4

Antonio Lioy, Tao Su, Adrian L. Shaw, Hamza Attak, Diego R. Lopez, and Antonio Pastor

4.1   Introduction

Network infrastructure is quickly evolving from a hardware-based switch-only layer to a full-fledged computational system. This is permitted by the advent of two new architectures, namely, software-defined networking (SDN) and network functions virtualisation (NFV).

The usage of SDN and NFV introduces new network abstractions and high-level .software-based primitives that are powerful and flexible. However, this also creates a trust gap for administrators as they cannot easily assess the correct behaviour of the software components of these architectures. Due to errors or attacks, the modules may act differently from their expected behaviour. Thus, in order to trust a softwarised network, the integrity of software modules is vital.

In a SDN/NFV environment, we envision that *a softwarised network can be trusted if and only if its expected behaviour can be guaranteed*. Following this definition, in order to trust a softwarised network, all software modules launched

A. Lioy (✉) • T. Su
Dipartimento di Automatica e Informatica, Politecnico di Torino,
corso Duca degli Abruzzi, 24, 10129, Torino, Italy
e-mail: antonio.lioy@polito.it; tao.su@polito.it

A.L. Shaw • H. Attak
Hewlett Packard Enterprise, Bristol, UK
e-mail: als@hpe.com; hamza.attak@hpe.com

D.R. Lopez
Telefonica I+D, Seville, Spain
e-mail: diego.r.lopez@telefonica.com

A. Pastor
Telefonica I+D, Distrito Telefonica, West 1 Building, Ronda de la Comunicación S/N, 28050, Madrid, Spain
e-mail: antonio.pastorperales@telefonica.com

© Springer International Publishing AG 2017   103
S.Y. Zhu et al. (eds.), *Guide to Security in SDN and NFV*, Computer
Communications and Networks, DOI 10.1007/978-3-319-64653-4_4

in network nodes and their load-time static and runtime dynamic configurations must be known, which implies that the operations performed and the corresponding behaviour are as expected.

Therefore, a novel technique is needed to achieve this goal. Currently, a lot of attention is paid to remote attestation (RA), a main feature of the trusted computing (TC) architecture which provides hardware-based authentic evidence of a physical node's software integrity state. In a nutshell, remote attestation relies on a specially designed hardware chip – namely, the Trusted Platform Module (TPM)[1] – to provide isolated storage, limited access capability, and a unique cryptographic identity whose private part never leaves the chip. Coupled with a proper firmware, it creates a platform where each software component is "measured" (i.e. its digest is computed and reliably stored) before being executed or accessed. When requested by an authorised actor, the platform can securely report the list of all software modules executed since initialisation. This may include also the configuration files and it should, as they influence the platform's behaviour as well.

Thanks to hardware-based countermeasures, this approach is resistant to attacks in the considered adversary model: by assumption, an attacker could launch network-based attacks against the SDN/NFV network nodes (e.g. to load a cracked software module or to change a critical configuration file for achieving some malicious result, such as mirroring traffic to a third party), but he could never get physical access to the nodes.

Although there are other hardware-assisted isolation and trusted execution environments, such as TrustZone in ARM-based systems, the remote attestation technique coupled with TPM is the only technique considered here because it is based on a standard specification, freely available, and its essential building block, i.e. TPM, is available in millions of devices, including server-class ones as needed by SDN/NFV infrastructures. This does not exclude solutions based on other technologies, provided that they support reliable, secure, and trusted reporting of the global software state of a platform, from the boot process up to the applications.

However, direct application of remote attestation to SDN/NFV environments requires various improvements over the basic technique.

First, remote attestation is not virtualisation friendly, as discussed in Sect. 4.3. This requires a full understanding of the limitations of integrity reporting in virtualised infrastructures and points to a research area which is worth investigating. This problem concerns traditional hypervisor-based virtualisation environments, while lightweight ones (such as the Linux containers as implemented in Docker) are more easy to couple with remote attestation, as discussed in Sect. 4.3.2.

Second, standard remote attestation is only able to attest the load-time integrity of the network nodes (i.e. the executed software modules and their static configurations), but it does not offer any guarantee of runtime properties. Solving this problem requires the introduction of a specific monitoring plane, with a dedicated element

---

[1]This paper directly considers TPM-1.2 which has been massively deployed in business class laptops, desktops, and servers, but the same concepts apply to the newest TPM 2.0 as well.

which retrieves the expected dynamic configuration from the SDN/NFV controller and compares it against the information directly obtained from the network nodes through remote attestation. This approach is discussed in Sect. 4.4.

Third, since SDN/NFV environments typically contains a plethora of nodes, management, scalability, and performance must be carefully addressed. To this extent, we consider the OpenAttestation framework [8] as an example of a management platform for attestation in a cloud-like environment and discuss the improvements needed to make it more scalable and push its performance to the limits imposed by the hardware components.

Last but not least, since network environments are often heterogeneous, standardisation is important as well. In this respect, we discuss the role of remote attestation in the management and orchestration of NFV environments, as currently addressed in the IETF and ETSI working groups.

4.2   Remote Attestation

Remote attestation is a main feature provided by the trusted computing technology. The overall scheme proposed by the Trusted Computing Group (TCG) for using trusted computing is based on a step-by-step extension of trust, called a *chain of trust*. It uses a transitive mechanism: if the first execution step can be trusted and each step correctly measures the next executable software for integrity, then the overall system integrity can be evaluated. A trusted computing platform "measures" (i.e. computes the digest of) each piece of software before execution, and the measure is stored inside a secure log. Later, at the request of an external party, the attesting platform (hereafter *attester*) can present this log, signed with a unique asymmetric key of the platform to prove its identity and integrity state. Verification of this log can be performed directly by the partner which requested the attestation, but, given its complexity, it is often delegated to an external trusted third party, named *verifier*.

From the chain of trust extension point of view, any component that needs to be loaded is considered an adversary, and it must be measured before it is loaded. The base case for the extension of the chain of trust is called the *root of trust for measurement*; it encompasses the minimal combination of hardware and software elements to be trusted by a remote verifier in order to validate the entire chain of trust. It is recommended to use a hardware device in combination with software components to create a strong unforgeable identity and provide safe storage of evidence. Therefore the main components of the Root of Trust for Measurement are: (i) a specialised hardware component to store the log and measurements away from the software access, (ii) an initial isolated component that is able to measure the first non-trusted software, which, if trusted, will measure the next untrusted software layer.

When using a TPM as root of trust, measurements of the software stack are stored in special on-board *Platform Configuration Registers* (PCRs). There are normally a small number of PCRs (at least 16) that can be used for storing measurements. For security reasons, it is not possible to directly write to a PCR; instead measurements must be stored using a special operation called *extend*. The extend operation can update a PCR by producing a global hash of the concatenated values of the previous PCR content with the new measurement, such as the following:

$$PCR^{new} = sha1(PCR^{old} \parallel measurement) \tag{4.1}$$

This approach brings two benefits. First, it allows for an unlimited number of measurements to be captured in a single PCR, since the size of the values is always the same, and it retains a verifiable ordered chain of all the previous measurements. Second, it is computationally infeasible for an attacker to calculate two different hashes that will match the same resulting value of a PCR extend operation. It should be noted that while TPM-1.2 always used the SHA1 algorithm for measurements and the extend operation, the newer TPM-2.0 permits also the use of the stronger SHA256 digest algorithm.

Besides strong isolated storage, the TPM also provides a unique key whose private part never leaves the TPM. This key is called *endorsement key* (EK), and it is created when the TPM is manufactured. To preserve the privacy of a platform identity, *attestation identity keys* (AIKs) are generated and used in the remote attestation process instead of the EK. The AIK is an alias of the EK; its private part also never leaves the TPM which generated it. However, binding the EK and the AIKs of a TPM must be done in conjunction with a third party – namely, a *privacy certification authority* (PrivacyCA) – which is trusted to not reveal the real platform identity but to act as an intermediary. The use of AIKs and PrivacyCA is not important when privacy is not at stake or, on the contrary, if a strong proof of the real identity of the node being attested is requested. This is typically the case of SDN/NFV nodes, whose management requires both strong integrity and identity evidence.

When a platform receives a remote attestation request, it sends back an integrity report which comprises the values stored in the PCRs and their digital signature computed with an AIK. Since the private part of the AIK is never released from the TPM, then the authenticity and integrity of the report are guaranteed.

To be more specific, the operation to get signed PCR values from a TPM is called *quote*. This operation is simple from both the verifier's and the attester's point of view. The verifier wishing to validate the integrity state of the attester sends a remote attestation request specifying an AIK for generating the digital signature, the set of PCRs to quote, and a nonce to ensure the freshness of the digital signature. After the TPM receives the remote attestation request, it validates the authorisation to use the AIK, fills in a structure with the set of PCRs to be quoted, and generates a digital signature on the filled-in structure with the specified AIK. Then, it returns the digital signature and the PCR values to the verifier, which in turn validates the integrity of the PCR values received by using the public portion of the AIK. If the PCR values are intact, then the verifier assesses the attester's trustworthiness by comparing the reported values with those in a whitelist database (Fig. 4.1).

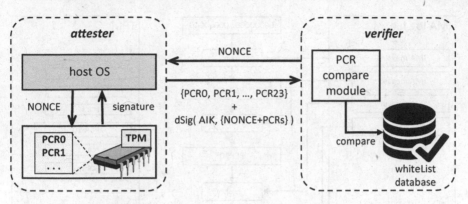

Fig. 4.1 The remote attestation process

4.2.1 Trusted Boot

Trusted boot is used to ensure that the platform is booted into a trusted state. It can be achieved by storing into different PCRs the digests of the components loaded during the boot phase. The following list describes which PCRs can be used during a trusted boot process, according to the TCG specification:

- PCRs 00-03 for use by the core Root of Trust for Measurement (initial EEPROM or PC BIOS);
- PCRs 04-07 for use by the bootloader stages;
- PCRs 08-15 for use by the booted base system (e.g. compartmentalisation system, hypervisor).

It should be noted that the PCR values are predictable if and only if the same boot components are always loaded in a specific fixed order. Thus, when a verifier receives a set of authentic PCR values, it can be sure that the platform was booted by using only known trusted components and the operating system is thus running in a trusted state.

4.2.2 Service Measurement

Once the operating system is booted into a trusted state, it will measure each service loaded through an appropriate component, such as the Linux *integrity measurement architecture* (IMA) [1]. These measurements are stored in a *Stored Measurement Log* (SML), and each measure is also extended into a PCR in the TPM (Fig. 4.2). Thus the integrity of the SML is implicitly authenticated by the TPM. Later, the measurements in the SML will be used during the remote attestation process, as an evidence to prove the integrity state of the loaded services.

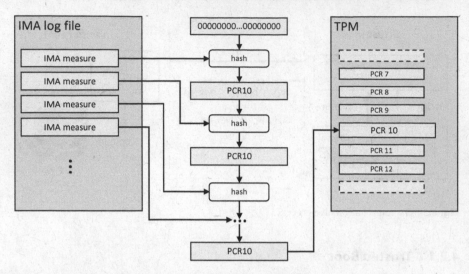

Fig. 4.2 The TPM extend operations for IMA measurements

```
PCR#  template-hash  template  filedata-hash    filename-hint
 10   fc465...848ee   ima      e4092...732e6c   /usr/sbin/iptables
 10   48327...9fed4   ima      f7655...43f45c   /etc/iptables-init
 10   bd57b...e45b3   ima      810cf...f821d6   /usr/sbin/sshd
 10   94ea2...eff6b   ima      960f7...a9728a   /etc/ssh/sshd_config
```

Fig. 4.3 An example of IMA measurements in ASCII format

Figure 4.3 contains an example of the SML content, displaying the four most important IMA measurements for a host firewall application:

- the file /usr/sbin/iptables is the iptables executable loaded by the system kernel, and /etc/iptables-init is its initial configuration when the system is booted;
- SSH is used to access the application host remotely, so the system measures the corresponding executable /usr/sbin/sshd and its configuration in the file /etc/ssh/sshd_config.

The filedata-hash column shows the hash value (i.e. digest) of the files, and these values are extended into PCR 10 in the way illustrated in Fig. 4.2.

4.2.3 Verification

When an integrity report is received by the verifier, it first checks the digital signature of the report with the public part of the AIK. Then it compares the received

PCR values to a whitelist database in order to check that the boot phase of the attester is trusted. Afterwards, the verifier extracts the IMA measurements from the integrity report and recomputes the final value of all the extend operations as illustrated in Fig. 4.2. If the final value equals to the PCR value in the received integrity report, then this proves the IMA measurement list is intact. Finally, the verifier queries the IMA measurements to a well-formed database with whitelisted custom configurations. In the case that a received PCR value or a measure in the integrity report does not match any element in the whitelist, then the verifier can assess that the node has not booted into a trusted state or a certain service in the application layer has been compromised. This is evidence that an unknown/manipulated component has been loaded or an unknown/altered configuration file has been read. In turn this problem may be traced back either to an attack or a management error (e.g. an unauthorised change to the node's configuration or an authorised change not followed by an update of the whitelist). So remote attestation is a technique which is useful to detect not only attacks but also system management problems.

4.3 Attesting Virtual Network Infrastructures

SDN/NFV environments make extensive use of virtualisation; hence, remote attestation of physical platforms is insufficient to guarantee integrity of these environments. Unfortunately, remote attestation is difficult in a virtualisation context for two main reasons. First, typically the virtualisation layer breaks the link amongst the services running in the virtualised instances and the hardware TPM. Second, the number of virtualised instances running on a single platform is significantly higher than the resources provided by the TPM, which makes the chip unable to provide authentic evidence for all the instances. In particular, the secure storage provided by the TPM has very limited size: although it is sufficient to store the integrity measures of a single operating system, it cannot store the measures of tens of operating systems coming from tens of virtual machines.

These problems may be addressed by introducing a software entity to simulate the TPM functionality [2, 3], which however cannot provide the same strong guarantees provided by a hardware trust anchor or by modifying the hypervisor to monitor the internal behaviour of the virtual machines [4,5], which brings additional performance loss and yet still misses the direct link to the hardware trust anchor. Both solutions are not completely satisfactory, but the first one is preferable to the second and it is described and discussed in Sect. 4.3.1, followed by a novel solution that may be used to attest Docker virtual containers (Sect. 4.3.2).

4.3.1   Virtual TPM and Xen Virtual Machine Attestation

The virtual Trusted Platform Module (vTPM) was proposed by Berger et al. in [2]. Its goal is to allow unmodified operating system and services running in virtual machines to use trusted computing techniques (such as remote attestation but also *sealing*[2]) with the help of a virtual TPM.

In general, the threats to a virtual machine (VM) are essentially the same as for a physical node, plus those coming from its virtual machine manager (VMM) or hypervisor. A VM needs to completely trust its VMM, because the VM cannot defend itself in any way against VMM attacks, e.g. a VMM can tamper its VMs' memory without being detected by the latter. For this reason, the integrity of the VMM itself must be established in the first place, and this is part of the basic attestation which addresses those components directly executed on the hardware. Depending on the VMM's type, it can be attested either as a component loaded at boot time (type I hypervisor) or as a service running in the host system (type II hypervisor); however, this distinction is not influent on the result: the VMM's integrity is attested as part of the base operating environment of the node.

The vTPM approach has general validity, but it has been implemented only for the Xen hypervisor [6] since v4.3 [7], so the rest of this section deals with this specific implementation.

4.3.1.1 Architecture

In Xen, each VM is represented as a domain. All domains are unprivileged by default, with the exception of one privileged domain called domain-0 (dom0 in short). Each unprivileged domain has front-end drivers that connect to the corresponding back-end drivers running in dom0, which offer access to hardware components.

The same model applies to the vTPM: each VM is provided with a vTPM front-end driver (or client-side driver) which is fully compliant with the TPM specification. It receives the TPM relevant commands from the VM operating system and forwards them to the server-side driver. The back-end driver (or server-side driver) is running in a separate domain, managed by a vTPM management module. The vTPM manager creates vTPM instances for each VM, isolates its storage, and forwards the request from a VM to its associated vTPM instance.

In the original proposed architecture, both the vTPM instances and the vTPM manager are processes running in the privileged domain, and dom0 has pass-through access to the hardware TPM to get strong integrity guarantees tied to thehardware

---

[2]Sealing is a technique by which a cryptographic key is bound to a specific software state so that it cannot be used in a different state (e.g. the platform has been somehow compromised).

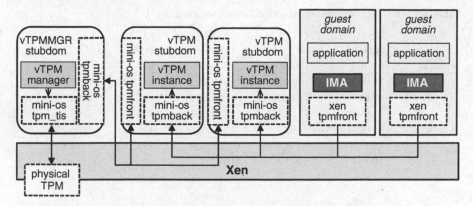

Fig. 4.4 vTPM implementation architecture

root of trust. However, the vTPM implementation in Xen is slightly different: the vTPM manager and the vTPM instances are no longer running inside dom0, but inside "stub domains"[3] (Fig. 4.4).

When a VM needs a vTPM instance, the system administrator enables inside the VM's configuration file the vtpm option before the VM is initialised, indicating which stub domain its back-end driver belongs to. Meanwhile, the front-end driver inside the VM is plugged into the general TPM kernel driver. Thus, the service running in the VM can invoke the vTPM front-end driver as a standard module.

4.3.1.2 Performance Analysis

In order to assess the current vTPM implementation in a real virtualisation environment with remote attestation support, we created a testbed using Xen v4.6.1 with the vTPM functionality enabled. The host system uses a 64 bit Intel Core CPU i7-4600U at 2.10 GHz (two cores four threads, and maximum clock frequency of 3.3 GHz) with 16 GB RAM. Each VM is assigned with one vCPU and 4 GB RAM.

In this setup, all domains are running the CentOS 7 Linux distribution, and the remote attestation framework used is OpenAttestation v1.7 [8], extended to include the IMA measurement list in the integrity report in a way compliant with the TCG's specification [9].

In order to identify the performance impact of vTPM, IMA, and remote attestation, each guest domain performs a simple test task: computation of the SHA512 digest on a 1 MB file. The test is repeated with each of the following four software configurations on the host platform:

- **basic** – guests with vTPM, IMA, and RA disabled;
- **vTPM** – guests with vTPM enabled, IMA, and RA disabled;

---

[3]Stub domains are the same as other guest domains, but are dedicated for special purposes, such as disaggregated device drivers.

Table 4.1 Total counts of operations with different configurations

#VM(s)	No vTPM No IMA No RA	vTPM No IMA No RA	vTPM IMA No RA	vTPM IMA RA	Index
1	39,095	39,024	39,006	38,019	97.2%
2	67,641	67,286	67,044	66,702	98.6%
3	114,991	114,564	114,067	109,873	95.5%
4	131,014	130,749	130,648	126,688	96.7%
5	130,930	130,893	130,660	124,140	94.8%
Index	100%	99.8%	99.5%	96.2%	

- **IMA** – guests with vTPM and IMA enabled, RA disabled;
- **RA** – guests with vTPM, IMA, and RA enabled.

The test works in the following way: dom0 coordinates the guests and the verifier, setting a flag to start/stop their jobs simultaneously. As a performance measurement, the benchmark counts the number of operations (i.e. SHA512 computations) performed by all guests during a period of 5 min. Each configuration is tested ten times in order to collect more reliable data, and then the results are averaged.

The results reported in Table 4.1 show that activation of the vTPM feature causes an average performance loss of 0.2% (0.5% in the worst case), but if IMA is enabled too then the average loss is 0.5% (0.9% in the worst case). When the remote attestation agent is also activated, then the loss is even bigger, with an average of 3.8% and a worst case of 5.2%.

4.3.1.3 Limitations of Xen with vTPM
Even if these performance figures could be considered acceptable in the tested case of five VMs, the expected performance hit would increase with the number of VMs, since a substantial portion of computing power would be used by each VM to prepare its own integrity report.

Aside from performance problems, there are actually more critical issues. First of all, the vTPM manager stub domain has its own TPM driver, which directly communicates with the physical TPM. This can cause a race condition if dom0 has its own driver activated at the same time. Hence, the privileged domain dom0 cannot use the TPM functionalities, neither using the physical TPM (which is not accessible due to conflict with the vTPM manager stub domain) nor via the vTPM (which is not yet available when dom0 is started).

A more elegant and secure solution would be to set a different *locality*[4] of the physical TPM for dom0 and the vTPM manager stub domain. However, in this case,

---

[4]Locality is an assertion to the TPM that a command is associated to a particular component. The purpose of setting different localities for dom0 and the vTPM manager is to permit them to use different PCRs and avoid conflicts.

another practical problem appears: the vTPM manager fails to start if using a locality different from the default one. [10]. This is a bug known to vTPM developers, and, at the time of writing, no solution is available to resolve this problem. Therefore dom0 cannot be attested when using the vTPM, which is unacceptable since dom0 is at the heart of Xen.

The second problem is related to the vTPM client-side driver, which is compiled as a module in the guest VMs' kernel. As explained in [11], the problem is that IMA is loaded with the kernel, and when it starts taking measurements, the client-side driver has not been loaded yet, and the vTPM instance is not available, with the consequence that the IMA measurements are not extended to any PCR. This problem also affects all the components loaded during the VM's boot process. For this reason, guest domains do not have access to a root of trust with high integrity guarantee, and this reduces the benefits of the remote attestation procedure.

The third problem is that, without an entity guaranteeing the integrity state of each vTPM instance stub domain, it is possible that a stub domain is compromised (e.g. an attacker changes the vTPM instance behaviour to not record its malicious actions), and this fact goes undetected. This problem poses a serious question about the integrity guarantee provided by the vTPM solution.

In conclusion, while vTPM is an attractive concept, it has both performance and practical issues that severely limit its application. For this reason, in a VMM-based virtualised environment, normally integrity verification is provided only for the host system/VMM, while the integrity guarantee for the VMs is limited to checking the image being loaded in a VM via a digital signature and/or download from a trusted repository. As a consequence, runtime integrity verification for the applications executed in the VMs is not provided.

4.3.2   Docker Virtual Container Attestation

Recently lightweight virtualisation techniques, and most notably Docker [12], have raised a lot of interest. These techniques incur a lower performance compared to full virtualisation as they create smaller and more agile execution environments named *containers*. Therefore lightweight virtualisation appears especially important for SDN environments, where the nodes have limited computational resources. For example, Deutsche Telekom is a major player that has already started to experiment with NFV in Docker [13].

Integrity verification (via remote attestation) for containers is an important yet unexplored area. While in principle the vTPM approach could be tweaked to work also with containers, its limits and heavy dependence on Xen make it an unlikely solution. We have studied this problem and developed a different solution that provides integrity verification by remote attestation of the services running inside Docker virtual containers. This solution introduces negligible overhead on the host machine and uses IMA as the core method to prove the integrity state of the executed binaries and applied configurations for both the hosts system and all the containers executed on top of it.

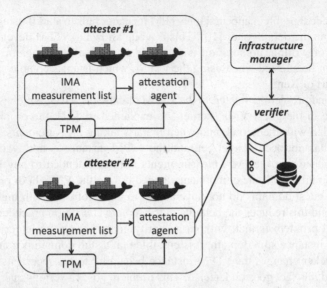

Fig. 4.5 Overall architecture of the Docker attestation system

4.3.2.1 Architecture

The Docker attestation architecture (Fig. 4.5) exploits three components: the *verifier*, the *attester*, and the *infrastructure manager*.

The manager creates the required containers for the users and keeps track of the identifier of both containers and nodes hosting them. When a user queries the integrity of a containerised service deployed on this cloud, the cloud manager initiates the remote attestation process: it sends to the verifier the list of containers to be checked, along with the list of the machines hosting these containers, and asks for their integrity state.

The verifier, after receiving the remote attestation request, first contacts the attesters in the list, asking them to send back their integrity reports that include evidence for both the host system and all the containers it runs. With the knowledge of the container list, the verifier then starts to check the measurements belonging just to the containers of interests. Finally, it generates an attestation report and sends it back to the infrastructure manager.

Since the manager is in charge of all the containers running in the infrastructure, it can start a rollback strategy if it notices tampering with any container. For example, the manager can replace the compromised container without rebooting the physical node hosting it. However, if the Docker container host is compromised, then the whole node must be rebooted because all containers could potentially have been compromised in subtle and unpredictable ways (e.g. in their application data).

Table 4.2 Number of operations and performance index for three settings of Docker

	No IMA No RA	IMA No RA	IMA RA
Min	134,855	133,849	133,799
Avg	135,284	134,623	134,440
Max	135,602	135,626	134,769
Index	100%	99.51%	99.37%

4.3.2.2 Performance Analysis

The same test environment used for the performance test of Xen with vTPM was set up (Sect. 4.3.1.2). Since containers are lighter than virtual machines, we activated 256 containers executing the test computations (SHA256 digest over a 1 MB file). The test was performed ten times for each of three different settings: basic Docker environment, Docker with IMA, and finally Docker with IMA and remote attestation. As for the vTPM, each run of the test lasts 5 min. The results are presented in Table 4.2.

These results show that the performance loss due to IMA is very small (about 0.49%) and also the activation of the remote attestation process does not affect seriously the performance, with a loss about 0.63%.

Compared to the impact of the vTPM solution, this approach has three main advantages:

- the available computing power is higher because there is only one operating system kernel, which limits the unnecessary performance efforts;
- the impact on performance of remote attestation is negligible, because each network node only needs to generate a single integrity report even though there are multiple virtualised instances running on it, so this removes the need to send duplicated IMA measures to the verifier;
- measurements of software modules and their static configurations are stored inside hardware TPM (rather than in the software-based vTPM), which provides strong integrity guarantees against network attacks.

In conclusion, we think that this approach – while not supporting all the features offered by TPM – provides a viable and efficient path towards integrity attestation of Docker containers.

4.4   Integrity Verification for SDN Environments

Until this point in the chapter, trust requirements in software networks have only been partially covered, since previous sections discussed how the integrity state of software modules and their static configurations can be reliably attested, with hardware-based evidence, even in a containerised environment. However, load-time integrity is not enough as attacks may happen at runtime; thus, this section presents a novel approach to attest dynamic configurations of SDN switches.

The SDN infrastructure paradigm makes managing and programming the network easier than with legacy networking. In particular, fine-grained network flows can be flexibly adapted within seconds and without any changes to the physical topology. This enables agile provisioning and removal of network services. However, SDN also brings its own set of problems, especially with regard to security. The programmable nature of SDN introduces new risks that could affect the behaviour of the network itself. Here, what these risks mean for the network *integrity* is discussed, and a solution to detect any deviations from the expected state of network elements is proposed.

The main concept of SDN is the separation of the control plane from the forwarding plane on the network. In practice, it is built around the combination of a centralised controller and switches, where the controller actively programs the forwarding rules of the different switches. If a network switch does not have a rule to deal with a certain network flow, it notifies the controller, which, in turn, updates the rule set of the switch based on application logic. Since the controller is centralised in this new paradigm, it needs to have direct connections to each of the switches. The controller has an indirect view of the network topology based on the rules it has programmed on the various switches. The latency incurred when updating forwarding rules implies a synchronisation problem between the controller's view of the network and the actual network configuration. Existing works, such as [14] and [15], propose solutions to solve this problem, although – as with all timing problems – there is no perfect answer.

Another way to look at the problem is to avoid trying to solve the synchronisation part of the problem and to focus on the discrete states taken by an SDN infrastructure. In fact, these states are represented by the combination of all the forwarding rules happening on each switch. The objective here is to ensure integrity of the desired forwarding behaviour of the SDN, such that it is always in a valid and expected state. The idea of this proposal, first introduced by Jacquin et al. [16], is to insert a trusted verifier in the SDN architecture and to make it perform continual verification of the controller's view of the network with respect to the actual configuration enforced on each switch (Fig. 4.6). This verification occurs at a discrete time, either when the verifier requests it or when the controller detects a new forwarding rule to apply.

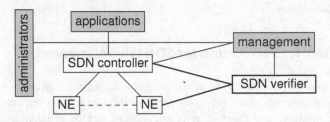

Fig. 4.6 Logical overview of the proposed SDN monitoring architecture

Trusted computing techniques are used to determine if a switch is running expected software. This is an important concept, since the switches need to be relied upon to report their configuration in a reliable fashion. This is achieved by computing a digest of each software component loaded on the switch and storing the digests in a tamper resistant log. Digests are computed and logged at each loading stage, such that only the first stage needs to be implicitly trusted for starting the measurement process. A log is typically guarded by a discrete security chip, such as the TPM discussed in Sect. 4.2. A remote verifier, which knows the expected software hashes, can recompute the aggregate values in an expected order to see if the PCR value contains a valid hash chain.

A commonly used implementation of the communication protocol for configuring SDN between the controller and the switches is OpenFlow [17]. In the context of OpenFlow-enabled switches and controllers, the forwarding rules are represented in rule tables. They are stored and managed in the kernel space and thus part of the trusted computing base (TCB) of this proposal. In the case of a virtual switch, such as Open vSwitch [18], each switch has a set of rules to apply to an ingress packet. In a correctly managed network, these rules are known by the controller, and it is therefore easy to verify if they actually match the rules applied on the real switches by comparing them.

The implementation of the solution is based on TPM-enabled hardware switches from Hewlett Packard Enterprise (HPE) and the HPE Virtual Application Networks (VAN) SDN controller. The verifier is tightly coupled with the controller in order to retrieve its view of the network. Also it permits the controller to notify the verifier upon the event of a rule update and therefore triggers an automatic verification of the infrastructure. The verifier takes the rule table in the controller as a reference. It also takes each rule tables present in each of the switches to be verified; this permits to acquire a potential view of the network through the currently applied rules. Finally, the verifier simply compares each of the rule table obtained from the switches with the expected tables taken from the controller and verifies if they match or not. A small portion of code present in the TCB of each switch takes care of extracting the relevant rules, hashes them, signs the hash with the local TPM, and then sends it to the verifier when requested. In addition to the hashes of the rules, the values of the PCR set are also sent to show that the rule hashes can be trusted.

Since the TPM is a slow device with a serialised interface, careful considerations must be taken to not limit the performance of this approach. Instead of storing hashes of the rules in a PCR one by one, or alternatively signing each rule one by one, the switch simply computes the hashes when requested and lets the TPM sign them directly with the TPM quote operation. Therefore, the number of rules does not change the number of slow TPM operations. Finally, it should be noted that communication between the verifier and the monitored elements is implementation specific, since it is common to have heterogeneous networking equipment. It lets the door open to manufacturers which could provide plugins that can verify a range of supported networking products.

4.5   Remote Attestation for Large Network Infrastructures

Since SDN/NFV networks are composed by thousands of nodes, scalability and performance of remote attestation in such large environments are issues. This section introduces an extension to the base OpenAttestation (OAT) framework, with the main purpose to push the performance of remote attestation to its limits in order to be able to manage large infrastructures. However note that there is a hard limit imposed by the speed of the TPM in the physical platform or the computing power of the host in a virtual environment.

4.5.1   Analysis Customisation

A first extension of OAT was to make possible for various user-defined external tools to analyse the integrity reports provided by the attesters and return a validation result to the infrastructure manager. This is important because it significantly improves the usability of remote attestation, by permitting various kinds of analysis. For example, IMA measurements can be verified by calling the tool described in [19], which identifies not only known good software components but also components for which a functional or security update is available. In this way, the system administrators can easily identify the critical nodes of the network.

4.5.2   Incremental Reporting

Analysing the whole integrity report with all the IMA measurements is a computing-intensive task for both the attester and the verifier. A new and complete integrity report must be sent to the verifier at each attestation request; otherwise, the obtained result may not reflect the current state of the attester.

However, two properties of IMA can be used to optimise the overall attestation process. First of all, once a measure is extended into a PCR, it cannot leave the IMA log file without compromising its integrity, because of the incremental nature of the extend operation. Second, each step of the measurement validation process relies on the previous value stored in the used PCR, so this value can be used as a starting point for verifying subsequent measurements instead of the default one.

These two properties permit the attester not to send all the IMA measurements at each attestation request but only those digests that have not already been sent to the verifier in the past. This greatly reduces the integrity report size and avoids querying former IMA measurements from the whitelist database every time.

The validation of an incremental integrity report (i.e. a report containing only the new IMA measurements) slightly differs from the verification of a complete integrity report. The main difference between the classic IMA validation process and the approach using incremental verification is just the starting point for the hash chain. Indeed, in the first case, it is a 20-byte long sequence of zeros, while in the second case, it is the last valid value of PCR10 (used by default in IMA for the extend operation with each new measure) in the previous integrity report of the attester.

4.5.3 Periodic Attestation

An additional improvement is related to the polling mechanism between the attester and the verifier, which necessarily affects performance of the overall attestation process (i.e. a remote attestation request must wait for a full set of operations, quote, and IMA measurements verification). For this reason, the concept of periodic attestation is important. This is a new kind of attestation request, augmented with two extra parameters: *timeThreshold* (the age limit for the integrity report used to evaluate the trustworthiness of the attester) and *expirationTime* (indicating how long the validity of periodic attestation is). Given these parameters, the verifier takes care of always having a valid attestation result that matches the request. To be more specific, the verifier periodically requests a new integrity report from the attester and performs the requested analysis; then the corresponding results are always available for asynchronous retrieval by calling a proper API.

4.6 Towards Management and Orchestration

The technical solutions described in the previous sections would have a limited impact if not endorsed by the players in the SDN/NFV field. Therefore, this section discusses how different Standards Developing Organisations (SDOs) are dealing with the problem of defining a framework able to support platform trust (in the sense of node and general infrastructure integrity) within the mechanisms defined for the orchestration of software-based network services, the management of these services and, more generally, of any security-related network function. We introduce the initiatives of the SEC working group within the ETSI NFV ISG,[5] focused on the NFV Management and Orchestration (MANO) components, and the initial results of the IETF I2NSF working group, which address how remote attestation is incorporated in the framework for security function management being defined by this group. Finally, the research reported within the IRTF[6] on the remote attestation of SDN-based network infrastructure is discussed too.

Management of trustworthiness is a permanent problem that has been faced by SDOs as one of the key elements to guarantee security. This issue has been historically addressed by using a combination of physical security in data centre premises, hardware security by means of hardened and tamper-proof physical

---

[5]http://etsi.org/nfv/

[6]Internet Research Task Force, focused on longer-term research issues compared to the shorter-term issues of engineering addressed by the IETF.

components, and software security methods applied in the basic components like the BIOS firmware or CPU microcode to avoid manipulation [20, Chapter 9].

The basis for this management mechanisms is the TPM specification by the TCGwhich provides a core reference for the software integrity protection on physical devices. The birth and expansion of virtualisation technologies create new attack surfaces that make the hardware protection model insufficient to guarantee the integrity of the now extended platform, and this is aggravated by the massive adoption of virtualisation in cloud IT frameworks. The TCG addresses the problem by extending TPM through the vTPM concept [2] that was standardised in the "Virtualized Trusted Platform Architecture" publication [21].

In 2013, ETSI initiated the standardisation of the NFV concept within the ETSI NFV Industry Specification Group (ISG), security issues were acknowledged from the beginning, and a dedicated working group (SEC WG) was created to address them. The first specification of the group, SEC001 [22], includes a discussion of the additional security threats introduced by virtualisation in the provisioning of network services and considers infrastructure attestation one of the essential techniques to deal with them. As a consequence, the SEC WG started working on a specific report about "Attestation Technologies and Practices for Secure Deployments", SEC007 [23], where attestation procedures in virtualised environments are introduced and discussed, and the mechanisms applicable to the attestation of VNFs are described, together with the required infrastructure capabilities to support them, and a series of recommendations for operational procedures. This document provides a description of the different levels of assurance (LoAs) that can be achieved by applying the different techniques discussed, with a range that goes from zero, limited to local verification of the hardware and virtualisation platform, up to four, requiring the remote attestation of hardware, virtualisation, and VNF software packages, along with the remote verification of the infrastructure network deployed to support the VNFs.

In 2016, the IETF has started the Interface to Network Security Functions (I2NSF) working group [24], focused on the definition of an open and consistent interface for network security function management. The WG has acknowledged from the beginning the need for attestation mechanisms to establish a trustworthy connection between network security functions and their consumers. This is reflected in the initial document defining the problem statement to be considered by the WG and the initial use cases [25], and a detailed discussion on attestation requirements applicable to security network function management and control is included in the document describing the I2NSF framework [26, 27]. While the target of I2NSF includes both physical and virtual network functions, the I2NSF framework contains specific considerations associated to the trustworthiness of virtualised functions and the methods to preserve it. At the moment of this writing, work continues in defining the requirements for the different management and control interfaces, and it is expected that remote attestation procedures will be included, connected with the LoAs described above.

There are also challenges regarding attestation of software-based networks, related both with general problems in software attestation (as it is the case of run-time attestation) and with particular network issues (in what is related to end-to-end service attestation) that are subject to active research nowadays. In the concrete space of infrastructure integrity, there is a specific problem that deserves special attention, related to the interplay of SDN and NFV. This problem is the attestation of the networking infrastructure supporting the virtualised network environment, directly related with the general problem of SDN verification. SDN verification requires to prove that the rules and configurations dynamically installed on the network forwarding elements by their controllers satisfy a set of original policy constraints. This goal is already complex when using physicals systems, though there are so-called operation and management (OAM) verification constructs in most of current protocols. The usage of a programmable software-based control plane makes this verification more easy and, at the same time, more difficult. As said before, this is a matter of research, and several results have already been reported at the IRTF groups dealing with NFV and SDN. The ETSI NFV SEC WG document mentioned above (SEC007) includes a summary of the current state-of-the-art on these open problems, and the work discussed in Sect. 4.4 is an important step in the right direction.

4.7   Conclusion

This chapter showed that remote attestation is able to provide hardware-based integrity guarantees in a distributed system, and its application to an SDN/NFV environment is an essential requirement to ensure the integrity of the network.

From the implementation point of view, we presented the current implementation of vTPM and its limitations, showing its poor performance and limited protection for a computational environment based on the virtual machine paradigm. On the other hand, the Docker operating system level engine provides lightweight instances and can be attested in a more reliable and easy way, which is a much more suitable option for virtualised network functions.

In the SDN context, it is important to verify the integrity of the network configuration not only at load-time but also at runtime. To this aim, a SDN verifier can be used to check the integrity of OpenFlow rules, which have been processed by a NFV node against the SDN controller, in order to verify the integrity state of the whole network.

In the end, we discussed how the remote attestation framework fits in the current management and orchestration model for software-based network environments.

In the future, we foresee integration of all these solutions together, in order to provide a complete solution to ensure the integrity state of the SDN/NFV environment. On the other hand, being alerted that a node is compromised is important, but avoiding its tampering would be even better. Along this line, proactive mechanisms could be used, such as the mandatory access controls mechanisms offered by SELinux [28].

Questions

1. What is *remote attestation* in the trusted computing concept, and what is its purpose?
2. What are the benefits of using TPM compared to other hardware-assisted isolation environments?
3. Why basic remote attestation cannot be directly applied in SDN/NFV environments?
4. What is the *extend* operation of the TPM and what benefits does it provide?
5. How does the TPM ensure the authenticity and integrity of the IMA measurement list?
6. What components are covered in the trusted boot?
7. What are the necessary steps to be performed for remote attestation verification?
8. Why is remote attestation difficult in a virtualised environment?
9. Why is the current vTPM implementation not capable of providing a complete trusted computing base for virtual machines?
10. Why an infrastructure manager is needed in the Docker attestation system?
11. What are the advantages of Docker attestation system compared to the vTPM solution?
12. Why is attestation of OpenFlow rules relevant in a SDN environment?
13. What is the problem of direct application of remote attestation to SDN configurations?
14. What is limiting the performance of remote attestation?
15. How does incremental integrity reporting work?
16. What does the ETSI NFV group propose related to remote attestation?
17. How does the IETF I2NSF group propose to use remote attestation?

Acknowledgements The research described in this paper has been supported by the European Commission under the FP7 programme (project SECURED, grant agreement no. 611458).

References

1. Sailer R, Zhang X, Jaeger T, van Doorn L (2004) Design and implementation of a TCG-based integrity measurement architecture. In: USENIX'04: 13th USENIX security symposium, San Diego, 27 June–02 July 2004, pp 223–238
2. Berger S, Cáceres R, Goldman KA, Perez R, Sailer R, van Doorn L (2006) vTPM: virtualizing the trusted platform module. In: USENIX'06: 15th USENIX security symposium, Vancouver, 31 July–4 Aug 2006, pp 305–320
3. Goldman K, Sailer R, Pendarakis D, Srinivasan D (2010) Scalable integrity monitoring in virtualized environments. In: STC'10: 5th ACM workshop on scalable trusted computing, Chicago, 4–8 Oct 2010, pp 73–78
4. Garfinkel T, Pfaff B, Chow J, Rosenblum M, Boneh D (2003) Terra: a virtual machine-based platform for trusted computing. In: 19th ACM symposium on operating systems principles, Bolton Landing, 19–22 Oct 2003, pp 193–206
5. Schiffman J, Vijayakumar H, Jaeger T (2012) Verifying system integrity by proxy. In: 5th International conference on trust and trustworthy computing, Vienna, June 13–15, 2012, pp 179–200

6. Xen project. https://www.xenproject.org/. Visited 27 Mar 2017
7. Fioravante M, De Graaf D (2012) Virtual trusted platform module (vTPM) subsystem for Xen, 12 Nov 2012. http://xenbits.xen.org/docs/4.6-testing/misc/vtpm.txt. Visited 27 Mar 2017
8. OpenAttestation SDK v1.7. https://github.com/OpenAttestation/OpenAttestation/tree/v1.7. Visited 27 Mar 2017
9. Trusted Computing Group (2006) TCG infrastructure working group integrity report schema specification. http://www.trustedcomputinggroup.org/wp-content/uploads/IWG-IntegrityReport_Schema_Specification_v1.pdf. Visited 27 Mar 2017
10. Xen project mailing list (2014) vtpmmgr bug: fails to start if locality not 0. https://lists.xen.org/archives/html/xen-devel/2014-11/msg00606.html. Visited 27 Mar 2017
11. Fioravante M, De Graaf D Virtual TPM interface for Xen. https://www.kernel.org/doc/Documentation/security/tpm/xen-tpmfront.txt. Visited 27 Mar 2017
12. Docker – home page, https://www.docker.com. Visited 27 March 2017
13. Brandon J (2015) Deutsche Telekom experimenting with NFV in Docker, 9 Feb 2015. http://www.businesscloudnews.com/2015/02/09/deutsche-telekom-experimenting-with-nfv-in-docker/. Visited 27 Mar 2017
14. Weijie Liu, Bobba RB, Mohan S, Campbell RH (2015) Inter-flow consistency: a novel SDN update abstraction for supporting inter-flow constraints. In: CNS-2015: IEEE conference on communications and network security, Florence, 28–30 Sept 2015, pp 469–478
15. Schiff L, Schmid S, Kuznetsov P (2016) In-band synchronization for distributed SDN control planes. ACM SIGCOMM Comput Commun Rev 46(1):37–43. doi:10.1145/2875951.2875957
16. Jacquin L, Shaw A, Dalton C (2015) Towards trusted software-defined networks using a hardware-based integrity measurement architecture. In: 1st IEEE conference on network softwarization, London, 13–17 Apr 2015, pp 1–6
17. McKeown N, Anderson T, Balakrishnan H, Parulkar G, Peterson L, Rexford J, Shenker S, Turner J (2008) OpenFlow: enabling innovation in campus networks. ACM SIGCOMM Comput Commun Rev 38(2):69–74. doi:10.1145/1355734.1355746
18. Pfaff B, Pettit J, Koponen T, Jackson E, Zhou A, Rajahalme J, Gross J, Wang A, Stringer J, Shelar P, Amidon K (2015) The design and implementation of open vSwitch. In: NSDI'15: 12th USENIX conference on networked systems design and implementation, Oakland, 4–6 May 2015, pp 117–130
19. Cesena E, Ramunno G, Sassu R, Vernizzi D, Lioy A (2011) On scalability of remote attestation. In: STC'11: 6th ACM workshop on scalable trusted computing, Chicago, 17–21 Oct 2011, pp 25–30
20. Skoudis E, Zeltser L (2004) Malware: fighting malicious code. Prentice Hall Professional, Upper Saddle River, pp 465–481
21. Trusted Computing Group (2011) Virtualized trusted platform architecture specification, Sept 2011. http://www.trustedcomputinggroup.org/resources/virtualized_trusted_platform_architecture_specification. Visited 27 Mar 2017
22. ETSI (2014) Network functions virtualisation (NFV); NFV security; problem statement, ETSI GS NFV-SEC 001 v1.1.1, Oct 2014. http://www.etsi.org/deliver/etsi_gs/NFV-SEC/001_099/001/01.01.01_60/gs_NFV-SEC001v010101p.pdf. Visited 27 Mar 2017
23. ETSI, Network function virtualisation (NFV); trust; report on attestation technologies and practices for secure deployments, ETSI GS NFV-SEC 007 (draft). http://docbox.etsi.org/ISG/NFV/Open/Drafts/SEC007_NFV_Attestation_report/. Visited 27 Mar 2017
24. IETF Interface to Network Security Functions Working Group. https://datatracker.ietf.org/wg/i2nsf/charter/. Visited 27 Mar 2017
25. Hares S, Dunbar L, Lopez D, Zarny M, Jacquenet C (2016) I2NSF problem statement and use cases. Internet-Draft draft-ietf-i2nsf-problem-and-use-cases-01, July 2016. https://datatracker.ietf.org/doc/draft-ietf-i2nsf-problem-and-use-cases/. Visited 27 Mar 2017
26. Lopez E, Lopez D, Dunbar L, Strassner J, Zhuang X, Parrott J, Krishnan RR, Durbha S, Kumar R, Lohiya A (2016) Framework for interface to network security functions. Internet-Draft draft-ietf-i2nsf-framework-03, Aug 2016. https://datatracker.ietf.org/doc/draft-ietf-i2nsf-framework/. Visited 27 Mar 2017

27. Pastor A, Lopez D, Shaw A (2016) Remote attestation procedures for network security functions (NSFs) through the I2NSF security controller, Internet-draft draft-pastor-i2nsf-vnsf-attestation-03, July 2016. https://datatracker.ietf.org/doc/draft-pastor-i2nsf-vnsf-attestation/. Visited 27 Mar 2017
28. NSA, Security-enhanced Linux. https://www.nsa.gov/what-we-do/research/selinux/. Visited 27 Mar 2017

Antonio Lioy (MS in Electronic Engineering and PhD in Computer Engineering) is Full Professor at the Politecnico di Torino (Italy), where he leads the TORSEC research group. Prof. Lioy has been working since 1994 in the field of cybersecurity, with special emphasis on network security (especially trust, optimization, and automatic configuration), PKI, electronic identity, and policy-based protection for large information systems. Prof, Lioy published more than 100 research papers and frequently acts as a cybersecurity reviewer and consultant for the Italian government and the European Commission.

Tao Su received his BS in Telecommunication Engineering and MS in Computers and Communication Network Engineering both from Politecnico di Torino (Italy), where he is currently working toward his PhD degree as a research assistant in the TORSEC research group. His research interests include distributed system security, mobile computing system security, and trusted computing.

Adrian L. Shaw is a senior researcher at Hewlett Packard Labs in Bristol. He specialises in operating systems security, and currently investigates the intersection between trusted computing and distributed systems. He works in close collaboration with product security architects around the world on improving HPE's products.

Hamza Attak is a research engineer at Hewlett Packard Enterprise in Bristol. Having a M.Sc. in general computer science, he has experience and interest from embedded system design to high-level software engineering. Recently, he is spending most of his time in the Linux kernel, mostly extending network and security functionalities.

Dr. Diego R. Lopez joined Telefónica I+D in 2011 as a Senior Technology Expert on network middleware and services. He is currently in charge of the Technology Exploration activities within the GCTO Unit of Telefónica I+D. Before joining Telefónica he spent some years in the academic sector, dedicated to research on network service abstractions and the development of APIs based on them. Diego is currently focused on identifying and evaluating new opportunities in technologies applicable to network infrastructures, and the coordination of national and international collaboration activities. His current interests are related to network virtualization, infrastructural services, network management, new network architectures, and network security. Diego chairs the ETSI ISG on Network Function Virtualization, and the NFV Research Group within the IRTF.

Antonio Pastor received the MS degree in industrial engineering from the Carlos III University of Madrid (UC3M), Spain, in 1999. Since then, he has been with Telefónica I+D, where he works on the engineering of different worldwide Telefónica networks. Since 2006 he has been working as an expert in network security, and recently he is working in SDN and NFV technologies oriented to security and research, where he is the holder of several patents and published various papers. He also holds several certifications from ISACA and GIAC in this area.

Part II

SDNFV Security Challenges and Network Security Solutions

Practical Experience in NFV Security Field: Virtual Home Gateway

5

Antonio Pastor and Jesús Folgueira

5.1 Introduction

Today, Internet service providers (ISPs) try to deliver more and more value-added services integrated with their residential Internet access offer, such as triple play (voice, Internet and video). This situation generates the need for more powerful and expensive home devices to cover these needs. This device receives different names, from customer premise equipment (CPE) to residential router and to home gateway (HGW), but all have a common ground: the trade-off between low-cost and rich functionalities, with a potential negative effect in the device security.

As a result, vHGW was one of the first scenarios that were adopted within the NFV paradigm, to demonstrate its potential in terms of efficiency and security.

In this chapter, we are going to describe the NFV architecture that Telefonica designed and implemented in a commercial trial, to evaluate its potentiality.

The commercial trial counted with several thousand customers and was run by Telefonica's operation in Brazil [1]. The required equipment was deployed in a network point of presence (PoP) and was partially integrated in processes and systems, which limited the number of customers. The Telefonica's vHGW architecture is described in Sect. 5.2.

Evaluation methodology was based on operational key performance indicator (KPI) measurements and comparison with a control group under the current technology and architecture. Promising efficiency results were reached.

It was precisely because of the commercial nature of the trial that a comprehensive security analysis (detailed in Sect. 5.3) was done. As a result, a set of security solutions were enforced, enumerated in Sect. 5.4.

A. Pastor (✉) • J. Folgueira
Telefónica I+D, Distrito Telefónica, West 1 Building, Ronda de la Comunicación S/N, 28050, Madrid, Spain
e-mail: antonio.pastorperales@telefonica.com; jesus.folgueira@telefonica.com

© Springer International Publishing AG 2017
S.Y. Zhu et al. (eds.), *Guide to Security in SDN and NFV*, Computer Communications and Networks, DOI 10.1007/978-3-319-64653-4_5

Additionally, vHGW is a vehicle for new service creation, including security services. Indeed, some security services were evaluated in the project laboratory test bed and partially in the commercial trial. Details are listed in Sect. 5.5.

5.2 Virtual Home Gateway: A Realistic NFV Use Case

One of the first approaches in NFV technology has been the virtualization of the home environment, through the virtualization of the home gateway (vHGW) device. This use case has been defined as very relevant use cases by ETSI NFV [2], mainly due to the increase of operational efficiency (OPEX[1] savings): a lower number of complaint calls from customers, a lower number of truck rolls to customer premises and a lower HGW replacement ratio. Moreover, in order to minimize network transformation CAPEX[1], existing HGW has been reused and adapted (by configuration upgrades).

The vHGW solution addresses this challenge by reducing local functionalities on the equipment installed in residential home premises: it just provides bare lower-layer connectivity (Wi-Fi access point, switch and modem functionalities). The upper-layer network functions, typically running in the HGW to support the delivery of network services, are offloaded to the network through virtualized network functions (VNFs) running on carrier-grade commercial off-the-shelf (COTS) servers.

vHGW leverages on the NFV paradigm to move the following higher-layer functionalities from the physical CPE to a network virtualized equipment: IPv4/IPv6 routing, NAT, DHCP, Universal Plug and Play (UPnP), IPv6 OSI layer 3 firewall, TR-069 [3] and web-based configuration interface, among others. Figure 5.1 depicts the HGW before and after this process.

vHGW is not only a matter of savings but also an enabler for new network services. It will also help to address new security risks that will arise as NFVI becomes ubiquitous in telco networks. These risks are part of the price to be paid for improving flexibility, efficiency and interoperability in our networks.

5.2.1 vHGW Architecture

A vHGW architecture design able to support better efficiencies requires that the different functionalities are shared across several network functions and elements. Figure 5.2 shows our proposal for the ISP's network environment, where the CPE network functions are highlighted.

The main internal components to build up the architecture are:

---

[1] Operating expense (OPEX) is associated to the concept of the economic cost of running a service, system or product, while capital expense (CAPEX) refers to new assets acquisitions. Both are part of the total cost of ownership (TCO).

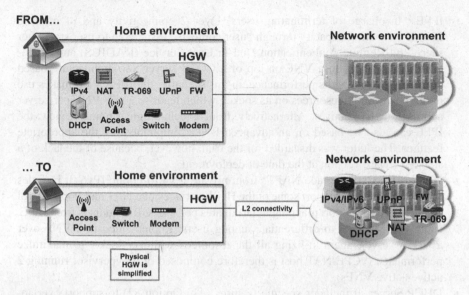

Fig. 5.1 vHGW model

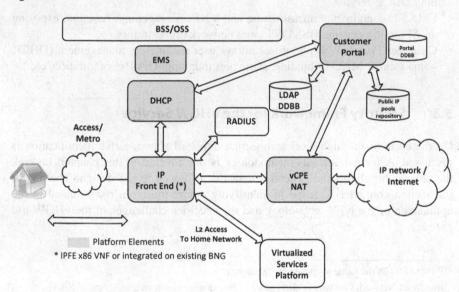

Fig. 5.2 Internal architecture for vHGW

- vHGW. Simplified residential CPE that delegates most of its functionalities on other network elements.

- IPFE.[2] In charge of terminating users' layer 2 connectivity and of offering IPv4/IPv6 routing capacity through "user contexts" associated to user state after successful Remote Authentication Dial-In User Service (RADIUS) authentication. Implemented in a VNF on top of a COTS server x86-architecture-based server. To maximize its performance, in this scenario, the IPFE VNF makes use of all the available resources on its socket, which leads to a two-VNF-per-server approach (active-active). Alternatively, from a technological point of view, the IPFE can also be based on an advanced BNG[3], implementing the appropriate features. The latter was discarded for the trial, however, because of the lack of a stable software version at the time of deployment.
- vCPE-NAT. Carrier-grade NAPT[4] from private IPv4 to public IPv6. It includes specific features to support some of the HGW services like NAT and Port Control Protocol (PCP) for port mapping. It terminates per-user GRE[5] tunnels from IPFE, using GRE key ID to differentiate among users. Implemented in a VNF over a COTS server, again utilizing all the resources within a socket to maximize performance (vCPE-NAT host is therefore composed of a hypervisor running 2 active-active VNFs).
- DHCP Server. It includes specific features (e.g. Option 82) to support overlapping DHCP service.
- EMS.[6] It contains the infrastructure and VNFs management function, exposing an API to the existing BSS/OSS[7], and network orchestrators.
- Customer Portal. Web portal that allows user parameters management (DHCP, home subnet, MAC-IP binding, static port mapping, UPnP configuration, etc.).

5.3   Security Framework for the vHGW Service

On the basis of the high-level architecture depicted above, a risk identification is discussed. A formal analysis methodology is not covered in this chapter. Instead, the chapter highlights the general framework followed in the design. The rest of the section content is focused in identifying where the main risks related to the application of the NFV technology and the specifics challenges of the vHGW use case are.

---

[2]IP Front End as the name proposed by Telefoniea.

[3]Broadband Network Gateway is also known as broadband remote access server or BRAS.

[4]Network Address Port Translation is a variation of NAT defined in RFC 2663 that extend the notion of translation to transport identifier, such as port.

[5]Generic Routing Encapsulation is protocol based on RFC 2784 to create tunnels with low overhead.

[6]Element management systems role is focused in managed and configure specific network devices. In our NFV context is associated with the VNF configuration, such as DHCP or IPFE.

[7]Operations support system/business support system. First cover the management of the network, such fault management or provisioning. Second include all customer related systems like billing or service orders.

5.3.1 Common Security Framework Requirements in Network Architectures

One of the most valuable methods to identify security risks and design and implement countermeasures that reduce the risks to acceptable values in a data network is to apply the telecom standard ITU x.805. This ITU guide defines a security architecture end to end for any type of network. It is based in two key concepts: security layers and planes. Around them, security measures or dimensions are applied (authentication, access control, confidentiality, etc.). Security layers are the way to hierarchically organize network elements and components (infrastructure, service and application). Finally, security planes are organized based in the type of activity to protect (management, control and end user). The x.805 guide basically proposes a method to protect networks from threats and vulnerabilities by applying the security dimensions in each layer/plane. The vHGW service as a network end-to-end service fits perfectly in this model. A detailed specification of the security architecture for a broadband residential fixed access would exceed the dimension of chapter. Instead, we highlight some relevant risk and requirements we identified:

- Management, control and data plane isolation. Sharing different types of traffic with different levels of criticality is a big risk. Separate management, or out-of-band, is one of the most important concepts. Extending this segmentation to the control plane and the user traffic (data plane) is also expected. This reduces the risk for several threats, from denial of service to fraud, including privacy breaches and data loss. This has been achieved historically by offering physical (network interfaces and devices) and logical (VLANs[8] and VPNs[9]) separate paths.
- Layer isolation is also a common security practice. Services and applications usually must implement different security protection against different threats (user data protection, XSS[10], SQL injection, etc.) than network devices (device monitoring, availability, low-level protocols authentication, etc.). NFV as a network "softwarization" solution is dissolving this application network frontier, requiring an enforcement of the software application isolation.
- Perimeter protection. This is a basic requirement in the legacy access models where the BNG applies a set of controls to the incoming end-user traffic: antispoofing, Martian or internal network address filtering and protocol filtering (routing and non-authorized services). Non-enforced perimeter can produce intrusion attacks, service disruptions and data theft.

---

[8] Virtual LAN, based on 802.1q protocol and tagging.

[9] Virtual private network are based in multiple technologies that allow extend private networks over public ones.

[10] Cross-site scripting is a family of well-known attacks in web applications to inject malicious scripts, especially web client side scripts.

- Segmentation based on the need-to-know principle. Services like DNS or DHCP are very attractive targets for attackers because without them, the service failure is general. As sensitive services, they must be supervised and isolated.
- Network devices and server default configurations. Devices offer by default multiple protocols and services that are not necessary, with default passwords, secure configurations disabled and leave the administrator the responsibility of securing them. VNFs and hypervisors suffer the same problem.

5.3.2   The NFV Variable in the Security Design Formula

NFV is a new technology, a paradigm shift. Fortunately, there is a valuable work in progress in ETSI NFV within the security area, where several stakeholders including ISPs are working on. This subsection details the main results of standardization works and how we applied them to identify relevant risks in the vHGW service.

5.3.2.1 Work in ETSI NFV Related to Security

ETSI NFV ISG security working group has been identifying where the new risks are and proposing solutions for them. The first result of the working group was related to the areas of concern in NFV [4] and addressed several problems. Relevant ones are detailed below.

Topology Validation and Enforcement   There is a risk in how the service graph path is instantiated in both the data and control planes and how it can be made visible and validated, when we include virtual functions and ports.

Availability of Management   If the management network cannot be kept out-of-band in all cases, the pervasive use of VNFs can impact in the management traffic affecting the function availability and must be considered and evaluated.

Secure Boot   There is a need for validating and assuring the boot process integrity, including the validation of the VNFs at the instantiation stage and periodically. A detailed analysis and recommendations are being proposed in the SEC007 draft, which includes the use of TPM[11] and remote attestation.

Secure Crash   Data backups and failover procedures are well-known technologies, but system crashes leave sensitive data (memory dumps with passwords, keys, tokens, etc.) that if not controlled are a source of risk, so a secure crashing process is needed.

---

[11] Trusted Platform Module, a secure cryptoprocessor standardized by Trusted Computing Group (TCG).

Performance Isolation Sharing resources can impact in security. A strict resource consumption isolation is needed, especially in some areas like network I/O partitioning, cores, memory, accelerated hardware and in general in the resources of the virtualization infrastructure.

User/Tenant Authentication, Authorization and Accounting (AAA) When multidomain and multilayer management is required, it is vital to avoid privilege escalation, secure data leakage and guarantee audit capacities, among others. These problems are deeply analysed and have produced a set of requirements in the SEC009 [5] document. Also, there is an agreement to apply AAA controls in sensitive workloads at host levels. These control definitions are in progress as part of the SEC012.

Authenticated Time Service This service has a high impact on general network service availability, with threats ranging from billing system fraud to system crashes produced by back-in-time clock references. Network Time Protocol (NTP) and time synchronization protocol protection are required.

Private Keys Within Cloned Images Cloning VNFs with sensible information must be addressed. One alternative is the use of certification authorities (CAs) with a public key infrastructure (PKI), and the related process to assign keys per VNF. SEC005 draft is working in offering a guide in certification management in NFV.

Backdoors Via virtualized test and monitoring functions. Software testing and debugging interfaces must be sanitized in VNFs before deploying in production environments.

Multi-admin Isolation This feature must be supported, especially in the case of LI[12] and other regulatory requirements have to be addressed.

Altered Procedures All procedures, especially those related to humans operating the network must be revised with the new virtualization model.

Software Vulnerabilities VNF software patch processes must be included in the security management cycle of NFV deployments. This makes sense especially if we consider that NFV allows more dynamic and nondisruptive updates.

These problems and new ones that likely arise along the maturity of the NFV technology are actively being considered and standardized. The following list shows some examples of the active work at the moment of the chapter preparation:

- NFV-SEC003 tries to offer a set of recommendations in the lifecycle among other guidelines.

---

[12]Lawful interception.

- NFV-SEC002 has focused in providing an OpenStack security hardening guide.
- Several work item documents (NFV-SEC004, NFV-SEC010 and NFV-SEC011) are focusing on the regulatory impacts, like data retention or LI compliance.
- NFV-SEC013 is working in securing the management and in particular the monitoring process.

5.3.2.2 Applying NFV Risk Analysis to vHGW

The vHGW architecture is fully aligned with the NFV concepts. This allowed us to apply the above-introduced ETSI NFV SEC insights to identify the risks that impact in our service definition. The following risks were analysed during the design phase of the trial:

Regulatory Compliance Internet residential services have a legal requirement to support LI and data retention. This is a relevant risk to solve in initial designs and deployment of vHGW scenario, i.e. complying with the law and in parallel solving the threats generated by these technologies. One simple example, root user privileges in generic Linux operating systems do not offer simple methods to conceal some processes and resources that LI needs. The most relevant risks identified in this area were illegal traffic interception, privacy data leakage, interception order failures, user identification and data delivery based on IPv4 address (all users share the same IPv4 private address range, 192.168.x.x, and through vCPE-NAT a dynamic public IPv4 address).

Topology Validation and Infrastructure Integrity The vHGW network topology is designed to be stable once it is deployed in an initial stage, any dynamic change, and therefore, the associated risk is related to user provisioning. New users create new virtual data paths, including isolated user contexts inside IPFE, GRE tunnels between IPFE and vCPE-NAT and NAT sessions. A set of controls are needed to avoid any security impact.

Management and Time Synchronization Management interfaces of all VNFs must be evaluated. Sharing physical interfaces, internal switching and external network could cause management failures. NTP is the common accepted protocol for physical network functions (PNF) and could not be supported by some VNFs. NTP has been relevant in recent years as a source of DDoS [6] if it is not well configured and protected.

COTS Server's Operating Systems (OS) Network functions in vHGW are executed on generic hardware (COTS) and with well-known and used software, e.g. Linux. This model has security implications:

- More reported and unreported (zero-day) vulnerabilities (i.e. Linux kernel vulnerabilities)
- More attack tools available, such as virus and rootkits (i.e. malicious kernel modules)
- More people trying to exploit commodity software (for fun, fame or finance)

Larger-Scale Disruption If hypervisors or physical servers are disrupted, all VNFs that host vHGW functions are affected and can generate service disruptions.

Backdoor Risk **Is Increased** More software components to cover vHGW functionalities (OS, hypervisors, VNF OS, applications) increase the opportunity for backdoor injections.

Maintenance by Patching PNF in carrier-grade versions provide procedures well tested for system upgrades, such as firmware ones. New VNF solutions based on generic software could not offer the same quality and generate disruptions or degradation.

Secure Boot/Crash VNFs must support a cold restart process, such as power outages. Base software of VNFs sometimes derives from generic operating systems, which could not manage well-crashing processes. Filesystem corruptions, temporal state files that alter the application behaviour or dumps garbage that fill partitions, are examples of insecure crash, which can also expose private information without correct access control.

Performance Isolation In the vHGW architecture, thousands of users share the same physical resources, e.g. IPFE, vCPE-NAT, DHCP, etc. If performance isolation fails, it can produce degradation or disruption of the service to multiple users.

5.3.3 Residential Internet Access Service, Inherent Risks in the Service

The next step in our secure design for the trial was to analyse those risks that are intrinsic for a residential broadband Internet access service. We applied the analysis and identify the risks keeping in mind that we are working with NFV technology.

We organized our study in two main areas: the HGW device and functionality, and other related risk in the services.

5.3.3.1 HGW Vulnerabilities

HGW has been traditionally identified as the main enabler for new residential services. There is a historical interpretation by CPE device vendors and ISPs around the need of enriching user experiences with new features to be supported by CPEs (firewalls, quality of service, VPNs, IPSec, IPv6, IPTV, VoIP, etc.). This model has created very complex devices while keeping resources (and prices) low. The direct consequence of this policy is prioritizing functionality and performance against security. NFV offers an opportunity to change this trend by lightening features in HGW devices and offloading their control onto the network management. It is not self-evident that *security can be increased almost without specific security configuration* in this architecture. This is an example where NFV security benefits can balance the risk of a new technology. We refer to this as NFV providing

Table 5.1 HGW inherent threats mitigated

Risk	Problem description	Solution by default
Surface attack	Multiple HGW features	Firmware disable unnecessary features
Code bugs	Software bugs	Less software in use
Wrong management	Easily configurable	ISP control most configurations
Remote management	Internet accessible	Only ISP accessible
Firmware configuration	Configuration loss between resets	Permanent configuration in Firmware

solutions by default. Table 5.1 summarize security threats commonly exploited through vulnerabilities in HGW. Let us enumerate these common vulnerabilities and how vHGW architecture can provide protection from them.

Surface Attack Extensive Surface Attack Caused by Multiple Supported Device Features *Solution by default*: After an analysis of the really need for features in a vHGW architecture, we can conclude that there is an extensive list of non-needed functionalities, especially those of them that require that the HGW acts as a local server. Some possible functionalities that disappear are device web server management, command line services (SSH or Telnet servers), local firewall and NAT, uPnP server, dynamic DNS clients and DMZ zones. Eliminating or disabling by default (in firmware) those features, we can reduce the risk for different well-known attacks like denial of service or Cross-Site Request Forgery (CSRF).

Code Bugs and Instability It is accepted that there is no software 100% clean of software bugs, backdoors, etc. The cost of secure the code increases with the complexity and time invested. This is also aggravated when HGW vendors integrate third-party software without security validation. For example, the openSSL [7] library has solved in recent years multiple security flaws (just in 2015, 29 CVE[13] were registered), which low-cost HGW vendors did not address. Some known examples of vulnerabilities exploited in home CPE devices are local web server attacks (XSS, SQL injection), weak passwords stored by default and exposure of private keys. *Solution by default:* If you have less functionalities, the probability of flaws is reduced proportionally, and the stability improved.

Security Risks Derived from Wrong Management A HGW could be altered by customers, because they have admin rights on the device (taken to the extreme, factory reset allows complete access). Wrong feature configuration by error can derive in increasing the security risks, such as opening sensitive ports to Internet, disable basic filtering or set weak passwords. This very often implies that the Internet access service is not affected while the user is exposed. *Solution by default:* Fewer opportunities for wrong management derive in fewer security risks.

---

[13]Common Vulnerabilities and Exposures is a dictionary of vulnerabilities identified maintained by MITRE corporation.

In vHGW, configurations are mostly offered through the ISP web portal, instead of local device management. This way, the ISP can apply stricter controls, such as centralized sanity checks on wrong configuration or monitoring.

Remote Management Network management for HGW is a necessity for ISP. This means that the HGW still needs an accessible IP address for remote management (firmware upgrades, remote configuration changes, inventory, monitoring, etc.). Not only an IP address is needed, but also a server and a protocol attending requests, i.e. a potential opportunity of attack. Some examples before mentioned are TR-069 or SSH protocols. This is usually solved by NAT and filtering rules in the local HGW itself, with the inherent risk of being easily removed by the user through the HGW web interface. *Solution by default:* In the vHGW model implemented, the physical HGW uses a private IP (the same for all users, as each one has their routing context inside IPFE). The rules of NAT and filtering that allow the connectivity from the server for management are defined and enforced by the network (web portal and vCPE-NAT) by the ISP and cannot be altered in the HGW device or by an external attacker.

Firmware Configuration The migration process from HGW to vHGW, having in mind the CAPEX reduction (one of the reasons for NFV), implies the use of existing legacy HGW already deployed but modified to behave as a vHGW. This process can be achieved by configuration (just commuting HGW from routing mode with PPP[14] tunnels to layer 2 bridging mode, supported today by most HGWs). This solution leaves available all the existing HGW features, and a factory reset would re-enable them, affecting the service availability. *Solution by default:* Based on the real trial experience, to avoid faults on the service caused by user factory resets, the best security solution consisted in modifying the HGW firmware with enabled specific functionalities in the HGW, such as bridge mode, disabling the rest of unnecessary functionalities.

5.3.3.2 Other Security Risks

Residential Internet access services have other risks beyond the HGW itself.

Home LAN Extensibility

Home network LAN attacks have been considered innocuous to the network essentially because of historical reasons:

- HGW switch functionality isolates protocols of layer 2 to the home local LAN, so any traffic at this level cannot be sent or received from the outside of the home.

---

[14]Point-to-point protocol allows multiple implementations. HGW common support includes PPP over Ethernet (PPPoE) or over ATM (PPPoA) and requires an authentication process.

- Private IPv4 addresses used in home networks do not allow communications with external networks by default (non-routable). Only by using NAT technologies, traffic and devices become accessible.
- HGW functionalities, like DHCP, uPnP, NAT, etc., are only accessible from the home network and not from the outside.

As a consequence, attacks and threats using layer 2 protocols or through HGW network functionalities have been considered harmless to the ISP network, affecting customers and their local environments. *This idea must be abandoned in the case of the vHGW scenario* because layer 2 accessibility is extended to the ISP network. Here are some of the identified risks:

- *Layer 2 attacks.* There are a set of well-known attacks inside the local area network (LAN) environment with potential impact on the ISP network (in particular to the IPFE) caused by the layer 2 extension. The attacks are based in several protocols: Address Resolution Protocol (ARP) in IPv4, ICMPv6[15] in IPv6, vLAN management (802.1q) and stacked vLAN (802.1ad). Some examples of attacks based on those protocols are:
  - *Manipulated* messages, to be used in MITM[16] attacks or denial of service in different devices or against the ISP service.
  - *Message* flooding could impact on the performance of the IPFE and therefore on other users allocated to the same device.
  - *Martian* or non-expected Ethernet MAC address values to bypass network filters.
  - *Malformed packets* to alter the protocol stack stability.
- *Virtualized HGW network functions* attacks. In traditional, non-NFV architectures, some possible attacks against the HGW functionality are limited to the device itself and do not have impact on the network, but in the new vHGW architecture, some functionalities are exposed to all users and devices. Some examples are:
  - *DHCP attacks.* Flooding of packets, lease consumption or manipulated packets can affect the DHCP server in the network.
  - *IP layer 3 attacks.* Flooding of different forged IPv4/IPv6 addresses to fill the routing tables. Also, if private or Martian IP address is used, they can affect the IPFE stability.
  - *IP routing attacks.* Malicious packets based on routing protocols like RIP, BGP and OSPF. Some of these protocols are occasionally supported by residential gateways, and in some services, these messages could be accepted by the network IPFE.

---

[15]Internet Control Message Protocol in IPv6 includes neighbour discovery as the alternative to ARP and others messages equally vulnerable.

[16]Man in the middle allows an attacker to be located in the middle of communications.

- *Port forwarding (NAT)*. Flooding NAT (translation table) with massive static-/dynamic requests and keeping them indefinitely alive could affect vCPE-NAT.
- *UPnP and multicast attacks*. Port mapping capacity based on UPnP protocol must be offered by the IPFE, synchronized with the vCPE-NAT. This functionality implies several risks from resource consumption in vCPE-NAT to improper port opening.

User Session Management
Residential access traditionally use PPP sessions for broadband Internet access services. HGW is in charge of PPP establishment. This process adds a new security layer with session IDs and also encapsulates and isolates traffic among users on the access network. Additionally, the use of VLAN IDs for user in access increases the security and makes really hard to alter the user identity or traffic. The layer 2 model of vHGW is based only on VLAN IDs, with the associated risk increase.

Internal Home LAN Security
Some user decisions or default factory configurations apply different security measures on the interfaces that are not exposed to the Internet. This is the case of LAN or Wi-Fi interfaces. The problem is that local HGW routing and NAT functionality hide any visibility of these security problems and any possible mitigation. It is also very commonly accepted the concept of unreachability of internal devices from external attackers, because of the same reason. This assumption has been demonstrated to be a false security concept. The next couple of examples are real situations supporting this statement:

- Weak passwords or protocol protection in Wi-Fi access
- Malware infection in home computers to be used as intermediate hop

These and other mechanisms can be used to obtain access to the internal home LAN and the HGW itself. One real, well-documented case is the DNSChanger [8]. This malware infected millions of users and several ISPs. The most sibylline behaviour of this malware consisted in modifying the HGW DNS clients to point to compromised DNS servers, to be used for fraud and illegal actions. ISPs had to invest in user notification and network policies to avoid service disruption in infected HGW by the shutdown of the malicious DNS.

5.4   Specific and Innovative Security Design in an NFV Model

This section tries to cover the overall measures applied after the risk assessment. Each subsection matches with a risk subsection previously detailed.

5.4.1 Common Security Architecture

The general rules for a good security design (read previous section 5.3.1 X.805 architecture) were followed. The most relevant ones are listed below.

Management, Control and Data Plane Isolation This was achieved by offering physical (network interfaces and devices) and logical (VLANs and VPNs) separate paths. This segmentation has been a challenge with the logical interface sharing, especially for VNFs that share the same physical server. In most of the situation, this was solved using what is called "pass-through" mode. This configuration allows to assign a physical interface to a specific VNF container (typically a virtual machine).

Layer Isolation of VNFs Based on Hypervisor In some PoP, physical servers could host different VNFs, e.g. a IPFE and vCPE-NAT. The Linux hypervisor Kernel-based Virtual Machine (KVM) has not shown any security problem in terms of segmentation and performance isolation, with adequate configuration.

Perimeter Protection The VNFs for the service, and in special IPFE and vCPE-NAT, support and implement perimeter security controls of a network node to the incoming end-user traffic (antispoofing, Martian or internal network address filtering, protocol filtering), expressed by the RADIUS attributes. It is true that some advanced features like access control list (ACL) could be improved, such as by user MAC address filtering. This is expected to be solved in next versions. Also, the filter application triggered by the session establishment, based on the first IP packet detection instead of PPP negotiation, has shown a robust behaviour. This mechanism managed the user context and traffic path isolation with the same assurance than a normal BGN.

Segmentation Based on the Need-to-Know Principle Internal network control services, such as DNS, DHCP or RADIUS, were isolated from the rest of the network and controlled by firewalls. The multi-tier model for services (presentation, logic and data) was applied in web portals, including the user portal for vHGW configuration (user DHCP leases, static IP address, NAT port forwarding rules, Wi-Fi password, etc.).

Hardening Network Devices and Servers There are multiple security templates for routers, operating systems, databases and applications. NIST guides [9] are a good example. These templates cover access controls and exposure of the protocols, enable audit and monitoring function and disable non-needed processes, to encrypt sensible information, such as passwords. Security engineers have assumed that these templates are different when you work with a network device than when you work with a server. NFV is telling us that this is not happening any more. Company-based security hardening templates were applied in each physical server. A specific procedure was introduced to verify the same hardening process in VNFs and hypervisor software.

5.4.2   NFV Design Solutions in vHGW

We enumerate some solutions, recommendations and tests derived from the risks identified using the ETSI NFV security documents as reference.

Regulatory Compliance In terms of regulation, each country has its own legal requirements. In general, most countries within the Telefonica footprint follow the reference from the ETSI LI model. There is still a work in progress as part of ETSI NFV SEC working group, as shown by the number of documents that refer to this aspect (SEC001, SEC004, SEC006, SEC011). The solution implemented for the trial was to incorporate the internal interception function (IIF), the element that executes the LI, and it is shown in Fig. 5.3, integrated as part of the VNF. This model allows to align the network security measurements with legacy systems: Network segmentation, filtering, monitoring and auditing. Using ETSI LI standard reference for functionalities and interfaces, in Fig. 5.3, we superimpose the vHGW architecture components as it is defined in Fig. 5.2. For example, IPFE generates the copy of the content of a communication (INI3), or vCPE-NET in conjunction with RADIUS provides intercept-related information (INI2). The most relevant security challenges solved here are:

- Access control of the interception functions inside VNFs
- Security controls (authentication, non-repudiation, integrity, confidentiality) in the protocol of the internal interfaces (INI).
- Integration between VNFs (IPFE, vCPE-NAT, RADIUS) to allow extract user identity, based in private IP address, Nas-Port-Ids[17], GRE tunnels id and RADIUS sessions

Topology Validation and Infrastructure Integrity Well-known logic and protocols are used to define the user paths across the network, such as BGP or GRE protocols. Diagnostic tools were also added in the design phase to verify the correct connectivity end to end. The diagnostic process includes a virtual client connected in the user home LAN through the IPFE and executing a traceroute[18] command to verify each hop.

Management and Time Synchronization Management interfaces of all VNFs have been evaluated in the general security architecture. NTP protocol hierarchy was defined to not depend only on VNFs as time servers. Also, all VNFs support security features in the NTP protocol: ACL and authentication.

---

[17]"Network Access Server Port Id" is a radius attribute which identifies the port of the NAS which is authenticating the user. IETF RFC 2869.

[18]Diagnostic command used almost since IP network existence. Display each IP node in a route between origin and destination, and the round trip time in each hop. Based on ICMP Time Exceeded Messages.

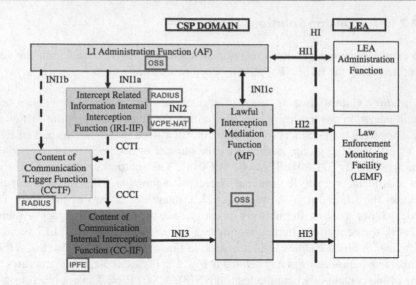

Fig. 5.3 Lawful interception mapping ETSI TR 102528 with vHGW

COTS Server OS Hardening guides for each VNF OS were required and tested. All VNFs were Linux based; no antivirus engine was added because of the potential resource impact, but audit and monitoring tools (host-based IDS) were proposed as an alternative. Backdoor presence risks were also covered by this model.

Larger-Scale Disruption Physical server redundancy, combined with VNF redundancy in active-passive mode, was defined. The solution involved allocating two different VNFs: IPFE1 and vCPE-NAT2 in one physical host and IPFE2 and vCPE-NAT1 in another, so if one host fails, the VNF could be activated in the other. A geographical redundancy between PoPs was also designed in case of expansion to more PoPs.

Maintenance by Patching Procedures similar to the one applied to network devices were established for patching and upgrading processes. The procedures include traffic diverging from the VNFs, VNF stop and image backup, VNF image replacement or image file patching, VNF start and testing and finally traffic restore. There is one interesting example of how a faulty patch procedure can have severe impact: During the certification phase, the VNF image backups were not systematically cleaned after successfully upgrades, at the end the host ran out of disk space, and all the VNFs went down.

Secure Boot/Crash All VNFs and physical servers were tested by the simple method of pulling the power cord. After correct powering, all filesystem and data were monitored to check a clean state.

Performance Isolation Hypervisor fine-grained low-level configuration was added, such as CPU pinning[19] or NUMA topology[20] assignment. Scalability tests validate the stability of the VNFs up to the nominal capacity. Pentesting as a customer verified that was not possible to escape from the vHGW user context.

5.4.3   Mitigating Inherent Risks

Apart from the previously analysed "solutions by default", the inherent risks we have described needed to be solved as well, in particular those impacting the home LAN. Let us see some of the solutions adopted.

5.4.3.1   Home LAN Extensibility
In the vHGW architecture, the security perimeter is shifted towards the network, and each network system has to solve the threats that were previously concentrated at the HGW. This is not a drawback, but an opportunity to use more powerful and efficient technology to apply security controls than the resource-limited HGW can support. Let us see some examples analysing previous identified risk and how they were solved in the trial:

- Layer 2 attacks. The IPFE implements layer 2 isolation between the user home networks. During the trial, a QinQ[21] double tagging for VLAN was used for user identification. The access node (DSLAM[22] or OLT[23]) was in charge of adding these tags and protect them by overriding any attempt of modifying them. Also, access nodes and the IPFE included a set of controls in the layer 2 protocols activated to protect the service:
  - ARP/ND packets rate limit
  - MAC learning and cache limit per users
  - Configurable lifetime for cache entries
  - MAC filtering
- Virtualized HGW network functions attacks. Each of the network systems that covers HGW functions implemented its own protection measurements at a carrier-grade scale capacity:

---

[19] Also known as processor affinity, binds and reserve CPUs to a specific virtual machine.

[20] Non-uniform memory access in x86 architecture allows faster memory access to co-located CPUs.

[21] QinQ is the informal name for 802.1ad.

[22] Digital subscriber line access multiplexer. Network device that allows broadband access in telephone lines, i.e. DSL. Multiple variants exist: ADSL, VDSL, etc.

[23] Optical line terminal. Network device endpoint and multiplexing for passive optical network. Commonly known as Fiber access. Multiple variants exists: FTTH, FTTB, FTTN, etc.

- *DHCP VNF*: Rate limits in packets and in number of IPs assigned per home and in total. Override DHCP invalid options, robust to malformed DHCP packets.
- *IPFE VNF:* Firewall rules, antispoofing [10], rate limits in several protocols including UPnP, multicast, logging, accounting for any IPv4/IPv6 traffic, robust to malformed IP packets.
- *vCPE-NAT VNF*: Rate limits in statics/dynamic translations per home and in total, configurable timeouts for different protocols (NAT-ALG[24], PCP, etc.), robust to malformed IP packets.

5.4.3.2 User Sessions Management

The lack of PPP sessions was one of the main concerns initially identified. The application of VLAN tagging robust solutions at the access nodes, outside of the user control, reduces greatly the risk. After a long trial period, the VLAN model for isolation did not show any vulnerability. Diagnostic tools were applied to evaluate the user traffic as monitoring tools to detect any incident related with this risk.

5.4.3.3 Internal Home LAN Security

User behaviour is someway difficult to enforce, but some of the previous solutions in vHGW can alleviate this problem.

Router access or Wi-Fi passwords are configured through the service web portal. This portal requests the user strong passwords, removing the risk of jeopardizing the security by weak passwords.

If malware or malicious users access the HGW, most of the functionalities are not usable, e.g. DNS, UPnP and NAT, because they are offloaded on the network. This will require more elaborated malware design (remember the DNSChanger case [8]).

Finally, some additional security capacities exist and can be deployed on demand. This is the focus for the last section: New security service opportunities for ISPs.

5.5   Innovation Through New Service Opportunities

One of the big opportunities of the vHGW service architecture is the capacity to deploy layer 2 services and in particular security services. The IPFE offers two key functionalities for this:

- Traffic mirroring by user. IPFE can mirror user layer 2 traffic on demand. The IPFE capacity could not allow a full traffic mirror of all of the users. This limitation made this technology valid for on-demand user services only.

---

[24]Application-level gateway NAT devices allow to apply address and port translation to the application layer, such as FTP.

- The Virtualized Services Platform (VSP) provides a way for cloudlike services to interact (inject traffic) with the end devices at layer 2. The general architecture of Fig. 5.2 includes the VSP. This VSP is deployed in a datacentre but connects with the IPFE using pseudowire Martini tunnels [11]. The tunnelling technology allows to extend layer 2 connectivity of any user home network to the VSP by means of Multiprotocol Label Switching (MPLS).

Some of the potential security services that our NFV use case offers have been tested in the field trial, such as mentioned below KPI collection, and others are in a state of design and analysis in the laboratory. The different services were studied from two different points of view:

- As ISP's internal services. By internal services, we cover a set of services that an ISP requires from the point of view of protecting its own assets: the network and service infrastructure, the security of its users or their quality of experience. No subscription option is offered to the end user in this modality.
- As residential services. End-user security services that could be based on a subscription model or included as part of the Internet access service.

5.5.1 Security KPIs

This service has the aim of collecting and analysing KPIs for the trial, including security ones. It was defined and tested as an internal service. The solution was implemented by the use of the IPFE mirror capacity, adding a vDPI (virtual deep packet inspection) VNF. This was an in-house solution deployed on a COTS server. The vDPI with capacity of collecting traffic higher than 20 Gbps allows to process, anonymize and store relevant data such as the number of devices per home, types of protocol most used and percentage of encrypted traffic, among others. From the point of view of security, a couple of algorithms were included:

- Spam generation detection. Identify spam behaviour from user networks
- Botnet activity detection. Based on DNS traffic analysis, such as DGAs,[25] Fast Flux[26] and blacklist

The results after the trial period include a set of relevant insights in the network traffic patterns and the vDPI demonstrated that it was able to detect several infected users. No notification was delivered because the data was anonymized.

---

[25]Domain generation algorithms used by several botnets families that produce thousands of potential domains where host the botnet controller.

[26]Fast Flux is a botnet technique based on DNS for hiding botnet controller with dynamic changes of compromised bots acting as proxy.

5.5.2   IDS at Layer 2

This residential service was tested in laboratory. Despite of not being deployed in the trial, very interesting capacities were evaluated in what relates to NFV. A virtual intrusion detection VNF (vIDS) based on open-source software SNORT was deployed in the network receiving the IPFE mirror traffic. In this case, user identification and notification through a captive portal were included. The vIDS was able to identify malware in user devices, thanks to the layer 2 visibility, including MAC address of the infected device and the operating system. This is very valuable information for the customer and/or for the ISP support call centre.

5.5.3   Diagnostic Tool

In order to help in the service monitoring during the trial phase, a diagnostic service was included. The solution was based on the use of a VSP. This service, internal to the ISP, includes a client virtually deployed in the home LAN. The client executes a set of tests to verify the correct state of the services. In what relates to security, it could detect malicious traffic. One of the most promising functionalities is the capability of injecting layer 2 traffic to block specific devices connectivity.

5.5.4   Third-Party Security Tools as VSP

Apart from the services described above, the opportunity for third-party services is enabled as well by the use of NFV technology for vHGW. There are multiple security aspects for residential and SME services where third parties' security solutions can be deployed as VSP. Some promising areas related to security services are:

- Parental control. Set up a VSP web proxy for the home LAN browsing traffic.
- DDoS detection. Interacting with network devices to mitigate the attack upstream.
- Advanced firewalls. VSP application layer and new-generation firewalls for SME.
- Private VPNs. Extend through the VSP the connectivity between users in a VPN style for resource sharing.

5.6   Conclusions

In this chapter, we have described a real example of NFV use case: the virtualization of residential home gateways in a commercial trial. Leveraging on this trial, the chapter has presented an analysis of the security risks, and the solutions adopted in a real deployment.

Successful trial of NFV technologies for vHGW from the operational point of view opens the opportunity to explore new services, with a special focus on security. Some alternatives and challenges to be addressed have been identified:

- Risk analysis methodologies for network security and IT security are still valid and necessary despite the NFV disruptive technology.
- Offloading and virtualizing network functions to the network from the low-cost end devices reduce several existing security risks without additional investment but open new ones like user authentication or layer 2 accessibility to attacks.
- Centralization on the network simplifies some security task for HGW, because they are now part of ISP standard procedures (patching, monitoring, redundancy) but they must be fully integrated in the company.

One important lesson learnt in the design and the security certification of the solution is that common security solutions did not fully cover the risk in vHGW, and by this reason, specific measures were needed. We had to resort to NFV available security standards, produced by the ETSI NFV SEC WG, which provided us valuable insight in the solution design space.

As a trip with no end, the implementation of this trial has allowed us to update the security procedures in service design and operation. Our future plans include applying this knowledge in new NFV-based services. Some of the most promising areas are vIMS, 4G/LTE backhaul or vBNG, all with the aim of increasing the efficiency and security of the network.

The objective of this work has not only been to secure the network, but also the study and validation of new opportunities for providing security services based on the NFV technology. Indeed, some of the laboratory tests discussed here are in the process of becoming future services for our customers.

Questions

1. What is the single most significant difference between a conventional HGW and vHGW?
2. How does the ITU propose to protect end-to-end network services?
3. What are the security advantages of vHGW versus classical HGW?
4. Based on ETSI NFV-SEC001, what are the most relevant requirements for vHGW?
5. Why is point-to-point protocol (PPP) not necessary from a security point of view?
6. How would you implement high availability of IPFE and vCPE-NAT if you only have two physical hosts?
7. Where do you apply BCP 38 in the vHGW architecture?
8. What is a VSP and what can it do for security?

References

1. Palancar RC, da Silva RAL, Chavarría JLF, López DR, Armengol AJE, Tinoco RG (2015) Virtualization of residential customer premise equipment. Lessons learned in Brazil vCPE trial. it-Infor Technol 57(5):285–294. doi:10.1515/itit-2015-0028
2. ETSI, G (2013) Network Functions Virtualisation (NFV); Use Cases. V1, 1, 2013–10. http://www.etsi.org/deliver/etsi_gs/nfv/001_099/001/01.01.01_60/gs_ nfv001v010101p.pdf
3. Bernstein, J, Spets, T, Bathrick, G, Pitsoulakis, G (2004) DSL Forum TR-069, CPE WAN Management Protocol. In: Proceedings of DSL forum
4. ETSI, G (2013) Network Functions Virtualisation (NFV); NFV Security; Problem Statement. V1, 1, 2014–10. http://www.etsi.org/deliver/etsi_gs/NFV-SEC/001_099/001/01.01.01_60/gs_NFV-SEC001v010101p.pdf
5. ETSI, G (2015) Network Functions Virtualisation (NFV); NFV Security; Report on use cases and technical approaches for multi-layer host administration. V1, 1, 2015–12. http://www.etsi.org/deliver/etsi_gs/NFV-SEC/001_099/009/01.01.01_60/gs_nfv-sec009v010101p.pdf
6. Czyz, J, Kallitsis, M, Gharaibeh, M, Papadopoulos, C, Bailey, M, Karir, M (2014) Taming the 800 Pound Gorilla: the rise and decline of NTP DDoS attacks. In: Proceedings of the 2014 conference on Internet Measurement Conference (IMC'14). ACM, New York, pp 435–448
7. OpenSSL Software foundation, Inc. (1999). https://www.openssl.org/
8. Meng, W, Duan, R, Lee, W (2013) DNS Changer remediation study. Talk at M3AAWG 27th
9. National Institute of Standards and Techonologies, National Checklist Program Repository. http://checklists.nist.gov
10. Ferguson, P, Senie, D (2000) Network ingress filtering: defeating denial of service attacks which employ IP source address spoofing, BCP 38, RFC 2827. http://www.rfc-editor.org/info/bcp38
11. Martini, L, Ed., Rosen, E, El-Aawar, N, Smith, T, Heron, G (2006) Pseudowire setup and maintenance using the Label Distribution Protocol (LDP), RFC 4447, doi:10.17487/RFC4447. http://www.rfc-editor.org/info/rfc4447

Antonio Pastor received the MSc. degree in industrial engineering from the Carlos III University of Madrid (UC3M), Spain, in 1999. Since then, he has been with Telefónica I+D, where he works on the engineering of different worldwide Telefónica networks. Since 2006 he has been working as an expert in network security, and recently he is working in SDN and NFV technologies oriented to security and research where he has several patents and papers. He also holds several certifications from ISACA and GIAC in this area.

Jesús Luis Folgueira Chavarría earned a Master's degree in Telecommunications Engineering at the Universidad Politécnica de Madrid (ETSIT-UPM) in 1994 and a Master degree in Telecommunication Economics (UNED) in 2015. From 1992 to 1994 he was working in Computational Electromagnetics research at UPM. After an internship in Spanish National Aeronautics Institute, he was working as a consultant in Data Services over Residential Cable Networks. In 1995 he joined to Telefonica I+D (Research & Development), in Network Engineering division. He was working in architecture and technology evolution of IP Networks and xDSL services. He became a Project leader in 1999. In 2004 he became Senior Manager, leading IP Services & Networks area, with responsibility on network technologies and OSS development. From 2009 to 2011 he has been leading network evolution areas focused on fixed access evolution (fibre and xDSL), new transport technologies and IP networks evolution. From 2011 to 2013, he was responsible of Network Transversal Projects within Direction of Network Transversal Projects & Innovation in Telefonica Global CTO, working on network evolution plans and projects, network evolution activities with Telefonica's OBs and techno-economical analysis for new technologies. Since 2014, he is responsible for Network Engineering and Transformation in Network Virtualization area of Telefonica Global CTO, working on first network virtualization deployments for Telefonica.

A Security Policy Transition Framework for Software-Defined Networks

6

Jacob H. Cox Jr., Russell J. Clark, and Henry L. Owen III

6.1 Introduction

Software-defined networking (SDN) [1] allows for a single controller to orchestrate the actions of an entire network of switches.[1] Meanwhile, southbound interfaces, like OpenFlow [2], provide network operators with a single, vendor-agnostic interface for creating network applications, allowing for more fine-grained orchestration. In addition, these interfaces are further augmented by programming frameworks, like Pyretic [3] and Ryuretic [4] to provide greater abstraction and shield network operators from the complexities inherent in network application development. Furthermore, as organizations seek to protect their network's clients, data, and resources, greater numbers of researchers and network operators are looking toward SDN to quickly produce network security applications that address various attack vectors as they are discovered.

Unfortunately, many security solutions lack a framework for reversing or updating security measures (e.g., port blocking, traffic redirection, and other policy enforcements) once they are activated. Without a transition framework, once a client is flagged for a policy violation, revoking (or updating) the triggered security

---

[1]This chapter only considers a single controller, though distributed, logically centralized controllers can be used for more robust control options (e.g., fault tolerance, scalability, etc.).

J.H. Cox Jr. (✉) • H.L. Owen III
School of Electrical and Computer Engineering, Georgia Institute of Technology,
North Ave NW, 30332, Atlanta, GA, USA
e-mail: jcox70@gatech.edu; henry.owen@ece.gatech.edu

R.J. Clark
College of Computing, Georgia Institute of Technology, North Ave NW,
30332, Atlanta, GA, USA
e-mail: russ.clark@gatech.edu

© Springer International Publishing AG 2017
S.Y. Zhu et al. (eds.), *Guide to Security in SDN and NFV*, Computer
Communications and Networks, DOI 10.1007/978-3-319-64653-4_6

measure is not possible without having the network operator manually update the controller with either a script or external command. In some cases, the network operator may even have to reset the controller. None of which are ideal. For in one case, network operators can become overwhelmed with a large number configuration requirements. Yet, in the other, resetting the controller can result in a loss of state for the network and deprive the network of orchestration while the controller reboots.

As Kim et al. [5, 6] observe, network operators may already be responsible for as many as 18,000 network configuration changes in a given month. On traditional networks, these changes often include adding, modifying, or deleting entries in access control lists (ACLs). Similar change requirements may exist on SDNs where network operators utilize *whitelists* and *blacklists* as part of their security strategy. In both cases, each additional configuration introduces an opportunity to add an error to the network. This task is further compounded when we consider that network operators may already be maintaining ACLs that contain roughly 10,000 entries, requiring updates as much as 4,000 times per year [5]. Such requirements represent a burdensome and tedious challenge for network operators. Moreover, this burden can be even more cumbersome for many network operators who lack programming experience. Thus, forcing network operators to manually handle policy enforcements prolongs a traditional requirement that is already seen as tedious and error prone. Additionally, future and emerging networks and services are likely to present levels of complexity that are currently unforeseen and unmanageable by the traditional means. Hence, as argued by Tsagkaris et al. [7], the design and implementation of more sophisticated tools are required to simplify network management and control and also to minimize human interaction.

For the above reasons, this chapter describes a security policy transition framework [8] to automate the process of updating policy enforcements in SDNs, which can assist network operators and benefit their clients by automating security policy transitions. For instance, a transition framework can help network operators reduce their manual configuration requirements, allowing them to avoid additional network errors and to pursue more complex tasks. Second, clients receive automatic notification of their violation and instructions for regaining their network privileges. Third, it eliminates erroneous trouble tickets by informing both clients and administrators of the violation. Finally, depending on the violation and validation requirement, this framework reduces the total time required to reinstate a client's network privileges. Having triggered a policy enforcement, the client need only enter a *passkey* into a web interface (i.e., a captive portal) to regain network privileges. Additionally, this framework is easily adaptable to other protocols and cloud infrastructures.

The rest of this chapter is outlined as follows. We first discuss the motivation for a security policy transition framework in Sect. 6.2. In Sect. 6.3, we discuss related work that best correlates to security policy transitions. The components of this framework are explained in Sect. 6.4, and the Mininet-based, test environment for this framework is explained in Sect. 6.5. Use cases for this framework are then introduced in Sect. 6.6. Finally, further discussion and future opportunities for this framework are offered in Sect. 6.7 before concluding this chapter in Sect. 6.8.

6.2   Motivation for a Security Policy Transition Framework

The primary goal of the security policy transition framework [8] is to reduce the number of manual network configurations in order to reduce network errors and improve network operator efficiency. Hence, it automates system functions to alleviate human error and reduce network operator workloads. Likewise, automating the revocation (or updates) of policy enforcements, once triggered by security policies, can significantly reduce a network operator's involvement with ACLs. For example, when a flagged client is added to a *blacklist* that triggers a policy enforcement, a security policy transition framework, like the one presented in this chapter, provides the client with preconfigured options for regaining access to network services. In other cases, where automated options are not possible, a help desk – employing less-skilled attendants – can be used to provide validation services for the flagged client. When the client does meet validation requirements, either the automated system or the help desk can provide the client with a *passkey*.

For instance, patch compliance can potentially be completely automated, while infected computers that require operating system reinstalls could be handled by help desk personnel. In either case, the transition framework handles the revocation of policy enforcements once the client obtains and provides a unique *passkey*. Since this process avoids network operator involvement, operational expenses (OPEX) and customer wait times can be further improved. We now offer a more detailed discussion of the security policy transition framework as seen in Fig. 6.1.

In this framework, the network operator sets the security policies for the controller as shown in (1) of Fig. 6.1. Then, as shown in (2), when the controller detects a violation that triggers a policy enforcement, the SDN controller informs the Trusted Agent, which serves as the framework's automated system for client services and controller updates, via an in-band communication and then updates the OpenFlow switch's flow table through its southbound interface. The flow table

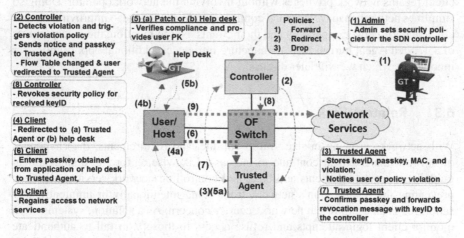

Fig. 6.1 Security policy transition framework [8]

modification results in the redirection of the flagged client's current and future traffic to a captive portal provided by the Trusted Agent. In (3), the Trusted Agent accepts and stores the client's *keyID*, *passkey*, MAC address, and violation. Thus, the Trusted Agent has knowledge of the client's violation when it presents the client with the web interface of its captive portal. This interface can then provide the client with a notice of the client's violation and instructions for regaining access to network services. For instance, if the client is flagged for patch compliance, then the Trusted Agent can make the patch available for download (4a or 5a). Once the software is installed and validated, the client can obtain a *passkey* from the validation authority (5a or 5b) and enter it into the web portal. Then, once the client enters the correct *passkey* (6), the Trusted Agent sends a revocation request to the controller (7), and the client's network privileges are reinstated as the policy enforcement is revoked (8). Hence, in this framework, the Trusted Agent services the flagged client and provides automated revocation requests to the SDN controller to remove policy enforcements.

A similar approach can be taken if the client inadvertently (or overtly) violates a network policy (e.g., packet spoofing, port scanning, rogue DHCP replies, etc.) requiring them to re-sign an acceptable use policy (AUP) after retraining. This requirement may also force the user to provide assurances that they will not repeat such actions in the future. The *passkey* can then be provided with a certificate of completion. Still, network operators may also wish to choose their level of involvement for certain policy violations. For instance, they may want to take action based on a first occurrence of a policy violation or a third, etc. In a corporation or government office, the network operator may even require the first line supervisor to login and acknowledge the incident before granting the certificate and *passkey*.

Another case occurs when clients are flagged for a computer virus that requires their system to be re-imaged. For such cases, a validation authority, such as a help desk can easily provide this service or verify that specific actions were completed. Once done, a *passkey* is provided to the client. For all of these examples, the client regains network privileges without involving the network operator. Doing so simplifies network management and control operations while also improving service efficiency for network operators and their clients. Not to mention, the incorporation of a Trusted Agent into an SDN architecture introduces additional opportunities for innovation, which we will later discuss.

6.3   Related Work

With networks growing in size, traffic volume, and requirements, the challenges of network management continue to increase. Likewise, enforcing organizational guidelines, protecting clients and data, and controlling network services all while preventing the organization's network from being intentionally or unintentionally sabotaged is an ever present network security concern. As a solution, systems often monitor client login attempts and refuse access to those who fail to authenticate or lack authorization. These solutions may even seek to monitor security policies and automatically adjust network parameters to ensure compliance. Accordingly, various methods for controlling network access and enforcing policies exist in traditional networks and SDNs.

Traditional security management methods often rely on access control lists (ACLs), client IDs and passwords, and terminal access controller access control to enforce prearranged policies on system networks [9]. However, these policies are often reconfigured by network operators each time a security violation occurs or when a client (who triggered the security measure) regains approval to be reinstated. Additionally, protocols like 802.1X [10] can shut down ports if they detect unapproved devices connected to them, but removing these policy enforcements to reactivate these ports is often left to the network operator to resolve via a trouble ticket. Hence, these solutions place considerable configuration burden on network operators, add additional software and hardware costs, and lack an automated security policy transition framework for reinstating clients. They also add to the ambiguity of trouble tickets created by clients who do not yet know the reason for their loss of network services. Likewise, due to the ambiguity of these trouble tickets, network operators can spend unnecessary time trying to troubleshoot and determine the cause of the client's loss of services.

Consider, for example, commercial network access control (NAC) solutions, like ForeScout [11] and Cisco NAC [12]. They mostly seek to ensure that access policies for the network (and its resources) are enforced on a per person basis. These systems may even move a device to a reconfigured guest network (e.g., walled garden), so it can receive system updates (e.g., antivirus software and patches). Previously, a major restriction of NAC solutions was that they were typically limited to devices that had specific operating systems installed and/or were capable of installing a NAC agent. For instance, IEEE 802.1X requires that end devices (i.e., a client) have a supplicant installed, which is used to communicate with the central authentication server. However, modern NAC solutions have grown to offer new features. For instance, the Aruba ClearPass Policy Management Platform, the Bradford Networks' Network Sentry/NAC, the Cisco Identity Services Engine (ISE), and the Pulse Secure Policy Secure NAC solutions all offer agentless support, extended policy capabilities, onboarding support, extended guest management, extended profiles support, extended endpoint compliance, optional advanced threat protection and mitigation, expanded monitoring and reporting, and extended system integration and interoperability [13].

Still, NAC solutions can also be complicated to set up, often becoming a long-term project requiring phased deployments and more suitable to robust/mature infrastructures. Since an authentication server is required, deployment also includes more power, space, and licenses, while support for random equipment, like printers, can also be problematic. Examples also exist for defeating NAC. For instance, a security researcher demonstrated that by attaching a hub to a port, they could simply wait for the authorized client to authenticate with the NAC server and then piggy back their communications over the network by spoofing the authorized client [14]. Other researchers have implemented bridging techniques using an authorized port and an active client to achieve better results [14]. Still, when port violations are detected, the port is generally blocked and manually cleared. So, despite a plethora of available protocols and software, network connectivity remains a manual process and a challenge to network management. Hence, network operators must still work with clients to address the flag's cause and to reinstate their privileges, which the security policy transition framework discussed in this chapter attempts to address. Additionally, NAC deployments also require proprietary switches that support NAC features, like 802.1X. However, such features are absent in SDN/OpenFlow switches, hence, SDN-based approaches are required.

SDN solutions have also developed in recent years to assist network operators with flexible network programmability for security management. For instance, PolicyCop [15] helps network operators detect policy violations. Action requests are either forwarded to an autonomic policy adaptation module or the network operator depending on the policy violation. As a result, the network operator is an essential part of this architecture having to provide manual configurations. Moreover, PolicyCop [15] does not directly consider the revocation of policy enforcements, yet it can be assumed that the network operator must provide manual interventions for those as well. Ethane [16], a precursor to SDN, provides a centralized network architecture with identity-based access control that allocates IP addresses as IP-MAC-Port associations. In this environment, clients authenticate via a webform, and their packets are then reactively evaluated by the controller for policy compliance. By doing so, Ethane allows network operators to define a single, fine-grain policy and apply it network wide. And, as a result, network clients can be held accountable for their traffic, yet Ethane also requires network operator intervention for flagged clients [16]. In contrast, FlowNAC [17] drops web-based authentication in favor of a modified 802.1X framework supporting extensible authentication protocol over LAN (EAPoL-in-EAPoL) encapsulation. In this framework, client traffic flows are associated with a target service. As a result, this system handles client access based on predefined authentication and authorization policies, but it does not consider policy violations where the client becomes flagged. Additionally, supplicant (client) software must be utilized to enable FlowNAC's features.

Kinetic, formerly known as Resonance, also represents a transition framework that offers an OpenFlow-based dynamic access control system [6]. It uses network alerts to support continuous monitoring and per interface policy control to automate dynamic security policies. Additionally, Kinetic verifies that prescribed changes align with operator requirements by employing a finite-state machine (FSM) having states that correspond to distinct forwarding behavior [6]. Transitions within the FSM are controlled by Kinetic's Event Handler, which monitors for events and triggers policy updates. However, Kinetic follows a similar vein to the solutions previously discussed in that it too requires network operators to supply the events that trigger its policy changes. In addition, since Kinetic is built atop the Pyretic [3] programming language and POX [18], which is limited to OpenFlow 1.0 [2] and only 12 packet header match fields, its packet inspection capabilities are substantially constrained. Moreover, Kinetic also lacks an automated framework for transitioning between security measures.

While all these solutions represent great strides toward better and more intuitive interfaces that simplify the application development process, they still do not provide a policy transition framework for automating the revocation or modification of a policy enforcement. Resultantly, network operators are still heavily involved in multiple, unnecessary configurations on a daily basis. Hence, we next introduce a security policy transition framework that can be implemented in SDN and NFV environments. By including this framework, network operators can improve the time associated with reinstating network clients while reducing network operator workloads and erroneous trouble tickets. Much like Kinetic [6], this framework implements an event listener (i.e., Event Handler); however, it works with a trusted entity (i.e., Trusted Agent) to determine when an activated security measure or policy enforcement should be changed. The SDN controller then assumes responsibility for implementing and enforcing security policies, while relying on the Trusted Agent to provide notification for when policy enforcements should be revoked.

6.4   The Framework

The security policy transition framework introduced in this chapter uses Ryuretic [4] for its SDN controller applications. Ryuretic [4] is a domain-specific language offering a modular framework for application development atop the Ryu [19] controller. It also provides an intuitively simple format for network operators to select header fields within a packet (pkt[*]) and then specify what operation (*ops[*]*) occurs when a match (*fields[*]*) is found. This platform also allows programmers to craft their own packets, which is utilized to establish a communication channel between the SDN (Ryuretic) controller and its Trusted Agent using ICMP packets. This communication channel is then used to submit policy enforcement updates or revocation requests. This is discussed in greater detail in Sect. 6.4.3. Additionally, this communication allows both the Ryuretic controller and the Trusted Agent to maintain corresponding state tables as we will also discuss in Sect. 6.4.3. These and the other components comprising the controller and Trusted Agent modules (shown in Fig. 6.2) are now discussed.

6.4.1   Controller

As shown in Fig. 6.2, the Ryuretic controller for this framework is an SDN controller comprised of an Event Handler, a Policy Enforcer, and a Policy Table. These components are implemented in Ryuretic [4], which serves as an abstraction layer residing atop the Ryu [19] controller and supporting OpenFlow 1.3 [2]. With Ryuretic, network operators can choose to forward, drop, mirror, redirect, modify, or craft packets based on match parameters that they define via objects.

As shown in Fig. 6.3, when a packet-in event occurs in the Ryu [19] controller, the Ryuretic coupler generates a packet object (*pkt*) that is forwarded to the Ryuretic

Fig. 6.2 Security policy
transition framework
components [8]

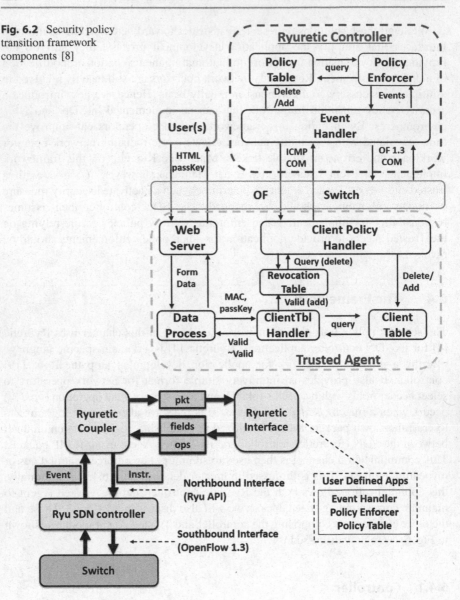

Fig. 6.3 Ryuretic controller

interface. This is where the network operator policies are specified. Based on these
policies, the interface returns two objects (i.e., *fields* and *ops*) specifying which
match-action rules to pass to the switch. These objects are then interpreted by the
Ryuretic coupler and forwarded as instructions to the Ryu controller, which installs
the rules to the switch. In Fig. 6.3, the Event Handler, the Policy Enforcer, and the
Policy Table all exist as user-defined applications in the Ryuretic interface.

6.4.1.1 Event Handler

The Event Handler serves as the primary interface for the controller, responding to network events from the switch, security events from the Policy Enforcer, and security policy transitions from the Trusted Agent. It also handles insert and delete messages for the controller's Policy Table to maintain state for each connected client. When a packet arrives from the switch, the Event Handler passes the packet to its Policy Enforcer. If a violation is detected (e.g., a spoofed ARP packet), then the Event Handler will receive notification of the violation along with a generated *keyID* and *passkey*. It then records this information, including the client's MAC address and input port number, into the SDN controller's Policy Table, which serves as an access control list for future packet decisions. It then notifies the Trusted Agent via the in-band communication channel (shown previously in Fig. 6.2 and discussed in Sect. 6.4.3) and includes the client's table information discussed above. Finally, it provides a match-action flow rule to the OpenFlow switch to direct future packets from the flagged client to the Trusted Agent. Should the Event Handler receive a policy enforcement revocation request from the Trusted Agent, then the Event Handler reinstates the client's privileges by removing the associated client entry from the controller's Policy Table.

6.4.1.2 Policy Enforcer

The Policy Enforcer handles events passed to it from the Event Handler. It first confirms that arriving packets are not already flagged in the Policy Table. If not, the Policy Enforcer next applies selected security policies against the arrived packet. If the packet passes specified checks, then it is passed to the Event Handler for normal forwarding. Otherwise, the Policy Enforcer returns *fields* and *ops* hash tables[2] to the Event Handler – resulting in the client's traffic being redirected to the network's Trusted Agent. If the client is flagged, the Policy Enforcer also generates a randomized *passkey* and a unique *keyID*, which is passed back to the Event Handler with the client's other unique flow information (i.e., input port, MAC, and violation).

6.4.1.3 Policy Table

The Policy Table simply stores the identification and flag state information for each client. As shown in Fig. 6.4, the Policy Table stores *keyID* (primary identification key), *passkey* (for client authentication), MAC address, input port, and violation code for flagged clients (of which, all but the input port are forwarded to the Trusted Agent).

6.4.2   Trusted Agent

The Trusted Agent serves as an intermediary between the client and the network operator. For instance, the Trusted Agent is able to send revocation messages to the controller and reinstate the client's privileges in lieu of the network operator once

---

[2]Hash tables (Python dictionaries) are Ryuretic's method for directing network operations.

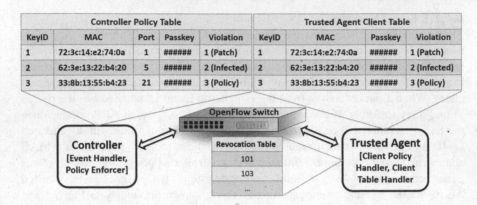

Controller Policy Table					Trusted Agent Client Table			
KeyID	MAC	Port	Passkey	Violation	KeyID	MAC	Passkey	Violation
1	72:3c:14:e2:74:0a	1	######	1 (Patch)	1	72:3c:14:e2:74:0a	######	1 (Patch)
2	62:3e:13:22:b4:20	5	######	2 (Infected)	2	62:3e:13:22:b4:20	######	2 (Infected)
3	33:8b:13:55:b4:23	21	######	3 (Policy)	3	33:8b:13:55:b4:23	######	3 (Policy)

Fig. 6.4 Controller – Trusted Agent communication

the *passkey* is provided. It can also provide clients with instructions for regaining network access. Its components (See Fig. 6.2) are next discussed.

6.4.2.1 Client Policy Handler

The Client Policy Handler establishes a communication link with the controller to receive policy activation notices and submit revocation requests. When the Trusted Agent is first notified of a policy enforcement activation, it records the provided *keyID*, *passkey*, MAC, and violation associations in its Client Table as indicated in Figs. 6.2 and 6.4. The Client Policy Handler also periodically queries the Revocation Table for *keyIDs* belonging to clients who have submitted a *passkey* and are awaiting the reinitialization of client privileges. In this framework, the query is arbitrarily performed every 30 s. Ideally, this query can be performed more frequently.

6.4.2.2 Client and Revocation Tables

The Client Table allows the Trusted Agent to maintain state for flagged clients. As shown in Fig. 6.4, this table maintains the client's *keyID*, *passkey*, MAC, and violation. It is also queried by the Client Table Handler to confirm client MAC and *passkey* pairs. Furthermore, the Client Table provides violation information to the Handler, so the Trusted Agent renders appropriate instructions to the client.

The Revocation Table (also shown in Fig. 6.4) allows the Trusted Agent to queue *keyIDs* for clients awaiting privilege reinstatement. The Client Policy Handler then routinely queries the table and sends *keyIDs* in revocation messages to the controller.

6.4.2.3 Client Table Handler

The Client Table Handler queries the Client Table to verify a client's *passkey* and MAC address. If successful, the Handler loads the client's *keyID* to the Revocation Table for delivery to the controller. As a security measure, the Client Table Handler can only query the Client Table and write to the Revocation Table.

6.4.2.4 Data Processor

The Data Processor is a Common Gateway Interface (CGI) module that provides server-side scripting for the Trusted Agent's web server. It receives as input the MAC and *passkey* from form data and provides them to the Client Table Handler. In turn, the Handler returns feedback information to the client's web interface via HTML.

6.4.2.5 Web Server

While any number of web servers could be used for this component, the lighttpd [20] web server is used due to its small memory footprint and support for CGI scripts. It serves as the client's primary interface while resolving flags. It also captures the client's MAC address via a PHP script when the client enters their passkey. The passkey and MAC address are then forwarded to the Data Processor for passkey validation. Note that the web server and the client must be on the same subnet for the PHP script to capture the client's MAC address. Otherwise, it captures the MAC address of the previous hop (e.g., a router's MAC address).

6.4.3   Communication Channel

The SDN controller and Trusted Agent communicate rule insertions, updates, and revocations via crafted ICMP packets having instructions in their modified data field. Both ICMP request and reply packets (see Fig. 6.5) are used. Normally, the data field of an ICMP packet header contains information for determining round trip times (e.g., time stamps), etc. However, the transition framework's communication channel repurposes this field. Additionally, identification (ID) and sequence (SEQ) fields are set to zero. Yet, while the Trusted Agent can receive ICMP packets having complete payloads, the SDN controller only receives the ICMP packet's header information and the up to 86 bytes of the packet's data – based on observations of the Open vSwitch and Ryu controller implementation used in this work. Hence, communications from the Trusted Agent to the Ryu controller are limited to 86 bytes, as shown in Fig. 6.5b.

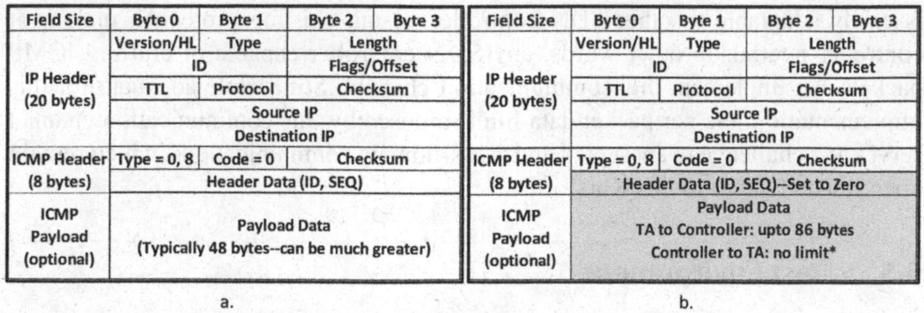

Field Size	Byte 0	Byte 1	Byte 2	Byte 3	Field Size	Byte 0	Byte 1	Byte 2	Byte 3
IP Header (20 bytes)	Version/HL	Type	Length		IP Header (20 bytes)	Version/HL	Type	Length	
	ID		Flags/Offset			ID		Flags/Offset	
	TTL	Protocol	Checksum			TTL	Protocol	Checksum	
	Source IP					Source IP			
	Destination IP					Destination IP			
ICMP Header (8 bytes)	Type = 0, 8	Code = 0	Checksum		ICMP Header (8 bytes)	Type = 0, 8	Code = 0	Checksum	
	Header Data (ID, SEQ)					Header Data (ID, SEQ)–Set to Zero			
ICMP Payload (optional)	Payload Data (Typically 48 bytes--can be much greater)				ICMP Payload (optional)	Payload Data TA to Controller: upto 86 bytes Controller to TA: no limit*			

a.   b.

Fig. 6.5 ICMP Packet modification. *Ideally, within network's max transmission unit (MTU) size. (**a**) Typical contents of ICMP packet. (**b**) Modified ICMP packet

Table 6.1 Abbreviations used for controller communication [8]

Abbr.	Meaning	Summary
i	Initialize	Establish Trusted Agent parameters
a	Acknowledge	Send table entry receipt for keyID
d	Delete	Request policy deletion for specified keyID

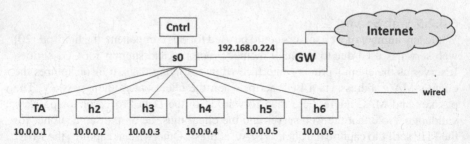

Fig. 6.6 Mininet test environment

To accommodate its data limitation and allow for future features, the Trusted Agent constrains it responses to *action*, *keyID* strings, consuming up to 8 bytes. The *action* (see Table 6.1) value is a single letter abbreviation. It identifies the message type (i.e., initialize, acknowledge, or delete). Messages not requiring a *keyID* (e.g., initialize) include a zero after the *action* value. For example, the Trusted Agent's initialization message to the Ryuretic controller appears as "i,0" in the data field of the ICMP's packet header. A revocation appears as "d,102," while an acknowledgment from the controller appears as "a,d,102."

Messages from the controller, however, have more flexibility. For instance, rule insertion methods destined for the Trusted Agent's Client Table will include MAC, *passkey*, violation, and *keyID* values in a comma-separated string. This format is recognized by the Trusted Agent and handled accordingly by its Client Policy Handler. It is through this communication channel and format that the Ryuretic controller and the Trusted Agent are able to maintain corresponding tables (the Policy Table for the Ryuretic controller and the Client Table for the Trusted Agent), which are shown in Fig. 6.4. Moreover, while limited, this solution is easily adaptable to other SDN controllers using existing protocols, making it controller neutral. In other words, any SDN controller capable of crafting ICMP packets can implement this communication channel. Still, while adequate for this implementation, the per packet data limit imposed by this communication channel serves as a challenge to encrypted and cross-domain communications, which remain open research areas in this work.

6.5 Test Environment

The test environment (shown in Fig. 6.6) is implemented in Mininet [21], a network emulator for creating virtual clients, switches, controllers, and links. All clients, including the Trusted Agent, are virtual machines with Ubuntu 14.04 operating systems. The switch is OpenFlow 1.3 [2] capable, and Ryuretic [4] applications run atop a Ryu controller to provide network control. The testbed also provides Internet access via a virtual network address translator (NAT) or gateway router (GW). Until a client is flagged, it can ping other clients and access web services via the GW. Web services are tested using curl and *wget* commands and the Firefox Internet browser. However, the flows of a flagged client are redirected to the Trusted Agent's web server until the client provides the appropriate *passkey*. Once that is provided, the client regains network privileges within 30 s of making the entry.

6.6 Example Use Cases

In this security policy transition framework, the Ryuretic controller enforces the policies defined by the network operator. In this section, we attempt to highlight just a couple of policy violations (i.e., ARP spoofing and unauthorized NAT) that a network operator might target. We implement these attacks in the test environment discussed in Sect. 6.5. In this environment, we assume a client is behaving maliciously, so we will discuss some of the key code listings contributing to the framework's detection and notification methods. This section will also allow us to explore Ryuretic's packet crafting feature.

6.6.1 Spoofed ARP Packets

Spoofed ARP packets can poison neighboring client ARP tables and serve as a springboard for more dangerous attacks (e.g., packet dropping (black hole) and man-in-the-middle (MitM) attacks). However, this framework allows the network operator to set an ARP spoofing detection protocol in Ryuretic [4] to trigger appropriate security measures. When Ryuretic detects an arriving ARP packet, it is forwarded to the appropriate handler (see Listing 6.1). The Policy Enforcer checks the Policy Table to determine if the incoming packet should be dropped, redirected, or forwarded.

Listing 6.1 Ryuretic ARP Event Handler

```
1  def handle_arp(self,pkt):
2    #Check Policy Table for MAC and input port
3    pkt_status = self.check_net_tbl(pkt['srcmac'],
4                                    pkt['inport'])
5    if pkt_status is 'flagged':
6      #If flagged, redirect flow
7      fields,ops = self.Redirect_Flow(pkt)
8    else:
9      #If not flagged, test for spoof
10     spoofed = self.detectSpoof(pkt)
11     if spoofed != None:
12       #Notify Trusted Agent of Policy Transition
13       self.notify_TA(pkt)
```

```
14              fields, ops = self.drop_ARP(pkt)
15          else:
16              # Handle ARP packet
17              fields, ops = self.respond_to_arp(pkt)
18          self.install_field_ops(pkt,fields,ops)
```

If the source MAC or input port is not flagged, then the packet is evaluated by the detectSpoof() method (see Listing 6.2). If the packet is flagged as spoofed, then the Policy Enforcer notifies the Event Handler, which forwards a notification message to the Trusted Agent with the client's MAC, *passkey*, violation, and *keyID*. It then sets Ryuretic's *fields* and *ops* objects to drop future ARP replies from the client. In turn, the Trusted Agent adds the flagged client to its Client Table.

Otherwise, the packet is forwarded to the *respond_to_arp()* method for normal forwarding. As seen in Listing 6.2, the *detectSpoof()* method builds a network view to associate each client's MAC and IP address to a switch port. If a packet arrives after the network view is built with an incorrect MAC or IP address, then it is flagged as spoofed, and its future traffic is sent to the Trusted Agent, which renders a web page to explain the violation and offer instructions for regaining access to the network (e.g., submit an acceptable use policy, AUP). Currently, the security policy transition framework discussed in this chapter relies on the help desk to serve as the validating authority; however, a future implementation could make the AUP available and provide compliance validation. Once the client obtains and submits the *passkey*, their network services are reinstated – generally within 30 s of entering the *passkey*. The complete implementation is available at [22].

Listing 6.2 Ryuretic ARP poison detection method

```
1   def detectSpoof(self,pkt):
2     policyFlag = None
3     # Has port been mapped?
4     if self.netView.has_key(pkt['inport']):
5       # Does srcmac match recorded value?
6       if pkt['srcmac'] != self.netView[pkt['inport']]['srcmac']:
7         policyFlag = 'ARP'
8         # Does srcip match recorded value?
9       if pkt['srcip'] != self.netView[pkt['inport']]['srcip']:
10        policyFlag = 'ARP'
11    else:
12      # Map the port
13      self.netView[pkt['inport']] = {'srcmac': pkt['srcmac'],
14                                     'srcip': pkt['srcip']}
15    # Set policy enforcement
16    if policyFlag == 'ARP':
17      self.net_MacTbl[pkt['srcmac']] = {'stat':'flagged',
18                                        'port':pkt['inport']}
19      self.net_PortTbl[pkt['inport']] = {'stat': 'flagged'}
20    return policyFlag
```

6.6.2   Network Address Translation (NAT)

Unauthorized network address translation (NAT) devices can also compromise local networks by giving unauthorized users access to network services. One way to detect these devices is to monitor IP packet headers for a decremented time-to-live (TTL) [23]. In this example, host 2 (h2) from Fig. 6.6 attempts to run NAT services. To detect this policy violation, the Policy Enforcer utilizes a *nat_detect* module, as defined in Listing 6.3, to inspect the TTL field of each IP packet passing through the switch (s0). Consequently, inspecting every packet can impact the controller's performance. A better solution would limit packet inspections to just a few packets per flow before installing rules for future flows. Instead, this listing shows a simple example that is implemented with just few lines of code.

We first observe that most network devices have TTL values of 64 or 128. If hosts are directly connected to the switch, then it should detect one of these values. However, if these devices are connected behind a rogue NAT device with TTL decrement enabled, then the NAT will be detected, and the value returned will signal the Ryuretic controller to flag the client for a rogue "NAT" violation. The controller then updates its Policy Table and notifies the Trusted Agent before updating the switch's flow table.

Listing 6.3 Ryuretic NAT detection method creation

```
1   def TTL_Check(self, pkt):
2     policyFlag = None
3     if pkt['ttl'] not in [64, 128]:
4       policyFlag = 'NAT'
5     return policyFlag
```

6.6.3   ICMP Packet Notifications

Packet creation is a feature developed for Ryuretic allowing programmers to craft packets via its *fields* and *ops* objects. Listing 6.4 demonstrates how messages are crafted using Ryuretic within the security policy transition framework. The controller generates a packet containing the *srcmac*, *passkey*, *violation*, and *keyID* (see lines 15–16). Additionally, while not shown, the MAC and IP addresses of the controller and Trusted Agent are defined elsewhere in the code. Other ICMP message examples can be found in the Ryuretic interface file located at [22] and [24].

Listing 6.4 Ryuretic packet crafting

```
1   def update_TA(self,pkt, keyID):
2     table = self.policyTbl[keyID]
3     agent, cntrl = self.t_agent, self.cntrl
4     fields, ops = {},{}
5     fields['keys'] = ['inport', 'srcip']
6     fields.update({'dstip':agent['ip'],
7                    'srcip':cntrl['ip']})
8     fields.update({'dstmac':agent['mac'],
```

```
 9                          'srcmac':cntrl['mac']})
10      fields.update({'dp':agent['dp'], 'msg':agent['msg'],
11                          'inport':agent['port'],
12                          'ofproto':agent['ofproto'],
13                          'ptype':'icmp','ethtype':0x800,
14                          'proto':1, 'id':0})
15      fields['com'] = table['srcmac']+','+str(table['passkey'])+
16                          ','+table['violation']+','+str(keyID)
17       ops = {'hard_t':None, 'idle_t':None, 'priority':0, \
18                  'op':'craft', 'newport':agent['port']}
19       self.install_field_ops(pkt, fields, ops)
```

6.6.4 Traffic Redirect

Once a client is flagged, the Ryuretic controller must next divert the client's traffic
to the Trusted Agent. An example using Ryuretic [4] is provided in Listing 6.5,
and additional code examples can be found at [22] and [24]. In this snippet, an IP
table is tied to the Ryuretic controller's Policy Table. Notice that line 2 first sets
the *fields* and *ops* objects to set match-action rules for the traffic flow. This snippet
also shows how additional fields can be updated in lines 4–28. Here we see that if
a client is flagged for "deny," then the traffic flow's destination information is saved
to a TCP table. Its packet header data is then modified, and the packet is forwarded
to the Trusted Agent. These actions occur in lines 4–17. Otherwise, if the packet
originates from the Trusted Agent, the Ryuretic controller performs a reverse table
lookup to associate the client with its packet, modifies the packet's source fields
to reflect its original destination, and forwards the packet to the flagged client, as
shown in lines 18–28 of Listing 6.5.

Listing 6.5 Ryuretic traffic redirect
```
 1   def redirect_TCP(self,pkt):
 2     fields,ops = self.default_Field_Ops(pkt)
 3     #IP address (src & dst) maintained in IP forwarding table
 4     if self.ipTbl.has_key(pkt['srcip']):
 5       if self.ipTbl[pkt['srcip']] in ['deny']:
 6         key = (pkt['srcip'],pkt['srcport'])
 7         # Copy srcmac and dstmac to modify packet header
 8         self.tcp_tbl[key] = {'dstip':pkt['dstip'],
 9                               'dstmac':pkt['dstmac'],
10                               'dstport':pkt['dstport']}
11         fields.update({'srcmac':pkt['srcmac'],
12                         'srcip':pkt['srcip']})
13         fields.update({'dstmac':self.t_agent['mac'],
14                         'dstip':self.t_agent['ip']})
15         # Modify and redirect packet to TA or flagged client
16         ops = {'hard_t':None, 'idle_t':None, 'priority':100,\
17                 'op':'mod', 'newport':self.t_agent['port']}
18     elif self.ipTbl.has_key(pkt['dstip']):
19       if self.ipTbl[pkt['dstip']] in ['deny']:
```

```
20          key = (pkt['dstip'],pkt['dstport'])
21          # Copy srcmac and dstmac to modify packet header
22          fields.update({'srcmac':self.tcp_tbl[key]['dstmac'],
23                          'srcip':self.tcp_tbl[key]['dstip']})
24          fields.update({'dstmac':pkt['dstmac'],
25                          'dstip':pkt['dstip']})
26          # Modify and redirect packet to TA or flagged client
27          ops = {'hard_t':None, 'idle_t':None, 'priority':100,\
28                  'op':'mod', 'newport':None}
29      return fields, ops
```

6.7   Discussion and Future Opportunities

The security policy transition framework presented in this chapter presents many opportunities for future improvements. For instance, while this framework's limited communication channel is suitable for multiple controllers and allows for automated revocations using existing protocols, more robust communication channels are still needed. These channels could allow an east-westbound interface to better enable policy enforcement and validation across domains (which is still an open research topic) or provide for more versatile communication between the SDN controller and the Trusted Agent. As presented, the framework covered in this chapter relies on existing unmodified network protocols to implement a limited communication channel for the invocation and revocation of policy enforcements.

The transition framework discussed in this chapter is also easily adaptable to a password-based authentication framework for clients seeking to join the network. In which case, a network view can be built as clients authenticate to the network. Additionally, within the context of this framework, there is potential to provide a variety of actions for clients to take once they are redirected to the Trusted Agent. For instance, the captive portal can include patches, courses, administrative documents, initial warnings, etc. Additionally, the Trusted Agent's responsibilities could expand to include other security features. For instance, a modified Trusted Agent could provide active testing for security threats where passive monitoring is either not sufficient or too intensive for the controller to handle. With minor updates to this framework's communication channel, the SDN controller could notify the Trusted Agent of testing requirements for clients, and the Trusted Agent could instruct the SDN controller to transition the security state of a client under "test."

Using a Trusted Agent in this framework also reduces burden on network operators by reducing the manual configurations needed to remove policy enforcements, while also providing clients with immediate feedback on the status of their network privileges. With regard to network access control (NAC) systems, it is not too far a stretch to have the Trusted Agent interact with NAC authorization servers to implement comparable features as already exist today. However, this remains a focus for future work. Furthermore, since this framework's functions and components are implemented using NFV, it is also viable for cloud and virtual network environments, which serves as another future research direction.

Of course, while SDN is capable of implementing numerous security features, we still do not suggest that all security features should be handled by the SDN controller. In fact, the introduction of the Trusted Agent in this chapter further provides for the incorporation of additional security features where secondary devices serve to provide more layers to a defense-in-depth security strategy. Likewise, this framework does not replace the need for application-level monitoring. Such services are still needed to identify a client's software version, provide patch compliance, detect malware, or even apply an application-layer firewall. However, the Trusted Agent could be configured to coordinate security efforts between application-layer products and the controller.

Furthermore, as the Trusted Agent serves as a key intermediary between the client and the network operator, this framework could also benefit from the inclusion of machine learning algorithms that better cater to the client's needs while providing more automated services. Doing so could offer a more human experience along with a greater range of services for client validation. Additionally, the Trusted Agent's functions could be expanded to coordinate with existing middleboxes, manage IoT devices, and/or provide system redundancy. For example, should a primary server (e.g., DHCP, DNS, etc.) fail, the Trusted Agent could serve as a backup until the primary server is again operational. IoT device security along the network's edge is also an open research topic for which this framework might be expanded to include.

Network operators using this framework must also consider that more clients than just subscribers will operate on their networks (e.g., M2M communication or Web service interaction). If not handled appropriately, the redirection of flagged clients to a self-service interface, as proposed in this work, could cause IoT devices or user agents to assume the network has failed. Such incidents could result in the generation of erroneous trouble tickets that once again task network operators to troubleshoot connectivity issues instead of policy violations. Ideally, the network operator will *whitelist* or set aside specific ports for such devices to provide notifications if the device becomes flagged. For such cases, the Trusted Agent could also run a mail server to notify the help desk when a nonuser device is affected. Additional applications could further augment the Trusted Agent to better handle such devices as well. For instance, should IoT devices deviate from expected traffic patterns, then their subsequent flows can be forwarded to the Trusted Agent for deep packet inspection or other analysis, isolated from the network, or recorded for future analysis. SDN is uniquely situated to provide edge-based analysis of IoT device traffic, and future work will explore how a security policy transition framework as discussed in this chapter can be applied to IoT management and security.

Of course, introducing the Trusted Agent into this framework also introduces yet another attack vector. If the Trusted Agent can be compromised, then its communications to the controller for policy revocations can also be affected. However, in this system, we assume the Trusted Agent to be at least as physically secure as the SDN controller. Likewise, we utilize the controller to monitor network access to the Trusted Agent and block unauthorized traffic. As a result, only clients who have already been flagged are able to interact with the Trusted Agent via its web server, which limits packets to HTTP(S) (i.e., port 80 and 443) and DNS (i.e., port 53) protocols. Moreover, further hardening of the transition framework should add additional network security. For instance, randomizing keyIDs, encrypting the passkey while in transit, and further securing communications between the client and Trusted Agent are all prudent measures. Another consideration is validation of this framework with standards specified by the Trusted Computing Group (TCG) [25] for Trusted Network Communications (TNC) and Security Content Automation Protocol (SCAP). However, additional security analysis, hardening, and standards compliance of this security policy transition framework, including its Trusted Agent, are left to future work.

6.8   Conclusion

With OpenFlow providing a vendor-agnostic platform for SDNs and enabling the orchestration of numerous switches, programmers are better able to implement novel network applications for security and traffic engineering. Yet, network operators still need additional measures for automating daily processes and configurations to fully utilize SDNs in physical and virtual environments. As a result, this chapter introduces the concept of a security policy transition framework, which provides automation by flagging clients, redirecting their network flows to a Trusted Agent, and revoking activated security measures once the client validates they have met specific requirements by entering a *passkey*.

In this framework, a *passkey* is obtained from a validating authority (e.g., a help desk or the Trusted Agent) and used by the client to prove that specified requirements have been met in order to rejoin the network. As a result of these features, frameworks such as the one discussed in this chapter can eliminate many daily network configuration requirements that must currently be manually performed by network operators. Other benefits include reduction of both erroneous trouble tickets and client wait times for regaining network access. However, these wait times may still vary based on the violation and system validation procedures.

Finally, this chapter introduces several potential directions that this framework may take in future iterations. For instance, machine learning could be leveraged to enhance user experience when interacting with the Trusted Agent. Additionally, the Trusted Agent may be further developed to implement active detection measures for security applications. Other future work includes security analysis and hardening of the framework itself, improving upon it communication channel with an east-westbound interface, and implementing security and management applications for IoT.

Questions

1. Overall, how will this framework or one like it aid network operators?
2. Regarding security, what additional challenges does introducing a Trusted Agent to an SDN create?

3. What features should be added to the Trusted Agent and the communication channel used in this work to support functions that go beyond policy enforcement revocation, for instance, active testing of clients?
4. Considering the ICMP-based communication channel utilized in this work, what are its primary limitations, and how might they be improved?
5. Does the communication channel used in this work represent an in-band or out-of-band form of communication? Explain your answer.
6. Is the communication channel developed in this work only applicable to the Ryuretic programming framework, or could it also be used with other controllers (e.g., POX, OpenDaylight, Floodlight, etc.)?
7. What ways might a client obtain a passkey to regain their network privileges?
8. How might network operators modify the security policy transition framework presented in this chapter to accommodate Internet of things (IoT) devices and other clients having neither access to a web browser nor an ability to respond to the Trusted Agent's web server?
9. Concerning Ryuretic, what SDN controller does it augment, and what are the objects it uses for monitoring, matching, and rule setting on packets?

References

1. McKeown N (2009) Software-defined networking. INFOCOM Keynote Talk 17(2):30–32
2. McKeown N, Anderson T, Balakrishnan H, Parulkar G, Peterson L, Rexford J, Turner J (2008) OpenFlow: enabling innovation in campus networks. ACM SIGCOMM Comput Commun Rev 38(2):69–74
3. Reich J, Monsanto C, Foster N, Rexford J, Walker D (2013) Modular SDN programming with pyretic. Technical report of USENIX
4. Cox JH Jr, Donovan S, Clark R, Owen H (2016) Ryuretic: a modular framework for RYU. In: IEEE MILCOM2016
5. Kim H, Benson T, Akella A, Feamster N (2011) The evolution of network configuration: a tale of two campuses. In: Proceedings of the 2011 ACM SIGCOMM conference on Internet measurement conference, Nov 2011. ACM, pp 499–514
6. Kim H, Reich J, Gupta A, Shahbaz M, Feamster N, Clark R (2015) Kinetic: verifiable dynamic network control. In: 12th USENIX symposium on networked systems design and implementation (NSDI 15), pp 59–72
7. Tsagkaris et al (2015) Customizable autonomic network management: integrating autonomic network management and software-defined networking. IEEE Veh Technol Mag 10(1):61–68
8. Cox JH Jr, Clark RJ, Owen HL (2016) Security transition framework for software defined networks. In: Proceedings of the 2016 IEEE the first international workshop on security in NFV-SDN (SNS2016), Nov 2016. IEEE
9. Cisco, Network management system: best practices white paper. http://www.cisco.com/c/en/us/support/docs/availability/high-availability/15114-NMS-bestpractice.html
10. Congdon P, Aboba B, Smith A, Zorn G, Roese J (2003) IEEE 802.1 X remote authentication dial in user service (RADIUS) usage guidelines (No. RFC 3580)
11. ForeScout. https://www.forescout.com/solutions/use-cases/network-access-control/
12. Cisco NAC. http://www.cisco.com/c/en/us/products/collateral/security/nac-appliance-clean-access/product_data_sheet0900aecd802da1b5.html
13. Wilkins S (2015) A guide to network access control (NAC) solutions, May 2015. http://www.tomsitpro.com/articles/network-access-control-solutions,2-916-2.html

14. Skip Al, A bridge too far: defeating wired 802.1X with a transparent bridge using Linux. https://www.defcon.org/images/defcon-19/dc-19-presentations/Duckwall/DEFCON-19-Duckwall-Bridge-Too-Far.pdf
15. Bari MF, Chowdhury SR, Ahmed R, Boutaba R (2013) PolicyCop: an autonomic QoS policy enforcement framework for software defined networks. In: 2013 IEEE SDN for future networks and services (SDN4FNS), Nov 2013. IEEE, pp 1–7
16. Casado M, Freedman MJ, Pettit J, Luo J, McKeown N, Shenker S (2007) Ethane: taking control of the enterprise. In: ACM SIGCOMM computer communication review, vol 37, no 4, Aug 2017. ACM, pp 1–12
17. Matias J, Garay J, Mendiola A, Toledo N, Jacob E (2014) FlowNAC: flow-based network access control. In: 2014 third European workshop on software defined networks, Sep 2014. IEEE, pp 79–84
18. POX. http://www.noxrepo.org/pox/about-pox/
19. Ryu. http://osrg.github.io/ryu/
20. Lighttpd. https://www.lighttpd.net/
21. Lantz B, Heller B, McKeown N (2010) A network in a laptop: rapid prototyping for software-defined networks. In: Proceedings of the 9th ACM SIGCOMM workshop on hot topics in networks, Oct 2010. ACM, p 19
22. Cox JH Jr, Ryuretic security policy transition project. https://github.com/Ryuretic/SecRev
23. Phaal P (2003) Detecting NAT devices using sFlow. http://www.sflow.org/detectNAT
24. Cox JH Jr, Ryuretic rogue access point detection. https://github.com/Ryuretic/RAP
25. Trusted Computing Group. https://trustedcomputinggroup.org/work-groups/trusted-network-communications/

Jacob H. Cox Jr. received his B.S. in EE from Clemson University, SC in 2002, and his M.S. in ECE from Duke University, NC, in 2010. He has also recently completed his Ph.D. in ECE under the supervision of Dr. Henry Owen and Dr. Russell Clark at Georgia Institute of Technology, GA. As an Army officer, Jacob served as an Army telecommunications engineer (2008–2014) with his most recent assignments being assistant professor at the United States Military Academy (2010–2013) and chief of Enterprise Operations for the South West Asia Cyber Center in Kuwait (2013–2014). His research interests include software-defined networking and network security.

Russell J. Clark received his B.S. in Mathematics and Computer Science from Vanderbilt University in 1987. He received his M.S. and Ph.D. degrees in Information and Computer Science from Georgia Institute of Technology in 1992 and 1995. For the years 1997–2000, he was a senior scientist with Empire Technologies, a network management software company. He is currently a senior research scientist at Georgia Tech's School of Computer Science where he engages hundreds of students each semester in mobile development, networking, and the Internet of things. Russell is also the founder and co-director of the Georgia Tech Research Network Operations Center (GT-RNOC) and research director for SoX/Southern Crossroads.

Henry L. Owen III received his BSEE, MSEE, and Ph.D. in Electrical Engineering from the Georgia Institute of Technology in 1980, 1983, and 1989 respectively. He joined the research faculty of the Georgia Tech Research Institute in 1980 and the Georgia Institute of Technology academic faculty in 1989. He is a member of the Computer Engineering and the Telecommunications technical interest groups at the Georgia Institute of Technology. His research interests include software-defined internetworking and security.

SDNFV-Based DDoS Detection and Remediation in Multi-tenant, Virtualised Infrastructures

7

Abeer Ali, Richard Cziva, Simon Jouët, and Dimitrios P. Pezaros

7.1 Overview

In this section we provide a definition and classification of DDoS attacks and give a few examples to them. Also, we discuss why do DDoS attacks pose a serious risk for the cloud and how can clouds be exploited to run attacks.

7.1.1 DDoS Definition, Types and Examples

Denial of service (DoS) attacks are one of the major threats networks are facing today. They mainly aim at disturbing the normal behaviour of a system by over-consuming compute or network resources at the victim site, making it inaccessible or slow to legitimate users and in some severe cases causing entire system failures. This is usually done by sending large volumes of traffic that leave the victim site in an unstable state, causing the system to deny some or all the services to legitimate users. Distributed denial of service (DDoS) attacks are DoS attacks with multiple synchronised attack sources that add more bandwidth and consequently amplify the damage [19]. To launch a powerful DDoS, attackers usually take control of a large number of machines (zombies or bots) by infecting them with malware which allows them to control the machine by sending instructions through a handler programme, Internet Relay Chat (IRC) or more recently HTTP requests [24, 60]. Bots make it harder to detect attacks due to their distributed nature and can cause rapid destruction even to the most well-provisioned systems due to large volume of generated traffic that reach over 600 Gbps in some cases [2]. Today, almost all

A. Ali (✉) • R. Cziva • S. Jouët • D.P. Pezaros
School of Computing Science, University of Glasgow, G12 8QQ, Glasgow, Scotland, UK
e-mail: a.ali.4@research.gla.ac.uk; r.cziva.1@research.gla.ac.uk; simon.jouet@glasgow.ac.uk;
dimitrios.pezaros@glasgow.ac.uk

© Springer International Publishing AG 2017
S.Y. Zhu et al. (eds.), *Guide to Security in SDN and NFV*, Computer
Communications and Networks, DOI 10.1007/978-3-319-64653-4_7

attacks are distributed in nature which makes DDoS a major threat to any computer system connected to a network. DDoS attacks can be classified in a number of ways according to attack layer, launching method and vulnerability exploited. In [47], Specht et.al. suggest a classification of DDoS attacks according to the impact as follows:

1. Bandwidth depletion attacks: the victim's network is flooded with traffic preventing legitimate users from reaching the victim, e.g. flooding attacks (UDP and ICMP) and amplification attacks (Smurf and Fraggle).
2. Resource depletion attacks: attack traffic consumes the victim resources preventing it from processing legitimate user requests, such as protocol exploitation attacks (e.g. TCP SYN) and malformed packet attacks (e.g. Land attack).
3. Application-level attacks: server resources, e.g. sockets, memory and CPU cycles, are exhausted or a vulnerability in the application layer protocol is exploited, e.g. HTTP fragmentation and HTTP GET attacks [24, 39].

7.1.2 DDoS Posing a Serious Threat for the Cloud

Virtualised environments such as cloud data centres are distributed systems that provide compute, network and storage resources as-a-service, on an on-demand basis. Recently, cloud services are increasingly becoming targets of attacks since many corporate and global ICT systems are moving their daily operations to the cloud (e.g. banking transactions, government services, online shopping, entertainment, etc.) in an effort to reduce their capital and operational expenditure [56]. While services are offered in a scalable, elastic and always-on manner, they are extremely prone to security vulnerabilities which cause downtime, economic loss and reputation damage to the infrastructure, service and application providers. Recently, cloud services have become a target of DDoS attacks with many incidents confirming the prediction in Alcatel security report [38] that DDoS attacks would shift to cloud-based servers. The attack on Microsoft and Sony gaming cloud-based servers by Lizard Squad on Christmas 2014 was the first of a series of many incidents. Linode, a cloud-hosting provider, was targeted by several DDoS attacks over a 10-day period across its worldwide data centres in late 2015 [55]. An attack on Dyn, a cloud-based Internet infrastructure company in October 2016, affected Internet users all over the East Coast of the United States [25]. Below, we discuss the inherent characteristics of the emerging, virtualised cloud environment and other factors that make it particularly vulnerable to DDoS [51].

Cloud Services: The way some of the cloud services are offered introduces new types of attacks that target cloud users. For example, on-demand resource provisioning introduces a new attack which is known in the literature as economic denial of service or sustainability (EDoS) [45, 51] or fraudulent resource consumption (FRC) [26]. It is a DDoS attack carried out over a longer duration of time which rather than causing the server to reach a denial of service state, it fraudulently increases the victim's resource usage over time. As a result of the increased resource utilisation, the victim's resources will automatically scale up in an attempt to maintain the target service level agreement (SLA) and therefore increase the cost of the hosting service. Thus, attackers exploit the "Pay-as-you-Go" pricing model which manages resource usage (e.g. server hours, bandwidth, storage, etc.) to hinder the victim's financial ability to host its services in the cloud [30]. In addition, such attacks can also affect cloud providers in the long term by driving customers away from cloud-based services [3].

Isolation: The lack of isolation and physical separation in a virtualised, multi-tenant infrastructure allows DDoS attacks to affect other parties that are not the actual targets, e.g. co-located virtual services sharing the same physical servers or network substrate [45]. This effect includes performance degradation, indirect EDoS, downtime and wider business losses to services other than the victim itself. Moreover, it affects the cloud service providers through increasing overall energy consumption as a result of handling the attack's traffic and VM migration/instantiation caused by new traffic patterns. Research has shown that, upon a (D)DoS attack, the performance of a non-virtualised (web) infrastructure degrades by 8%, while the equivalent degradation in a virtualised environment can be up to 23% [41].

Availability of Large-scale, Aggregated Services: DDoS attacks highly affect the availability of services which is one of the main features of cloud services. DDoS floods the network with fake traffic that requires a certain amount of time to be processed by servers which decrease the availability of the cloud to process other legitimate requests. While this impacts the general availability of the cloud to their users and consequently the reputation of a cloud service provider (CSP), most cloud services are offered under SLA, and any violations will impose losses to the CSP. Furthermore, in some cases, it is also required for cloud services to meet certain availability requirements such as allowing maximum 5 min downtime per year due to national legislation which can impose even further financial losses to service providers [39].

Increasing Scale of DDoS Attacks: Recently, there has been a large increase in DDoS attacks in volume and rate. In November 2016, Akamai confirmed a 5-day attack on a website that peaked at 623 Gbps generated traffic, consisting of six DDoS attack vectors: GRE floods, SYN floods, NTP amplification, ACK floods at the network level and both PUSH and GET floods at the application layer. Apart from this concrete case, Akamai also reported 71% increase in total DDoS attacks compared to the same time in 2015 and 58% increase in attacks over 100 Gbps compared to the previous quarter of 2016. This can be attributed to two main factors:

1. Indirect attacks resulting in massive volumes of aggregate traffic only by generating small initial attack vectors which make it harder to detect [56]. For example, a DNS amplification attack exploits open DNS resolvers to issue requests with the victim's spoofed IP address. In the attack on Spamhaus in 2013, a 36-byte malicious request converted to a 3,000-byte response, and an aggregate 75 Gbps attack volume was launched with 30,000 unique DNS resolvers [54].

2. The outbreak of botnet services (DDoS-as-a-service or malware-as-a-service) that become more powerful and inexpensive as described below.

The rapid increase of volume and rate of attacks transforms the cloud from a promising solution to mitigate the effects of DDoS attacks due to the over-provisioning of resources to a potential target. With attack traffic reaching 1 Tbps, even global cloud service providers are being tested, while successful attacks can take down parts of the Internet as seen on the Dyn attack [25].

The Outbreak of Botnets: The recent outbreak of botnets provides attackers with a powerful launching platform for their attacks which can be attributed to (1) services like DDoS-as-a-service and malware-as-a-service that enable even inexperienced attackers to create a powerful attack vector with little expense [54, 56]; (2) cloud clones of VM instances that allow an attacker with usually hijacked cloud account to easily and rapidly create bots by duplicating instance that does not need much memory or disk space [56]; and (3) the wide penetration of insecure consumer devices (e.g. tablets, smartphones, laptops and IoT devices) with broadband connectivity capabilities [56]. For example, 150 K compromised IoT devices were recently used to launch a 623 Gbps attack on the *Kerbs on security* website [29] and Dyn. The attack on Dyn disrupted services such as Netflix, Twitter, Amazon, Spotify, Reddit, CNN, PayPal, Pinterest and Fox over the East Coast of United States. The attacks were the result of the source code of the Mirai malware released to public which took control of IoT devices with a weak/default password. This kind of malware demonstrates the ability to launch attacks with billions of the devices around the world. Reports that are yet to be confirmed claim that the Dyn [25] attack reached 1 Tbps in volume [25].

Attacks from Inside the Cloud: The cloud's on-demand resource provisioning model can itself be exploited for launching attacks with virtually unlimited resources using cloud VMs as bots. In 2014, Kaspersky Labs confirmed that attackers take advantage of a vulnerability in the distributed search engine software *Elasticsearch* to install DDoS malware on EC2 instances and possibly other cloud servers too. UDP-flood-based attack has been subsequently launched using the infected EC2 instances against multiple victims across a large regional US bank and a large electronics maker and service provider in Japan. The attack creates a substantial amount of traffic that Amazon had to notify their customers because of potential unusual charges resulting from the excessive resource usage [6].

7.2   DDoS Detection and Remediation

In this section we evaluate the challenges in legacy defence systems in clouds and introduce how SDN and NFV can be exploited to tackle these challenges.

7.2.1   Deployment Challenges of Legacy Defence Dystems in the Cloud

In enterprise systems, the main defence against DDoS is a combination of prevention, detection and mitigation techniques [46]. Prevention is usually done by filtering any suspicious traffic before it reaches the destination hosts. For instance, prevention can be done using Turing tests in form of CAPTCHAs or puzzles to identify legitimate users and block spoofed traffic [46]. Detecting attacks is accomplished by installing dedicated security components by system administrators, such as anti-malware, firewalls and intrusion detection or prevention systems (IDS/IPS) that usually perform deep packet inspection (DPI). These security components are commonly hardware-based middleboxes deployed in fixed locations across the network [5]. On the other hand, mitigation techniques are based on filtering attacker's traffic and do not guarantee full elimination of the attack [24]. As a common mitigation technique, malicious traffic identified by the detection process can be filtered in upstream routers to mitigate the attack; however, this process is prone to false positives and results in legitimate traffic filtered as malicious one. Alternative mitigation techniques aim at surviving attacks by scaling up resources until the attack is over. However, this can only be used on infrastructures where scaling is provided on-demand (e.g. in clouds).

Most of the above mentioned solutions are not effective against massive attacks that can scale up to overwhelm most traditional on-premises equipment and resources available at cloud providers. As a popular option, third-party mitigation services (e.g. Cloudflare, Akamai) can be used to mitigate such attacks, as they have massive amounts of network bandwidth and DDoS mitigation capacity at multiple locations around the world that can absorb and filter any type of network attacks. Using these services is effective since these providers are fine-tuned to cope with extremely high demand but are often expensive due to their infrastructural requirements. They can also raise privacy concerns since user traffic is redirected to third-party servers [46]. As the ineffectiveness of the legacy on-premise detection systems is caused by the inherited problems of hardware-based middleboxes, resolving some of these problems such as the inflexible deployment can increase the system's ability to handle large volume attacks without using expensive mitigation add-on services.

Management of network services (or "functions") should support basic operation such as insertion and deletion of services (and service chains) between any two endpoints. Traditionally, network services have been implemented as middleboxes deployed across different parts of the network to process the bulk of the ingress and egress traffic. However, this approach prevents middleboxes from being efficiently managed and updated, as any maintenance on the network function requires all the traffic to be redirected to an alternative path until maintenance is completed. This approach is even more problematic in legacy infrastructure where the management protocols are limited and most traffic redirections require physically changing cabling of the network devices. Also, while many companies (e.g. Cisco, Juniper,

Fortinet, Blue Coat, IBM, Radware and Intel security) offer line-speed appliances that provide firewall, IDS, IPS and DPI functionality, these appliances are allocated manually based on a static risk management process [40,43]. For example, a firewall function is used to deny or allow specific traffic based on IP addresses, protocols or ports; it is installed at the entry points of the system to examine all egress and ingress traffic [37]. In the case of IDS appliances, Cisco, for instance, recommends installing them in centralised positions around the protected network (e.g. between the network and the Internet to protect connection with a business partner or to protect a specific Internet connection to, e.g. a web server) [12]. Moreover, with the appearance of next-generation firewalls (NGFW), many security systems are integrated to a single appliance and therefore designed to detect and block attacks combining all security function classes (e.g. firewall, IDS or DPI) [59]. However, the effectiveness of these approaches can be greatly limited, for example, by the capabilities of the hardware or the fixed allocation of the security functions that reduce the system's ability to respond to attacks such as DDoS. We detail these challenges below.

Lack of Deployment Flexibility: The functionality of a defence system is measured by the accuracy of detection and the performance stability over time. An efficient defence system must adapt to traffic changes (e.g. volume or distribution), infrastructure changes (e.g. failures, reconfiguration) and policy changes without degradation. These changes can occur under normal conditions or as a result of an attack. For a virtualised environment like the cloud, the rapid resource reallocation such as VM migration is a typical change that a security system must adapt to, and the adaptation must come into effect in short timescales [52]. The manual and ad hoc placement of physical security appliances results in reconfiguration and maintenance of the network becoming a challenging process and affects the ability of the system to react rapidly to changes or respond to attacks [28]. Furthermore, as system administrators deploy middleboxes in specific locations, steering traffic to non-shortest paths can seriously affect the performance of the system [61].

Cost and Inefficient Management of Resources: To mitigate the aforementioned problems of deployment inflexibility and performance and to increase system-wide fault tolerance, administrators tend to deploy more security middleboxes on network links which cause underutilised, expensive middleboxes to be deployed across the network. The survey by Sherry et al. [42] shows that for an enterprise network (between 10,000 and 100,000 hosts), the hardware cost of middleboxes alone can reach $1 m every 5 years. Besides, because they are not scaled up or down easily, the traditional approach is to provision for peak demand in order to handle traffic spikes [34]. Thus, most middlebox resources are idle most of the time, something that increases the capital expenditure for underutilised resources.

Vendor Lock-in: The variations across vendor-specific middleboxes result in complex, specialised functions and different configuration interfaces for each vendor and device. Thus, security administrators are required to have a per-vendor expertise for each type to effectively allocate and manage them, increasing expenses as a team of specialists is required to manage the appliances [20]. Besides, compatibility issues can arise every time a security system upgrade is required [42].

Limited Functionality: A security system must continuously adapt to respond to the latest threats [42]. This includes changing the implemented security functionality, e.g. updating the attacks' signature database and changing or extending the functionality of the security service itself. However, extending or updating a hardware-based appliance is usually very limited as there is tight coupling between hardware capabilities (e.g. memory, TCAM, ASIC or NPUs) and the software running on them [20]. Although reprogrammability for network equipment has been suggested by academic projects such as P4 [9], these projects have not reached widespread adoption among vendors.

Customised Services: As users run different applications in clouds, they require different levels of security per application. For example, a web server would only require protection against HTTP flooding attacks, while critical servers may require deep packet inspection and/or a combination of signature-based and anomaly-based intrusion detection. As hardware appliances are designed to process all traffic passing through with very limited capabilities to specify different operations on specific parts of the traffic, there is no opportunity to specify different services for different users [5].

7.2.2   Exploiting SDN and NFV to Address These Challenges

SDN and NFV are two complimentary technologies that can be exploited to address the challenges identified in Sect. 7.2.1. In the following section, we are identifying the capabilities of both technologies.

7.2.2.1 SDN for DDoS Defence

Software-defined networking (SDN) promotes the decoupling of data and control planes of the network. The control plane is centrally managed by a controller that orchestrates the entire infrastructure, while the data plane is responsible for forwarding packets based on the flow rules specified by the controller. This separation and abstraction allow for new network control services to be implemented without changes in the underlying infrastructure [57]. Moreover, SDN increases manageability, scalability and dynamism of the network, something that also enhances the capability of the system to handle security challenges [27,52,56]. We introduce some of these capabilities below and their relation to security challenges in the cloud.

Centralised Control: In SDN, forwarding elements are directly connected to and controlled by controller software (e.g. Ryu[1] or OpenDaylight[2]). This centralisation of the control plane enables a defence system to rapidly respond to network changes from a central controller through updating the forwarding rules of the entire network infrastructure.

Programmability: The ability to apply custom routing policies in SDN through programming the controller instead of by statically configuring each network element individually provides the ability to programmatically steer traffic through network services hosted at any physical location of the network. Additionally, it can improve the efficiency of a security system through the dynamic control of traffic to achieve load balancing between security functions.

Global View of the Network: In contrast to a traditional network, in an SDN environment, the controller is able to maintain a global view of the network status and operation. The controller can query all the flow entries across the network to identify individual traffic paths, request per-switch statistics of the ports as well as flow utilisation. Furthermore, the controller can build a full topological representation of the network allowing (re-)routing decisions to be made. Combining all the data available at the controller, it is possible to have a fine-grained view of the network-level utilisation as well as identifying the flows, ports and hosts responsible for the bulk of the traffic. Using this information can increase a security system's ability to monitor and analyse network behaviour and reconfigure the network in response to changes.

While there has been a considerable research on using SDN for security functions, most approaches only focus on network management. As an example, in [57], routing to security functions such as firewalls and IPSs is managed from a Floodlight SDN controller. The particular SDN application can update flow rules to forward traffic to the appropriate security function that is connected to a specific interface of the switch. In contrast to this approach, we advocate the use of SDN not only for flexible traffic steering but also as the underlying mechanism to dynamically distribute network functions where and when required across the network.

Another related example of utilising SDN for improving security is presented in [11]. In this work, the authors distribute security functions between switches and a SDN controller. Specifically, a local detection component is installed on each SDN switch, and a global detection component is installed on the controller to detect attacks that can only be seen on the global view. Implementing security functions on switches and/or controller introduces scalability issues where resources are limited to detect intrusions in the case of high-volume attacks or traffic changes. Therefore, security functions from switches and controller should be offloaded programs running on commodity servers (as network functions (NFs)). On the other hand, SDN introduces programmability and centralised control in other fields that require situation-aware management such as unmanned aerial vehicles (UAVs) [53].

---

[1]https://osrg.github.io/ryu/

[2]https://www.opendaylight.org

7.2.2.2 NFV for DDoS Defence

Network functions virtualisation (NFV) aims at replacing hardware-based equipment with software-based network functions (NFs). It enables implementing and running NFs on off-the-shelf servers by using commodity programming languages, frameworks and virtualisation techniques. NFV therefore offers faster deployment and provisioning of service functions, addresses the problem of compatibility of vendor-specific hardware and reduces the capital and operational expenditure associated with network services [35]. Implementing security functions, e.g. firewalls and IDSes, in software also has the potential to increase efficiency and flexibility of a defence system for cloud environments [10, 22, 34]. Some of these potentials are detailed below:

Software-Based Network Functions: NFV introduces the benefits of software-based solutions to security systems. NFV offers cost reduction, solving compatibility and updating issues. Software solutions are inexpensive compared to hardware appliances as they eliminate the cost of the periodical rebuild or upgrade of the security system and the cost of maintaining vendor-specific knowledge. Pure software solutions can also benefit vendors: they allow them to put more effort in reducing the complexity of managing and reconfiguring their products by providing easy-to-use programming interfaces. Furthermore, updating or upgrading software services is a matter of dynamically retrieving new source code of software components rather than extending or replacing hardware equipment.

Efficient Resource Provisioning: The rapid and easy deployment of NFs increases the system's flexibility to react to changes such as traffic dynamics, dynamic resource (e.g. VM) allocation or the adding of new security functions. Therefore, it increases the efficiency of the system to handle attacks and maintain a consistent security policy. NFs also offer dynamic up and down scaling on-demand, leveraging the system's ability to handle traffic changes and attacks and at the same time maintaining an efficient management of resources which is considered a more efficient approach to the fixed underutilised resources of hardware middleboxes.

Flexibility of Placement: NFs can be developed and run on commodity x86 servers. While NFs are usually encapsulated in VMs, we advocate the use of lightweight containers for NFs to lower the hardware requirements and increase the NF-to-host ratio [13–15]. By using containers, NFs can be started and teared down in a matter of seconds, compared to weeks (the time it takes to design, purchase and deploy a new middlebox in a traditional network).

Modularity and Chaining NFs: As NFs are implemented in software, they allow efficient modularisation of security services and small component reuse to build more complex and customised security systems. The modularisation encourages developers and vendors to focus on building more efficient but standalone modules instead of large monolithic applications. As a concrete example presenting modularity, one could build a high-performance IDP (intrusion detection and prevention) NF by using a high-performance packet processing library (e.g. Intel DPDK), a software switch (e.g. Open vSwitch [21]) and an open-source IDP software (e.g. Bro). Moreover, modularisation allows the chaining of NFs to apply complex security policies. As an example, a common service chain consists of packet classifiers and firewalls or IDPs functions that are only used for specific set of traffic (identified by the packet classifiers).

While there has been considerable amount of work in NFV, most of it has focused on particular aspects of an overarching architecture. Some projects, e.g. ClickOS, focus on high-performance data plane NFs using the Click modular router [34]. While such platforms offer small and high-performance network functions, they use a custom hypervisor and restrict users to a specific programming language. However, a cloud-specific, dynamic DDoS defence system should utilise generic, widely deployable, yet lightweight NFs. On the other hand, a plethora of research is targeted towards a sophisticated management and orchestration framework for NFV. As a prominent example, in [4], the Slick programming framework is proposed to manage fine-grained functions that can be shared and composed into more complex packet processing sequences. While Slick elements can be allocated at arbitrary locations and traffic can be steered through them, they do not provide a comprehensive defence system targeting DDoS attacks.

7.3   A SDNFV-Based Security Framework

In this section, we are describing the benefits of using NFV and SDN technologies in synergy for a novel security framework that addresses the challenges of legacy and monolithic security through providing elastic service provisioning, avoiding vendor lock-in and offering easily extensible functionality. A high-level architecture of such framework is presented in Fig. 7.1.

In Fig. 7.1, we are proposing a framework that is managed from a central SDNFV controller. This controller manages the virtualised network and computes resources available. As shown, our proposed security modules are encapsulated in lightweight container-based network functions (NFs) based on the Glasgow Network Functions (GNF) virtualisation framework [14]. Containers have been chosen for NFs as they provide fast lifecycle management (100 s of containers can be started in the matter of seconds), exhibit only a slight overhead over native software installations and have widespread availability (container NFs have been demonstrated to run from full x86 architectures down to low-cost, commodity home routers, cf. [16]). Moreover, containers can offer excellent chaining properties due to sharing the same kernel space, hence avoiding packet copying as in the case of traditional machine virtualisation where packets are copied multiple times while traversing a chain of NFs. Finally, our NFs are linked to the SDNFV controller via a notification channel, where NFs can notify the controller about events such as traffic changes, intrusion(s) detected, etc. Moreover, the controller is responsible for traffic steering between all NFs and the cloud VMs that the NFs are attached to (these cloud VMs are omitted

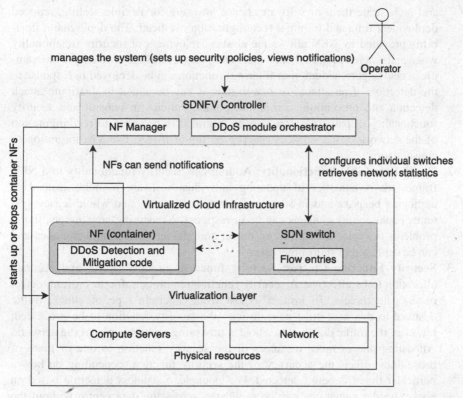

manages the system (sets up security policies, views notifications)
Operator

Fig. 7.1 SDNFV security framework architecture

from Fig. 7.1 for clarity). Traffic management is done by setting up OpenFlow flow entries on SDN switches and periodically retrieving flow and port statistics from all network devices. Apart from supervising the NFs and managing traffic routing, the SDNFV controller runs the concrete implementation of a specific security system itself which is a "DDoS module orchestrator" in our case. These modules can access the collected traffic statistics and the notification received from NFs. This information defines the behaviour of the security system. In our particular example (described in Sect. 7.4 below), once a DDoS attack is detected by a detector NFs, a notification can be raised to the DDoS module orchestrator to react by setting up mitigation and remediation NFs in the infrastructure. The main characteristics of this system are detailed below.

7.3.1   Framework Characteristics

1. **Elastic Security Provisioning**: The framework implements security functionality as a series of NFs with logically centralised management to allocate, deploy

and orchestrate them in software, hence allowing for flexible scaling, reduced deployment time and minimal reconfiguration overhead. The deployment flexibility provided by NFV allows the elastic deployment of security functionality when and where required, hence increasing resource usage efficiency. For example, a new (e.g. remediation or filtering) function can be deployed in response to the detection of an attack, or new instances can be added to distribute attack detection and prevention to multiple points. Policies in general and security functionality in particular can also be migrated in response to reconfiguration of the network or the services running on top of it (e.g. live VM migration or consolidation).

2. **Easily Extensible Functionality**: Adding new security functionality to a NFV framework is a matter of updating individual software modules instead of deploying bespoke and in some cases hardware-accelerated whole legacy systems. Functionality changes can be in response to emerging new threats, fixing problems or replacing with more recent and efficient detection techniques and can be deployed in short timescales.

3. **Security Function Classes**: Security functions require careful and accurate allocation to be effective. A security function monitors traffic to prevent, detect or mitigate threats. To protect a host from a certain type of attack, traffic destined to this host must pass through the security function to be processed; however, the traffic destined to a host is traversing multiple links of the network. Allocating one or more instances of the security function to one or more of those links affects the accuracy of the security function, depending on how a particular threat is being detected. For example, a stateless detection based on packet header signatures can be replicated across the data centre without the need for further coordination between duplicate modules so long as the entire traffic destined to a particular service is monitored. On the other hand, anomaly detection based on statistical properties of the aggregate traffic (e.g. exponential weighted moving average) needs coordination between multiple measurement vantage points in the network. Hence, to effectively allocate a security function, the specific functionality of each module must be considered. We have produced a set of equivalence classes of security functions based on the detection method of different attacks, as illustrated in Fig. 7.2:

   (a) **Stateless (Packet-based) Detection**: The first equivalence class of attack detection techniques consists of modules that process traffic at the individual flow or packet level. Detection decisions are made based on state of a single packet, while the flow specification upon which the detection algorithm performs can be parameterised based on the (number of) services a given module is trying to protect. Placement of security modules under this class is very simple, since intrusions matching a given signature can be detected independently at different links. Replicated instances of this class can be distributed across multiple network locations so long as they capture the entire traffic matching a given specification. This can be achieved by per-flow routing and by placing duplicate detection modules at diverse network locations where traffic matching a certain specification is being split, due to equal

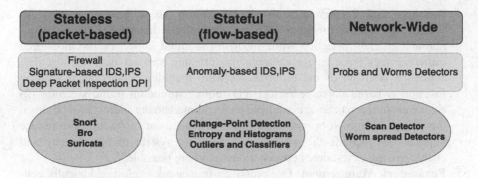

Fig. 7.2 Security function equivalence classes

cost multipath (ECMP) routing being employed by the underlying topology. Examples of this equivalence class include access control list (ACL)-based stateless firewalls that evaluate packet contents statically, stateful firewalls that keep track of the bidirectional state of network connections (e.g. TCP streams, UDP communication) [33] and signature-based IDS and deep packet inspections (DPI) [1] systems where header/payload data are processed against a database of known attack signatures (e.g. Snort [44], Bro [49], Suricata [50]).

(b) **Stateful (Flow-Based) Detection**: The second equivalence class consists of security modules that process packets or flow aggregates destined to the protected service to extract anomalies. They detect anomalies based on changes in traffic volume (e.g. change point detection [48]), deviations in a given traffic feature distribution (e.g. entropy, histograms) [7] or more complex machine learning techniques (e.g. outlier detectors [32], classifiers, neural networks and SVM [8]). They are based on extracting information that forms flow aggregation features that are used to construct a model for normal behaviour and compare this model to current behaviour to detect anomalies. Therefore, all the intended monitored flows must be steered to one instance of this type to be processed for accurate construction for the normal behaviour model. However, processing flows at different locations and sending the summarised (meta)data to one instance can be an alternative to steering the entire flows to one instance.

(c) **Network-Wide Detection**: The third equivalence class consists of modules detecting network-wide threats such as probes and worms. For example, network-wide attacks such as scans for vulnerable ports and worm spreading cause distribution changes in traffic features that can be observed at high aggregation level [31]. Therefore, this class monitors aggregate packets/flows between multiple destinations, and consequently they can be allocated to centralised/core locations where all aggregate traffic to multiple destinations can be processed.

4. **Resource and Performance-aware Allocation**: The allocation strategy for placing the security functions ensures capturing the indented traffic for accurate and efficient detection while incurring minimal impact on the monitored traffic/services through, for example, maintaining shortest path routing. The allocation decision of the different software modules comprising a security function is based on three factors: (1) require minimum traffic steering, (2) ensure enough resources are available to accommodate the additional module on the chosen host platform and (3) efficient management of resources to reduce duplications, increase the network-wide security system usable capacity and enable sharing of resource between modules where possible.

5. **Framework Management**: Our proposed framework exploits a logically centralised controller that maintains a network-wide view. The framework controller is responsible for monitoring and managing the different security components (e.g. diverse detection and prevention modules) and handles communication to and from the network infrastructure. It monitors the system components, their temporal resource utilisation and the network state (e.g. traffic distribution, network failures, VM migrations) and subsequently responds to reflect any operational changes. For example, typical response can include the dynamic scaling of a security function to accommodate intensified attacks or traffic changes and the automatic migration of security detection NFs alongside live migration or consolidation of client VMs. In addition, the controller manages the overall security service model. It keeps track of the active security functions deployed for each tenant and coordinates service requests with respect to the individual components involved. For example, a tenant request for new security functionality might include the allocation and deployment of the equivalent NFs, as well as the steering of traffic to diverse network elements.

6. **Modularisation**: We envisage security functionality being composed of a set of modular components that can be shared among services to save computational resources. For example, a basic function such as a traffic filter based on packet header fields can be shared among multiple modules, while common flow statistics, e.g. number of bytes/packets, average flow size, etc., can be shared among diverse anomaly detection modules. Common resources, e.g. attack signature databases, can also be shared between modules. Hence, the management system should also handle the joint placement of shared resources and modules to minimise state duplication. The modularisation and NFV implementation permit multiple heterogeneous security functions to be deployed in the same framework. Decoupling functionality from the platform encourages third-party vendors to compete building new and open security modules.

7.3.2   Framework Challenges

While we detailed many benefits coming from both SDN and NFV technological evolutions, a few challenges are also mentioned here that need to be taken into consideration when deploying a converged SDNFV security framework. First and foremost, as SDN requires continuous communication between all switches and a controller, a poorly performing controller can introduce delay in the network [52]. To mitigate this scenario, one could use physically distributed controller platforms, such as ONOS.[3] Also, as SDN switches and SDN controllers can also become the new targets of DDoS attacks, special care has to be taken to isolate them from untrusted networks (where user traffic is carried) [52].

While NFs also provide many benefits for security systems, it is worth mentioning the challenges they face. For instance, the performance properties of generic software NFs are inferior to their hardware counterparts, since general purpose hardware and software have originally not been designed for high-speed packet processing. In order to tackle the performance challenge without sacrificing deployability, many research projects are focusing on new, open-source packet processing techniques (e.g. the Intel Data Plane Development Kit).[4] Another challenging aspect is performance isolation between network services sharing the same physical host which is highly relevant to the lightweight container technologies we are proposing. However, through exploiting the right configuration options (e.g. using SELinux or AppArmor to implement kernel-based access control), even containers can be adequately isolated and run safely. Also, as using NFV also means redirecting traffic to hosts that are not always on the shortest path, the experienced end-to-end latency will undoubtedly grow. However, this penalty is only considerable for internal VM-to-VM communications, since for external traffic, it is expected to be only a fraction of the overall latency. To mitigate the latency penalty for communications inside the cloud, operators need to make sure that VNF servers are deployed as close as possible to the VM's hosting servers (e.g. at the ToR switches).

Furthermore, in large production networks designing an orchestration algorithm that considers network traffic, resources utilisation and the multiplexing of different services and physical machines is a complex optimisation problem that initiated many research projects. However, as an example, in [58] the authors provide a multi-objective resource scheduling algorithm for NFV infrastructures, while in [23] the authors address policy-based orchestration of NFV services in SDN networks in a practical example. In [17], authors exploit SDN to build communication-aware management system for VMs in cloud data centres.

7.4   A Proposed Approach for DDoS Detection and Remediation

In this section, we present and evaluate a concrete SDNFV DDoS mitigation system that we have built using open-source tools. We provide details on how the proposed system distributes detection and remediation modules across a fat-tree network topology.

---

[3]http://onosproject.org
[4]https://dpdk.org

7.4.1   Impact of DDoS

At the onset of a DDoS attack, the amount of traffic accumulating at the ingress of a cloud infrastructure can increase drastically at very short timescales. Even though most cloud infrastructures are provisioned for very high demand, if the attack is widely distributed and amplification is used, the network can quickly saturate [18]. Augmentation attacks have been used in the recent years since they provide an easy way to saturate remote networks without the need for an equivalently high-bandwidth infrastructure at the attackers' side(s). The most common amplification attacks have exploited the Domain Name System (DNS) and the Network Time Protocol (NTP) and rely on the fact that the reply is significantly larger than the request. Coupling this property with the fact that DNS and NTP operate over UDP, an attacker can send malicious requests to a DNS or NTP service with the source IP altered to point to the host that should be compromised. Through this approach, many small malicious requests can be issued from the attacker over low bandwidth connections, subsequently generating a very large volume of traffic at the ingress of the targeted network or host.

In this section, we show experimentally the impact of a DDoS attack over a cloud infrastructure and how the attack affects the targeted host as well as the rest of the target's network. This evaluation is performed over Mininet [36] HiFi 2.3 for a cloud data centre fat-tree (k = 4) topology, as shown in Fig. 7.3. OpenvSwitch 2.6 is used as the software switch, and OpenFlow 1.3 and the Ryu controller are used to insert the flow table entries and configure the buckets necessary for ECMP

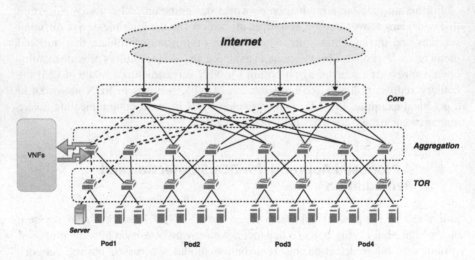

Fig. 7.3 Fat tree topology

Table 7.1 Network properties of a cloud infrastructure under a DDoS attack

Location	Average RTT (ms)	Packet loss %	RTT jitter	RTT Standard deviation (σ)
Normal operation	3.53 ms	0.0%	0.044	0.07
Attacked host	323.18 ms	79.8%	36.289	171.08
Edge	177.40 ms	50.2%	28.144	33.81
Pod	61.21 ms	0.0%	34.583	34.40

routing to distribute the flows across the multiple redundant paths.[5] We simulate an amplification attack by generating enough UDP traffic to saturate the ingress of the four core switches with the first host in the first pod (bottom-left) being the target of the attack. The attack is initiated by hosts connected to the core switches, to represent an ingress attack from the Internet. Using hping version 3 in flood mode on these attacking hosts, enough UDP traffic is generated to saturate the links in the topology. The network properties are measured using the TCP ping approach, with the initial SYN packet acting as the request and the response SYN/ACK or RST as the reply. This approach to measure the network characteristics is used instead of traditional ICMP packets as their static header prevents the hashing function within the switches to select multiple paths and therefore ignores all but one of the available ECMP paths.

In Table 7.1, we present the characteristics of the network in its normal operation mode and under attack, respectively. Under normal condition the latency of the network is around 3.5 ms, with a delay of 1ms between the core and aggregation switches, a delay of 0.5 ms between the aggregation and edge switches and a delay of 0.25 ms between the edge and the host, summing up to a round-trip latency of 3.5 ms. The table shows the impact in connectivity with the attacked host, hosts under the same edge switch in the topology and hosts within the same fat-tree pod. From this table, we can observe than under normal conditions, the cloud data centre provides the typical high performance, low latency expected of such an environment, with stable RTT over a long period of time. After a DDoS attack is started, the victim host suffers the most due to the fully utilised paths to this host at every layer of the topology. Under these conditions, the attacked host becomes practically unreachable with close to 80% packet loss making the retransmission feature of TCP ineffective. The 20% of the packets that are able to go through the topology suffer from very high latency and high jitter, with more than 320 ms to traverse the topology back and forth. Even if this poor performance of the attacked host is expected, it is evident that the attack also impacts the rest of the infrastructure significantly, with hosts under the same edge switch suffering 50% packet loss and very high latency making them very hard to reach, while hosts within the same pod also suffer an order of magnitude higher latency and significant jitter.

---

[5]Source code and instructions to replicate this experiment are available at https://github.com/UofG-netlab/sdnfv-ddos

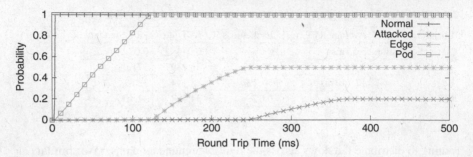

Fig. 7.4 Cumulative distribution function (CDF) of a cloud infrastructure RTT for the duration of a DDoS attack

Figure 7.4 shows the cumulative distribution function (CDF) of the RTT for the network under normal operating conditions and under the augmentation attack, respectively, as also previously shown in Table 7.1. In this CDF, all the points are included whether the measurement was successful or not, and packet loss is represented as an infinite RTT since the response is never received. As a consequence, the probability on the Y-axis also represents the packet loss too. We can see that, under normal operating conditions, the latency is very low and very stable with a 100% probability of getting a few milliseconds RTT. The host under attack, however, suffers the most with a best-case latency of 250 ms and a worst-case latency of 370 ms for only 20% of the packets (while the rest are being dropped). All hosts under the same edge switch suffer very similarly to the host under attack, with a wide range of latency from 120 to 250 ms and a 50% packet loss. Finally, all hosts under the same pod remain accessible but with a degraded performance and a latency varying over two orders of magnitude.

7.4.2 Distributed Detection and Remediation

Following the SDN+NFV framework proposed, we evaluate the impact and benefits of deploying security modules throughout the infrastructure at the onset of DDoS attacks. In the following experiments, we evaluate the benefits of deploying a DDoS remediation module of the stateless, packet-based class at multiple layers of the infrastructure. A security module can be deployed according to its ability to be distributed (e.g. stateless vs. stateful), on the amount of network traffic it needs to observe (i.e. how many services it tries to protect) and on the resource availability at each layer. The most straightforward approach is to deploy the module at the edge switch, the device closest to the host to be secured. This would be the equivalent of a bespoke, monolithic IDS deployed at the edge (or top-of-rack) to protect the target system (physical or collocated). In this particular case, module deployment is simple since the entirety of the traffic from and to the target host will flow through this switch, not requiring the processing logic to be distributed. However, this limits protection against the effects of the attack to the final hope of the path. Alternatively, duplicate modules can be installed at the aggregation switches, in which case the monitored traffic will include the attack vector as well as all other hosts within the same pod. Depending on the network coverage necessary for the module to operate properly, the module can be deployed on one or more aggregation switches. The amount of traffic analysed is dependent on the multipath routing and the number of modules deployed, requiring every aggregation switch within a pod to host the module in order to cover the entirety of the traffic. Finally, the modules can be hosted directly at the core layer of the network to filter traffic immediately at the ingress of the cloud infrastructure with the requirement to deploy one module per core switch to achieve full coverage of the attack vector to the single host.

In Fig. 7.5, we show the CDF of the RTT when the DDoS remediation modules are deployed at different layers of the infrastructure. In Fig. 7.5a, DDoS traffic is blocked at the edge switch, the last hop of the path. In this case, we can see that the traffic to the hosts within the same pod remains unchanged; however, the network characteristics of all the hosts under the same edge become similar, with a 100 ms reduction in latency and packet loss decreasing by 30% compared to the unprotected case shown in Fig. 7.4. Subsequently, in Fig. 7.5b, we deploy the remediation module at the aggregation layer, requiring two (duplicate) modules to be instantiated to cover the entirety of the traffic. By placing the modules higher in the infrastructure and distributing across multiple nodes to cover all the traffic, the performance of the network becomes uniform with all the hosts under the same pod performing equivalently, achieving a low packet loss and a high but usable latency. Lastly, the modules are deployed across all four of the core switches to block the traffic at the ingress of the network and, as presented in Fig. 7.5c, the network is restored very close to a normal state except a marginally higher jitter and standard deviation on the RTT and latency due to the high link utilisation at the ingress from DDoS traffic. In Table 7.2, we summarise the network properties shown in Fig. 7.5 with the modules deployed at the different layers of the infrastructure.

7.5   Summary

ICT services are shifting from legacy, vertically integrated infrastructures to cloud computing, seeking for low cost, more reliable and flexible service deployment. At the same time, attacks have also started to target cloud-based services or cloud infrastructure providers themselves. One of the most popular and major risks to clouds, DDoS, is growing in both volume and intensity from year to year. Moreover, with the proliferation of botnets, DDoS attacks can bring down large-scale public Internet services as, for example, this was recently experienced during the attack against the DNS services of Dyn in October 2016 that made millions of websites unavailable. Additionally, as cloud infrastructures are shared between services and tenants, it is extremely challenging to protect resources through physical isolation.

Traditional defence systems are generally tightly integrated to the infrastructure, using dedicated and optimised middleboxes in fixed locations of the physical infras-

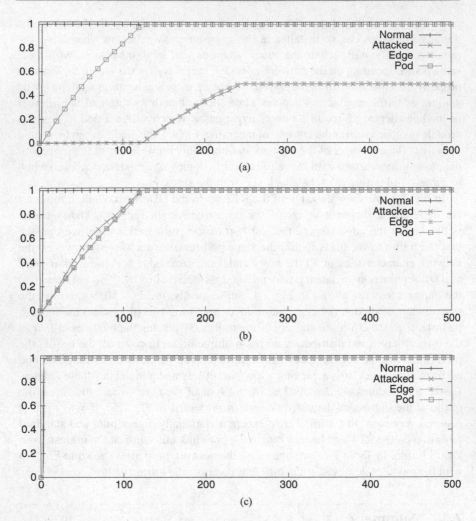

Fig. 7.5 CDF of RTT of cloud data centre under DDoS attack with remediation modules deployed at different layers of the infrastructure. (**a**) Edge switch (1 node). (**b**) Aggregation switches (2 nodes). (**c**) Core switches (4 nodes)

tructure. This inflexible deployment, combined with the high cost and expensive management of a bespoke infrastructure, makes legacy DDoS defence system unsuitable for dynamic cloud environments that incur frequent changes in traffic patterns, hosted services and service physical locations. Moreover, the limited extensibility, access and vendor lock-in of hardware-based systems hinder their ability to be flexibly updated in response to frequent operational changes in an evolving and dynamic environment.

To overcome these limitations, two recent technologies, software-defined networking (SDN) and network functions virtualisation (NFV), have been explored

Table 7.2 Network properties of a cloud infrastructure under a DDoS attack with remediation modules deployed at different layers of the infrastructure

Location	Average RTT (ms)	Packet loss %	RTT jitter	RTT standard deviation (σ)
Normal operation	3.53 ms	0.0%	0.044	0.07
Remediation at the edge (1 node)				
Attacked host	179.62 ms	50.65%	26.674	35.26
Edge	178.14 ms	50.36%	25.329	32.89
Pod	57.90 ms	0.0%	36.378	35.28
Remediation at the aggregation (2 nodes)				
Attacked host	54.88 ms	0.02%	34.689	34.25
Edge	59.91 ms	0.04%	37.220	35.64
Pod	59.38 ms	0.02%	35.731	34.58
Remediation at the core (4 nodes)				
Attacked host	3.53 ms	0.0%	0.302	0.53
Edge	3.50 ms	0.0%	0.280	0.48
Pod	3.49 ms	0.0%	0.255	0.42

as an alternative framework for offering network-wide security in virtualised ICT environments. The global view and centralised control inherent in SDN enable a security system to keep updated with network state and operation and rapidly change the data plane from the SDN controllers (e.g. through updating switches' forwarding rules) in case of infrastructure changes (e.g. when a VM migration is detected). At the same time, NFV enables software-based solutions to be introduced as network services (e.g. firewalls, packet classifiers, etc.) and allows their flexible deployment on commodity hardware. Moreover, NFV allows extending the functionality of the security infrastructure through simply updating software elements.

In this chapter, we have discussed the challenges of DDoS attacks on the infrastructure and introduced a novel DDoS defence framework to detect and remediate their effects using modular software components. The proposed SDNFV framework uses lightweight, centrally orchestrated container-based virtual network functions (NFs) to implement components of the DDoS defence system and dynamically distribute them across the infrastructure to minimise the adversarial impact of an attack. The allocation of NFs is based on temporal resource utilisation and the actual functionality of the deployed modules. For example, a packet header-based detection module can be duplicated statelessly, whereas statistical anomaly detection might require all affected traffic to be steered towards a single detection point in the network. However, this can be done seamlessly and dynamically through the exploitation of SDN flow rules and centralised NFV orchestration. We have evaluated the proposed system using an emulated DDoS augmentation attack that triggers the deployment of remediation modules at different layers of a simulated fat-tree cloud network topology. The experiments show the benefit of flexibly distributing the remediation modules across the different layers of the network and demonstrate the cost-benefit trade-off between performance and resource consumption.

Chapter Exercises

1. What are the three main classes of DDoS attacks and which vulnerability is exploited to deny access to the victim's services?
2. What is the reason behind the continuous increase of the volume and intensity of DDoS attacks and how do they relate to Cloud service providers?
3. What is the traditional approach used as a defence system to mitigate the impact of DDoS attack and why is this approach unattractive for Cloud operators?
4. What are the benefits of Software Defined Networking (SDN) and network functions virtualisation (NFV) that make them an attractive alternative for deploying DDoS detection and remediation systems?
5. How can SDN and NFV be leveraged in tandem to provide a Cloud security framework and what are the advantages over traditional legacy approaches?
6. What are amplifications attacks and why are they commonly used for large scale DDoS? Experiment with DNS amplification by analysing the difference in size between a DNS request and a DNS reply using, for example, the *dig* Linux utility: *dig ietf.org ANY*.
7. Using Mininet, the Ryu controller and the code provided in Sect. 7.4, create a multi-path fat-tree topology and observe the impact of DDoS as shown in the experiments.

Acknowledgements The work has been supported in part by the UK Engineering and Physical Sciences Research Council (EPSRC) projects EP/L026015/1, EP/N033957/1, EP/P004024/1 and EP/L005255/1 and by the European Cooperation in Science and Technology (COST) Action CA 15127: RECODIS – Resilient communication services protecting end-user applications from disaster-based failures.

References

1. AbuHmed T, Mohaisen A, Nyang D (2008) A survey on deep packet inspection for intrusion detection systems. arXiv preprint arXiv:0803.0037
2. Akamai, Akamai state of the internet security report (2016). https://content.akamai.com/pg7425-uk-soti-report.html. Accessed on 18 Nov 2016
3. Alosaimi W, Alshamrani M, Al-Begain K (2015) Simulation-based study of distributed denial of service attacks prevention in the cloud. In: 2015 9th international conference on next generation mobile applications, services and technologies. IEEE, pp 0–65
4. Anwer B, Benson T, Feamster N, Levin D (2015) Programming Slick network functions. In: Proceedings of the 1st ACM SIGCOMM symposium on software defined networking research. ACM, p 14
5. Basile C, Pitscheider C, Risso F, Valenza F, Vallini M (2015) Towards the dynamic provision of virtualized security services. In: Cyber security and privacy forum. Springer, Cham, pp 65–76
6. Baumgartner K, Elasticsearch Vuln abuse on Amazon cloud and more for DDoS and profit – Kasperskylab Blog. https://securelist.com/blog/virus-watch/65192/elasticsearch-vuln-abuse-on-amazon-cloud-and-more-for-ddos-and-profit/
7. Bereziński P, Jasiul B, Szpyrka M (2015) An entropy-based network anomaly detection method. Entropy 17(4):2367–2408
8. Bhuyan MH, Bhattacharyya DK, Kalita JK (2014) Network anomaly detection: methods, systems and tools. IEEE Commun Surv Tutorials 16(1):303–336

9. Bosshart P, Daly D, Gibb G, Izzard M, McKeown N, Rexford J, Schlesinger C, Talayco D, Vahdat A, Varghese G et al (2014) P4: programming protocol-independent packet processors. ACM SIGCOMM Comput Commun Rev 44(3):87–95
10. Bremler-Barr A, Harchol Y, Hay D (2016) Openbox: a software-defined framework for developing, deploying, and managing network functions. In: Proceedings of the 2016 conference on ACM SIGCOMM, SIGCOMM'16. ACM, New York, pp 511–524. doi:10.1145/2934872.2934875, http://doi.acm.org/10.1145/2934872.2934875
11. Cabaj K, Wytrebowicz J, Kuklinski S, Radziszewski P, Dinh KT (2014) SDN architecture impact on network security. In: FedCSIS position papers, pp 143–148
12. Cisco, Installing the IDS Appliance – Cisco. http://www.cisco.com/c/en/us/td/docs/security/ips/4-0/installation/guide/
13. Cziva R, Pezaros D (2017, in press) Container network functions: bringing NFV to the network edge. IEEE Commun Mag Adv Netw Softw. http://eprints.gla.ac.uk/138001/
14. Cziva R, Jouet S, White KJS, Pezaros DP (2015) Container-based network function virtualization for software-defined networks. In: 2015 IEEE symposium on computers and communication (ISCC), pp 415–420. doi:10.1109/ISCC.2015.7405550
15. Cziva R, Jouet S, Pezaros DP (2015) GNFC: towards network function cloudification. In: 2015 IEEE conference on network function virtualization and software defined network (NFV-SDN), pp 142–148. doi:10.1109/NFV-SDN.2015.7387419
16. Cziva R, Jouet S, Pezaros DP (2016) Roaming edge vNFs using glasgow network functions. In: Proceedings of the 2016 ACM SIGCOMM conference, SIGCOMM'16. ACM, New York, pp 601–602. doi:10.1145/2934872.2959067, http://doi.acm.org/10.1145/2934872.2959067
17. Cziva R, Jout S, Stapleton D, Tso FP, Pezaros DP (2016) SDN-based virtual machine management for cloud data centers. IEEE Trans Netw Serv Manag 13(2):212–225. doi:10.1109/TNSM.2016.2528220
18. Deep inside a DNS amplification DDoS attack. https://blog.cloudflare.com/deep-inside-a-dns-amplification-ddos-attack/
19. Douligeris C, Mitrokotsa A (2004) DDoS attacks and defense mechanisms: classification and state-of-the-art. Comput Netw 44(5):643–666
20. Enguehard M (2016) Thyper-NF: synthesizing chains of virtualized network functions. Master's thesis, School of Information and Communication Technology, KTH Royal Institute of Technology
21. Foundation L (2017) Linux foundation open vswitch. https://LinuxFoundationOpenvSwitch. Accessed on 28 Mar 2017
22. Gember A, Krishnamurthy A, John SS, Grandl R, Gao X, Anand A, Benson T, Akella A, Sekar V (2013) Stratos: a network-aware orchestration layer for middleboxes in the cloud. Technical report
23. Giotis K, Kryftis Y, Maglaris V (2015) Policy-based orchestration of NFV services in software-defined networks. In: 2015 1st IEEE conference on network softwarization (NetSoft). IEEE, pp 1–5
24. Gupta BB, Badve OP (2016) Taxonomy of DoS and DDoS attacks and desirable defense mechanism in a cloud computing environment. Neural Comput Appl 1–28. doi:10.1007/s00521-016-2317-5, http://dx.doi.org/10.1007/s00521-016-2317-5
25. Hilton S, Dyn Analysis Summary Of Friday October 21 Attack | Dyn Blog. http://dyn.com/blog/dyn-analysis-summary-of-friday-october-21-attack/
26. Idziorek J, Tannian M, Jacobson D (2011) Detecting fraudulent use of cloud resources. In: Proceedings of the 3rd ACM workshop on cloud computing security workshop. ACM, pp 61–72
27. Jammal M, Singh T, Shami A, Asal R, Li Y (2014) Software defined networking: state of the art and research challenges. Comput Netw 72:74–98
28. Joseph DA, Tavakoli A, Stoica I (2008) A policy-aware switching layer for data centers. In: Proceedings of the ACM SIGCOMM 2008 conference on data communication, SIGCOMM'08. ACM, New York, pp 51–62. doi:10.1145/1402958.1402966, http://doi.acm.org/10.1145/1402958.1402966

29. Krebs B, Krebs on Security website. http://krebsonsecurity.com/
30. Kumar MN, Sujatha P, Kalva V, Nagori R, Katukojwala AK, Kumar M (2012) Mitigating economic denial of sustainability (EDoS) in cloud computing using in-cloud scrubber service. In: 2012 fourth international conference on computational intelligence and communication networks (CICN). IEEE, pp 535–539
31. Lakhina A, Crovella M, Diot C (2005) Mining anomalies using traffic feature distributions. SIGCOMM Comput Commun Rev 35(4):217–228. doi:10.1145/1090191.1080118, http://doi. acm.org/10.1145/1090191.1080118
32. Lazarevic A, Ertöz L, Kumar V, Ozgur A, Srivastava J (2003) A comparative study of anomaly detection schemes in network intrusion detection. In: SDM. SIAM, pp 25–36
33. Liu AX (2005) A model of stateful firewalls and its properties. In: Proceedings of the 2005 international conference on dependable systems and networks, DSN'05. IEEE Computer Society, Washington, DC, pp 128–137. doi:10.1109/DSN.2005.9, http://dx.doi.org/10.1109/ DSN.2005.9
34. Martins J, Ahmed M, Raiciu C, Olteanu V, Honda M, Bifulco R, Huici, F (2014) Clickos and the art of network function virtualization. In: Proceedings of the 11th USENIX conference on networked systems design and implementation, NSDI'14. USENIX Association, Berkeley, pp 459–473. http://dl.acm.org/citation.cfm?id=2616448.2616491
35. Mijumbi R, Serrat J, Gorricho JL, Bouten N, De Turck F, Boutaba R (2015) Network function virtualization: state-of-the-art and research challenges. IEEE Commun Surv Tutorials 18(1):236–262
36. Mininet, Mininet (2017). http://mininet.org/. Accessed on 24 Mar 2017
37. Modi C, Patel D, Borisaniya B, Patel H, Patel A, Rajarajan M (2013) A survey of intrusion detection techniques in cloud. J Netw Comput Appl 36(1):42–57. doi:http://dx.doi.org/10.1016/j.jnca.2012.05.003, http://www.sciencedirect.com/science/ article/pii/S1084804512001178
38. Motive Security Labs (2014) Motive Malware Report 2014 H2. Technical report, Motive Security Labs. https://resources.alcatel-lucent.com/asset/184652
39. Osanaiye O, Choo KKR, Dlodlo M (2016) Distributed denial of service (DDoS) resilience in cloud: review and conceptual cloud ddos mitigation framework. J Netw Comput Appl 67:147–165
40. Qazi ZA, Tu CC, Chiang L, Miao R, Sekar V, Yu M (2013) Simple-fying middlebox policy enforcement using SDN. SIGCOMM Comput Commun Rev 43(4):27–38. doi:10.1145/2534169.2486022, http://doi.acm.org/10.1145/2534169.2486022
41. Shea R, Liu J (2013) Performance of virtual machines under networked denial of service attacks: experiments and analysis. IEEE Syst J 7(2):335–345. doi:10.1109/JSYST.2012.2221998
42. Sherry J, Hasan S, Scott C, Krishnamurthy A, Ratnasamy S, Sekar V (2012) Making middleboxes someone else's problem: network processing as a cloud service. In: Proceedings of the ACM SIGCOMM 2012 conference on applications, technologies, architectures, and protocols for computer communication, SIGCOMM'12, ACM, New York, pp 13–24. doi:10.1145/2342356.2342359, http://doi.acm.org/10.1145/2342356.2342359
43. Shin S, Wang H, Gu G (2015) A first step toward network security virtualization: from concept to prototype. IEEE Trans Inf Forensics Secur 10(10):2236–2249
44. Snort intrusion detection system. https://www.snort.org/
45. Somani G, Gaur MS, Sanghi D (2015) DDoS/EDoS attack in cloud: affecting everyone out there! In: Proceedings of the 8th international conference on security of information and networks, SIN'15. ACM, New York, pp 169–176. doi:10.1145/2799979.2800005, http://doi. acm.org/10.1145/2799979.2800005
46. Somani G, Gaur MS, Sanghi D, Conti M, Buyya R (2015) DDoS attacks in cloud computing: issues, taxonomy, and future directions. arXiv preprint arXiv:1512.08187
47. Specht SM, Lee RB (2004) Distributed denial of service: taxonomies of attacks, tools, and countermeasures. In: ISCA PDCS, pp 543–550

48. Tartakovsky AG, Rozovskii BL, Blazek RB, Kim H (2006) A novel approach to detection of intrusions in computer networks via adaptive sequential and batch-sequential change-point detection methods. IEEE Trans Signal Process 54(9):3372–3382
49. The Bro Network Security Monitor. https://www.bro.org/
50. The Suricata open source IDS, IPS, and NSM. https://suricata-ids.org/
51. VivinSandar S, Shenai S (2012) Economic denial of sustainability (EDoS) in cloud services using http and xml based DDoS attacks. Int J Comput Appl 41(20):11–16
52. Wang B, Zheng Y, Lou W, Hou YT (2015) {DDoS} attack protection in the era of cloud computing and software-defined networking. Comput Netw 81:308–319. http://dx.doi.org/10.1016/j.comnet.2015.02.026, http://www.sciencedirect.com/science/article/pii/S1389128615000742
53. White KJ, Pezaros D, Denney E, Knudson M, Marnerides AK (2017) A programmable SDN+NFV-based architecture for uav telemetry monitoring. http://eprints.gla.ac.uk/130944/
54. Wong F, Tan CX (2014) A survey of trends in massive DDoS attacks and cloud-based mitigations. Int J Netw Secur Appl 6(3):57
55. Yan Q, Yu FR (2015) Distributed denial of service attacks in software-defined networking with cloud computing. IEEE Commun Mag 53(4):52–59
56. Yan Q, Yu FR, Gong Q, Li J (2016) Software-defined networking (SDN) and distributed denial of service (DDoS) attacks in cloud computing environments: a survey, some research issues, and challenges. IEEE Commun Surv Tutorials 18(1):602–622. doi:10.1109/COMST.2015.2487361
57. Yoon C, Park T, Lee S, Kang H, Shin S, Zhang Z (2015) Enabling security functions with SDN: a feasibility study. Comput Netw 85:19–35. http://dx.doi.org/10.1016/j.comnet.2015.05.005, http://www.sciencedirect.com/science/article/pii/S1389128615001619
58. Yoshida M, Shen W, Kawabata T, Minato K, Imajuku W (2014) Morsa: a multi-objective resource scheduling algorithm for NFV infrastructure. In: 2014 16th Asia-Pacific network operations and management symposium (APNOMS). IEEE, pp 1–6
59. Zapechnikov S, Miloslavskaya N, Tolstoy A (2015) Modeling of next-generation firewalls as queueing services. In: Proceedings of the 8th international conference on security of information and networks, SIN'15. ACM, New York, pp 250–257. doi:10.1145/2799979.2799997, http://doi.acm.org/10.1145/2799979.2799997
60. Zargar ST, Joshi J, Tipper D (2013) A survey of defense mechanisms against distributed denial of service (DDoS) flooding attacks. IEEE Commun Surv Tutorials 15(4):2046–2069
61. Zhang Y, Beheshti N, Beliveau L, Lefebvre G, Manghirmalani R, Mishra, R, Patneyt R, Shirazipour M, Subrahmaniam R, Truchan C, Tatipamula M (2013) Steering: a software-defined networking for inline service chaining. In: 2013 21st IEEE international conference on network protocols (ICNP), pp 1–10. doi:10.1109/ICNP.2013.6733615

Abeer Ali received the MSc degree in computer engineering from Cairo University, Egypt, in 2012. She is currently a PhD candidate at the Networked Systems Research Laboratory in the School of Computing Science, University of Glasgow. Abeer's research focuses on the softwarisation and modularisation of security functionality using network functions virtualisation (NFV) and software-defined networking (SDN).

Richard Cziva received the BSc degree in computer engineering from the Budapest University of Technology and Economics, Hungary, in 2013. He is currently a PhD candidate at the Networked Systems Research Laboratory in the School of Computing Science, University of Glasgow, where he has previously worked as a research assistant. Richard's research focuses on software-defined networking (SDN) and on designing lightweight, container-based network functions virtualisation (NFV) frameworks for next-generation networks. Richard has also been involved in SDN and network measurement projects with a number of wide-area network providers (e.g. NORDUnet, GEANT and REANNZ).

Simon Jouët received the MEng degree in electronic and software engineering from the University of Glasgow in 2012. He is currently a research assistant in the School of Computing Science, University of Glasgow. His research focuses on the cross-layer benefits of centralised control in cloud data centres in order to optimise resource utilisation, network and compute performance and energy efficiency. His current research focuses on the centralisation of network state, topology, routing and forwarding through software-defined networking (SDN) and orchestration through network functions virtualisation (NFV).

Dimitrios P. Pezaros received the BSc (2000) and PhD (2005) degrees in computer science from the University of Lancaster, UK. He is currently senior lecturer (associate professor) and director of the Networked Systems Research Laboratory (netlab) in the School of Computing Science, University of Glasgow, which he joined in 2009. His research is focusing on the resilient and efficient operation of future virtualised networked infrastructures through the exploitation of converged network-server resource management mechanisms, software-defined networking (SDN) and network functions virtualisation (NFV). He has published widely and has received significant funding for his research in the above areas from the UK Engineering and Physical Sciences Research Council (EPSRC), the European Commission, the University of Glasgow, the London Mathematical Society (LMS) and the industry. Prior to joining Glasgow, he worked as a postdoctoral and senior research associate on a number of EPSRC- and EU-funded projects in the areas of performance measurement and evaluation, network management, cross-layer optimisation, QoS analysis and modelling and network resilience. Dr. Pezaros has been a doctoral fellow of Agilent Technologies (2000–2004). He is a chartered engineer, a fellow of the UK higher education academy, and a senior member of the IEEE and the ACM.

SHIELD: Securing Against Intruders and Other Threats Through an NFV-Enabled Environment

8

Hamza Attak, Marco Casassa-Mont, Cristian Dávila,
Eleni-Constantina Davri, Carolina Fernandez, Georgios Gardikis,
Bernat Gastón, Ludovic Jacquin, Antonio Lioy, Antonis Litke,
Nikolaos K. Papadakis, Dimitris Papadopoulos, Jerónimo Núñez,
and Eleni Trouva

8.1   Introduction and Motivation of the SHIELD Project

Cybercrime techniques continuously evolve to target carefully selected victims, subvert critical data in information technology and exploit devices with a new type of attacks. It is expected that the emergence of the IoT (including mobility and heterogeneity of devices), as well as big data environments, will be two of the main cybercrime targets in the years to come. An example of these new targets is that most of the devices involved on the massive and sustained Internet attack on October of 2016 were IoT devices [1]. Previously, a Norton report [2] estimated economic losses due to consumer cybercrime – and for Europe alone – at 13 billion dollars.

H. Attak (✉) • M. Casassa-Mont • L. Jacquin
Hewlett Packard Labs, Longdown Avenue BS34 8QZ Stoke Gifford, Bristol, UK
e-mail: hamza.attak@hpe.com

C. Dávila • C. Fernandez • B. Gastón
Fundació I2CAT, Barcelona, Spain

E.-C. Davri
Orion Innovations P.C., Athens, Greece

G. Gardikis
Space Hellas S.A., Athina, Greece

A. Lioy
Politecnico di Torino, Dip. Automatica e Informatica, Turin, Italy

A. Litke • N.K. Papadakis • D. Papadopoulos
Infili Technologies PC, Athens, Greece

J. Núñez
Telefonica I+D, Madrid, Spain

E. Trouva
Institute of Informatics and Telecommunications NCSR "Demokritos", Agia Paraskevi, Greece

© Springer International Publishing AG 2017
S.Y. Zhu et al. (eds.), *Guide to Security in SDN and NFV*, Computer
Communications and Networks, DOI 10.1007/978-3-319-64653-4_8

Moreover, Ponemon study also points out that the tendency of these economic losses is increasing [3]. The consequences of successful attacks are multifaceted: loss of sensitive data and intellectual property, brand image and company reputation damage, contractual penalties and compensations after service disruptions, costs (insurance, countermeasures, mitigation strategies and recovery from cyberattacks) and loss of carried out work [4].

Towards a Universal Cybersecurity Solution

Nowadays, the current defence mechanisms and monitoring entities lack some capabilities to take advantage of the knowledge extracted from previous attacks. All these entities and mechanisms need to evolve towards effective collection, reporting and sharing of data and statistics about previous attacks: the goal is to provide readily available and potentially useful information in order to enable better decision about the state of networks. The recent surge of interest in analytic capabilities suggests data analytics as enabler for a more rapid detection of and reaction to coordinated attacks. The result of data analytics leads to the creation of a general view of networks in their geographical or logical vicinity. This allows to detect attacks and understand malicious or suspect behaviours, permits to confront attacks at an earlier stage and also anticipates future vulnerabilities in order to reinforce the network.

The lack of information sharing is not the only key issue that hampers the efficient and effective utilisation of cybersecurity techniques. Currently, the deployment of specialised hardware-based security appliances is expensive. This deployment generates significant costs (mostly capital expenditure – CAPEX) that can be prohibitive for small and medium enterprises (SMEs) in particular. However, a detect-react strategy that can be applied efficiently across the whole range of the IoT, the end consumer devices and the back-end infrastructure has to be based on mechanisms that allow deploying security functionalities at a fraction of the current costs of today's dedicated hardware.

Thus, security solutions should also move from hardware-based solutions to network virtualisation technologies that permits to build equivalent software solutions. Network virtualisation technologies allows to offer detection and prevention functionalities as services rather than hardware appliances. Moving towards a security-as-a-service (SecaaS) [5] paradigm enables dedicated service providers (SPs) to offer different types of security functionalities. SHIELD aims at empowering both Internet and telecommunications SPs and data centre (DC) centric IP deployment to use SecaaS. Furthermore, this approach reflects one of the main trends for SPs identified by [6]: it attributes the steady growth in the demand for hosted (or cloud-based) security to SMEs, which keep moving from on-premises security tools to cloud-based security services.

Behind SHIELD's approach, there is a move towards network function virtualisation. This reflects a major trend in the network telecommunication community, which is currently driving this technology through an ETSI standardisation process [7]. This reflects the increasing number of dedicated network appliances and functionalities, being migrated to software running on virtual machines (virtual network functions, VNFs). In technical terms, the infrastructure on a data centre is extended by a certain number of computing clusters in order to accommodate VNFs at various locations in the network. The VNFs are typically combined to provide a specific network service (NS), and either a vNSF or a NS can perform a wide variety of operations, including security-related ones. According to the type and complexity of cyberthreats, these VNFs can identify and detect them or mitigate their consequences; hence, virtual network security functions (vNSFs) may implement virtual firewalls, network traffic data analysers, VPN concentrators, etc.

Moreover, following the paradigm of NFV orchestrators (NFVOs), the SHIELD approach aims at deploying specific vNSFs to protect the environment, monitor a segment of the network when required and notify for further actions.

SHIELD: A Tailored Solution for Virtual Security Infrastructure as a Service
SHIELD aims at delivering IT security as an integral service of virtual network infrastructures. These services can be tailor made for ISPs and enterprise customers – including SMEs. vNSFs provide software instantiations of security appliances which can be dynamically deployed into the desired network infrastructure. In order to be in line with the NFV concept and to go beyond traditional SecaaS offers, the vNSFs can be deployed close to the user/customer, allowing radical performance improvements while reducing the response time.

In addition, the SHIELD infrastructure needs to be trustworthy in order to bridge the trust gap introduced by separating the controlling logic from the enforcement plane. Leveraging TC methods and technologies, the virtualisation (or containerisation) software stack and the vNSFs are measured and attested against their expected state. Similarly, the software-defined network (SDN) use to steer users' packets through their vNSFs is also attested to ensure the correct vNSFs chain is applied for each user.

All data and logs collected from vNSFs are aggregated into a data-driven intrusion detection and prevention system (IDPS) platform called data analysis and remediation engine (DARE), where analytical components are capable of predicting specific vulnerabilities and attacks. These predictions are archived along with capturing the relevant network traffic to enable later learning from them and building adversarial options, behaviours and intents. Furthermore, the DARE learns from incoming intrusions through a reinforcement learning process in order to adjust or create new countermeasures and create richer and more correct conclusions. An additional challenge arises on the large networks: a general view of the network – rather than on a specific part of it – is required in order to be able to infer the specific events that cannot be detected by individual vNSFs. The DARE capability helps to solve this problem by storing the traffic produced on the network without having to focus upfront on specific parts. The analysis may be geared at indicators for malicious behaviours in the network (network behaviour analysis – NBA) or filter activity based on an event-based system detection (looking for activity or events on the system at the host, virtual and application layers). Moreover, the system permits to combine multiple types of observations in order to enable monitoring and decision support or autonomously decide and act on the network configuration in order to detect, predict and thwart malicious behaviour.

To summarise, the main components of SHIELD are responsible of:

- Retrieving raw monitoring data and logs from vNSFs deployed on the network
- Aggregating such information to be processed by intermediate engines
- Deploying additional vNSFs for further data gathering or attack countering
- Visualising such information and recommend actions
- Supporting new security capabilities and the reconfiguration of existing security controls, as deemed necessary to protect the infrastructure

Section 8.2 presents the SHIELD overall architecture, the main components and the underpinning security paradigms. Section 8.3 delves into the technical details about SHIELD key technology enablers, including infrastructure verification, virtualisation of security appliances and orchestration and big data for security. Finally, Sect. 8.4 draws conclusions and future work.

8.2   Architecture and Rationale of SHIELD as a Security Paradigm

The current high-level technical architecture of SHIELD is shown in Fig. 8.1. Three main layers create the SHIELD architecture: the deployment network, the vNSF layer and the DARE layer. For each layer, the main components' functionality is described in this section, while Fig. 8.2 presents a simplified example of the SHIELD framework detecting and protecting an attack.

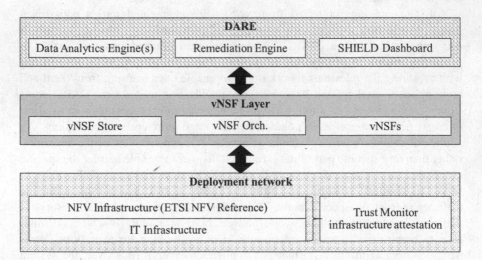

Fig. 8.1 High-level SHIELD architecture

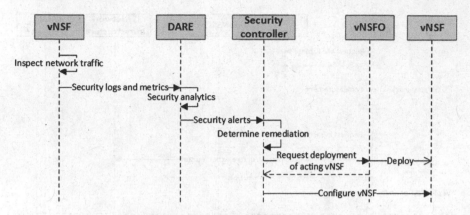

Fig. 8.2 SHIELD components' interaction to detect and protect against an attack

Assuming a vNSF is monitoring the network traffic of the deployment network, SHIELD's internal functioning could be summarised as follow:

1. Each monitoring vNSF (multiple instance of the same vNSF scattered on the network) analyses the network traffic crossing it. It extracts security-related logs and metrics, which are sent to the DARE's storage.
2. Security modules in the DARE analyse the data in the storage. Upon threat or attack detection by one of the security module, the DARE notifies the security controller.
3. The security controller warns the SHIELD operators through the dashboard. Once a remediation procedure has been decided – for example, deploying a firewalling vNSF with a given configuration – it requests deployment of this vNSF (only one in this example, but it could be multiple ones).
4. As soon as the new vNSF is ready, the security controller configures its security policy which leads to blocking the attack.

8.2.1 The Deployment Network

• The IT Infrastructure, inclusive of distributed edge devices, hosts and networks, represents the controlled and managed environment in SHIELD. Using TC-enabled platforms to run the components (including the vNSFs), along with well-defined security and integrity protocols (like secure wake-up procedures), SHIELD is able to measure the infrastructure integrity. The infrastructure interacts with the attestation authorities, Trust Monitor, to assess its trustworthiness. The Trust Monitor verifies the network infrastructure against the known-good state which is retrieved from vNSF store and vNSF orchestrator. This process is visualised in Fig. 8.3. In addition to the immediate action when detecting

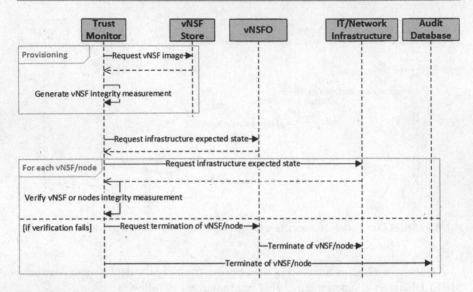

Fig. 8.3 Network infrastructure verification process

a misbehaviour by one component (isolation of the component, migration of
the vNSFs, modification of the network topology), SHIELD centralises the
measurement in an audit database.

- On top of the IT infrastructure, SHIELD runs a standard NFV infrastructure,
  compatible with the one described in the ETSI NFV reference framework [7]
  and architecture [8].

8.2.2 The vNSF Layer

The vNSF layer is composed mainly of three software components.

The vNSFs

The vNSFs can be categorised by their final target as follows: (1) traffic monitoring
(monitoring vNSFs) and (2) policy enforcement to block/filter/redirect traffic
(reacting vNSFs). Monitoring vNSFs can be instantiated anywhere in the network,
from the edge to the core (provided available resources exist). Monitoring functions
act as flexible network probes that gather information from the network. Reacting
vNSFs are expected in an automated and sustainable environment, where corrective
measures can be adopted. These measures may be performed – when possible – in
an automatic and fast fashion, prior consent of the user. Within the IDPS-related
environment, a reaction can be of two types: (1) acting as response to identified
threats and (2) preventing potential attacks (i.e. malicious patterns). When reacting,

the network functions are able to block, filter or redirect network traffic so as to stop malicious behaviours or minimise impact from an active attack.

The vNSF Orchestrator

The vNSF orchestrator instantiates, deploys and monitors the NSs and vNSFs, by means of its NS and vNSF managers (NSM, vNSFM), respectively. It also delegates the management of the life cycle of the vNSFs to the vNSFM.

As a standard NFV environment, SHIELD introduces a vNSF orchestrator (vNSFO), capable of orchestrating the creation and deployment of virtual resources, when provided with NS or vNSF descriptors (NSD, vNSFD). Internally, the NSM and vNSFM take each over the responsibility of controlling part of the network and computing resources, respectively, and ensuring a consistent state in the virtualised infrastructure manager (VIM). On the other hand, operations such as start, stop or scale vNSFs are delegated to the vNSFM, where it is left to interact with vNSFs deployed at specific points of placement (PoPs, according to standard NFV terminology).

The vNSFO is also in charge of arbitrating intercommunications between the different modules, in order to retrieve network functions from the vNSF store and deploy them in the network. The components described are aligned with the basic functions of the NFV management and orchestration domain, as laid out in current ETSI recommendations [9].

The vNSF Store

The vNSF store is a centralised digital repository for vNSFs, similar as [10]. This approach allows SPs to offer new security features to protect the network or extend already existing functionalities without the need of modifying the NFV platform nor the hardware of the underlying network. The store acts as a repository for vNSFs that have been previously published by developers, such as security agencies or other trusted source. The information contained in the store include (1) a vNSF definition to describe the vNSF requirements as per infrastructure, organised in a separate document (vNSF descriptor, in line with the ETSI VNF descriptor/VNFD), and (2) a vNSF image to be deployed. The store exposes two APIs: first, a developer API, which permits to deploy new vNSF in the store, and, second, a client API, enabling the acquisition of an existing vNSF in order to be deployed in a network. The basis for the development of the vNSF store is the marketplace component that is used to facilitate the interaction between different stakeholders in various NFV business scenarios. SHIELD is going to be able to integrate different existing vNSFs storage solutions.

The vNSF layer – besides the store, the orchestrator and the vNSFs themselves – contains additional components that support the onboarding, the deployment and management of the network functions, namely, the vNSFs catalogue, the infrastructure repository, the vNSF manager, the orchestration and data engines.

8.2.3   The DARE Layer

The DARE component encompasses several modules dedicated to identifying possible threats using network monitoring information as well as diverse learning and classifying mechanisms, eventually proposing possible actions to remediate them.

The Data Analytics Engines

The data analytics engines are responsible for detecting threats by using pattern discovery techniques. SHIELD leverages two different data analytics modules while opening the platform for the inclusion of others in the future. These modules also produce feedback to the data topologies, improving the efficiency of the processing area and carrying out threat remediation activities by using vNSFs.

The Cognitive Data Analysis Engine

This module leverages on machine learning techniques, such as naive Bayes classification and support vector machine (SVM) [11] methods, to analyse events and data. In particular, the data analytics engine studies the deployment of state-of-the-art frameworks for big data analysis based on Apache Mahout and Scala frameworks.

The Security Data Analysis Engine

This module leverages existing research work in the space of big data for security. This work has already been successfully trialled within production-like networking infrastructure with customers. This analytical engine is further enhanced and adapted to address the needs and requirements of this project. It includes processing and analysing a wide range of security data sets (e.g. DNS, networking information, web proxy, IP-MAC address mappings, etc.) collected via vNSF. Algorithms include data aggregation; analysis; correlation and detection of unusual networking traffic, domain names and correlations; and anomaly detection techniques based on current and historical data. This module is adapted to the SHIELD proposal in order to collaborate with the cognitive module covering different techniques and approaches that improves the detection capabilities of SHIELD.

The Remediation Engine

The remediation engine uses the results from the data analytics engines to produce recommendations to the dashboard users and/or to directly apply remediation when possible through the use of the vNSF orchestrator.

The reports produced by the analysis and remediation engines, either in real-time or by aggregating historical data, can be used to assist SP and CERT management decision-making process.

The Dashboard

The last component to be considered, the dashboard, facilitates the interaction of the various actors with the SHIELD platform. All the users of the SHIELD platform access the functionalities via the dashboard. For this purpose, the latter features a graphical web-based UI, as well as a RESTful API for third party applications. The dashboard allows access to authorised users, such as the SP, or a third party (e.g. a granted and legally empowered cybersecurity agency or a client requesting SecaaS). These interactions are directed to (1) the remediation and recommendation module and (2) the vNSFO to know the state of the network and the available functionalities and to manage the deployment of vNSFs. Through the dashboard, users are able to retrieve event information, recommendations regarding the current security status of the framework (e.g. through events), short-term predictions and to access a history of performed operations.

Based on the identification and functional specifications of the different components of the DARE framework, a more detailed overall architectural blueprint can be seen in Fig. 8.4.

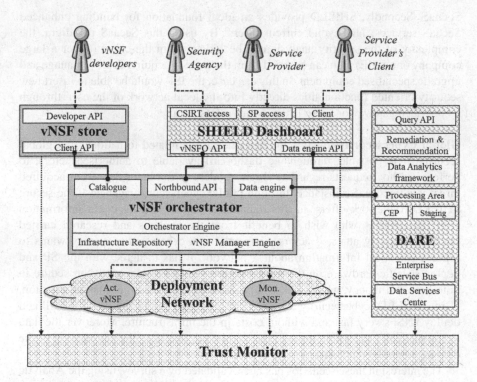

Fig. 8.4 Functional SHIELD architecture

8.2.4   Use Cases

The SHIELD project addresses three market-oriented use cases relevant to the industry. These use cases propose to deploy a SHIELD platform in different scenarios: protection of a company infrastructure, offering a security-as-a-service solution and creation of a global security environment.

ISP Firstly, we consider the case where, in order to protect their own network infrastructure, ISPs have to deploy purpose-specific and expensive hardware in enough quantity to fit the required dimension of the systems and deal with the expected traffic to process. At the same time, this hardware shall be updated and maintained by specialised operators. The virtualisation offered by SHIELD in this use case aims to dramatically reduce this cost by replacing specific hardware by vNSFs, to ease the swapping of vendors, to decouple hardware and software which breaks market barriers for software vendors as well as to provide a central interface (dashboard) to understand the gathered information and to act in the network.

SecaaS Secondly, SHIELD provides an ideal foundation for building enhanced SecaaS services, far beyond current offers. By using this SecaaS paradigm, the complexity of the security analysis can be hidden from the client (either a large company or a SME) who can be freed from the need to acquire, deploy, manage and upgrade specialised equipment. In this use case, the ISP would be able to insert new security-oriented functionalities directly into the local network of the user, through its provided gateway or in the ISP network infrastructure.

Global Cybersecurity Finally, the last use case is related to national and global security. It is possible, through the dashboard available to authorised actors, to perform ad hoc requests regarding threat models or to obtain data from acquired threat intelligence, for instance, through public cybersecurity agencies. The secure SHIELD framework offers, in this manner, a way of sharing threat information with third parties who wish to benefit from the analysis and research carried out by previously attacked actors. Currently, if a cybersecurity agency wants to retrieve statistical information about a network, it has to agree with the SP and deploy specific hardware on the infrastructure. This is a very costly procedure in both time and money, which makes it prohibitive for the current market situation. Using SHIELD, cybersecurity agencies can establish agreements with the SP and deploy vNSFs very fast and without costs in the infrastructure. Moreover the data is automatically accessible through the dashboard, thanks to the aggregation of the data treatment by the DARE.

The interest in these scenarios has been validated by a survey, using the Analytic Hierarchy Process [12] methodology. A panel of experts – distributed between SMEs, industry, research institutes, academia, ISP operators and government agencies and from various European countries (France, Greece, Luxembourg, Portugal, Spain, Italy and the United Kingdom) – answered the survey.

An important outcome is that experts believe that the SecaaS use case is the most relevant to fight against threats and vulnerabilities; this is a clear indication that SHIELD could start in the market as a service. As a result, SHIELD focuses primarily on an ISP providing advanced SecaaS offers to its customers as the initial solution.

From a societal impact standpoint, the survey shows that the global cybersecurity use case is the most important. Cybersecurity agencies can establish agreements with SP to deploy vNSF to protect against EU-wide attacks.

Finally, the ISP use case is considered relevant for SPs to replace the specialised hardware while keeping the same levels of protection, confidentiality/privacy and operational efficiency.

8.3 Building Blocks and Technology Enablers

The architectural components described in the previous section focus on the capture of data via vNSFs, big data for security and remediation, for continued security monitoring and reaction in the infrastructure. They are mapped to software components and modules. Additional SHIELD components provide security support functionality to the hardware and systems running this critical software, including ensuring proper verification (attestation) of a secure state of both computing and networking infrastructures. This section provides additional technical details about all these SHIELD components.

8.3.1 Infrastructure Verification

As trust in the computing/network nodes and a proper execution of vNSFs are critical to the functionality of SHIELD, the project employs state-of-the-art techniques to protect these components. Namely, it adopts trusted computing (TC) technologies – and specifically the remote attestation procedure – to measure the integrity of the distributed platform executing the vNSFs, isolate the misbehaving nodes and redeploy vNSFs to other nodes. Software integrity of vNSFs is measured both at deployment time and then periodically during execution, for example, by using Open Cloud Integrity Technology [13]. Trust is established through several attestation techniques and the introduction of an attestation architecture, described in Fig. 8.5.

First of all, a hardware root of trust must be present on the different nodes in the architecture. In SHIELD's case, this is implemented in the form of a TPM (Trusted Platform Module) [14] that permits to create a software stack (from the boot environment up to the application layer), where each component is "measured" (i.e. its integrity's hash is computed before being loaded), the measurements are accumulated in a secure way and they are reliably reported with a digital signature, uniquely identifying the node. A trust agent is part of the host system on each node, to reliably report the measurements to an external verifier.

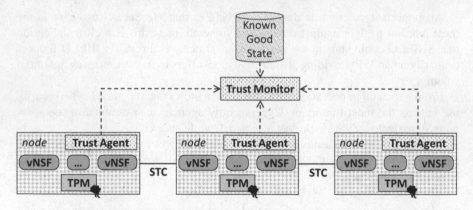

Fig. 8.5 Attestation architecture in SHIELD

Second, there is mutual authentication and creation of a secure channel (MACsec or IPsec) between the nodes themselves. The public key certificate used for authentication of the node is part of the measurements reported for attestation. This way, the channel-binding is created: the end point being attested is the same as the one managing the secure channel, and relay attacks – as demonstrated by Asokan et al. [15] – become impossible. This setting is represented by the "secure and trusted channel" (STC) in Fig. 8.5.

Finally, since comparing the measurements can be a complex task, a dedicated trusted third party – hereinafter named Trust Monitor (TM) – is used to check the reported measurements against a specific whitelist of components. Note that the whitelist contains the measurements of both the software components and their configurations, which are equally important for a correct behaviour.

These principles permit to perform five main practical steps to complete the attestation procedure between the nodes (such as two vNSF) and the TM:

1. *Secure channel*: creation of a secure channel between two nodes, mutually authenticated; the channel is not yet trusted.
2. *Node attestation*: each node asks the TM to attest the channel endpoint node, via the remote attestation procedure, followed by comparing the node's measurements with known-good states.
3. *Attestation result*: the TM returns to each node the integrity status of the other one. If untrustworthy, the secure channel created in step 1 is closed, the orchestrator is involved to isolate the compromised node and connect to another one. If trustworthy, then a STC has been created, since the attestation procedure includes the cryptographic key used for channel creation in step 1.
4. *vNSF attestation*: every time a new vNSF is deployed on the node, the TM is involved to check its integrity and report it (similar to steps 2 and 3 above). If integrity of the vNSF is compromised, then it is not activated and removed from the network.

5. *Periodic attestation*: steps 2, 3 and 4 are repeated periodically, to promptly detect events that could modify the behaviour of a node or of any of the vNSFs that it hosts. In this way, compromised elements can be isolated and replaced with good ones.

This procedure exploits current technologies as well as the results of past EC-funded projects, such as Open TC (open-source TC Linux-based platform) [16], TClouds (TC-based cloud computing platform) [17] and SECURED (which technology paves the way towards trusted VNFs) [18]. The latter project has contributed significantly to make remote attestation a viable technique for a virtualised network environment by making it more scalable and suitable for lightweight virtualisation environments, such as Docker containers.

Additionally, this procedure is also aligned with the work of the ETSI NFV standardisation group, which is going in the direction of applying TC techniques to protect generic virtualised network architectures.

SHIELD also improves over the state of the art by looking also at the security of the network infrastructure itself and coupling it with that of the vNSFs. Recent developments have proven that remote integrity attestation is possible also for network switches – even in the context of SDN [19] – and it can be coupled with that of the computational nodes and the vNSFs executed on them. This way, SHIELD creates a trusted and secure chain of components from the network level up to the vNSFs level.

It should be noted that SHIELD uses an SDN-fashioned architecture in order to configure the network; hence, the computing and networking nodes, running the vNSFs, are supervised by an SDN controller. It pushes the specified forwarding rules to the switches accordingly to the needed network architecture. The controller has a global view of the network topology through a rules table for each switch it manages. Having two representation of the actual network, a local view on the switches and a remote one on the controller, raises an obvious concern about their synchronisation. In fact, an attacker could fake the controller view by feeding it rules setup acknowledgements and steer the traffic completely differently on the actual network. To answer that matter, a novel integrity verification technique was proposed in [19]. This solution ensures that the underlying SDN rules applied on the switches match the SDN controller view of the network. It actually takes the SDN rules from the controller rules table for a given switch and compares them to their representations on the actual switch.

8.3.2   Virtualised Security Appliances and Their Orchestration

SHIELD builds on the network functions virtualisation (NFV) and security-as-a-service (SecaaS) concepts to provide an extensible, adaptable, fast and low-cost security solution based on virtual security infrastructure as a service, tailored for both service providers and enterprise customers, including SMEs. Security appliances –traditionally deployed as expensive and proprietary hardware modules– are bundled into software-only virtual computing nodes.

The aim of NVF is to decouple a given network function from the purpose-specific hardware device where it would traditionally run. The continued activity on research and on deployment of solutions support the NFV ecosystem goes in pair with an increasing number of dedicated network appliances and functionality (VNFs) that is migrated to software being hosted in virtual nodes. There are some typical network security functions that are eligible for this decoupling, such as firewalls or gateways, but also embedded solutions for network traffic monitoring and inspection. This decoupling process provides control over the network functions, which can be dynamically deployed – within commodity server – based on any desired orchestration logic. NFV is a softwarisation attempt to increase manageability of the networks, reduce capital and operational expenditures incurred by hardware devices (i.e. time and cost of deployment and management) as well as increase the homogeneity of the networking infrastructure and provide a broad spectrum of network functionalities that are deployed on top of common hardware.

In technical terms, a data centre infrastructure is extended by a certain number of distributed computing clusters to instantiate and accommodate VNFs at various locations in the network – that is, PoPs. They are clusters of compute nodes distributed into the network to allow hosting of virtual appliances. SHIELD aims to exploit NFV technology and provide security services in the form of virtual network security functions (vNSFs). As with any VNF, vNSFs can be deployed, migrated, restarted or deleted in the order of seconds. SHIELD implements two types of vNSFs, monitoring and reacting security services.

Although NFV technology offers many advantages, moving from hardware appliances to virtualised services carries an important shortcoming, which is especially critical to security; the performance cost associated with virtualisation. The use of virtualisation brings many challenges particularly in achieving the same level of performance in comparison to the traditional fixed appliance approach. To avoid sacrificing performance in exchange to the numerous benefits and savings obtained by NFV adoption, research and industry are investigating possible options to accelerate packet processing in NFV deployments. Emerging techniques attempt to fine-tune performances by adapting the virtualisation layer to offload some of the networking data plane functions (e.g. match-action processing based on flow rules, tunnel initiation and termination and others) on the servers. Other techniques provide methods that allow servers to process packets, bypassing virtualisation bottlenecks. There are several solutions available, some of which are based on hardware (e.g. PCI pass-through, single root I/O virtualisation, CPU pinning, NUMA nodes), some on software (e.g. Data Plane Development Kit) or on a combination of both.

Monitoring vNSF

Monitoring vNSFs enable gathering information regarding network flows, intrusion detection or suspicious/unwanted activity. Monitoring vNSFs can be placed in any PoP, close to the end points or in the middle of the backbone, and in multiple layers. Monitoring functions act as flexible network probes that gather information regarding network flows and thus can be used to identify potential intrusions as well as suspicious or malicious activity and monitor it. The monitoring vNSFs may be generic or purpose specific and shall provide either raw or filtered data.

Reacting vNSF

Reacting vNSFs act as a response to identified threats and apply policies to block/filter/redirect traffic, mitigating potential attacks. Traditionally the placement of reacting security functions is at the end points of the network, which results in an early mitigation of attacks, and therefore prevents malicious traffic from entering the core network.

The implemented vNSFs are integrated into a network service (NS) and instantiated close to the customer, thus tightly coupling them with the customer's infrastructure (as opposed to offloading security "to the cloud"). At the same time, this offers total or shared control of vNSFs to service providers and to their customers. In this way, similar benefits of SecaaS can be delivered (e.g. reduced CAPEX due to displacement of proprietary hardware with commodity off the shelf hardware, continuous upgrades and unlimited resources) while at the same time eliminating the disadvantages of cloud-based security. Depending on the type of cyberthreats meant to be detected or mitigated by the vNSFs, those may implement virtual firewalls and web security appliances, content filters, e-mail scanners, virtual DNS servers, VPN concentrators or honeypots.

The SHIELD vNSF environment leverages the most relevant network monitoring techniques in use for threat detection and mitigation. The specific functionalities developed in SHIELD for network security depend on the analysis of the security requirements and on the threats to be addressed on the project's selected use cases. The considered vNSFs are described as follows:

- Deep packet inspection (DPI) and intrusion detection vNSFs that are able to set inspection points, searching for packets that are unable to pass them and triggering events when such situation happens
- Honeypot vNSFs which can attract the adversary to a controlled environment to investigate its behaviour, in an effort to understand the attacker's intent
- Vulnerability scanning vNSFs that actively and periodically scan the network for vulnerabilities and weaknesses
- Packet sniffing vNSFs, responsible for detecting unauthorised network monitoring
- Penetration testing vNSFs that attempt to test the security level of the network
- Monitoring vNSFs, which inspect the traffic passing through the network

In addition to the monitoring functions, SHIELD implements several reacting vNSFs. Reaction/remediation is expected to be performed ideally in an automatic and fast way, to allow corrective measures to be timely deployed on the network. Within an IDPS environment, a reaction can be of two types: acting as a response to identified threats or preventing potential attacks (i.e. malicious patterns). When reacting, the network functions are able to act in the network by blocking, filtering, redirecting or adjusting traffic to stop malicious behaviours or minimise impact of an active attack. These vNSFs are also able to fix networking problems, vulnerabilities and weaknesses. Possible reacting vNSFs considered for implementation by SHIELD are:

- Firewall vNSFs, able to protect against attacks by filtering the passing traffic based on a set of predetermined security rules.
- Intrusion Prevention Systems (IPS) vNSFs, which are IDS deployments augmented with capabilities for firewall interaction, rejecting or dropping packets in the case a security threat has been detected.

The vNSFs contain separate logic that is to be placed, monitored and initialised in the network. The life cycle of these functions must also be managed. In a standard NFV environment, the life cycle of NSs is expected to be managed by an NFV orchestrator platform. In this aspect, SHIELD introduces a vNSF orchestrator, which is responsible for the deployment and management of virtualised security services composed of one or more vNSFs.

vNSF Orchestrator

The vNSFO administers the workflows for basic operations on NSs and vNSFs, such as the placement of the functions to selected PoPs, the deployment of network services comprised of a single or more VNFs/vNSFs, their termination or –whenever required– their scaling to cope with changing conditions. The vNSFO is also in charge of arbitrating as deemed the intercommunication between different modules, to retrieve network functions from the vNSF store and deploy them in the network. To fulfil its role, the vNSFO maintains internal catalogues and repositories containing information about underlying resources, available and established network services, available VNFs/vNSFs and deployed instances of them, as well as infrastructure resources. Specifically, the following key components support the vNSFO functionalities:

- *The orchestrator engine* is the kernel of the orchestrator platform. This module manages all the execution workflows of the orchestrator itself. It is responsible for the intercommunication of the different modules and for the catalogue and repositories' management.
- *The data engine* provides the communication with the DARE to provide security events and coordinate the network functions deployed in the infrastructure to react accordingly.
- *The vNSF manager* is the component responsible for the management of the vNSFs that have already been deployed. Following the instructions of the orchestrator engine, it is the component responsible for the scaling, provisioning and monitoring the status of the vNSFs and the infrastructure where they are deployed. Its northbound API permits the management of the SHIELD orchestrator, which is used to communicate with the dashboard.

- *The vNSF catalogue* at the orchestrator level contains metadata about the different vNSFs available in the vNSF store to the service provider to be deployed over the infrastructure. The SP can then decide which ones to compose with and deploy to provide the expected service. The catalogue contains both the vNSFD document, which describes the specific hardware requirements of the vNSF and its various components (virtual deployment units, VDUs) to be deployed, as well as the vNSF image, so the deployment process is accelerated up to operational timescales. Some examples of existing valid VNF repositories are those developed within the FP7 T-NOVA project [20], the ETSI Open Source Mano (OSM) [21] or the 5G-PPP SONATA [22] project, all providing catalogues of descriptors in different granularity, whether that targets a VNF, a NS or a package descriptor (PD).
- *The infrastructure repository* contains all details and resources of the underlying infrastructure in which the vNSFs are to be hosted. The repository shall communicate with some other specific systems to retrieve all required information on the physical infrastructure, which is later used to make the vNSF placement (using some specific mapping strategy) and scheduling decisions.

SHIELD introduces big data analytics and remediation capabilities on top of the NFV infrastructure, to detect both known and unknown security attacks and remediates them.

8.3.3   Security Through Big Data Analytics

This section focuses on how security is provided by applying big data analytics and the overall threat detection process, while the next section further discusses remediation and recovery actions, triggered by the detection of threats.

The deployment of big data as a technological foundation for security incident and event management (SIEM) systems is a common approach in the information security industry today. Managing the output of SIEM and logging systems is bringing a significant cost for all IT departments, and big data is seen as a potential solution. Big data is a change of paradigm in the technology that deals with big amounts of heterogeneous data, and hence, we can say that big data is about processing techniques. These techniques could play a key role in helping detect threats at an early stage, using more sophisticated pattern analysis, combining and analysing multiple data sources. For instance, logs are often ignored unless an incident occurs. Big data provides the opportunity to consolidate and analyse logs automatically from multiple sources rather than in isolation. This could provide insight that individual logs could not give, and this potentially enhance intrusion detection systems (IDS) and intrusion prevention systems (IPS) through continual adjustment and effectively learning "good" and "bad" behaviours.

Dealing with Advanced Threats

The core goal of SHIELD is to leverage a network-wide security view so that it can address distributed attacks such as advanced persistent threats (APT). These attacks manifest themselves over a potentially long-time period (e.g. weeks, months) and involve attack steps that are typical of a kill-chain [23]:

- *Initial compromise*: a device is initially compromised by an internal/external attacker by using one of the available attack mechanisms, including exploitation of vulnerabilities and social engineering. As a consequence, malware is deployed within the system and its malicious activity starts.
- *Command and control*: deployed malware might periodically communicate with the attacker's remote malicious systems to receive information from the affected systems and/or use it to perform remote actions on the latter.
- *Reconnaissance and lateral movements*: the active malware might start exploring the networking neighbours to identify valuable targets, e.g. other networked devices that might contain sensitive business information, IPs, etc. This includes scanning for vulnerabilities of networked devices and trying to break into them, hence repeating steps 1–3 for each further compromised device.
- *User account compromise*: the malware might need to escalate its privileges to achieve specific actions and malicious activities. It might try to compromise critical admin accounts or privileged accounts.
- *Data exfiltration and damages*: the malware might eventually try to exfiltrate sensitive data outside the organisation by connecting to remote sites and/or damaging enterprise infrastructure and services, e.g. with DDoS attacks.

In order to detect this type of advanced attacks, a wide range of networking and system events needs to be collected, stored and processed over time. SHIELD collects the relevant data through vNSFs and detects threats using its big data solution applied to security.

The Role of vNSFs in Threat Detection

Let us consider the enterprise scenario where a very high number of distributed networked devices are connected to one or more network edge devices (e.g. in campus-size networks). Some of these devices might lack basic security capabilities or only have installed some common security controls (antiviruses, firewalls, etc.). They rely on the underlying networking capabilities to share with other devices the data they locally collect (and potentially process). As discussed in Sects. 8.3.1 and 8.3.2 the networking edge devices are instrumented to further collect information about networked devices, in particular about their networking events and behaviour. They run virtual network security functions (vNSFs) under the control of a user/administrator and are orchestrated by SHIELD management and orchestration modules.

In this context, specialised vNSFs collect overall networking events that are relevant for threat detection. This includes (but it is not limited to) the following types of events that are extracted by network packets and processed on the fly:

- *DNS events*: they are relevant to understand which sites/devices are trying to connect to, their properties, the nature of queried domains, the way to resolve IP addresses, etc. Attacks in involving Command&Control and exfiltration activities might leave DNS footprints when trying to communicate with remote malicious sites.
- *Netflow events*: they are relevant to understand network communication patterns between networking devices, including which device is trying to connect to another one, communication successes and failures, amount of involved traffic, etc. Attacks involving reconnaissance and lateral movements are usually leaving footprints that can be detected by analysing netflow events.
- *HTTP/S events*: as for DNS events, attacks in involving Command&Control and exfiltration activities might leave footprints in web proxy logs when trying to communicate with remote malicious sites. These logs include additional information such as files and data exchanged via URLs and HTTP/S protocols.

Connecting the Pieces

The aforementioned events are locally processed; non-relevant events are filtered (e.g. whitelisted DNS logs are filtered out) and finally shared with centralised big data analytics solutions. Figure 8.6 provides additional details about SHIELD components of specific relevance to SHIELD big data for security and remediation capabilities:

- Data processing pipelines are in place to ensure that events collected from vNSFs are cleaned, enriched with additional metadata (e.g. geolocation of IP addresses, flagging suspicious IP addresses and domains based on threat intelligence, etc.) and stored in high-performance data repositories (inclusive of SQL and noSQL ones). Open source event brokering and processing frameworks, including Apache Kafka [24] and Apache Storm [25] are used in the data processing pipeline.
- A set of analytics engines processes the collected data both in near-time and on a historical basis (e.g. spanning from data collected in the last few hours back to weeks/months). They include rule engines and Apache Spark-based analytics engines. These engines support a wide range of threat detection mechanisms, which are classified as:
  - Pattern-based analytics: they check for well-known attack patterns and mechanisms, driven by deep security knowledge and expertise in the field. They adapt to specific context, by using statistical analysis of data, and apply prebuilt knowledge to identify threats and minimise false positives.
  - Machine learning-based analytics: they use machine learning techniques to identify abnormal entities and user behaviours, including Bayesian networks, peer anomaly detection, decision trees, etc. After an initial phase of training and contextualisation, classifiers are deployed within SHIELD analytics engines (e.g. based on Apache Spark) to identify issues in real and near time.
  - Both types of analytics are used to detect new, unknown security threats happening at different stages of complex and advanced attacks, during potentially long-time periods (weeks/months). This includes all attack steps

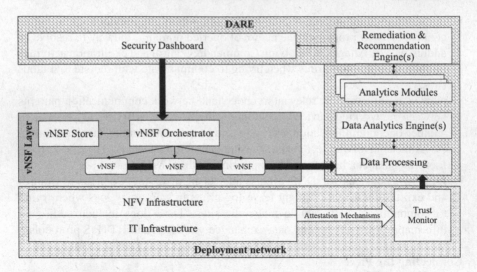

Fig. 8.6 SHIELD architecture components

    in the previously mentioned kill chain: initial compromise of a system/device, command and control by an external attacker site, lateral movements within an organisation network and exploitation/damage.
- Alerts are triggered from detected threats, further aggregated (e.g. across various engines) to determine their level of evidence/relevance and visualised to security analysts via a security dashboard UI. The next section discusses how detected issues are used to trigger remediation steps.

The end-to-end security approach provided in SHIELD ensures that known/unknown security threats within an organisation are quickly detected by using trustworthy data, collected from a programmable NFV infrastructure and automatically remediated (or risks mitigated) by using the same NFV infrastructure and programmable vNSF functions. The key value proposition is drastically reducing the time needed to remediate an attack, from its initial detection, hence reducing risk exposure and damages within an organisation.

Exploiting Machine Learning in Threat Detection
The implementation of big data analytics in the scope of SHIELD and regarding its capabilities becomes a demanding process, considering the properties of big data (commonly referred to as the "5Vs"):

- Volume – the quantity of data
- Velocity – the speed/rate at which data is provided
- Variety – the different formats and semantic models in which data is provided
- Variability – the variation in data being provided
- Value – the accuracy/truthfulness, and therefore usefulness, of the data

Thus, SHIELD have to contemplate the management of large, distributed aggregations of loosely structured data which may be often incomplete and inaccessible, possibly involving time-stamped events and/or connections between data elements that must be probabilistically inferred. The above factors render the traditional analytics tools insufficient to acquire the full value of the information contained in big data, as they merely offer a systematised extension of basic analytics that still relies on human perception to direct activities and specify the computational procedures. Machine learning, on the other hand, is the ideal method for exploiting the information hidden in big data, as it extracts values from data sources with far less reliance on human direction. Furthermore, being data-driven, it is well suited to the complexity of dealing with disparate data sources and the huge variety of variables and amounts of data involved, specifically on growing data sets.

Machine learning uses several approaches to solve problems. The two most commonly used ones are supervised and unsupervised learning, depending on the nature of the feedback available to a learning system:

- Supervised learning is tasked with learning a function from labelled training data in order to predict the value of any valid input. Common examples of supervised learning include classifying e-mail messages as spam, labelling web pages according to their genre and recognising handwriting. The most common algorithms used in supervised learning include neural networks, support vector machines (SVMs) and naive Bayes classifiers.
- Unsupervised learning is tasked with inferring a function to describe hidden structure from unlabelled data. Since the examples given to the learner are unlabelled, there is no error or reward signal to evaluate a potential solution, which is the main distinction between unsupervised learning and supervised learning. It is commonly used for clustering similar inputs into logical groups, in order to reduce the number of dimensions in a data set and to focus on only the most useful attributes or to detect trends. Common approaches to unsupervised learning include k-means hierarchical clustering, generative statistical models and self-organising maps.

The main machine learning tasks that are commonly used in big data applications and implemented in SHIELD are clustering and classification. Here is a brief explanation of each method:

- Clustering calculates the similarity between items of a collection, in order to create groups of similar items. In many implementations of clustering, collection items are represented as vectors in an n-dimensional space. Given the vectors, one can calculate the distance between two items using measurement techniques such as the Manhattan distance, Euclidean distance or cosine similarity. Then, the actual clusters can be calculated by grouping together the items that are close in distance.

- Classification is the problem of identifying to which of a set of categories a new observation belongs, on the basis of a training set of data containing observations whose category membership is known. The training algorithm is given a sample set of data, in order to recognise patterns and learn a model. This model is then used on new unlabelled data, to generate predictions for pattern matching. In the terminology of machine learning, classification is considered an instance of supervised learning, while clustering belongs to the unsupervised learning methods. Since the majority of the threats that will be confronted by SHIELD are either unknown or unique, clustering methods are more expected to be applied than classification methods –the latter being limited to known threats.

Configuration of a Functional Big Data Analytics Engine

An emerging issue concerning the structure of the DARE is the selection of the appropriate big data framework that serves the purposes of distributed computing. This is decided based on the data processing techniques utilised by each known framework. There are two common processing techniques that can facilitate big data analysis, namely, batch data processing and real-time data processing:

- Batch data processing is an efficient way of processing high volumes of data, where a group of transactions is collected over a period of time. Data is collected, entered and processed, and then the batch results are produced. Batch processing requires separate programs for input, process and output.
- In contrast, real-time data processing involves a continual input, process and output of data. Data must be processed in a small-time period (or near real time). Typically, frameworks that utilise real-time data processing execute many parallel operations on a cluster and support a cyclic data flow and in-memory processing.

It is understandable that real-time data processing techniques seem to correspond better to the nature of the project than batch processing techniques, based on its expected capabilities.

SHIELD's DARE should be able to produce packet and flow analytics, by providing ingest and appropriate transform of data, scalable machine learning and interactive visualisation of threat identification in network flows and DNS packets. By utilising open-source solutions like Apache Spot [26], billions of events can be analysed in order to detect unknown threats, insider threats, and achieve a higher level of visibility into the network.

The solution consists of a three-step procedure for its overall threat detection process. A parallel ingest framework is used to decode binary flow and packet data, then loading the data in HDFS and data structures inside Hadoop. The decoded data is stored in multiple formats so it is available for searching, being used by machine learning, being transferred to law enforcement or being inputted to other systems. Subsequently, the system uses a combination of Apache Spark tools to run scalable machine learning algorithms, not only as a filter for separating bad traffic from benign but also as a way to characterise the unique behaviour of network traffic in an organisation. Finally and in addition to machine learning, a process of context enrichment, noise filtering, whitelisting and heuristics are applied to network data, in order to present the most likely patterns that may comprise security threats. These three discrete procedures are shortly referred to as ingestion, machine learning and operational analytics:

- The ingest component is responsible for the data that is captured or transferred into the Hadoop cluster, where they are transformed and loaded into solution data stores. As a prerequisite, both Kafka service and Spark-streaming Kafka support are needed.
- The machine learning component is responsible for the detection of anomalies in network traffic and the prevention or mitigation of potential threats. For this purpose, latent Dirichlet allocation (LDA) [27] is used. LDA is a generative probabilistic model used in discrete data, more specifically a three-level hierarchical Bayesian model, in which each item of a collection is modelled as a finite mixture over an underlying set of topics. This is similar to probabilistic latent semantic analysis (pLSA), except that in LDA the topic distribution is assumed to have a Dirichlet prior. In practice, this results in more reasonable mixtures of topics in a document. As a prerequisite for the machine learning component, MPICH is required to support different computation and communication platforms, including commodity clusters.
- The operational analytics component provides modules and utilities to extract and transform data, by loading the results into output files. It supports basic data types as flow, DNS and proxy that correspond to the most common types of network threats. The output of the OA component can be used to activate task-specific countermeasures in the form of security functions from vNSF store. Therefore, our solution is able to provide layer-specific threat monitoring according to the OSI model, as network flow correlates to the transport layer, DNS to the network layer and HTTP/S to the application layer.

The proposed configuration of the above system consists of at least four nodes (physical or virtual machines). The edge node is responsible for the ingest component that handles the incoming network traffic. After the relevant transformation, data is passed to the worker nodes (at least two) which operate the machine learning components. Finally, the UI node executes the operational analytics and is intended as a monitoring, management and alert-triggering interface. This configuration is shown in Fig. 8.7.

8.3.4   Remediation and Recovery

Along with the DARE, the remediation engine is fed with alerts and contextual information to determine a plan for mitigating existing threats and risks. This engine considers the alert details and context (e.g. infected device, network location,

Configuration Overview

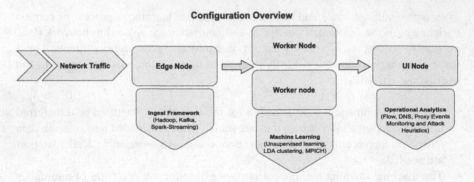

Fig. 8.7 Data analysis and remediation engine configuration overview

business priority, etc.), coupled with existing playbooks (workflows of steps and actions) to determine which remediation actions need to be carried out.

Examples of remediation actions might include:

- Getting security personnel authorisation to automatically remediate the threat
- Contacting device owners
- Intervening at the networking level, e.g. by blocking networking flows or redirecting them
- Enabling further logging activities at the networking level

The network-level remediation automatically happens when the remediation engine contacts the NFV management and orchestration modules. The vNSFO identifies which are the appropriate vNSFs to deploy and carry out the desired reaction in the network.

Finally, an audit service is used in SHIELD to log diverse collection, detection and remediation steps to provide an audit trail for future forensic analysis and incident management purposes.

8.4   Conclusions and Future Work

The SHIELD project focuses on three main pillars:

1. The analysis of the network events through big data techniques to provide remediation suggestions
2. The deployment of the appropriate secure network functions to monitor and react
3. The attestation of the secure state of the infrastructure to ensure traffic is not intercepted or tampered with

Processing and analysis of large amounts of data are carried out in three differentiated phases. During the first phase, the data acquisition phase, data from the several vNSFs is gathered and converted into a unified structure, marked with a certain level of reliability. In the second phase – data storage and processing phase – a data topology is created from the previously stored information. The real-time analysis of the gathered information, snapshots of the network state and interaction with the data analytics engine are also included in this phase. Throughout the third phase (the data analytics phase), various data analysis engines can be plugged to work with data topologies in the extensible analysis platform. This platform consists of two main modules: the data analytics module that is responsible of detecting threats by using pattern discovery techniques and the remediation module that uses the analysis done before to produce recommendations to the users either directly or using the dashboard.

The deployment of secure network functions is key in providing infrastructure protection. These are made available in a sort of repository (vNSF store) where developers (SP or security agency) publish their developed network functions. The variety of available vNSFs strengthens the ability of SHIELD to stop and prevent attacks and threats.

On the other hand, trusted computing techniques are employed to protect critical components. The remote attestation procedure measures the integrity of the distributed platform where the vNSFs run, isolating the nodes that misbehave and moving vNSFs to other nodes. Since remote integrity attestation is possible also for network switches, within SHIELD, integrity attestation for both computational nodes and switches can be coupled. In this way, SHIELD focuses on the creation of a trusted (and secure) chain of components from the network level up to the application-level vNSFs.

Throughout its lifetime, SHIELD aims to deploy specialised vNSFs (for specific monitoring and different types of reacting), combined with the DARE, a highly predictive analysis and remediation engine that feeds on the monitored data to identify current and possible incidents and threats in the network.

Compared to the current monitoring, detection and protection systems, this solution aims to provide easier configuration and deployment, reduce maintaining and integration costs on existing hardware, secure management and integrity validation of the hardware and enable a full coverage and protection of the network by deploying vNSFs transparently across the infrastructure.

As the targeted outcome of the project affects transversal disciplines and actors, SHIELD brings together telecom operators, technology platform vendors and integrators, SMEs and cybersecurity agencies. This aims to jointly gather a better understanding of the different scenarios and actors and implement appliances tailored for their needs. The benefits for the aforementioned actors are diverse:

- The telecom operators can take advantage of new revenue streams from cyber-security solutions, such as offering SecaaS to clients, further securing current infrastructure with the SHIELD big data engine and vNSFs for detection and remediation.
- The vendors, integrators and SMEs can benefit from the opportunity of extending their business, as they can collaborate to facilitate a strategic position by entering early in the market of global cybersecurity solutions. They have a common goal

to develop both platform capabilities and sell new vNSFs, such as the network monitoring and placement closer to the edge.

- The authorised national cybersecurity agencies and specific CERT/CSIRT teams can be provided with further information from enabled interfaces on the threats gathered by the SHIELD monitoring, analytics and remediation engine that are deployed on infrastructures external to them.

Besides the objectives achieved by the building blocks to be developed and deployed in the project, there is plenty of other interesting work to consider as possible extension of a secured VNF and big data environment. Some candidates to consider are the attestation of virtual network devices, for those infrastructures minimising the number of hardware equipment, or additional secure operations with different granularity (e.g. inside the vNSFs, between them and between any component interacting with the network functions) to ensure secure transmission of data.

Questions

1. Which use cases have been addressed in the project?
2. What is the methodology used to validate the importance of the use-cases?
3. What makes a secure channel also trusted?
4. Are trusted computing technologies only applicable to servers?
5. How will the SHIELD platform deal with the latency introduced by the software elements (vNSFs, analytics engine)?
6. To which extent will the SHIELD platform allow automation of threat mitigation (and which are the main restrictions or motivations not to do so)?
7. What are the benefits of deploying the reacting vNSFs close to the end points of the network?
8. What are the main factors that highlight the importance of big data analytics in cybersecurity applications?
9. Would you suggest a batch or a stream/real-time data processing approach for the analysis of network traffic? What are the advantages and disadvantages of each method?
10. What kind of engines and capabilities are applied in the DARE?
11. With regards to decision-making in cybersecurity, is SHIELD following a centralised or a decentralised apporach? What about the monitoring functionalities? What about the reaction functionalities?

References

1. Kochetkova K (2016) Kaspersky Lab official blog. https://blog.kaspersky.com/attack-on-dyn-explained/13325/. Accessed 6 Apr 2017
2. Paganini P (2013) 2013 Norton Report, the impact of cybercrime according Symantec. In: Security Affairs. http://securityaffairs.co/wordpress/18475/cyber-crime/2013-norton-report.html. Accessed 6 Apr 2017

3. Ponemon Cyber Crime Report: IT, Computer & Internet Security. In: Hewlett-Packard Enterprise. http://www8.hp.com/us/en/software-solutions/ponemon-cyber-security-report/. Accessed 6 Apr 2017
4. Paganini P (2013) 2013 – the impact of cybercrime. In: InfoSec Resources. http://resources.infosecinstitute.com/2013-impact-cybercrime/. Accessed 6 Apr 2017
5. Security as a Service: Cloud Security Alliance. https://cloudsecurityalliance.org/group/security-as-a-service/#_overview. Accessed 6 Apr 2017
6. Messmer E (2013) Gartner: cloud-based security as a service set to take off. In: Network World. http://www.networkworld.com/article/2171424/data-breach/gartner--cloud-based-security-as-a-service-set-to-take-off.html. Accessed 6 Apr 2017
7. Network Functions Virtualisation. http://www.etsi.org/technologies-clusters/technologies/nfv. Accessed 6 Apr 2017
8. (2014) Network Functions Virtualisation (NFV); NFV Security; Security and Trust Guidance. http://www.etsi.org/deliver/etsi_gs/NFV-SEC/001_099/003/01.01.01_60/gs_NFV-SEC003v010101p.pdf. Accessed 6 Apr 2017
9. (2014) Network Functions Virtualisation (NFV); Management and Orchestration. http://www.etsi.org/deliver/etsi_gs/NFV-MAN/001_099/001/01.01.01_60/gs_nfv-man001v010101p.pdf. Accessed 6 Apr 2017
10. Herbaut N (2015) D5.1 Network Function Store. http://www.t-nova.eu/wp-content/uploads/2016/03/TNOVA_D5_1_Network_Function_Store_v1.0.pdf. Accessed 6 Apr 2017
11. Vapnik V, Cheryonenkis A (1974) Theory of pattern recognition
12. Gerdsri N, Kocaoglu D (2007) Applying the analytic hierarchy process (AHP) to build a strategic framework for technology road mapping. Math Comput Model 46:1071–1080. doi:10.1016/j.mcm.2007.03.015
13. (2017) Open Cloud Integrity Technology (Open CIT). In: Intel Open Source. https://01.org/opencit. Accessed 6 Apr 2017
14. (2017) Trusted Platform Module (TPM). http://www.trustedcomputinggroup.org/trusted-platform-module-tpm-summary/. Accessed 6 Apr 2017
15. Asokan N, Niemi V, Nyberg K (2005) Man-in-the-Middle in Tunnelled Authentication Protocols. Security Protocols 28–41. Doi:10.1007/11542322_6
16. OpenTC – Open Trusted Computing. In: Technikon. https://www.technikon.com/projects/former/opentc. Accessed 6 Apr 2017
17. TClouds – Trustworthy Clouds. In: Technikon. https://www.technikon.com/projects/former/tclouds. Accessed 6 Apr 2017
18. SECURED – SECURity at the network EDge. https://www-secured-fp7.eu. Accessed 6 Apr 2017
19. Jacquin L, Shaw A, Dalton C (2015) Towards trusted software-defined networks using a hardware-based Integrity Measurement Architecture. In: Proceedings of the 2015 1st IEEE conference on Network Softwarization (NetSoft). Doi:10.1109/netsoft.2015.7116186
20. TeNOR, FP7 T-NOVA. https://github.com/T-NOVA/TeNOR. Accessed 6 Apr 2017
21. Open Source Mano. https://osm.etsi.org. Accessed 6 Apr 2017
22. (2016) Catalogue and Repository, 5G–PPP SONATA. https://github.com/sonata-nfv/son-catalogue-repos. Accessed 6 Apr 2017
23. Kill chain. In: Wikipedia. https://en.wikipedia.org/wiki/Kill_chain. Accessed 6 Apr 2017
24. Apache Kafka, distributed streaming platform. https://kafka.apache.org. Accessed 6 Apr 2017
25. Apache Storm, open source distributed real-time processing of data. http://storm.apache.org/. Accessed 6 Apr 2017
26. Apache Spot, open source solution for packet and flow analytics. https://spot.apache.org. Accessed 6 Apr 2017
27. Blei D, Ng A, Jordan M (2003) Latent dirichlet allocation. J Mach Learn Res 3:993–1022

Hamza Attak (Hewlett Packard Labs, Hewlett Packard Enterprise).

Hamza Attak graduated in 2011 with an MSc in computer science and modelling from the ISIMA in Clermont-Ferrand, France. After spending 3 years as a researcher at NIST in the High Performance Computing Group working on the National Vulnerability Database, he is now a research engineer at Hewlett Packard Enterprise in Bristol where he focusses on cybersecurity. Recently, he is spending most of his time in the Linux kernel, mainly extending network and security functionalities.

Marco Casassa-Mont (Hewlett Packard Labs, Hewlett Packard Enterprise).

Marco has been working at HP Labs since 1996. He holds an MSc in computer science from the University of Turin. He is a technical leader and security software architect. His current work focuses on big data for security: creating new solutions and novel security data analytics to detect and mitigate unknown threats. He was a member of the EU PRIME project and the lead of the UK TSB EnCoRe collaborative project.

Cristian Dávila (Fundació i2CAT, Internet I Innovació Digital a Catalunya).

Cristian Dávila holds a computer science engineering degree from the Universitat Politècnica de Catalunya and an MSc degree in artificial intelligence. He has researched in artificial neural networks field, drug discovery and learning by demonstration on robotics. His expertise is in the field of computer science, cybersecurity and machine learning. His research interests include artificial intelligence, machine learning, robotics, data engineering and big data.

Eleni-Constantina Davri (Orion Innovations Private Company).

Eleni-Constantina Davri holds an electrical and computer engineering diploma from the University of Patras, Greece (2009). Since 2012, she has been a PhD candidate in radio networks at Information and Communication Systems Department of the University of the Aegean. She has participated in GREENET project (GA 264759) as a Marie-Curie early stage researcher (2011–2014). Davri is the R&D project manager of ORION Innovations for the projects MENTA (GA 318389) and SHIELD (GA 700199).

Carolina Fernandez (Fundació i2CAT, Internet I Innovació Digital a Catalunya).

Carolina Fernández holds a computer science engineering degree from the Autonomous University of Barcelona (UAB, 2011). Her work deals with software networks-based applications and infrastructures, their management and federation, as applied in several FIRE projects. Her research interests include SDN, NFV, virtualisation, automation and security.

Georgios Gardikis (Space Hellas S.A.).

Dr. Georgios Gardikis received his diploma (2000) and PhD (2004) in electrical and computer engineering from the National Technical University of Athens. He is currently R&D manager at Space Hellas SA, supervising a number of national and European research projects and coordinating the company's R&D activities. He is project manager for the ESA CloudSat study and the EU H2020 SHIELD project.

Bernat Gastón (Fundació i2CAT, Internet I Innovació Digital a Catalunya).

Dr. Gastón holds a degree in computer science engineering from the Autonomous University of Barcelona (UAB, 2008), an MSc degree in data science (Compression, Codification and Security) and a PhD in distributed and cloud data storage (UAB, 2013), which received a "summa cum laude" mark. He is currently the head of the "Big Data Architectures and Techniques" unit in Fundació I2CAT.

Ludovic Jacquin (Hewlett Packard Labs, Hewlett Packard Enterprise).

Dr. Ludovic Jacquin holds an MSc in applied mathematics and computer science by ENSIMAG (Grenoble, France) in 2006 and received his PhD in computer science from Grenoble University (France) in 2013. His current research focuses on trust and attestation of the network infrastructure in the new paradigm of SDN and their application to related environment such as cloud or NFV. He contributed to the EU FP7 SECURED project and is Hewlett Packard Labs leader in the H2020 SHIELD project.

Antonio Lioy (Politecnico di Torino).

Antonio Lioy (MSc in electronic engineering, PhD in computer engineering) is full professor of computer engineering at the Politecnico di Torino, where he leads the TORSEC research group active in ICT security. Professor Lioy has been working since 1994 in the field of computer and network security, with special emphasis on PKI, e-identity, network and application security and policy- and ontology-based design of the protection for large information systems.

Antonis Litke (Infili Technologies Private Company).

Dr. Litke is cofounder and business development director at Infili Technologies PC. He holds a diploma in computer engineering and informatics from the University of Patras (1999) and a PhD in electrical and computer engineering from the National Technical University of Athens (2006). He has more than 14 years of experience as a professional IT engineer in several organisations and positions.

Nikolaos K. Papadakis (Infili Technologies Private Company).

Nikolaos Papadakis (MSc in electrical and computer engineering, PhD in computer engineering from NTUA) is an assistant professor of computer engineering at Hellenic Army Academy, where he leads the research lab "Artificial Intelligence and Distributed Systems". Dr. Papadakis has been working since 2001 in the field of distributed systems and intelligence agents for large information systems. He is cofounder and CTO at Infili Technologies PC.

Dimitris Papadopoulos (Infili Technologies Private Company).

works as a systems engineer at Infili Technologies PC. He received his diploma degree in mechanical engineering from the National Technical University of Athens (2014) and his master's degree in systems engineering from the Hellenic Army Academy and the Technical University of Crete. He is currently a PhD candidate at the same institution. His research interests include distributed machine learning and data mining, big data processing and analysis, cybersecurity and threat detection.

Jerónimo Núñez (Telefónica Investigación y desarrollo S.A.).

Jerónimo has a degree as technical engineer of telecommunications in the Polytechnic University of Madrid (UPM) in 1995. He joined Telefonica I+D in 1998. He has developed skills in networking, security and NFVs. His current work is focused on the design and certification of NFV architectures aimed at enhancing the optimisation and deployment of virtualised IP Edge solutions and network services.

Eleni Trouva (National Center for Scientific Research "Demokritos").

Ms. Eleni Trouva received her diploma in computer engineering from the University of Patras, Greece, in 2006 and a master of science in computer science from the Athens University of Economics and Business in 2009. She then joined the i2CAT, where she initially contributed in the GEANT3 project and then in the IRATI project. In 2013 she joined the Institute of Informatics and Telecommunications of NCSR Demokritos, where she is currently working on the CHARISMA and SHIELD projects.

Part III

Security Implications of SDNFV in Future Networks

Addressing Industry 4.0 Security by Software-Defined Networking

Rahamatullah Khondoker, Pedro Larbig, Dirk Scheuermann,
Frank Weber, and Kpatcha Bayarou

9.1 Introduction

Preceded by three industrial evolutions with the virtue of innovation in basic technologies such as mechanics (first evolution, beginning in the 1780s), electricity (second evolution, beginning from the 1870s), and electronics and computation (third evolution, starting from the 1970s), the vision for the fourth industrial evolution (in German called Industrie 4.0) has been started by the German government in 2011 [1]. German activities are mostly driven by the German association with the title Platform Industrie 4.0. The aim of this campaign is to improve the economy of the European (especially German) region by creating platforms for smart factories where the key enablers are interconnection (Internet) of all of the components by information and communication technologies (ICT) including cyber-physical systems (CPS) and the Internet of things (IoT) [2].

Similar to Industrie 4.0, coexisting approaches are seen internationally, e.g., by the Advanced Manufacturing Partnership and Industrial Internet Consortium (IIC) in the USA, by Industrial Value Chain Initiative (IVI) in Japan, and Made in China 2025 and Internet Plus initiatives [3] in China. These associations also work together with the previously mentioned German association. There exist different concerns in the different countries, depending on the individual business structures and strategies, and the term of the fourth industrial evolution is synchronized with

R. Khondoker (✉) • P. Larbig • D. Scheuermann • F. Weber • K. Bayarou
Fraunhofer Institute for Secure Information Technology (Fraunhofer SIT), Rheinstr. 75, 64295,
Darmstadt, Germany
e-mail: rahamatullah.khondoker@sit.fraunhofer.de; pedro.larbig@sit.fraunhofer.de;
dirk.scheuermann@sit.fraunhofer.de; frank.weber@sit.fraunhofer.de;
kpatcha.bayarou@sit.fraunhofer.de

© Springer International Publishing AG 2017
S.Y. Zhu et al. (eds.), *Guide to Security in SDN and NFV*, Computer
Communications and Networks, DOI 10.1007/978-3-319-64653-4_9

the German initiatives. However, the general idea is always the same: Production machines shall be connected via the Internet and be equipped with automatic control of production processes and protection against attacks from inside and outside.

The International term for Industrie 4.0 is Industry 4.0/Integrated Industry [4], and we will use the term Industry 4.0 for the general idea mentioned above. The technologies that are currently available in the production, i.e., preceding Industry 4.0, will be referred to as "pre-Industry 4.0" in this chapter. The assumption is that "pre-Industry 4.0" production machines have only very limited Internet connectivity; hence, they have very limited usage of security functionalities and do not fulfill the security requirements necessary for Internet connectivity.

Similar to office/enterprise networks, IT security (with a dedicated focus especially on network security) is considered as one of the most important aspects of Industry 4.0 as the enabling information and communication technologies (ICT) may bring threats to production networks (e.g., due to vulnerabilities in the enabling technologies, lack of protection capabilities of industrial control systems protocols, etc.). Therefore, especially to ensure network security in Industry 4.0, the IUNO project has been launched by the German Federal Ministry of Education and Research (BMBF) [5].

The aim of IUNO is to identify security threats and risks for Industry 4.0 factories (sometimes called smart factories), develop proactive measures to tackle the identified threats and risks, and implement those measures in application scenarios corresponding to the four items *secure process* (customer-specific production), *secure data* (technological data market), *secure service* (remote maintenance), and *secure network* (visual security control room), respectively.

To contribute in achieving the aim of IUNO, software-defined networking (SDN) is investigated for Industry 4.0 since it can be used intelligently to automate manifold tasks, including, but not limited to, user administration, routing, monitoring, controlling, security, and configurability. These tasks could also be accomplished using traditional non-SDN-based proprietary networking devices (such as switches and routers), which however require manual effort. The proprietary networking devices are statically placed in a particular location in a network, necessary to configure each of those devices individually, complex (hardware part of a device contains billions of gates, and the software part consisting of OS and applications is the implementation of more than 6000 standard documents), not programmable (contains no open/standard API), and difficult to manage (having no centralized configuration/management possibilities).

To tackle these issues, SDN decouples control plane of a networking device from the data plane where the planes communicate with each other by using protocols such as OpenFlow [6] so that the data plane can be directly programmed. As shown in [7] which is authored by Open Networking Foundation (ONF), the SDN architecture consists of three layers: infrastructure layer, control layer, and application layer (see Fig. 9.1). The control layer consisting of a network operating system, also called SDN control software, enables programmability of the network devices located in the infrastructure layer through the so-called SDN southbound interface (SBI) protocols. Some examples of SBI protocols are OpenFlow, the Network

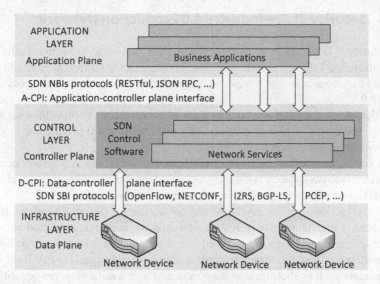

Fig. 9.1 SDN architecture from Open Networking Foundation [7]

Configuration (NETCONF) protocol, Interface to the Routing System (I2RS), Path Computation Element Protocol (PCEP), and Border Gateway Protocol with Link State (BGP-LS). The interface between the application plane and the controller plane is called application-controller plane interface (A-CPI). The application layer which implements business logics communicates with the controller located in the control layer through the so-called SDN northbound interface (NBI) protocols such as Representational State Transfer (REST/RESTful) and JavaScript Object Notation Remote Procedure Call (JSON-RPC). The interface between the controller plane and the data plane is called data-controller plane interface (D-CPI). There are many open-source and proprietary controllers in the market. Most prominent open-source ones are the Open Network Operating System (ONOS), OpenDaylight, Python version of network operating system (POX), and Ryu. A comparison of some controllers considering the criteria such as interfaces used, GUI availability, REST API support, documentation, programming languages support, TLS, and OpenFlow protocol support can be found in [8].

Motivated by the utilization of SDN architectures to improve network security such as OrchSec [9, 10] and AutoSec [11], this chapter describes how the security of Industry 4.0 could be improved by SDN. The architecture described in Sect. 9.2 is just an example for a pre-Industry 4.0 factory and its respective security status. From this state of the art, the requirements for Industry 4.0 are derived in Sect. 9.3. For example, two of the Industry 4.0 security functionalities, namely, industrial IDS/IPS and secure remote maintenance service, are explained in Sects. 9.4.1 and 9.4.2. Section 9.5 gives a short discussion on the relevance of the proposed SDN-based solutions for the security requirements mentioned before. Finally, the chapter is concluded with the summary in Sect. 9.6.

9.2   Security of Pre-Industry 4.0 Production Network

Pre-Industry 4.0 production machines and their network were not built to be connected to the Internet; therefore, their characteristics are different from office/enterprise IT components which were built considering Internet connectivity as shown in Table 9.1.

By deploying intermediate devices such as middleboxes (firewall/packet filter), however, industries started to connect their pre-Industry 4.0 production machines and networks to the Internet.

The protocols that are used within pre-Industry 4.0 production networks can be categorized into two types: classical Fieldbus and industrial Ethernet protocol. Some examples of protocols for production networks are shown in Table 9.2.

The production network protocols are not secure by design, therefore, lack of basic security mechanisms to provide confidentiality, authentication, and integrity.

Encryption mechanisms are required to ensure data confidentiality; however, no such mechanisms exist in these protocols as these were designed to fulfill the safety requirements such as short transmission time and high availability, not security. The encryption mechanisms from IT may not fulfill those requirements.

Authentication mechanisms (password based, certificate based, biometrics, multifactor, single sign-on, etc.) are required to protect from threats including message/identity spoofing and non-repudiation. Except Secure DNP3 (the security extension of DNP), no other classical Fieldbus and industrial Ethernet protocols in Table 9.2 provide authentication mechanism.

To protect data from tampering by man-in-the-middle attacks (i.e., message spoofing, identity spoofing, and replay attacks), integrity protection mechanisms

Table 9.1 Comparison of pre-Industry 4.0 production machine and enterprise IT component

Criteria	Production machine	IT component
Example	Shaping machine	Web server
Longevity (approximately in years)	10–30	0.5–3
Internet connectivity	No	Yes
Security (methods available)	Yes (isolated by air gap)	Yes
Safety (mechanisms available)	Yes	Yes
Updatability requirement	Seldom	Often
Availability requirement	High	High

Table 9.2 Examples of production network protocols

Classical fieldbus	Industrial Ethernet protocol
PROFIBUS	EtherCAT
Modbus	SERCOS III
DNP3	PROFINET
ControlNet	EtherNetIP
DeviceNet	ModbusTCP
Secure DNP3	POWERLINK

such as Secure Hash Algorithm 3 (SHA-3), Message Digest 5 (MD5), and Hash-based Message Authentication Code (HMAC) are required. However, no other classical Fieldbus and industrial Ethernet protocols except DNP3 and Secure DNP3 in Table 9.2 provide this mechanism. It is worthy to note that cyclic redundancy check (CRC) and checksum are not integrity protection mechanisms but error detection mechanisms.

In pre-Industry 4.0 production network, add-on security was used to protect the network, for example, Common Industrial Protocol Security (CIP Security) [12] was used as an add-on to protect the Ethernet/IP protocol by integrating authentication, encryption, and integrity check mechanisms.

For Industry 4.0, well-known, secure, and standardized protocols of the office networks such as Transport Layer Security (TLS), Internet Protocol Security (IPsec), Secure Socket Shell (SSH), Wi-Fi Protected Access 2 (WPA2), Open Platform Communications Unified Architecture (OPC UA), Data Distribution Service (DDS), Message Queue Telemetry Transport (MQTT), and Datagram Transport Layer Security (DTLS) could be used to secure the production networks. However, these protocols add latency and cannot guarantee any safety properties.

To improve the security of pre-Industry 4.0 production network, one or more security (hardware/software) devices such as a firewall or packet filter is used, though they cannot handle some security threats, for example, malware, when brought into the network using a memory stick (as happened in the Stuxnet scenario). Two general approaches are followed to deploy such a security system. One option is to place a complementary hardware device which consists of several security functionalities such as firewall and packet filter. Another option is to deploy a router which connects the production network with the Internet and can be configured to enable, for example, firewall, packet filter, etc. functions. In this case, no additional hardware device is needed for security.

In some cases, firewalls are used between the pre-Industry 4.0 production network and the Internet so that only the packets/flows matching the firewall rules are allowed to enter the production network and the unmatched packets/flows are rejected. Each packet/flow that is sent to the production network from the Internet is checked by the firewall against a set of rules that are called firewall rules and are defined either by the network administrator or by firewall vendor (these default rules are used when no expert network administrator is available). Some simple firewall rules are shown in Table 9.3 where each rule consists of a *rule number*, the *protocol* for which the rule is valid, the particular network or port the packet departs *from*, the particular network or port *to* which the packet is sent, and the *action* to be taken where two valid actions are *allow* and *deny*.

Besides firewall, a network address translation (NAT) is also used in pre-Industry 4.0 production network. Though the original purpose of NAT was to alleviate the problem of "Shortage of IPv4 addresses to identify all devices in the Internet as it can address 2^{32} devices uniquely," however industries mistakenly use it as a security module. A NAT, which is usually integrated in the edge router, translates from the private IP address to the public IP address (in case of outgoing traffic) so that only that public IP address is visible in the outside world while keeping the address of

Table 9.3 Some exemplary firewall rules

Rule No.	Protocol	From	To	Action
1.	IP	217.224.0.0/11	217.10.48.0/20	Allow
2.	IP	217.10.48.0/20	Any	Allow
3.	TCP	Any	5060	Deny
4.	UDP	Any	69	Deny
5.	DNS	Any	Any	Allow
6.	SMTP	Any	Any	Allow

the production machines hidden. In case of incoming traffic, the NAT translates from the public IP address to the private address. However, NAT alone (without firewall) does not protect from stateless NAT devices that allow all types of traffic even from the attackers. Besides, NAT alone cannot prevent outbound attacks from Stateful NAT hosts [13].

The disadvantages of these security solutions are stated below:

1. Proprietary/vendor locked and therefore these solutions are not programmable.
2. Static in nature as, for example, the firewall rules are predefined for a long duration and placed in a particular point.
3. Difficulty in configuration when there exist many such devices which are managed one by one.
4. No central overview of the configuration as each of the security devices is treated individually.

Considering a large company which requires to configure several security devices, each of these devices is configured manually. To configure several devices manually in a consistent way could be difficult to manage as there is no central overview of the configuration. As manual configuration is also time-consuming, the production machines may not be online during that time period which could result in production downtime.

Therefore, Industry 4.0 production networks will require network devices which will be programmable and centrally managed so that new security policies could be deployed immediately as a response to attacks.

9.3 Industry 4.0 Production Network: A Scenario

An architectural scenario for Industry 4.0 production network is shown in Fig. 9.2. Such a network may include production network, office network, SDN switches, and central platform. Several machines including shaping, drilling, and milling are connected to the production network.

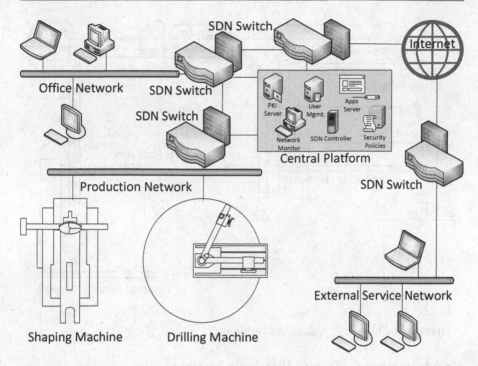

Fig. 9.2 A scenario of Industry 4.0 production network

In this scenario, the central platform server consists of components such as PKI server, application (app) server, user administration and management, network monitor, SDN controller, security policies, routing, etc.

One of the expectations for the success of Industry 4.0 is to increase protection of production machines and components without sacrificing their availability. Therefore, Industry 4.0 production network should support both proactive (encryption, firewall, etc.) and reactive (IDS/IPS) mechanisms. One way to achieve this aim is that the configuration efforts for the firewalls should be minimum which can be achieved by employing SDN-based switches in the networks that can be automatically programmed to create dynamic firewalls. Another way is to be able to detect and mitigate machine faults and illegitimate intruders automatically. This requires an intrusion detection system (IDS), referred to as industrial IDS here to differentiate it from the IDS of an office network. Whereas an office network IDS supports TCP/IP, UDP/IP protocol stacks, industrial IDS supports classical Fieldbus and industrial Ethernet protocols as well.

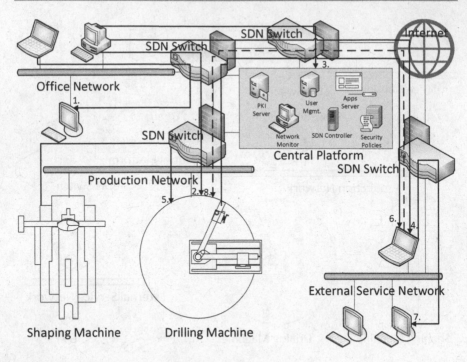

Fig. 9.3 Attack scenario of Industry 4.0 production network

9.3.1 Attack Model

Industrial networks with their often sophisticated structure, involving several network segments and hierarchies, are not easy to protect efficiently against illegitimate traffic originating from sources located at both the outside (outsider threats) or the inside (insider threats) of the network. The threat surface of an Industry 4.0 production network scenario is shown in Fig. 9.3 where the bold black color and dashed black color lines represent insider and outsider threats, respectively.

Some of the insider threats are shown in the figure marked with the bold black color lines and are enumerated in the following:

1. A node in the office network attacks another node(s) in the same network.
2. A node in the office network attacks one or more production machines located in the production network.
3. A node in the office network attacks the central platform.
4. A node in the office network attacks one or more nodes in the Internet.
5. A production machine attacks another production machine.
6. A production machine attacks one or more nodes in the Internet.
7. A node in the external service network attacks another node in that network.

Besides, employees may (un)intentionally download the malwares (virus, Trojans, worms, etc.) from the Internet using e-mail, browser, or other applications. They might also bring the malwares in their USB or other external memory drives. These malwares could be the source of insider threats.

Outsiders could attack the central platform, the office network within the factory, or the production network. This outsider threat is marked as threat no. 8 with the dashed black color line.

To protect industrial networks from both insider and outsider threats, some security functionalities are described in the following: industrial IDS, dynamic firewall, and secure remote maintenance service. These applications are hosted in the app server.

9.4   Examples of Industry 4.0 Security Functionalities

In industrial communication, protection mainly focuses on reactive security, that is, detecting and mitigating any unwanted actions (such as network traffic originating from untrusted sources). This comes naturally as, in contrast to office IT installations, availability and safety have the top priorities for production networks and confidentiality only plays a minor role there. Additionally, these requirements must often be fulfilled by equipment that uses unsupported and outdated software [14] not well suited for the use in industrial installations. A major problem results from the fact that while production machines are built to run multiple decades, the computer operating system that executes the machine-controlling software is typically considered archaic after only a few years. Furthermore, it is a typical case that neither operating systems nor control software are patched or upgraded during the lifetime of a production machine. This aversion to software updates in production machines is justified by the very fragile update processes of the most used operating systems that pose a significant threat to a machine's availability.

Still, attacks on these vulnerable machines were hardly possible since they were only connected to a local network. They did not communicate with the world outside the factory and thus never had to deal with everyday malware activities. However, with the advent of the new industrial revolution, more and more direct or indirect ways are built to send data to those machines in order to allow customers to customize their products or to let maintenance providers work remotely. If these data exchange corridors are established with legacy machines which still run unmaintained and vulnerable software, it can enable attackers and competitors to take control of production.

In the long run, these vulnerable systems will become replaced, and new technology is required that introduces update processes which do not interfere with a system's operation [15, 16]. In the short term, however, it is crucial to protect the existing technology as good as possible while not interfering with its functionality and safety properties.

Thus, we propose an extensive monitoring layer to be introduced by factory operators that passively collects and correlates input data from multiple data sources:

- **Communication data, traffic samples:** Network taps and monitor ports extract copies of packets observed on Ethernet-based field bus installations, SCADA networks, and office networks. The major challenge here is the sheer number of protocols in use. Almost every influential vendor of industrial automation products has established its own protocol. In order to be able to efficiently extract the relevant data out of the captured traffic data, parser generators (like HILTI [17] and Spicy [18]) and packet processing languages (like P4 [19]) can be used, as shown by Udd et al. [20].
- **Event management:** Existing security information and event management (SIEM) systems provide access to log files from the office IT world, including the perimeter firewalls. Additional collectors need to be developed by SIEM integrators to read out and forward events from the SCADA systems and logic controllers to the central IDS.
- **Enterprise management sources:** These sources add metadata to the pool of information provided to the IDS by making information available that describes what to expect when and where. This does contain sets of assignments. Examples are:
  - Employee timetables provide assignments between employees and work time. This can be used to detect account abuse (i.e., log-in, while employee is not working).
  - Inventory listings provide assignments between MAC addresses and device owner.
  - Quality assurance reports provide assignments between time and production quality to correlate system changes to overall production efficiency.
- **Engineering sources:** Provides boundary conditions of operation inside machine specification. Specification documents and data sheets of the devices used in production help in interpreting the field bus traffic to decide if the observed messages might indicate a sabotage attempt, in order to ensure that the software that is being sent to the devices is known to operate inside these specifications. Thus, this data source can also contain hashes and/or signatures for known PLC software to assess any programming actions.

The data that is collected should be preprocessed by the source and then sent to the central intrusion detection system that is outlined in the following section. Preprocessing and filtering are required to reduce the amount of data that is sent to the central IDS, as some data sources can be quite data intensive. Especially modern field bus protocols can generate continuous streams of control data at high bit rates [21] while not providing relevant input as long as the known cycles are performed. Still, a small and unexpected change can be a clear indicator of compromise.

This process can employ reporting protocols using incident descriptors as proposed by the Intrusion Detection Message Exchange Format (IDMEF, [22]) and Incident Object Description Exchange Format (IODEF, [23]) Requests for Comments (RFC) in order to transport the information to the IDS.

9.4.1   Industrial IDS

The ultimate goal of an intrusion detection system for industrial networks is identical to that of a conventional IDS: detecting unwanted actions in the protected networks. These actions include attack attempts from external sources as well as sabotage acts from employees. However, the approaches differ in detail as an IDS in a production environment must not modify or suppress any communication since it may be relevant for safety. This results in the fact that an industrial IDS has to be deemed a passive device that relies on human interaction to counter any detected threats.

Another difference from conventional networks is the complexity of the observed processes in industrial network scenarios. While in IP-based office communication there is a small set of protocols (such as TCP) transporting all kinds of information (e.g., HTTP), in industrial networks, a large set of protocols (see Table 9.2 in Sect. 9.2) is used to transport machine control data. Thus, the complexity is based on the variety of means of transport and not on the transmitted data itself. This simplifies the processing of the payloads which in turn allows multiple approaches on how to generate IDS events out of the observed traffic and traffic patterns:

- **Rule-based anomaly detection:** This standard approach uses attack signatures to detect well-known malicious actions inside the network. All incoming communication is matched against a signature database in the IDS which triggers an alarm in case of a match. While this technique is rather basic, it also has some valuable advantages in industrial networks: The rules can be audited and verified to ensure correct operation and a low amount of false positives. Occurring threats can be classified into risk levels to make prioritization easier when an attack on multiple targets is launched. Additionally, signatures can be exchanged between networks and users to profit from the experience gathered in other installations. However, a major drawback is the inflexibility of this approach when targeting new attacks that have not been known before. If the attackers know what signatures are in place, they can easily circumvent the detection mechanism.
- **Machine learning:** Typically, industrial machines are operated for long periods of time without any significant changes of the production process. At the same time, industrial automation protocols often transport fixed-size and well-defined payloads to be processed by the machines. This fact makes the data exchanged in those networks a good candidate for input of machine learning algorithms that can be used to identify traffic anomalies. When introducing such mechanisms in a network, the algorithms usually start a learning phase first to accommodate to the expected traffic in the environment. In this period of time, the network operators must make sure that no unwanted or malicious actions take place and that all use cases are covered. After the learning phase is completed, the algorithm will then compare any incoming traffic with the previously seen patterns and raises an alert when the deviation between them is too high. On the positive side, an IDS based

on machine learning is very versatile and can be compatible with many protocols and use cases, as it dynamically adapts to the data that is presented. While this saves work for the IDS vendor, the users have to cope with several problems: First, they need to conduct a well-planned learning phase where nothing must interfere with this process or the resulting detection mechanism may be erratic. Also, if anything is changed in the way the machine works, another learning phase must be started to adapt to the changes made. The whole system is rather obscure as there is no easy way to audit and verify the resulting mechanisms. Additionally the output of the learning process can hardly be transferred to other machines and networks, most likely only to relatively similar installations.

- **Programmatic incident investigation:** This new approach supplies the users with tools that enable mimicking the actions of a human network administrator in case of a detected anomaly. Such a system shall provide a way to define actions that are taken after an initial detection to further substantiate the suspicion of a malicious activity. An incident investigation system thus needs access to external data sources that supply the required metadata that enables it to reach a verdict. These sources are mentioned in the beginning of Sect. 9.4. Obviously, the advantages of such a system are the very low amount of false positives combined with the fact that it instantly supplies the administrators with crucial details in case of an attack. Additionally, those systems can be configured to not only trace signs of attacks but also to monitor and manage production efficiency. This can put the high price of setup and maintenance of such systems into perspective.

These three approaches can and should be applied concurrently within an industrial IDS to improve the overall detection mechanism. These approaches could be implemented as SDN applications within the SDN controller when efficiency is given more priority than flexibility or outside of it when flexibility and multiple controllers support are given more importance. The advantage of SDN-enabled hardware in those scenarios is apparent, as they enable fine-grained control over the type of data to extract and send to the IDS for further inspection. When using OpenFlow protocol as an SDN SBI protocol, it supports 12 matchable fields in version 1.0 and 41 fields in version 1.4 [24]. The filtering and preprocessing of data, which can be done efficiently in SDN hardware and SDN controllers, can substantially reduce the load on the IDS and reduce or mitigate the impact of, e.g., denial of service (DoS) attacks.

9.4.2 Secure Remote Maintenance Service

There is no standard definition of the term remote maintenance or administration. For administrating (i.e., accessing, monitoring, repairing, controlling, etc.) an IT system component (such as a server, router, switch, computer) from a remote site (the remote place where the service engineer is located), a remote maintenance service is used. As there is no specific "remote" distance, it can range from several meters to several thousand kilometers. In terms of Industry 4.0, the components to be remotely managed, configured, or maintained are parts of industrial production machines located in the production site.

Remote maintenance does not only reduce OPEX for the enterprises by saving travel and accommodation costs for their employees to be physically in the production site but also increase production efficiency by maintaining (e.g., monitoring, identifying, and repairing) the problem with no travel delay. By intelligently utilizing wireless and wired communication technologies, remote maintenance is possible [25]. Therefore, from the 1990s, several approaches have been proposed to access, monitor, and maintain control processes remotely. Some of these approaches are Distributed Aircraft Maintenance Environment (DAME [26]), SCADA.web [27], and e-Diagnostics. However, security was not their main focal point. e-Diagnostics considered security in the guidebook revision 2.1 [28].

Until now, the main application of remote maintenance in IT and office environment was remote desktop, that is, accessing a computer from another computer where the screen of the remote computer is seen in the screen of the local computer and the remote computer can be operated using the local computer's keyboard and mouse. The mostly used software for remote desktop is Virtual Network Computation (VNC) which uses Remote Framebuffer Protocol (RFP) [29]. The VNC server (VNC server and X client) is installed in the remote computer, and the VNC client (VNC client and X server) is installed in the local computer. The problem with the VNC software is the high configuration effort required for both the client and the server. Besides, according to RFC 6143, "VNC Authentication is cryptographically weak and is not intended for use on untrusted networks."

To solve the abovementioned problems of the VNC software and to offer manageability and add-on security, a central server between the client and the server is used in products like TeamViewer and Netviewer. Irrespective of licenses (free and proprietary), there are around 80 remote desktop software (such as rdesktop, TeamViewer, and GoToMyPC) that are available in the market. Extensive comparison of those software (OS supports, features) can be found at [30]. In terms of security, on the one hand, software like TurboVNC has no built-in encryption and access permission request; on the other hand, software like TeamViewer has AES-256 built-in encryption and requires access permission requests.

The main features of remote desktop and remote maintenance are opposed to each other in Table 9.4. Teradici Personal Computer over Internet Protocol (PCoIP) solution [31] is similar to remote desktop; however, the product is optimized for performance (supports two or four displays, 60fps). In terms of security, it supports AES-128/AES-256 Suite B ciphers. According to their secure remote connections feature, "Mitigate the risk associated with remote data storage on desktops and laptops with Workstation Access Software. Our PCoIP protocol encrypts and authenticates all transmissions – and only transmits encoded pixels, not data."

9.4.2.1 Commercial Solutions for Remote Maintenance

Several providers such as Netbiter [32], Genua [33], Phoenix Contact [34], and Siemens [35] offer products for remote maintenance security in industrial context. Netbiter remote management provides three different communication gateways (EasyConnect 220, 310, 350) to be placed in the production site. These gateways are connected to the system to be monitored using Modbus (Serial or Ethernet),

Table 9.4 Remote desktop versus remote maintenance

Criteria	Remote desktop	Remote maintenance
OS supports	Windows, Linux, Mac, iOS, Android, BlackBerry, OS/2, Windows Mobile, FreeBSD	Windows (e.g., Siemens SIMATIC IPC), Linux
Security protocols	AES, SSH, SSL/TLS	SSL/TLS, AES
Application protocols	RDP, VNC, X11	
Communication protocols	Ethernet, TCP/IP	CIP, EtherNet/IP, DeviceNet, CompoNet, ControlNet, process automation (i.e., PROFIBUS, Modbus), ICS (MTConnect, OPC)
Managed by organization	FCC, ITU, CEPT, CITEL	ODVA, Object Management Group (OMG)
Applications	Working in a remote computer	Building automation, substation automation, automatic meter reading, vehicle automation

EtherNet/IP, and I/O. In addition to providing hardware products, Netbiter offers three different services for their customers: remote access, view and control, and manage and analyze. The first two services which support one remote user and one production system to be remotely accessed are free with hardware gateways, but the last one which supports multiple remote users and multiple production systems to be remotely accessed is subscription based. In terms of security, on the client side, Netbiter QuickConnect software creates a secure tunnel to the Netbiter gateway through a mobile or fixed network. The communication between the client and the gateway is encrypted. Optionally, Netbiter also provides a two-step verification method (password log-in and SMS-based verification). Netbiter stores data received from Netbiter gateway to Netbiter Argos data center in the cloud so that these data can be used for different purposes including visualization, forensic, error investigation, and forecasting. Netbiter's monitored data between the gateway and the cloud is encrypted.

Similar to Netbiter communication gateways, Genua offers a hardware box called genubox which is also installed in the production site where the machine (called supervised machine) is located which will be remotely monitored by the service engineer. Locally, a wired connection is established between the genubox and the supervised machine; however, the communication between the genubox and the supervised machine is not encrypted. For the global connection, genubox has both firewall and VPN functionalities, and all of the communication between the service engineer computer (the client) which is located outside the production site (remote site) and the gateway which is located in the production site is encrypted. To protect from repudiation, Genua records all of the activities of the remote maintainer in a video file. In addition, Genua offers a graphical user interface (GUI) for the settings of the remote access, for example, a service personnel is allowed to access a machine remotely on Monday between 10:00 and 12:00 o'clock.

Phoenix Contact offers a platform called mGuard Tele Service for the secure remote maintenance. In the production site, it uses a hardware called mGuard industrial rs to connect to the machine to be monitored/supervised. This hardware has integrated mGuard firewall technology and hardware-based encryption. On the client/service center side, a hardware is used, called mGuard bladepack, which provides both a firewall and VPN gateway. Therefore, all of the communication between the remote site (mGuard bladepack) and industrial site (mGuard industrial rs) is transmitted through an IPsec tunnel. Phoenix Contact has mGuard device manager (mdm) to centrally manage all of the mGuard devices. Siemens offers an industrial modem SCALANCE M which ensures remote access to distant plants with the integrated firewall and VPN security functions [35].

9.4.2.2 Standards for Secure Remote Maintenance Service

In the area of remote maintenance, standardization activities currently haven't progressed very far. Actual activities mainly concentrate on the definition of security recommendations by the German Federal Office for Information Security (BSI). A set of security recommendations for remote maintenance solutions for IT in enterprises [36] and in the production [37] have actually been defined. BSI defined eight basic access rules for remote maintenance for IT in enterprises (three rules for home and small enterprise networks, three rules for big companies and governments, and two rules for security protection means for remote maintenance service providers) [37]. Though these rules are for IT in enterprises, they also generally apply for the production network. For improving the security of remote maintenance for industrial production, BSI defined a set of recommendations categorized into architecture, secure communication, authentication mechanisms, organizational requirements, and miscellaneous [38]. To improve industrial control system (ICS) security, BSI defined possible internal threats and mitigation mechanisms [37], top 10 threats and countermeasures for the years 2012 and 2014 (intrusion via remote access was the fifth threat in 2014 and was the topmost threat in 2012) [39], and two use cases swimming pool [40] and service technician [41]. In the first use case, the remote control interface of the component in the swimming pool (for heating, chlorine mixture, etc.) that was directly connected to the Internet was misused by the attacker. In the second use case, several control centers were infected by a virus that was unintentionally brought by the service technician in his USB stick from his personal computer.

9.4.2.3 Requirements for Secure Remote Maintenance Service for Industry 4.0

Existing solutions are based on well-known operating systems (OSs) such as Linux and Windows. According to [42], Kaspersky is building an industrial operating system (IOS) considering "Security by Design." As results of the Industry 4.0 or similar campaign, many such OSs might be developed in the future considering parameters such as security, performance, host/network size, SDN, virtualization environment, cloud, etc. Therefore, one of the requirements of the Industry 4.0 solution is to be independent of the OS. In addition, existing solutions do not provide any centralized management and control facilities for access rights where the access rules must be deployed on several machines concurrently.

9.4.2.4 Dynamic Firewalls for Secure Remote Maintenance

Dynamic firewalls are the most important component to realize the secure remote maintenance service for industrial networks to protect from both the insider and outsider threats. Typically, considering a real-world industrial network, several firewalls (see Sect. 9.2) have to be applied to effectively shield sensitive passages (both physical and organizational) between different networks and their segments against potentially harmful traffic. Hence, in most cases, gaining access to a certain network port of a specific industrial machine from outside the industrial network (e.g., from the Internet) is typically prevented by a cascade of firewalls. However, such a serial arrangement of shields also complicates a legitimate reach-through from foreign networks to components inside the industrial network. For example, this might be required in scenarios where machine condition information have to be monitored more or less frequently by the machine manufacturer or where software updates have to be uploaded to a production device (hence, in typical remote maintenance scenarios). Manually opening pinholes of every concerned firewall (and closing them again after the legitimate access mission has been completed) would cause unfeasible expenditure. SDN-based dynamic firewalling provides a solution for the automated instant reconfiguration and synchronization of rules for an arbitrary number of firewalls on a data path between defined sinks and sources within a network.

SDN-based dynamic firewalling rests upon an approach first described in the year 2012 in [43] to define and enforce individual-related or role-specific firewall policies. In this approach that emanated from a research project called DynFire funded by the German Federal Ministry of Education and Research, a novel central network entity called firewall manager is introduced. Besides being able to gain and dynamically maintain an overview on the network topology including further security-related network characteristics, the firewall manager administers access policies for every individual (or their functional roles, respectively, such as service technician for device X). In case of an access request from an authenticated individual to a specific network resource (such as a production device connected to an industrial network), by analyzing the network topology, the firewall manager identifies the network intersections that will be passed by the traffic flow caused by the intended access. Subsequently it will update the rules of all concerned firewalls in the network to allow the required data flows to pass. Once the access session involving the data flow has been completed, the firewall manager will again update the firewall rules, now closing the pinholes that had been opened before upon the access request.

9.4.2.5 SDN-Based Remote Maintenance Security Architecture

To achieve secure remote maintenance, as mentioned previously, several rules were defined by the BSI [36]. To go into more detail, for home or small business, the following rules should be considered:

1. Remote maintenance/diagnostics session must be started by the machine operator.
2. The remote maintenance connection must be encrypted.
3. The remote user or technician must be authenticated before accessing the system.

In addition to these rules, the following rules should be considered especially by
large enterprises and government offices:

4. At least during the remote maintenance session, the object to be repaired should
   be isolated from the rest of the networks to avoid any (intentional/unintentional)
   access to other machines or servers. At least one packet filter should be used for
   the isolation.
5. Configuration effort for the security gateway should be minimal.
6. The activities of the technician should be logged.

To fulfill these requirements, especially minimizing configuration efforts for the
security gateway, the SDN-based security architecture is proposed as shown in
Fig. 9.4.

The architecture works are as follows:

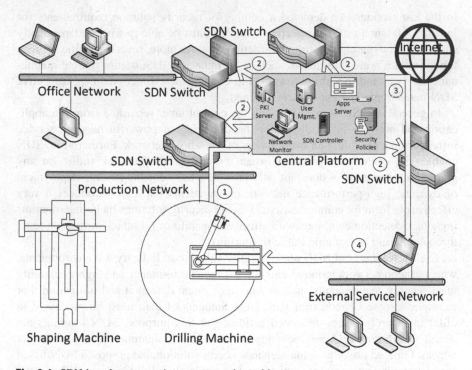

Fig. 9.4 SDN-based remote maintenance security architecture

1. Whenever an event is triggered by the production machine, for example, in a result of some error, one component is detached or a forged component is attached, the production machine sends a message to the central platform (where the SDN controller is located) for an action.
2. The central platform then checks the security and other policies (e.g., responsible person for the maintenance, security assertions, etc.) for this particular event. After selecting the maintenance engineer who is online, the central platform uses the SDN controller to configure all of the SDN switches between the engineer and the production machine conforming security policies. The assumption here is that the laptop/computer is online. If this is not the case, then an e-mail/SMS/IM is sent to the engineer to bring his/her device online.
3. The central platform then configures the engineer's laptop/computer according to the security policies. After that, it signals the engineer to start maintenance.
4. The maintenance engineer has now a connection with the production machine which conforms the security policies.

9.5   Discussion on Relevance of Proposed SDN-Based Security Solutions

In the last sections, we depicted a number of security solution requirements for Industry 4.0 (such as that respective solutions must be able to work independently and allow for dynamic and automatic action). Furthermore, several specific security functionalities were introduced, such as an industrial IDS, secure remote maintenance service, and dynamic firewalls. For each of these functionalities, respective SDN-based implementations were outlined.

In general, the SDN approach with the control layer separated from the application and network layer allows for the designing of powerful network service infrastructures providing an overall view of the whole network. Furthermore, SDN enables the central analysis and instant control of the network traffic on any given link. Hence, SDN does not only provide a basis for the flexible deployment of dynamic high-performance network environments but also introduces a very effective platform for comprehensive IT/cyber security solutions including monitoring/attack detection combined with effective capabilities for attack mitigation (e.g., through filtering or dynamic traffic re-routing).

These advantages of SDN are especially valuable in Industry 4.0 environments, where general network requirements such as high performance and high availability meet security requirements such as automatic threat detection and mitigation. For example, in case of industrial IDS, large amounts of data must be processed in order to securely detect unwanted actions. For this purpose, SDN solutions are useful for filtering and preprocessing the data and mitigating DDoS and further attacks. For a secure remote maintenance access solution, the proposed SDN-based security architecture provides a platform to completely fulfill the given BSI security guidelines.

9.6   Conclusion

In this chapter, we discussed the potential to use SDN as a basis for IT/cyber security solutions for Industry 4.0. Legacy firewalls with their static behavior and the lack of a central network/security policy overview and configurability will no longer be acceptable in modern and industrial networks connecting industrial machines and their components with the Internet. Industry 4.0 needs dynamic, easily configurable, and central policy-based security mechanisms that can be provided by intelligently using/adapting SDN technologies. Toward this, as examples, two security functionalities for Industry 4.0 were discussed in this chapter: an industrial intrusion detection system (IDS) and a secure remote maintenance service. When SDN will be used as a basis technology for Industry 4.0, more security components and services will be created and deployed easily as this will provide an innovation platform for the next industrial evolutions let alone Industry 4.0.

Exercise

1. What is the meaning of the number in "Industry 4.0," and what is the meaning of the preceding numbers 1–3?
2. What are the two general types of protocols to be used in production networks?
3. What are the Industry 4.0 similar initiatives from the USA, Japan, and China?
4. How many layers ONF SDN architecture have, and what are those layers and their functions?
5. Why is security an important aspect for Industry 4.0?
6. Please name some classical Fieldbus and industrial Ethernet protocols.
7. As an add-on to Ethernet/IP protocol, which security mechanism is used?
8. What are the disadvantages of non-SDN-based security solutions?
9. Why is current IDS/IPS not appropriate for Industry 4.0?
10. What are the advantages of remote maintenance compared to local maintenance?
11. Which protocol is used by the VNC software that is defined in RFC 6143? What are the advantages and drawbacks of this protocol?
12. BSI defined eight access rules for remote maintenance. What are those rules?
13. According to BSI top 10 threats and countermeasures document, what was the topmost threat in 2012?
14. Similar to the Table 9.3, please create a firewall rule to disable all connections from the IP address 46.38.224.0/24 to 217.224.0.0/11.

Answer

1. Check 9.1
2. Check 9.2
3. Check 9.1

4. Check 9.1
5. Check 9.1
6. Check 9.2
7. Check 9.2
8. Check 9.2
9. Check 9.4.1
10. Check 9.4.2
11. Check 9.4.2
12. Check 9.4.2
13. Check 9.4.2
14. **Solution:** Protocol: IP, From: 46.38.224.0/24, To: 217.224.0.0/11, Action: Deny

References

1. Zukunftsprojekt Industrie 4.0. https://www.bmbf.de/de/zukunftsprojekt-industrie-4-0-848. html. Online; Accessed 18 Nov 2016
2. Hermann M et al (2016) Design principles for industrie 4.0 scenarios. In: 2016 49th Hawaii international conference on system sciences, pp 3928–3937
3. Heilmann D et al (2016) Industrie 4.0 im Internationalen Vergleich. Eine Studie des Handelsblatt Research Institute, pp 1–144
4. Deutsche Bank Research, Taking point industry 4.0: huge potential for value creation waiting to be tapped. Created on 23 May 2014. http://www.dbresearch.com/servlet/reweb2. ReWEB?rwsite=DBR_INTERNET_EN-PROD&rwobj=ReDisplay.Start.class&document= PROD0000000000335628. Accessed 18 Nov 2016
5. IUNO, Nationales Referenzprojekt, IT-Sicherheit in Industrie 4.0. http://www.iuno-projekt.de/ (German national research project, available in German only). Online; Accessed 18 Nov 2016
6. McKeown M, Anderson T, Balakrishnan H, Parulkar G, Peterson L, Rexford J, Shenker S, Turner J (2008) OpenFlow: enabling innovation in campus networks. SIGCOMM Comput Commun Rev 38(2):69–74
7. ONF (2014) SDN architecture. ONF Technical Report TR-502, Open Networking Foundation, June 2014
8. Khondoker R, Zaalouk A, Marx R, Bayarou K (2014) Feature-based comparison of software defined networking (SDN) controllers. In: ICCSA, pp 1–7
9. Zaalouk A, Khondoker R, Marx R, Bayarou K (2014) OrchSec: an orchestrator-based architecture for enhancing network-security using network monitoring and SDN control functions. In: NOMS, pp 1–9
10. Zaalouk A, Khondoker R, Marx R, Bayarou K (2014) OrchSec demo: demonstrating the capability of an orchestrator-based architecture for network security, academic demo. In: ONS, pp 1–2
11. Khondoker R, Larbig P, Senf D, Bayarou K, Gruschka N (2016) AutoSecSDNSemo: demonstration of automated end-to-end security in software-defined networks, IEEE NetSoft 2016. In: IEEE NetSoft, pp 1–2
12. Batke B, Wiberg J, Dube D (2015) CIP security phase 1, secure transport for EtherNet/IP. In: 2015 ODVA industry conference
13. Davis R, The myth of network address translation as security. White paper, F5. https://f5.com/ Portals/1/Cache/Pdfs/2421/the-myth-of-network-address-translation-as-security.pdf. Online; Accessed 02 Dec 2016
14. Higgins KJ (2014) Windows XP Alive & Well in ICS/SCADA networks. Information week darkReading, Oct 2014

15. Poimboeuf J, Jennings S (2014) Introducing kpatch: dynamic kernel patching. Technical report, Red Hat, Feb 2014
16. Pavlík V (2014) kGraft – live patching of the Linux kernel. Technical report, SUSE, Maxfeldstrasse 5 90409 Nuremberg Germany, Mar 2014
17. Sommer R, Vallentin M, De Carli L, Paxson V (2014) HILTI: an abstract execution environment for deep, stateful network traffic analysis. In: Proceedings of the 2014 conference on internet measurement conference. ACM, pp 461–474
18. Sommer R, Amann J, Hall S, Spicy: a unified deep packet inspection framework dissecting all your data. Technical Report TR-15-004, International Computer Science Institute Berkeley, 1947 Center Street, Suite 600, Berkeley, California, 94704, Nov 2015
19. Bosshart P, Daly D, Gibb G, Izzard M, McKeown N, Rexford J, Schlesinger C, Talayco D, Vahdat A, Varghese G et al (2014) P4: programming protocol-independent packet processors. ACM SIGCOMM Comput Commun Rev 44(3):87–95
20. Udd R, Asplund M, Nadjm-Tehrani S, Kazemtabrizi M, Ekstedt M (2016) Exploiting bro for intrusion detection in a SCADA system. In: Proceedings of the 2nd ACM international workshop on cyber-physical system security. ACM, pp 44–51
21. PROFIBUS User Organization, Haid-und-Neu-Str. 7 76131 Karlsruhe Germany. PROFINET design guideline, version 1.04 edition, Nov 2010
22. Debar H, Curry D, Feinstein B (2007) The intrusion detection message exchange format (IDMEF). RFC 4765 (Experimental), Mar 2007
23. Danyliw R, Meijer J, Demchenko Y (2007) The incident object description exchange format. RFC 5070 (Proposed Standard), Dec 2007. Updated by RFC 6685
24. GT/Coursera SDN Course Travelogue – Week 5, https://www.sdnskills.com/learn/gtcoursera-sdn-course-travelogue-week-5/. Online; Accessed 04 Apr 2017
25. Thompson HA (2004) Wireless and internet communications technologies for monitoring and control. Control Eng Pract 12:781–791
26. Distributed Aircraft Maintenance Environment from 2002, http://www.cs.york.ac.uk/dame. Online; Accessed 03 Mar 2016
27. SCADA.web, https://www.scada-web.net/default.aspx. Online; Accessed 03 Mar 2016
28. Wohlwend H, e-Diagnostics guidebook: revision 2.1. http://www.sematech.org/docubase/document/4153deng.pdf. Online; Accessed 03 Mar 2016
29. Richardson T, Levine JR (2011) The remote framebuffer protocol. RFC 6143, Mar 2011. https://rfc-editor.org/rfc/rfc6143.txt
30. Comparison of remote desktop software, https://en.wikipedia.org/wiki/Comparison_of_remote_desktop_software. Online; Accessed 03 Mar 2016
31. Teradici PCoIP (PC over IP) solution, http://www.teradici.com/products-and-solutions/pcoip-products/remote-workstation-card. Online; Accessed 03 Mar 2016
32. Netbiter remote management, http://www.netbiter.com/. Online; Accessed 03 Mar 2016
33. Genua genubox, https://www.genua.de/loesungen/fernwartungs-appliance-genubox.html. Online; Accessed 03 Mar 2016
34. Remote Services Security / Secure Remote Maintenance, http://www.phoenixcontact-cybersecurity.com/en/solutions/remote-services-security. Online; Accessed 03 Mar 2016
35. Siemens Industrial Network Security, http://www.industry.siemens.com/topics/global/en/industrial-security/network-security/Pages/Default.aspx. Online; Accessed 03 Mar 2016
36. Recommendation: IT in the Company. BSI publications on cyber security. Basic rules for protecting remote maintenance accesses. BSI Recommendation, June 2013. https://www.allianz-fuer-cybersicherheit.de/ACS/DE/_/downloads/BSI-CS_054E.pdf?__blob=publicationFile&v=4
37. Recommendation: IT in Production. Industrial Control System Security. Inside threat. BSI Recommendation, May 2013. https://www.allianz-fuer-cybersicherheit.de/ACS/DE/_/downloads/BSI-CS_061E.pdf?__blob=publicationFile&v=2. Online; Accessed 04 June 2016
38. BSI Empfehlung: in der Produktion, Fernwartung im industriellen Umfeld. BSI Recommendation, Jan 2015. https://www.allianz-fuer-cybersicherheit.de/ACS/DE/_/downloads/BSI-CS_108.pdf?__blob=publicationFile&v=3 [available in German only]. Online; Accessed 04 June 2016

39. BSI recommendation: IT in production, industrial control system security, top 10 threats and counŧermeasures 2014. BSI recommendation, May 2016. https://www.allianz-fuer-cybersicherheit.de/ACS/DE/_/downloads/BSI-CS_005E.pdf?__blob=publicationFile&v=2. Online; Accessed 04 June 2016

40. BSI Empfehlung: IT in der Produktion, Fallbeispiel Schwimmbad. BSI Recommendation, Feb 2014. https://www.allianz-fuer-cybersicherheit.de/ACS/DE/_/downloads/BSI-CS_095a. pdf?__blob=publicationFile&v=3 (available in German only). Online; Accessed 04 June 2016

41. BSI Empfehlung: IT in der Produktion, Fallbeispiel Servicetechniker. BSI Recommendation, Mar 2014. https://www.allianz-fuer-cybersicherheit.de/ACS/DE/_/downloads/BSI-CS_095c. pdf?__blob=publicationFile&v=2 (available in German only). Online; Accessed 04 June 2016

42. Bruner J (2013) Industrial internet the machines are talking, 1st edn. O'Reilly Media, Sebastopol

43. Marx R, Kuntze N, Rudolph C, Bente I, Vieweg J (2012) Trusted service access with dynamic security infrastructure configuration. In: 18th Asia-Pacific conference on communications (APCC). IEEE, 2012

Rahamatullah Khondoker is with Fraunhofer SIT and TU Darmstadt since January 2013. Before that, he worked in TU Kaiserslautern from where he completed Dr.-Ing. in computer science on the topic "Description and Selection of Communication Services for Service Oriented Network Architectures" after completing M.Sc. in computer science from the University of Bremen. He was selected as a top ten researcher in 2015 by the academics.de. In addition, he was awarded from Ericsson in the year 2008 and from the FIA Research Roadmap group in October 2011. On 8 July 2015, he completed "University Teaching Certificate" from TU Darmstadt. He worked with the DFG project (PoSSuM), BMBF projects (G-Lab, G-Lab Deep, FutureIN, IUNO), EU projects (PROMISE, EuroNF, PRUNO), and several industry projects. Currently, his focus is on the security of Future Internet Architectures including SDN, NFV, 5G, IoT, and Industry 4.0.

Pedro Larbig studied computer science at the Technical University of Darmstadt and was hired as a research assistant by the Center for Advanced Security Research Darmstadt (CASED) where he developed tools for testing security properties of wireless routing protocols. As a long-term developer of software in C for network encryption and authentication protocols, he gained a deep practical understanding of these mechanisms. Joining Fraunhofer SIT in 2011, he now works on designing and implementing new cryptographic systems and analyzing the flaws of existing ones. While he implements cryptographic authentication algorithms, a strong focus is put on managing secrets securely. He gained intensive knowledge about how attackers can use or abuse protocols to leak information and how they gain control over remote systems or networks, broadening the spectrum to an adversary's perspective.

Dirk Scheuermann completed his diploma in mathematics at Technical University Darmstadt in 1994 and his Ph.D. at Justus-Liebig University Giessen in 1998. Both his diploma thesis and his Ph.D. thesis were done in cooperation with Fraunhofer SIT and dealt with cryptography. Since 1998, Dirk Scheuermann is working as a researcher at Fraunhofer SIT. His major interests are cryptography, smart card technology, data formats, protocols, and anomaly detection. In the last years, he worked in several EU projects (e.g., EVITA) and BMBF projects (ESUKOM, ANSII) in these areas. Actually, he is strongly involved into the IUNO project with the major task of designing cryptography-based piracy protection concepts for Industry 4.0.

Frank Weber is the deputy head of the Mobile Systems and Mobile Networks Department at Fraunhofer SIT. He holds a diploma with a focus on computer engineering and a Ph.D. in network technologies. Before joining Fraunhofer SIT in 2013, from 2003, he has contributed to a number of both public- and company-funded R&D projects in the fields of network technologies and real-time communications, first as a member of the Research Group for Telecommunication Networks at Frankfurt University of Applied Sciences, Germany, and from 2009 as a freelancing engineer.

From 2006 to 2012, he has been an associated member of a research cooperation team of the Centre for Security, Communications and Network Research (CSCAN) at Plymouth University, UK. His current research focus is on various security aspects of upcoming and future network architectures, such as SDN and 5G, and their applications, such as real-time communications and Industry 4.0.

Kpatcha Bayarou received his diploma in electrical engineering/automation engineering in 1989, a diploma in computer science in 1997, and his doctoral degree in computer science in 2001, all from the University of Bremen in Germany. He joined the Fraunhofer Institute for Secure Information Technology (Fraunhofer SIT) in 2001. He is the head of the Mobile Systems and Mobile Networks Department that focuses on cyber-physical systems and future Internet including vehicular communication. In addition, he managed several EU and nationally funded projects and published several conference papers related to security engineering of mobile communication systems, mobile network technology, NGN (next-generation networks), and future network technologies like SDN/NFV and 5G.

Security Requirements for Multi-operator Virtualized Network and Service Orchestration for 5G

10

Mateus Augusto Silva Santos, Alireza Ranjbar, Gergely Biczók, Barbara Martini, and Francesco Paolucci

10.1 Introduction

The next generation of communications systems, 5G, will enable the deployment of diverse services with different networking requirements. Unlike earlier generations which consider a general purpose network for all services, 5G will be able to assign network services based on specific networking needs. As it is envisioned by the 5G-PPP community, 5G will empower a diverse set of verticals such as factories of the future (FoF), health, automotive, and media and entertainment. In order to enable the deployment of differentiated capabilities, 5G employs the end-to-end network slicing approach based on virtualized resources [2, 3]. These slices require multi-operator orchestration at both the business and technical levels. From the business point of view, operators should negotiate and agree on a set of services that they are

M.A.S. Santos (✉)
Ericsson Telecomunicações S/A, Rod. Eng. Ermênio de Oliveira Penteado,
Km 57.5, 13337-300, Indaiatuba, Brazil
e-mail: mateus.santos@ericsson.com

A. Ranjbar
OY L M Ericsson AB, Hirsalantie 11, Jorvas, Finland
e-mail: alireza.ranjbar@ericsson.com

G. Biczók
CrySyS Lab, Department of Networked Systems and Services,
Budapest University of Technology and Economics, Budapest, Hungary
e-mail: biczok@crysys.hu

B. Martini
Consorzio Nazionale Interuniversitario per le Telecomunicazioni (CNIT), Pisa, Italy
e-mail: barbara.martini@cnit.it

F. Paolucci
Scuola Superiore Sant'Anna, Pisa, Italy
e-mail: fr.paolucci@sssup.it

© Springer International Publishing AG 2017
S.Y. Zhu et al. (eds.), *Guide to Security in SDN and NFV*, Computer
Communications and Networks, DOI 10.1007/978-3-319-64653-4_10

able to provide. From the technical point of view, operators should be able to assign (virtual) resources to services in an agile and flexible manner. Technologies such as NFV and SDN are key enablers for providing high flexibility and manageability in service allocation and orchestration through 5G slices. Moreover, since end-to-end 5G slices may span across different operators, security becomes of utmost importance. Operators should be able to negotiate and deliver services without revealing sensitive configurations or part of their virtual or physical resources to others. In addition, end-to-end slices may require high level of isolation at the control, management, and also at the resource layer. Some control operations of each slice may need to be isolated from other slices, and there should be a way to authenticate and monitor a large number of virtual services deployed across multiple operators.

In the following, we review SDN and NFV as key technologies in 5G and introduce our 5G multi-operator service orchestration architecture.

10.1.1 The Role of NFV and SDN in 5G

NFV and SDN will be an important part of 5G enabling the flexible, rapid, and cost-efficient deployment of network services. NFV decouples software from hardware and provides higher resource efficiency and scalable service deployability by virtualizing the network functions and resources. The virtualized services can be deployed on demand to achieve higher coverage or capacity. Another major benefit of NFV is that it allows operators to implement network services independent of the location. In fact, virtualized services are not anymore bounded to physical networks, and depending on the desired functionality, they can be implemented close to base stations (i.e., at the edge) or on a centralized data center.

While NFV is focused on virtualizing the network functions, SDN aims at offering a higher level of control over network resources by centralizing the control and management functions. SDN separates the control plane from the data (forwarding) plane; the control plane consists of a logically centralized and programmable controller, which has an abstract view of network resources. The higher programmability and abstraction in SDN allow operators to define customized 5G logical slices with different sets of services. NFV and SDN are complementary technologies in 5G. In fact, SDN can be part of NFV framework, particularly to enhance the controllability and manageability of NFV components.

10.1.2 Multi-operator Orchestration Architecture

In order to have a common view of 5G resource sharing and orchestration between operators, the 5GEx innovation project [1] proposed a hierarchical architecture shown in Fig. 10.1. At the highest level, customers and operators negotiate and agree on services; at the lowest level, virtual and physical network resources are assigned to customers.

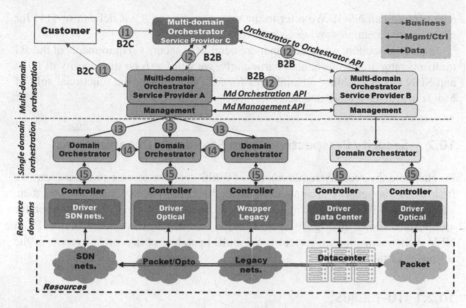

Fig. 10.1 5GEx multi-operator orchestration architecture [16]

The architecture illustrates the relation between different entities with a set of interfaces (I1 to I5). In this architecture, business agreements between an operator and a customer (i.e., business-to-customer, B2C) will happen through interface I1, while the operators negotiate (i.e., business-to-business, B2B) for service allocation through interface I2. Based on the agreements, the management entity in each provider network will request the domain orchestrators through interface I3 to map resources to a specific network slice. To offer end-to-end services, domain orchestrators may interact with each other through interface I4. Lastly, domain orchestrators instruct controllers to assign resources based on the technology deployed in the domain (e.g., SDN, optical, etc.). It is important to emphasize that the 5GEx project focuses on interfaces I1, I2, and I3.

The interaction between multi-domain orchestrators (MdOs) enables a service to be orchestrated in a multi-provider environment. Specifically, MdOs enable VNF instantiation on a third-party infrastructure through two fundamental components: Network Service Orchestrator (NSO) and Resource Orchestrator (RO) [11]. NSO manages the life cycle of network services in coordination with VNF Managers. RO provides an overall view of the resources within an administrative domain. An interesting observation is that operators' ROs can interact to expose slices in an abstracted and unified view which can be consumed by an NSO that will expose services to a customer. Thus, the split architecture of an MdO allows use cases such as network services provided using multiple administrative domains (i.e., multiple NSOs that compose services using cross-domain VNFs) as well as a network service provided using multiple infrastructure providers (i.e., multiple ROs expose a virtual data center to an NSO). We refer to the use cases #1 and #3 as defined in [11] for more specific examples and descriptions.

In the next section, we discuss in more details the security requirements of the 5G multi-operator architecture, and, particularly, we will focus on the security of NFV and SDN as key enabling technologies for 5G. We consider the functional split of MdOs to provide a more detailed analysis.

10.2 Security Perspectives from Standards Organizations

To elaborate the security requirements of multi-operator service orchestration, we first review the security architecture provided by ITU-T X.805 standard, and then, we apply ITU-T security recommendations to interfaces of the 5GEx multi-operator architecture shown in Fig. 10.1. In addition, we also review some of the ETSI NFV recommendations for security of multi-operator service orchestration in the following of this section.

10.2.1 ITU-T X.805

The ITU-T X.805 [17] provides recommendations for end-to-end network security regardless of the underlying networking technology. Even though it was published more than a decade ago, the recommendations are still very useful to understand potential types of protection needed against threats. The reason stems from the fact that the X.805 architecture is generic enough to accommodate the existing challenges in network security, as we explain next.

X.805 Security Architecture. Figure 10.2 shows the X.805 security architecture, which comprises three architectural components: security dimensions, security layers, and security planes. Eight security dimensions are used to measure specific aspects of network security. Three security layers (infrastructure, applications, and services) provide a hierarchical structure for applying the security dimensions to certain categories of network resources. Three security planes (management, control, end user) consist of a particular group of network activities that should be protected by security dimensions.

The infrastructure security layer measures the security in network components (i.e., switches and routers) and their communication links. The services security layer applies security at services offered by a service provider, while the applications security layer addresses the security of network-based applications. Since security for multi-operator networks is dealing with services, we only need to apply the security dimensions to the services security layer in the scope of each security plane.

According to the X.805 standard, the concept of protecting a network by security dimensions at each security plane provides a comprehensive security solution. As illustrated in Fig. 10.3, different security dimensions protect security planes. Focusing on the services security layer, we can define the security planes as follows [17]:

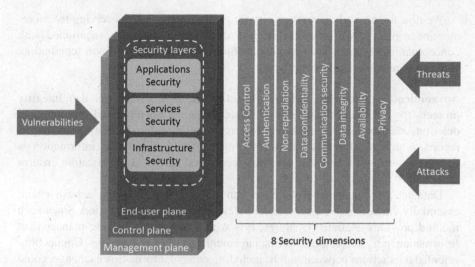

Fig. 10.2 X.805 security architecture

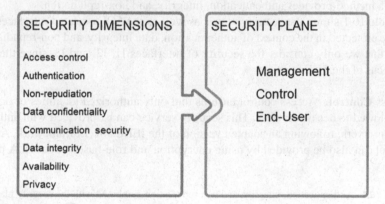

Fig. 10.3 Architecture rationale: security dimensions protect security planes

- Management plane: concerned with securing the operations, administration, maintenance and provisioning functions of network services.
- Control plane: securing the control or signaling information used by a network service, including control messages of network devices participating in the service.
- (End-)user plane: securing user data as it uses a network service. In the context of multi-operator networks, the term "user" is the same as "customer" in Fig. 10.1, which refers to either a service provider or an enterprise customer. We replace the term end-user plane by user plane.

We now review and discuss security for each dimension by observing the afore-mentioned planes. We group the security dimensions previously mentioned with conceptual intersections such as authentication and integrity with non-repudiation, and data confidentiality with privacy.

Authentication, Integrity, and Non-repudiation. X.805 states that data integrity protects the information of network services against unauthorized modification, deletion, creation, and replication. Non-repudiation is enabled by providing a record, which identifies activities performed. We highlight that information is defined according to the security planes mentioned earlier. Authentication ensures that claimed identities are verified.

Data integrity and non-repudiation can be provided by using a hash chain; essentially the successive application of a cryptographic hash function. Since such method provides onetime signatures, it is well suited for protecting management information, e.g., keeping track of management activities or past logs. Connection-oriented interactions between MdOs, including control information exchange, could be better secured with public-key cryptography schemes such as digital signatures. Such a method provides authentication, integrity, and non-repudiation.

Table 10.1 shows the security planes as well as the 5GEx-related interfaces that can be protected in the context of authentication, data integrity, and non-repudiation. Note that we only consider the security of interfaces I1, I2, and I3, since they are the focus of the 5GEx project.

Access Control. Access control ensures that only authorized identities or devices are allowed to access services. This security service can be provided with authentication servers, following an adapted version of the IEEE 802.1x framework. Access control can also be provided by using encryption and role-based controls. A policy

Table 10.1 Authentication, integrity, and non-repudiation combined with the security planes of X.805

Planes	Data authentication, integrity, and non-repudiation	Interfaces affected and possible countermeasures
Management	Protect management information and provide a record identifying management activities performed	I1, I2 for service management and VNF life cycle management. Protection with digital signatures or hash chains
Control	Protect control information and provide a record identifying the origin of control messages. Verify identity that originates control information	I1, I2 for service exposure. I2, I3 for resource orchestration. Protection with digital signatures
User	Protect user data being transported, verify its origin, and provide a record identifying each user and device that accessed and used the network service and the action that was performed	Not directly applicable

Table 10.2 Access control combined with the security planes of X.805

Planes	Access control	Interfaces affected and possible countermeasures
Management	Ensure only authorized identities are allowed to perform management activities of the network service	I1, I2 for requesting the instantiation and configuration of VNFs and SLA management. Protection can be provided with encrypted requests or authentication servers
Control	Ensure that control information for a network service originates from an authorized source before accepting it	Not directly applicable if user service request is granted and persisted
User	Ensure that only authorized users and devices are allowed to access and use the network service	I1 for requesting services. Protection with authentication servers that persist the authorization

Table 10.3 Data confidentiality and privacy combined with the security planes of X.805

Planes	Data confidentiality and privacy	Interfaces affected and possible countermeasures
Management	Protect the network service's configuration and management information. Ensure that no information can be used to identify the network management service system	I1, I2 for service management and VNF life cycle management. Protection with encryption
Control	Protect network service control information. Privacy for network devices or communications links participating in a network service	I1, I2 for service exposure I2, I3 for resource orchestration. Protection with encryption
User	Protect user data that is being transported, processed or stored by a network service against unauthorized access or viewing. Privacy for information pertaining to the user's use of the service	Not directly applicable per interface. Still an existing trust issue (with regard to user data flowing through a provider without having an established relationship)

database could be provided for user access differentiation. Table 10.2 shows how the security planes can be applied to 5GEx in the context of access control and authentication. We emphasize that only interfaces I1, I2, and I3 are taken into account.

Data Confidentiality and Privacy. Confidentiality protects the information from unauthorized access or viewing. Privacy ensures that no information will be available to be used to identify the network service. Encryption schemes are useful for implementing confidentiality and privacy. Table 10.3 shows the 5GEx interfaces that could be affected by the security planes for data confidentiality and privacy.

Availability. The availability security dimension ensures that there is no denial of authorized access to services. Considering that access policies are effective,

Table 10.4 Availability combined with the security planes of X.805

Planes	Availability	Interfaces affected and possible countermeasures
Management	Ensure the ability to manage network service cannot be denied for authorized entity	I1, I2 for SLA management, VNF instantiation and configuration as well as VNF life cycle management. Protection with multiple NSOs
Control	Ensure that network devices participating in a network service are always available to receive control information from authorized sources	I2, I3 for resource orchestration. Protection with multiple ROs
User	Ensure no denial of access to the network service by authorized users	I1 for request of services. Protection with multiple NSOs

availability can be provided by using logically centralized and physically distributed orchestrators per administrative domain. Table 10.4 presents the 5GEx interfaces affected in the context of availability.

10.2.2 ETSI NFV

ETSI Network Functions Virtualization (NFV) Industry Specification Group (ISG) provides technical recommendations and standards for the adoption of NFV, based on the network operator requirements. The ETSI NFV ISG has published a list of security issues [9] which we discuss next with respect to the multi-operator networks while taking into account ETSI's recommendations on security [8]. It should be noted that other concerns about security of individual network elements or VNFs are out of the scope of this document.

Topology Validation. Operators should be able to validate the connectivity between all network elements; however, this process is often complex especially because of the large number of virtualized functions. The topology validation of VNFs is particularly important considering the end-to-end slices in 5G, which require VNF orchestration across several virtual networks. Operators should verify that the network connectivity satisfies the forwarding policy of VNF chains and each VNF deploys the intended functionality. Also, it should be verifiable that the VNFs are connected to the correct virtual network and the topology of VNFs should be free of loops, which could be introduced accidentally or maliciously.

To improve VNF chaining across different operators, multi-domain orchestrators should be able to instruct local SDN controllers to set up a path for a specific chain of VNFs. However, orchestrators are expected to possess an abstract view of network topology. Depending on the level of abstraction, the ability of computing specific paths for VNFs is limited, leaving such task to an SDN controller. Moreover, the SDN controller becomes a trusted entity to hold information about physical and virtual network resources. As a consequence, if not secured, attackers may break into the centralized controller and gain access to the physical and virtual topology information.

Performance and Network Isolation.   Considering the 5G multi-operator scenario in which a service spans across multiple administrative domains, virtual networks might be deployed on several shared physical resources. Therefore, it is important to isolate the virtual networks by creating logical slices across all operators involved in the service. End-to-end slices will require a standardized interface between multi-domain orchestrators so that each operator may provide its own performance characteristic and network isolation method.

Multi-Administrator Isolation.   The hierarchy of administrators can become a potential source of threats when it comes to delegation of control or privileges between orchestrators of different administrative domains. It is important to consider the privileges of administrators of virtualized networks and functions.

User/Tenant Authentication, Authorization, and Accounting (AAA).   The multilayer virtualization introduced by NFV may lead to AAA-related issues. Authentication may lead to the disclosure of end-user's identities in a federation of different NFV infrastructure providers. One solution is to validate all identity tokens in VNF layers. Authorization can also introduce new privilege challenges, as it requires rich policies to identify the authorized users and tenants. The deployment of accounting for resource usage and billing purposes can also be challenging especially because the VNFs may be deployed at/by different operators. This requires granular traffic classification and accounting between orchestrators.

Back-Doors via Virtualized Test and Monitoring Functions.   Operators may provide a set of monitoring interfaces which can be used remotely for provisioning, configuring, debugging, and testing the VNFs. While operators may give certain privileges to each other, for example, for performance and quality monitoring, these interfaces should be properly hardened and restricted against any unauthorized access by attackers or even by other operators.

10.3   Threat Analysis Method

We provide a threat analysis over multi-operator networks according to the method illustrated in Fig. 10.4. Using a multi-provider scenario to specify interactions, we consider a selective list of threats and their reasons. Then, we provide a list of potential security schemes that can protect the system against the threats. Standards are also considered based on the study in Sect. 10.2. Finally, we elaborate on gaps identified from schemes and standards.

Fig. 10.4 Proposed method for threat analysis

10.3.1 Multi-provider Scenario

In order to understand the security aspects of a multi-provider environment, we consider the scenario of a wholesale infrastructure service, combining network, storage, and compute resources from multiple operators. A given service provider, SP_A, can create a service that involves other service providers' infrastructure in a process that consists of the following steps:

1. Customer sends a service request to SP_A;
2. SP_A MdO decomposes the service into smaller service components;
3. SP_A MdO maps service components to an inter-provider resource topology, defining the SPs that will cooperate to deliver the network service and their respective resources;
4. SP_A MdO sends requests to other SPs MdOs involved in order to instantiate the service components required (e.g., compute, storage).

Figure 10.5 illustrates the scenario. 5GEx Interface 1 (I1) is used in the first step of the aforementioned process, while the other steps are mostly defined in Interface I2 (I2). Examples of control messages that should be exchanged between MdOs are advertisement of resource topology and service catalog. The former exposes available resources that a service provider intends to share and the latter exposes available services. Exchange of control data between peers of MdOs is subject to threats that we elaborate in the next sections.

10.3.2 Threat List and Reasons

Before discussing threats and their reasons, it is important to understand the relationship between an orchestrator and an SDN controller in terms of security. Threats to an SDN controller can affect its corresponding orchestrator, and vice versa.

An orchestrator usually operates right atop an SDN controller using a defined interface for communication in the hierarchy. Such method is advocated by European projects such as Unify [25] and 5GEx [1], with potentially significant influence on the definition of future 5G networks. ETSI also acknowledges the importance of an interface between an SDN controller and an NFV orchestrator,

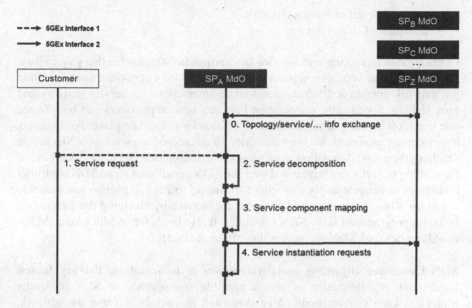

Fig. 10.5 Interactions subject to threats in a multi-provider scenario

being direct or indirect [10]. As an example of interaction, a controller should be able to push network decisions in the data plane using high-level requests generated by orchestrators. Conversely, an orchestrator should be able to receive network topology information from an SDN controller, possibly with a level of abstraction (e.g., hiding specific details of network devices). Moreover, ETSI states that topology information may be passed along in both directions [10].

The list of threats provided here is inspired by the study of ITU-T X.805 security architecture (Sect. 10.2.1). In addition, recent studies identifying attacks and vulnerabilities pertaining to the SDN/NFV domain are considered (e.g., [4, 6, 24]).

Potential threats for the scenario discussed in Sect. 10.3.1 are as follows:

- Destruction of information and/or other resources;
- Disclosure of information;
- Interruption of services;
- Loss of confidence in secure trading between service providers.

The above-mentioned list of threats is not exhaustive but covers a broad security spectrum for multi-operator networks as we discuss throughout this section. The following threat reasons will be taken into account in the discussions:

- Hijack the orchestrator or the SDN controller;
- Malicious/compromised applications;
- Configuration issues;

- Distributed denial of service (DDoS);
- Repudiation of shared data.

Orchestrator Hijacking and Service Interruption. An attacker that gains access to an orchestrator or SDN controller can disrupt any kind of communication within the network domain and affect inter-domain interactions for service delivery and provisioning. Specifically, cooperation between service providers can be affected due to packet loss or malicious forwarding behavior in the data plane. For instance, a service may require packets to be diverted to an ordered sequence of VNFs before reaching their final destination, a process known as service chaining. Such kind of forwarding behavior can be realized over the SDN paradigm, i.e., an SDN controller configures switches to apply a specific forwarding strategy to packets associated to a service. Thus, an attacker can interrupt the service by changing the forwarding behavior programmed at the SDN controller. It also holds for an MdO, since MdOs could interact with SDN controllers directly or indirectly.

SDN Controller Hijacking and Destruction of Information, Privacy Issues. Destruction of information is also a possible consequence of SDN controller hijacking. Data can be modified or corrupted as packets traverse the network, since SDN-enabled switches can be programmed to modify packet fields. Even though OpenFlow, the most noted SDN realization, mostly enables the controller to program the forwarding elements up to layer 4 in the stack, it is still possible to use SDN-enabled switches to modify any packet field (e.g., using P4[1] programs). Also, some types of applications running atop an SDN controller can be enabled to provide complete packet inspection and modification, possibly resulting in privacy issues due to disclosure of information encapsulated in data packets.

A question that arises from the above discussions is the method that makes it possible for an attacker to hijack orchestrators or SDN controllers. **Malicious applications** can be used for hijacking purposes [4]. Northbound applications atop an SDN controller or orchestrator should be provided with security features so that remote access is only performed by authorized entities. Any change in a resource state (e.g., forwarding element, database system, computational resource) should be restricted to trusted applications or monitored in real time. Also, controllers and orchestrators should have strong isolation properties to prevent applications from interfering with one another.

Configuration Issues and Disclosure of Information. Threat reasons are not restricted to malicious activities. In fact, misconfigurations in an orchestrated network can lead to serious threats such as disclosure of information. Configuration mistakes can lead the orchestrator to originate data without authorization. In addition, configuration issues can lead to mistaken or incorrect data sharing such

---

[1]http://p4.org/

Table 10.5 Summary of threats and their reasons

Threat	Reasons
Destruction of information and/or privacy issues	SDN controller hijacking
	Malicious/compromised applications
Disclosure of information	Orchestrator/SDN controller hijacking
	Configuration issues
Interruption of services	Distributed denial of service (DDoS)
	Orchestrator/SDN controller hijacking
Trading confidence between SPs	Repudiation of shared data

as the case in which an orchestrator exposes resources which the operator does not actually own.

Flooding, DDoS, and Interruption of Services. DDoS attacks in which multiple compromised hosts flood the network with packets are a notable form of service interruption. A large number of requests to an orchestrator such as service requests can prevent its functional modules from working properly. For example, services offered by an MdO can become unavailable in case advertisements of service catalog or resource topology are not performed as expected. In addition, a large number of coordinated packets that traverse the data plane can overload the SDN controller, requiring it to process too many packets for flow rule decisions which can lead to service disruption in the controller.

An important discussion is how an SDN controller and an orchestrator make the network more susceptible to DDoS in comparison with other networking paradigms. A centralized element for the control plane is the main reason for such vulnerability which also holds for an orchestrator. However, the control plane can be physically distributed, enabling the use of methods for controller placement to mitigate DDoS attacks. It is worth noting that distributed SDN controllers will have to perform synchronization in order to keep network state in a logically centralized fashion.

With respect to **repudiation of shared data**, an operator could claim to not have originated data units. Specifically, the operator could have agreed to share network resources but still denies such agreement or sharing. Non-repudiation issues can affect the confidence to encourage trading opportunities between service providers. A brief discussion on non-repudiation over ITU-T X.805 is provided in Sect. 10.2.1.

Table 10.5 presents an example of mapping threats and their reasons based on the discussions above

10.3.3 Security Schemes

Before reviewing potentially applicable security schemes and countermeasures, it is important to emphasize cryptographic protocol suites that provide basic services such as authentication and encryption. For example, Internet Protocol Security

Table 10.6 Potential security schemes and countermeasures

Threat Reason	Possible countermeasure
Orchestrator/SDN controller hijacking	Restrict malicious/compromised applications with application containerization
Configuration issues	Real-time policy checker
DDoS	Physically distributed SDN controllers; detect attack and redirect legitimate traffic to a new server address
Repudiation of shared data	Digital signatures over ITU-T X.509

(IPSec) provides end-to-end security in the IP layer. IPSec can be used to protect data flows between a pair of hosts, a pair of security gateways, or between a security gateway and a host. Another example is Transport Layer Security (TLS), which allows client/server applications to communicate in a way that is designed to prevent eavesdropping, tampering or message forgery [7]. TLS is designed in particular for communications over a reliable transport protocol such as TCP. A brief comparison between IPSec and TLS draws the attention to the fact that the latter protects application streams, while IPSec connects hosts to entire private networks, including across a public network.

Table 10.6 presents potential countermeasures against the threat reasons (thus, threats).

The impact of malicious application behavior can be restricted or prevented by using (or providing support to) application containerization [24]. Note that network applications can be statically compiled with the controller code or instantiated as a dynamic module with the controller software. Containerization allows for authenticating the application during setup, and controlling the application's access rights on the infrastructure. In addition, containerization can limit and isolate the resource usage for each application.

To detect disclosure of information caused by configuration issues, it is possible to use policy checker mechanisms such as the work in [18]. In an SDN network, the controller is aware of the network state because it is responsible for flow rule decision and creation. Thus, SDN allows the verification of correct forwarding behavior. A policy verification example is "traffic originated from hosts A and B should never leave the domain during working time." One of the major challenges in policy verification is the separation of different types of traffic using fine-grained policy checking, since the SDN controller can set forwarding rules based on network identifiers, and it has a limited view on the type of traffic, e.g., application identifiers. This can be improved by using external traffic classifiers and deep packet inspection mechanisms in the network. To perform policy checking in case of multiple controllers in the network, it is also important to synchronize the network-wide state among all distributed controllers.

Since centralization of control makes an SDN network more susceptible to DDoS attacks, the immediate solution is to physically distribute the control plane. Detecting DDoS is another possible countermeasure, having traffic volume as a trigger for an SDN application that also blocks malicious traffic. For instance, the work in [19] provides the following method: a blocking application sits atop the SDN controller and establishes a secure channel with the server under protection against DDoS – the server can be an orchestrator or an MdO. The secure channel is used by the server to notify the blocking application in case of DDoS attacks, and subsequently, the blocking application safely provides the server with a new IP address at which the service should resume. As a result, legitimate traffic is redirected from the attacked server address to a new address. Another method to prevent DDoS attacks is to use rate limiters at the data plane to detect the abnormal traffic that goes beyond a threshold value.

10.3.4 Gaps

Mapping security requirements to existing solutions in the literature, including recommendations from standards, draws the attention to at least three important topics: trust, Path Computation Element confidentiality, and privacy between operators. We next discuss these gaps before providing final considerations and concluding this chapter.

Trust Relationships Between Operators. A certification authority (CA) allows trust relationships by building, maintaining, and revoking digital certificates. These processes can be used within any given NFV context [8]. Note that a certificate verifies that a public key is owned by a particular entity, but it does not imply the trustworthiness of the key owner. This and other aspects of trust should be taken into account when using public-key infrastructure (PKI).

Should PKI be used for trust, we refer to the ITU-T X.509 to address some of the security requirements. The ITU-T X.509 can be seen as a hierarchical trust model for authentication [15]. It defines a certification authority tree in which a certificate within a local community is signed by a CA that can be linked into this tree. Such a rigid hierarchical structure may not be aligned with NFV-specific trust goals, since trust is highly dynamic and trust measures can combine a variety of assurance elements that include identity, attribution, attestation, and non-repudiation [8]. Thus, as far as trust is concerned, a trust objective should be defined before considering the use of PKI over the recommendations of ITU-T X.509.

PCEP Confidentiality in Multi-Operator Networks. In the context of 5GEx, a candidate mechanism for establishing inter-NSP (Network Service Provider) connectivity is the combined usage of BGP-LS (Border Gateway Protocol-Link State) for abstracted topology dissemination at provider level and PCE (Path Computation Element) for the actual path computation and instantiation of connectivity. In the case of inter-domain path computation, the end-to-end inter-domain path is a concatenation of intra-domain path segments resulting from cascaded PCE-to-PCE cooperative communications. Definitely, the PCE architecture can be considered as de facto standard to effectively deploy TE in multi-domain networks [22]. However, despite the authentication, authorization, and encryption mechanisms [20], confidentiality issues still might arise inherently due to the exchange of information on network resource availability (e.g., link bandwidth) aimed at the inter-domain LSP setup. In fact, the information exchanged in inter-PCE communications can be used in a malicious way. Although the inter-NSP topology exchanged by means of BGP-LS represents an abstract topology with aggregated TE metrics and values, confidential information (e.g., the amount of available bandwidth in a inter-provider link) may be inferred. In fact, a requester PCE is not forced to actually set up the returned path by triggering a signaling in the network. Thus, a malicious requester PCE might issue a sequence of bogus, although formally licit, computation requests to a PCE belonging to a different domain with the only purpose of processing the returned replies to infer network resource availability information in other domains. For instance, multiple requests with the same destination node and different values of requested bandwidth might be submitted to a PCE. Instead of establishing the path, the obtained replies with bandwidth availability can be used to derive possible bandwidth bottlenecks toward the specified destination. This represents a security weakness that might be exposed by a NSP for obtaining valuable advantages in terms of market share by leveraging on potential failures and weaknesses of concurrent providers. Such a misuse of the path computation services might prevent a beneficial cooperation among PCEs belonging to different NSPs and compromise the dynamic provision of end-to-end LSPs. In fact, a PCE might not have an interest in processing a request if it is arriving from a competitor provider or if some security threat is perceived that is likely to cause any operational or economic damage. Therefore, inter-PCE interactions could be extended with (1) malicious PCEP usage discovery techniques [13, 21] and (2) trust-based and incentive-compatible mechanisms to discourage the misuse of path computation services while stimulating effective interactions among PCEs [12, 14].

Privacy in Collaborative Service Delivery. Cross-domain orchestration of resources over multiple administrative domains enables collaborative service delivery, i.e., services can be realized via chaining (or sequence) of VNFs over domains of multiple operators. In this case, while a VNF runs on the infrastructure of one operator, policies can come from another operator, which motivates an operator to encrypt its traffic in order to hide business or technical strategies. The aforementioned example is only one out of many possible use cases for privacy in collaborative service delivery. For instance, user data traffic could also be impacted (see Fig. 10.6). Thus, there is a need for security mechanisms and standards for enabling private VNFs [5].

10.4   Research Challenges and Future Directions

Resource sharing in a multi-party service delivery requires, among other things, a flexible and programmable infrastructure. Such flexibility is a key enabler for efficient 5G services through network slices [3], adapting to service demands and meeting the requirements of emerging use cases.

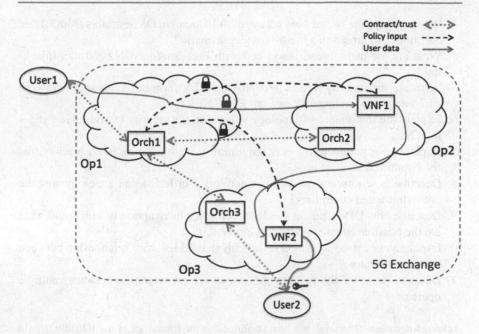

Fig. 10.6 Multi-operator service chaining and information flow [5]

In the context of security, network slices require strong isolation properties. Slices should not interfere with one another so that faults are not propagated through the network. Resilience and robustness are important in mission-critical business services such as public safety networks in which hierarchical SDN controllers can provide increased security features [23]. Other research challenges include trust, confidentiality, and evolved privacy solutions, as discussed in Sect. 10.3.4.

Multi-operator service orchestration and delivery in 5G bring intensified security concerns. This chapter has provided discussions on security requirements and threats related to service orchestration; moreover, potential solutions for securing 5G networks have been discussed. As operators want to be completely confident when hosting third-party service components in their infrastructures, such mapping of the threat landscape and threat mitigation strategies is essential. We argue that with the right design choices, future 5G networks will be able to meet the increasingly complex security requirements.

Questions

1. Explain how security dimensions can protect the management plane in multi-operator orchestration based on ITU-T X.805 standard?
2. Based on ITU-T X.805 standard, which security dimension can prevent the denial of authorized access to services in 5G?

3. What are possible interactions between Multi-domain Orchestrators (MdOs) that are subject to threats in a multi-provider scenario?
4. What are the main threats associated with orchestrator/SDN controller hijacking?
5. What are the security threats in deploying NFV in multi-operator 5G network based on the recommendations from ETSI NFV?
6. Explain the importance of topology validation for security of end-to-end slices in 5G?
7. Explain your rationale why it is important to deploy strong AAA mechanisms for virtualized services in 5G?
8. Describe how misconfigurations in network can lead to an attack against the orchestrator and controllers?
9. Describe how DDoS attacks can lead to service interruption in MdOs and what are the possible countermeasures to prevent it?
10. Explain your reasoning why it is difficult to establish trust relationship between multiple operators?
11. Describe some of the privacy challenges for orchestration between multiple operators?

Acknowledgements This work has been performed in the framework of the H2020-ICT-2014 project 5GEx (Grant Agreement no. 671636), which is partially funded by the European Commission. Gergely Biczók has been supported by the János Bolyai Research Scholarship of the Hungarian Academy of Sciences.

References

1. 5GEx EU H2020-ICT-2014-2, http://www.5gex.eu/. Accessed 01 Dec 2016
2. 5G White Paper, NGMN Alliance (2015). https://www.ngmn.org/uploads/media/NGMN_5G_White_Paper_V1_0.pdf. Accessed 5 Apr 2017
3. 5G Systems, Ericsson White Paper (2017). https://www.ericsson.com/res/docs/whitepapers/wp-5g-systems.pdf. Accessed 5 Apr 2017
4. Akhunzada A et al (2015) Securing software defined networks: taxonomy, requirements, and open issues. IEEE Commun Mag 53(4):36–44
5. Biczók G et al (2016) Private VNFs for collaborative multi-operator service delivery: an architectural case. In: Network operations and management symposium, 2016 IEEE/IFIP. IEEE, pp 1249–1252
6. Dabbagh M, Hamdaoui B, Guizani M, Rayes A (2015) Software-defined networking security: pros and cons. IEEE Commun Mag 53(6):73–79
7. Dierks T, Rescorla E (2008) The transport layer security (TLS) protocol version 1.2. RFC 5246
8. ETSI (2014) NFV Security and Trust Guidance. Technical Report ETSI GS NFV-SEC003
9. ETSI (2014) NFV Security Problem Statement. Technical Report ETSI GS NFV-SEC001
10. ETSI (2015) Report on SDN usage in NFV architectural framework. Technical Report ETSI GS NFV-EVE 005
11. ETSI (2016) NFV MANO Report on Architectural Options. Technical Report ETSI GS NFV-IFA 009
12. Fung CJ et al (2014) Quality of interaction among path computation elements for trust-aware inter-provider cooperation. In: 2014 IEEE international conference on communications. IEEE, pp 677–682

13. Gharbaoui M, Paolucci F, Giorgetti A, Martini B, Castoldi P (2013) Effective statistical detection of smart confidentiality attacks in multi-domain networks. IEEE Trans Netw Serv Manag 10(4):383–397
14. Gharbaoui M et al (2016) An incentive-compatible and trust-aware multi-provider path computation element (PCE). Comput Netw 108:40–54
15. Grandison T, Sloman M (2000) A survey of trust in internet applications. IEEE Commun Surv Tutorials 3(4):2–16
16. Guerzoni R et al (2016) Analysis of end-to-end multi-domain management and orchestration frameworks for software defined infrastructures: an architectural survey. Trans Emerg Telecommun Technol 28(4):1–19. http://onlinelibrary.wiley.com/doi/10.1002/ett.3103/full
17. ITU-T (2003) Security architecture for systems providing end-to-end communications. X.805
18. Kazemian P et al (2013) Real time network policy checking using header space analysis. In: Presented as part of the 10th USENIX symposium on networked systems design and implementation, pp 99–111
19. Lim S, Ha J, Kim H, Kim Y, Yang S (2014) A SDN-oriented DDoS blocking scheme for botnet-based attacks. In: 2014 sixth international conference on ubiquitous and future networks. IEEE, pp 63–68
20. Lopez D, de Dios O, Wu W, Dhody D (2016) Secure transport for pcep. Internet-Draft draft-ietf-pce-pceps-10, IETF Secretariat, July (2016). http://www.ietf.org/internet-drafts/draft-ietf-pce-pceps-10.txt
21. Paolucci F, Gharbaoui M, Giorgetti A, Cugini F, Martini B, Valcarenghi L, Castoldi P (2011) Preserving confidentiality in PCE-based multi-domain networks. J Opt Commun Netw 3(5):465–474. art. no. 5759822
22. Paolucci F et al (2013) A survey on the path computation element (PCE) architecture. IEEE Commun Surv Tutorials 15(4):1819–1841
23. Santos MAS et al (2014) Decentralizing SDN's control plane. In: 39th annual IEEE conference on local computer networks. IEEE, pp 402–405
24. Scott-Hayward S, Natarajan S, Sezer S (2015) A survey of security in software defined networks. IEEE Commun Surv Tutorials 18(1):623–654
25. UNIFY EU FP7. http://www.fp7-unify.eu/. Accessed 01 Dec 2016

Mateus Augusto Silva Santos received his M.Sc (2009) in Computer Science and Ph.D. (2014) in Electrical Engineering from Universidade de São Paulo (USP), Brazil. From 2013 to 2014 he was a research scholar with the Inter-Networking Research Group at UC Santa Cruz. He was also a postdoctoral researcher with University of Campinas (UNICAMP). His research interests are in software-defined networking, network security and wireless networks. He has industry experience in the following organizations: Hewlett-Packard and EMBRAER. He is currently a researcher at Ericsson in Brazil.

Alireza Ranjbar received his M.Sc degree with distinction from Aalto university, Finland in the field of Communications Engineering in 2015. Currently, he is working as a researcher at Ericsson Research, Finland. His current research interests include Software-defined networks, Security, and Cloud computing.

Gergely Biczók is an assistant professor at the CrySyS Lab at the Budapest University of Technology of Economics, where he received his PhD in Computer Science in 2010. Previously, he was a postdoc at the Hungarian Academy of Sciences and the Norwegian University of Science and Technology, a Fulbright scholar at Northwestern University and a research fellow at Ericsson Research. His research interests center around the economics of networked system including security, privacy and 5G systems.

Barbara Martini after getting her degree in Electrical Engineering, she worked at Italtel first and later at Marconi Communications, in Italy. Since 2003 she has been a research engineer at the CNIT National Laboratory of Photonics Networks in Pisa, Italy and she is affiliated Researcher within TeCIP Institute of Scuola Superiore Sant'Anna. Her research interests include transport network management, GMPLS/SDN control and service architectures for next generation networks and clouds, orchestration in software-defined infrastructure. She has been involved in several research project funded by EU FP7 (NOBEL, NOBEL Phase 2, BONE, OFELIA, FED4FIRE, 5GEx). She authored more than 80 papers in scientific journals and international conference proceedings. She is a co-chair of the Workshop on Orchestration for Software-Defined Infrastructures (O4SDI) held at IEEE ICC2016 and NFV-SDN2016. She is currently serving as a TCP Member of several IEEE conferences (ITU Kaleidoscope, ONDM, IEVC, APNOMS, NETSOFT) and as reviewer for IEEE journals (JLT, JOCN, IEEE Network, TNSM). She is also involved in IEEE P1903 WG on Next-Generation Service Overlay Networks (NGSON), IETF NFV-related initiatives and IEEE SDN Standardization Committee.

Francesco Paolucci received the Laurea degree in Telecommunications Engineering in 2002 from the University of Pisa, Italy and the Ph.D. degree in 2009 from the Scuola Superiore Sant'Anna, Pisa, Italy. In 2008 he was granted a research Merit Scholarship at the Istitut National de le Recherche Scientifique (INRS), Montreal, Quebec, Canada. Currently, he is Assistant Professor at the TeCIP Institute of Scuola Superiore Sant'Anna, Pisa, Italy and Affiliate Researcher of CNIT, Italy. His main research interests are in the field of optical networks control plane, including Generalized Multi Protocol Label Switching (GMPLS) and Software Defined Networking (SDN) protocol extensions, impairment-aware routing based on Path Computation Element (PCE), inter-domain traffic engineering and flexible optical node architectures. Other research activities include network services for Grid/Cloud Computing applications, optical network fault tolerance, inter-domain security and confidentiality. He is co-author of one IETF Internet Draft, 4 international patents, more than 100 papers on international journals and conference proceedings. He has been involved in European research projects on next generation optical networks and innovative control and management of transport networks (BONE, NOBEL, STRONGEST, IDEALIST, PACE, 5GEx). He has served as Work Package Leader within the PACE Project (CSA).

Improving Security in Coalition Tactical Environments Using an SDN Approach

11

Vinod K. Mishra, Dinesh C. Verma, and Christopher Williams

11.1 Introduction

The principles of software-defined networking (SDN) can be used in many types of networking environments and in particular for addressing challenges related to security and operations of these networks. The design philosophy embedded within SDN has applicability far beyond the control of data center networks where it first originated. However, in order to address the unique requirements of new environments, the implementation and architecture of SDN need to be modified suitably so that it can be applied in an efficient manner to them.

In this chapter, we explore how SDN can be used to improve the security and situational awareness in tactical networks in general and in coalition tactical networks (CTN) in particular. We assume that the reader is already familiar with the principles of SDN, which have been elaborated upon in other chapters of this book. However, tactical networks and coalition tactical networks are special type of networks which the reader may not be familiar with. Therefore, we first introduce these two types of networks with emphasis on their special security and networking requirements. After an introduction to the networks, we will look at the ways in which the SDN concepts can be applied to them to address their networking and security requirement.

V.K. Mishra
U.S. Army Research Labs, APG, Aberdeen, MD, 21005, USA

D.C. Verma (✉)
IBM T J Watson Research Center, Yorktown Heights, NY, 10598, USA
e-mail: dverma@us.ibm.com

C. Williams
Defence Science and Technology Laboratories, Porton Down, Salisbury, Wiltshire, SP4 0JQ, UK

© Springer International Publishing AG (outside the USA), and Her Majesty the Queen in Right of United Kingdom 2017
S.Y. Zhu et al. (eds.), *Guide to Security in SDN and NFV*, Computer Communications and Networks, DOI 10.1007/978-3-319-64653-4_11

As we apply the concepts of SDN to CTN, we adopt the approach that is the defining feature of the SDN architecture, namely, the separation of data plane (DP) from the control plane (CP), and consolidate the CP functionality at a central location in the network. The function of any computer communication network is to accept data packets (also known as protocol data units) from one computer and deliver it to another computer. The network consists of several elements, each of which performs some operations on receiving the packet, e.g., (1) deciding which of several possible outbound interfaces to choose for forwarding the packet or (2) whether to drop the packet due to a security reason. These per-packet operations are the DP functions. In order to perform them, it is necessary to complete some operations earlier, e.g., (1) populating the entries within data forwarding tables, (2) setting up virtual connections, or (3) defining any packet filtering rules. These types of operations are the CP operations. In a traditional network, both DP and CP functions are carried out using a distributed algorithm; e.g., in an Ethernet, a forwarding table which follows the links of a spanning tree among all participating switches is established as part of the CP using a distributed protocol implemented within each switch. This results in both CP and DP functions residing on the same network device and is the ultimate reason for the inflexibility of non-SDN networks.

In SDN, the CP operations of individual network devices are replaced with CP operations run from a centralized SDN controller (SDNC). The SDNC implements the control plane operations as software running on standard IT servers. This moves the CP functions from each device in the network to a logically centralized controller and enables more flexibility. The high-speed DP that is responsible for actually forwarding packets remains in the network devices. As an example, in an Ethernet, the logically centralized controller can be configured to implement algorithms that compute not just a spanning tree but a more complex graph for forwarding packets which use links not on the spanning tree. Thus, it is not necessary to implement a distributed protocol, which is more complex, and may require standardization among different devices manufacturers to work properly.

Another key component of SDN is a set of programming interfaces called northbound interface (NBI) and southbound interface (SBI). NBI allows network applications and policy commands to be communicated to the SDNC. Similarly SBI is used by SDNC to·control the data plane in network devices like switches and routers. These interfaces allow applications and control programs to automate network operations through well-defined, open APIs enabling much more agile interaction with the network than traditional methods, such as scripted command line interfaces (CLIs) and proprietary interfaces. Currently OpenFlow [1] is the dominant open SBI interface. It has been standardized by the Open Networking Foundation (ONF). There is at present no universally accepted open NBI, but attempts to define one are continuing.

For reasons discussed later in the chapter, having an SDNC as a physically centralized entity is not a good solution for tactical networks. Nevertheless, many benefits can be obtained by separating CP and DP functions in a CTN. The logically centralized SDNC can be also implemented in a physically distributed manner to improve its security and resilience.

11.2   Tactical Environments

In both military and civilian contexts, there are several situations when a group of people need to perform a task in an area where there may not be adequate infrastructure for communications. As an example, a platoon of soldiers or policemen may be asked to surround and secure a building in which suspected insurgents may be hiding. Similarly, a group of firemen may be dispatched to handle a fire in a mine or a forest where they may be outside cellular communication coverage. These environments, where a group needs communication without reliance on an existing infrastructure for a limited period of intense activity, are referred to as tactical environments.

In the tactical environment, the people who are involved in any operation would have mobile devices with them. Depending on the technology available to the group, they may be using autonomous vehicles like mules or drones to perform their tactical mission, and they may also be carrying equipment with built-in smart communications capabilities. Also network nodes themselves may move erratically; e.g., firemen may have to beat a hasty retreat if a sudden conflagration occurs, or a soldier may have to make sudden movements to avoid enemy fire.

Within a tactical environment, the nodes carried on person may be supported by more powerful (off-body) support system nodes. Firemen may have a supporting fire truck, which can carry an access point connected to a satellite network. Similar type of supporting infrastructure may be available to soldiers through one or more vehicles being driven in the area of operations. Furthermore, if the operation is being conducted in an urban area, the personal devices can even have cellular connectivity, and thus nodes in the tactical environment may be connected to the infrastructure at least some of the time, if not always.

11.2.1 Segments of a Tactical Network

Although the details vary widely in different countries and military and civilian organizations, one can create a simplified and abstract model of the network of any organization with a tactical environment component as shown in Fig. 11.1.

The model shown presented above has four segments:

- The first segment consists of the devices and the network used by people at the very edge of the operation. This will contain many different handhelds; unmanned aerial vehicles (UAVs); intelligence, surveillance, and reconnaissance (ISR) devices; mobile networking; and computing environments to be carried onto various platforms such as tanks, ships, or vehicles. These devices may establish an ad hoc network among themselves or use satellite communications to interconnect themselves. Thus, the tactical environment would be a mobile ad hoc network (MANET), but instead of being completely ad hoc, the tactical

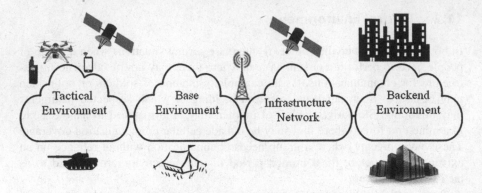

Fig. 11.1 Simplified model of a single organization network

environment can usually rely on a limited amount of infrastructure support from other components in the single organization network.

- The second segment connects tactical environment to the base environment found in bases and buildings used as support operations. In a military context, base environments may use portable laptops, desktop computers, storage devices, and networking equipment that usually create a temporary network infrastructure. It may also reflect the computing environment in a base that has been set up for a temporary period, ranging from a few days to a few months. The base is set up to provide logistics support to soldiers who may need to operate over a large area. In a civilian context, the base may be a temporary camp setup for operations in a disaster recovery area; e.g., it may be the place where people affected by a flood can find shelter, or it may be the command center of teams of firefighters trying to put down a forest blaze.

- The third segment consists of the infrastructure network which connects to the second segment of the base networks. It may contain satellite communications or may leverage installed infrastructure such as cellular communications networks. Depending on base's lifetime, it may also leverage fixed network infrastructure, such as a wired cable of fiber network to connect to the fourth segment of the backend environment.

- The fourth segment consists of the computing infrastructure found in buildings and military headquarters. In general, computing and communication resources in infrastructure and backend environments are plentiful and tend to be static in nature. It should be remembered that this bandwidth abundance becomes quite scarce by the time it reaches the tactical edge.

11.2.2 Security Considerations in Tactical Networks

One of the key attributes of a tactical network is that it is formed quickly and is decommissioned once the mission is completed. As a result, the security considerations in tactical networks are very different from those in the fixed infrastructure networks.

Many tactical networks need to operate in hostile environments. In the context of a fire, there may be a sudden conflagration, and due to the need to move suddenly, the firefighter tactical network may lose a node unexpectedly. In a military tactical network, enemy action may bring down a node at any time. A tactical network needs to be able to provide a high degree of resilience in the face of these sudden node failures. Adversarial action may also include less dramatic activities, such as an arsonist putting in a malicious node in the firefighter scenario or an enemy putting in malicious nodes to join the tactical network in an attempt to intercept and manipulate communications. Every tactical network needs an approach by which only authenticated and authorized nodes are able to join in the tactical environment. In addition, the communication needs to be encrypted so that they are not intercepted easily off the air.

The need for authentication needs to be balanced with the need to be able to form the network rapidly. This means that the process for authenticating nodes that can join the tactical network needs to be very agile and rapid. When a platoon of firefighters (or that of soldiers) is called upon to take on a mission, they cannot go through a complex manual process for establishing keys and certificates for authentication and encryption of communications. The process for establishing the required keys/certificates needs to be extremely agile and not add to the preparation time for the platoon members.

Another consideration in preparing the nodes that will constitute the tactical network is the fact that in a tactical network, all nodes may not be initially present at the formation time. New members in the tactical network may need to be added later. In the case of a platoon of firefighters, some firefighters may arrive late to the site of fire due to traffic delays. In the case of a military tactical network, additional troops may be added to a mission, and their nodes need to be able to join the existing nodes in the tactical network. Thus, the authentication mechanism needs to be able to support new authorized nodes while preventing access by unauthorized or malicious nodes at the same time.

The communication among nodes in a tactical environment would need to be encrypted, but the bandwidth capabilities and processing capabilities of the nodes are usually limited. As a result, the encryption mechanism needs to be a lightweight one. Either a shared key mechanism or popular TLS/SSL protocols can be used depending on the processing capabilities of the mobile node devices. These protocols use certificates and public key cryptography approaches to set up the shared keys that can be used for a brief period of time. In either case, the right shared keys or the right certificates including the public keys need to be set up in the nodes.

In addition to having a lightweight configuration, the nodes in the tactical environment also need to react to impending threats that they observe in the environment during the operations. These include having nodes react to sudden movements that are caused due to mission requirements, dealing with sudden loss of neighboring nodes, reacting to any intrusion attempts that an adversary may be making, and dealing with attempts of an adversary to jam communications. Each node needs to have the appropriate intelligence and insight to deal with these situations as they arise.

11.3   SDN Architecture for Tactical Environments

The SDN approach to networking was applied initially to the regular data center or fixed infrastructure IP and wireless networks. There are three key differences between such networks and tactical environments which need to be accounted for when using the SDN approach in tactical environments.

- *Bandwidth Constraints*: The bandwidth on wireless links is significantly lower than that on wired networks. Due to mobility, electromagnetic interference, and spectrum limitations, tactical network link's effective bandwidth is in the order of a few kilobits per second for platoon level links, and trunked wireless links can go up to a few megabits per second. This is significantly smaller than the available bandwidth in data center high-speed networks, where optical technology can easily offer hundreds of gigabits per second or higher bandwidth. Loss in wireless networks also tends to be high, from 1 to 10% [2], and this causes additional challenges for communication.
- *Disruptions and Failures*: Nodes in the tactical environment can fail suddenly, and due to the mobile nature of the network, a network node may not always have connectivity to the SDNC.
- *Short lifetime*: The lifetime of a traditional network is a few orders of magnitude larger than the time it takes to set up them or tear them down. In contrast, the lifetime of a tactical network is comparable to the time it takes to set up or tear down the network. As a result, the SDNC for a tactical network needs to take on additional functions, which may not be considered by the SDNC of a backend or data center network. Specifically, an SDNC for a tactical network needs to also handle the situation in which a node needs to join or leave the network.

Despite these challenges, SDNC architecture confers significant advantages in managing the security and operations of tactical environment. We propose such an architecture, in which the SDNC controller is part of the support infrastructure for the tactical environment. In the case of firefighters addressing a building fire, the SDNC may be a computer on a fire truck near the scene of the fire. In the case of a military operation, the SDNC could be a computer on a support vehicle. Nodes that join the tactical environment communicate for a brief period with the SDNC to get the appropriate security credentials for them to join the network. The SDNC can also provide policies to drive the operation of the nodes in the tactical network for routing and traffic control. Once a node is part of the network, it may or may not be connected to the SDNC. The SDNC needs to make provisions for enabling the network node to function properly even when it is not connected to the node. When nodes leave the network, they can briefly communicate with the SDNC to make a graceful exit from the network.

11.3.1 Challenges of SDN Architecture in Tactical Environments

The traditional SDN architecture requires a node to contact the SDNC whenever it encounters a situation in which it needs to make a decision for a DP operation for which it does not have the required CP information already within its control. In an environment like a data center where there are few losses and the bandwidth not constrained, having the node contact the SDNC for every decision is a nonissue. However, in wireless environments, where connectivity to SDNC cannot be assured, bandwidth is limited, and communication is lossy; contacting the SDNC for every CP decision is not a viable approach.

In order to deal with this situation, we propose an architecture in which the SDNC provides each node with the appropriate configuration and policies when the node first contacts it for access to the tactical environment. Configuration refers to any information that is needed by the software on the node to perform its operations and consists of files which include various parameters such as the type of security protocol to use and the size of encryption keys to negotiate for, along with any required security certificates or security keys. The policies provide a set of rules which tell the node how to react in different situations that may be encountered by the node and consist of actions to be taken under those conditions.

Using the model described above, the implicit assumption is that each node has an agent which invokes a standard interface to communicate with the SDNC. The agent considers its local configuration and policy data to be a cached copy of the information at the controller. The cached information can be maintained in sync with the information at the SDNC by using traditional cache coherency approaches, e.g., by having the agent check for any updates periodically with SDNC or by having the agent check that the configuration or policies have not changed when it needs to be invoked for a CP operation. Unlike a traditional node architecture, the agent can support not just policies that are common across nodes but also node-specific policies that are determined by the SDNC.

With this model, the traditional set of APIs defined in the SDN architecture get modified slightly as shown in Fig. 11.2. In the figure, the left-hand side shows the standard API definitions for the SDNC with an NBI exposed to the user/application to define the policies or configuration to the controller and a SBI that enables the communication of those policies and configuration to different network nodes or more specifically the DP component in each of the nodes. In the tactical environment, the device contains a DP as well as an agent that acts like a proxy for the SDNC. The SBI provides the interaction between the DP and the agent, the NBI remains unchanged in its functions, and an additional interface, the configuration coherency interface (CCI), is introduced between the nodes and the controller.

The CCI allows the DP elements to interact unmodified with the SDNC in coalition contexts, except that the interaction is now happening with the agent. In a tactical environment, the agent may frequently lose its network connectivity with the SDNC. The CCI deals with this loss of connectivity. In an environment when the device may only be connected with the SDNC occasionally, the agent

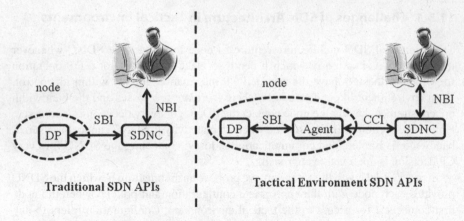

Fig. 11.2 APIs for SDN in tactical environments

can get the configuration and policies that are needed for the DP from the SDNC while connected. When it is disconnected, the agent is still capable of providing the required interaction between the DP, which is unaware that the real SDNC is disconnected. When the SDNC is reconnected, the agent can use the CCI to refresh its policies.

An obvious implication of the architecture for SDN in tactical environments is that the value of a standardized SBI in tactical environment is significantly less than that in traditional SDN environments. On the other hand, the need for defining a standard CCI for maintaining coherence between the agent and SDNC is important to enable devices and controller from different manufacturers to interoperate.

The other key difference in SDNC for tactical environment requires looking into the life cycle of a tactical network as well as that of nodes within the tactical network in more detail.

11.3.2 Life Cycle of a Tactical Network

The life cycle of a tactical environment can be described in a three-stage process as shown in Fig. 11.3.

These stages have specific functions:

1. In the first or the planning stage, the network functions like the type of authentication mechanism, encryption protocols, and policies for the operation of the network are defined.
2. In the second or the operation stage, the network is active, and it helps the performance of the mission.
3. In the third or the decommission phase, the mission of the network has been achieved, and the nodes are in the process of leaving the network.

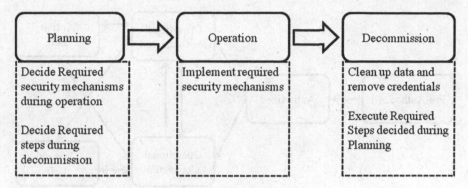

Fig. 11.3 Life cycle of a tactical environment

In each of these three stages, the SDNC needs to be able to provide the right control instruction for the different nodes in the network as the network progresses through each of these three stages. During the decommission stage, attention needs to be paid to the fact that some of the nodes may need to purge themselves of sensitive information if they are being taken out of service.

The policies and configurations needed for each of these stages is provided using the NBI to the controller. The NBI can either be invoked by a human administrator or by another software program. These policies and configuration will be provided to the agent in different network nodes as each of the network nodes goes through various states in its life cycle in the network.

11.3.3 The Tactical Network Node States

The tactical network nodes go through several states as they join the network during different life-cycle stages of the network. Some of the typical node states are shown in Fig. 11.4. In each of these states, the network node needs to determine what its configuration ought to be depending on the current network situation.

- Pre-authorized state: When a node has not been configured with the right credentials to join the tactical network, it is in the pre-authorized state.
- Authorized state: When that node talks to the SDN controller and gets the right keys and certificates to connect to the tactical network, it is in the authorized state. The node can then become operational when it joins the network and is connected to the other nodes in the network.
- Operational connected state: In this state, the node should typically have connectivity to the SDNC.
- Operational disconnected state: The node itself may be part of the tactical environment and connected to the network but still be unable to reach the SDNC. In that case, it is shown in an operationally disconnected state.

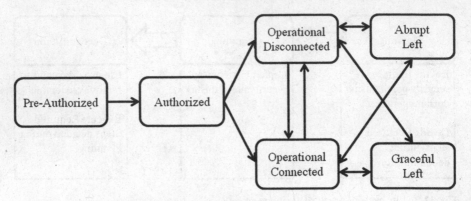

Fig. 11.4 States of a node in tactical environment

- Graceful left: After the mission in the tactical environment is over, the node may leave the network gracefully, i.e., after it communicates with the SDNC and performs the required cleanup procedures, if any.
- Abrupt left: On the other hand, some of the nodes may leave the network in an abrupt manner, e.g., leave the network without having this exchange with the SDNC.

When the SDNC is contacted by a node in the pre-authorized state, it needs to provide the node with all the configuration and policies needed for its operation in each of the stages of the life cycle, at least for those states where the node may not be connected to the SDNC. The SDNC may choose not to provide this configuration and policies for the node when it is able to connect to the SDNC, i.e., for the operational connected or graceful left states. However, it would be more bandwidth efficient for the SDNC to provide any configuration, policy, or other information needed for the control plane operations for those states as well.

When the node arrives in the pre-authorized state and contacts the SDNC, its credentials to access the network are validated, and on passing the validation checks, it is provided with the control plane information needed for operational disconnected state, as well as the abrupt left state. The operational connected state control plane information can also be provided. On receiving this information, the state changes to authorized. In this state, the node has the appropriate configuration allowing it to connect to the tactical network and communicate with other nodes in the network in a secure manner. Once it is operational, the node can check if it has a connection to the SDNC. It can then change its state to operational disconnected or operational connected state, appropriately.

In the disconnected or abrupt left state, the node uses the information provided by the SDNC during the authorized phase to perform its operations. In the connected state, the node uses the information provided in that phase as cached information. It can check if the set of configuration and policies have changed and use the locally cached information if it has not changed. It can download the changed control plane information if any update is available.

Table 11.1 Typical DP and CP functions at different life-cycle stages

Node state	DP function	CP information
Authorized	Joining the network	Security credentials
		Network configuration (e.g., SDNC address)
	Routing information	Routing configuration,
		Routing table
Operational	Forwarding	Forwarding table entries
	Filtering	Packet filtering rules/policies
	Encryption	Encryption keys/certificates
	Security monitoring	Intrusion detection/prevention policies
	Situational awareness	Situational awareness policies
Left	Reporting	Reporting policies
	Cleanup/retention	Data retention policies, data cleanup policies

The state of the network node defines the nature of the DP functions that need to be performed and the CP information to enable the DP functions. Table 11.1 shows some of the typical DP functions and associated CP information at different states of the network.

11.4 SDN-Based Operational Security and Situational Awareness

A tactical network node in the operational states (either disconnected or connected), as defined by the life cycle in Fig. 11.4, needs to obtain control plane information. The manner in which it is done is similar to that of SDN in backend networks, with the exception of caching that we described in the previous section. However, in order for the node to react to the security threats in the operational environment in an agile manner, it needs to be aware of its security situation and threats. In this section, we examine how situational awareness can be provided in a tactical environment.

11.4.1 The OODA Loop

In the human decision-making process, a common approach for situational awareness is the use of the OODA loop [3]. It explains that activity as consisting of the four stages of observe, orient, decide, and act as shown in Fig. 11.5.

The four phases are the following:

- Observe phase: All relevant information available from the environment is collected.
- Orient phase: The observation is analyzed further to get a deeper understanding of its implications; e.g., one may try to determine a root cause from the various observations.

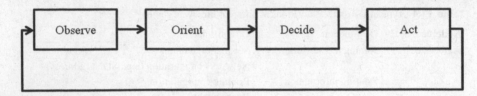

Fig. 11.5 The OODA loop for decision making

- Decide phase: The trade-offs involved in different courses of action are considered, and the right course of action is determined.
- Act phase: The action is actually undertaken, which results in a change to the environment, again leading to an observation of the environment. This completes the first loop. The next loop starts again with observing the changed environment.

As an example, suppose one hears the sound of a gunshot.

- During the observation phase, the sound of the gunshot is heard.
- In the orient phase, additional determination, e.g., the location of the gunshot, is determined, or other information sources, e.g., a camera video input, are used to get more information.
- In the decide phase, the possible options to deal with the gunshot is determined.
- In the act phase, the resulting action is then taken.

Although developed for the human behavior, the OODA loop can also be applied to tasks performed by a computer and in particular to the task of security in military networks. The application of SDN to cybersecurity situational awareness deals with using the OODA loop for cybersecurity to get humanlike situational awareness implemented within computer software.

11.4.2 Control and Data Plane Components of OODA Loop

In order to apply SDN principles, we need to differentiate between the control part and the data part of the cybersecurity situational awareness, as well as define what the implementation of the OODA loop means in this context. The architecture that we envision for cybersecurity situational awareness implements the OODA loop in software in the elements of environment which is described in Fig. 11.2.

It should be noted that there are actually two layers of OODA loops in operation: an outer or network-level OODA loop that directs the decisions and actions of the SDNC and an inner or device-level OODA loop that directs the operation of the DP with delegated authority (through policy) to act autonomously as directed by the SDN agent. The two-layered OODA loop architecture is shown in Fig. 11.6. The OODA loop software is responsible for performing the tasks required in the OODA loop as follows (for both device-level and network-level decision loops):

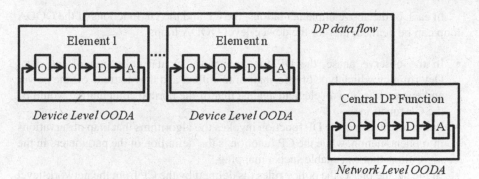

Fig. 11.6 Data plane with two layers of OODA loop

- The O (observe) part of the OODA loop consists of capturing portions of the network traffic that an element is seeing. Such data observations can be achieved by activating a variety of data collection elements. A data collection element may be collecting a subset of network packets, or looking at performance metrics within a computing system, or keeping track of the number of processes that are active within a computing device.
- The O (orient) part of the OODA loop needs to determine if anything abnormal is taking place in the network environment. The orient part of the system tries to map the observed data into higher-level phenomenon [4], implementing algorithms for root cause analysis to determine why specific observations might be happening. This may require the application of artificial intelligence (AI) and machine learning (ML) principles to discern patterns and classify the environmental cues.
- The D (decide) part of the OODA loop needs to process the collected information and assess the ongoing threat situation. On the basis of this assessment, a course of action (COA), which may comprise multiple parts, is then chosen as the response. Several approaches for making decisions, e.g., using policies or rules, utility maximization, and game theory, can be used at this stage. In the decide phase of the device-level OODA loop, one of the decisions may be to send the collected information or a subset of the information the network-level OODA loop for processing.
- The A (act) part of the OODA loop then implements the COA activities. For cybersecurity purposes, the action may consist of installing new network access control rules, information filtering policies, reconfiguration of security parameters, or switching to a different mode of encryption for secure communication, or specifically for the device-level OODA loop, the transmission of information to the network-level OODA loop. For the network-level OODA loop, one of the actions may be to update the policies and configuration of one or more device-level OODA loops

In each of the above implementations, the CP and the DP functions of the OODA loop can be defined, first for the device-level OODA loop:

- In the observe phase, the DP function is the actual collection of the data. Determining which type of information to collect and how to trade off the power and energy needs of an element against that of the normal computation would be the CP functions.
- In the orient phase, the DP function invokes the algorithms that map observations into phenomenon, while the CP function is the definition of the parameters in the algorithms that can enable such a mapping.
- In the decide phase, the policy rules (as defined by the CP from the network-level OODA loop) are implemented in the DP which leads to a decision. If a course of action cannot be identified to meet the required objectives within the policy constraints, then the DP can refer back to the SDNC for further guidance on the appropriate action to take.
- In the act phase, the DP functions then actuate the desired action of the data flow or sensors.

As an example, if a set of rules are being used to map observations into phenomenon, the rules are determined by the CP, while the rules are enforced by the DP. Similarly, the utility functions, policies, or defining the parameters of the game are CP functions, while the actual decision making is a DP function. The actual invocation of the action is a DP function.

The network-level OODA loop is similar to the device-level loop, though it has a global situational awareness derived from information provided by the network elements. So the OODA description above is modified to the following:

- In the observe phase, the DP function is still the actual collection of the data. Determining which type of information to collect and how to trade off the power and energy needs of an element against that of the normal computation would be the CP functions.
- In the orient phase, the mapping of observations into phenomena is a joint process, where some local fusion and processing may occur at the DP (to minimize network loading) and then part-processed observations are sent to the SDNC that will carry out global fusion and processing (e.g., threat correlation). Again, the CP function is the definition of the parameters in the algorithms that can enable the mapping of observation to phenomena, including the division of processing responsibilities.
- In the decide phase, the policy rules provided to the SDNC via the NBI are implemented in the CP which leads to decisions covering policies/rules/configuration on traffic handling, security configuration, and measurement functionality (to support the observe phase in both inner and outer loops).
- In the act phase the policies/rules/configurations are sent via the CCI to the individual DPs.

11.4.3 Orientation Phase Algorithms

As mentioned in Sect. 11.4.2, the primary task of the orientation phase is that of mapping observed data into a higher-level concept of phenomenon. The essential algorithm in the orientation phase is to take the input data and map it into a phenomenon. The input data consists of the network traffic (e.g., packet header logs, packet payload information), system logs (indicating errors and alerts), management data (e.g., information collected from SNMP MIBs or other management information on a device), etc. The phenomenon is a high-level description of the security situation in the environment, e.g., determining if there is an intruder node, if there is a misconfiguration in the environment, if a network or link is being overwhelmed because of a denial of service attack, etc.

The orientation phase algorithm can be viewed as a classification problem where the input data needs to be mapped into one or more classes, each class indicating the existence of one particular phenomenon. The classification problem can be solved by a variety of approaches, many of which borrow heavily from the field of artificial intelligence. In the classification problem, the input data is distilled down into one or more sets of features, and a combination of those features can be used to determine which phenomenon is being experienced. As an example, the input traffic data can be mapped into features such as the values defined for configuration parameters, values measured from system and network load, and distribution parameters of network traffic (e.g., the most popular and the least popular addresses and ports used by a given machine in the network and the relative ratios among them). Each of these features can be viewed as one dimension in a multidimensional plane, with the specific value of the features determining a point in the plane. Each observation (e.g., observing the network traffic at some interval of time) provides such a point, and one needs to determine which point belongs to which class (this indicating its corresponding phenomenon).

There are a variety of algorithms that can be used to address the classification problem. These include the k-nearest neighbor algorithm, support vector machines, neural networks, decision trees, and Bayes classifiers. A survey of these algorithms and how they are used for intrusion detection are found in [10].

Another set of algorithms that can be used to map input data to phenomenon consist of root cause analysis algorithms used in system management. These algorithms map input data into symptoms (which are essentially same as the features described earlier for AI-based algorithms) and try to figure out the root cause (or the phenomenon) which is causing the symptoms to exhibit themselves. These algorithms include network topology analysis, rule-based methods, decision trees, dependency graphs, and case-based reasoning. These algorithms and their use for root cause analysis are described in more detail in [11].

11.4.4 SDN for OODA-Based Cybersecurity

In the SDN architecture for cybersecurity, cybersecurity software on various devices
implements the DP functions. These use the SBI to get their configuration and
policies from the SDN agent on the same device. The SDN agent uses the CCI for its
configuration, rules, and policies from an SDNC, which provides them with the right
information needed for the DP operation. Each device implements its device-level
OODA loop and gets its CP information using the CCI. Similarly, the network-level
OODA loop also needs to get its CP information, which is also provided by the
SDNC using the CCI. The contents of the CP information would be very different
for the network-level OODA loop and the device-level OODA loop, but they can
use the same protocol to communicate with the SDNC. The structure is as shown in
Fig. 11.7.

The SDN approach ensures that the rules and configurations determined by
the SDNC are provided to different elements. In tactical environments, where
bandwidth is limited, disruption tolerant approaches would be needed to keep the
configuration parameters and policies of different elements in synchronization with
the values determined by the SDNC.

In the two-tier architecture, the DP consists of both the processing in the device-
level OODA loops at various devices and the network-level OODA loop. The
device-level OODA loops can communicate with the network-level OODA loop
using data flows that do not go through the SDNC1. These data flows are not shown
in Fig. 11.7.

As an example of data path communication between the various device-level
OODA loops and network-level OODA loop, consider an environment where one
wants to perform an intrusion detection function for the network, using an approach
like deep packet inspection. In this approach, protocol headers at higher levels are
reconstructed, and they require that network exchanges, both from a client to a
server (forward path) and from a server to a client (reverse path), be observed and

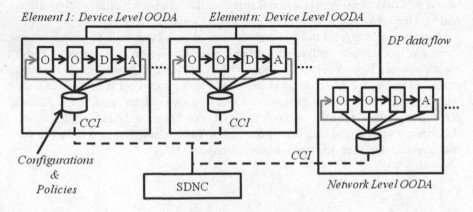

Fig. 11.7 OODA loop-based cybersecurity architecture using SDN

the results be combined to infer the progress of the higher-level protocol. However, in Internet Protocol (IP)-based communication, it is not unusual to have the forward path of a network exchange using the Transmission Control Protocol (TCP) to go through a set of devices that is different in the reverse path. In those cases, a device can only see half of the total packets being exchanged. The device-level OODA loop seeing the packets of the forward path and the device-level OODA loop seeing the packets on the reverse path can send a copy of the packets to the network-level OODA loop, which now has the information on both paths to perform the complete intrusion detection function processing.

Note that both the device-level and network-level OODA loops are data plane functions. The network-level OODA loop may or may not be collocated with the SDNC. When it is collocated with the SDNC, the benefit is that the number of points of vulnerability which can be used to attack the situational awareness system is reduced. When it is located on a separate device, the SDNC needs to be aware of that location and provide the appropriate CP information to that location. The advantage of separating the two is that the network-level OODA loop, which requires more resources, can be managed for scalability. An example of such manageability would be the ability to create multiple processes or virtual machines that perform the network-level OODA loop and to adjust the number of such processes and virtual machines depending on the amount of work needed. For the control path functions of SDNC, such scaling up and down for performance is not likely to be needed. The choice between the two modes, collocating the network-level OODA loop and the SDNC or having them on different machines, is dependent on the environment.

11.5 Coalition Tactical Environments

In a coalition environment, networks from two or more organizations need to work together. In a military coalition, the militaries from two or more nations need to come together to perform a joint mission [5]. In civilian coalitions, two independent agencies, e.g., firefighters and policemen need to work together.

The current state of the art is to have such collaboration mostly in the backend or base environments. Using SDN and the new architecture we propose, we can enable collaboration among coalition partners in the tactical environments as well. In general, coalition operations would set up their environments independently and have some level of network connectivity among them. They may have one or more tactical environments within each nation's network. In a typical coalition operation, a community of interest (CoI) is dynamically formed to conduct joint coalition operations. In a military context, the CoI can be an ad hoc team consisting of several coalition partners executing many concurrent missions including border/perimeter reconnaissance and surveillance, camp site surveillance, and detection/classification of human activities in concealed/confined spaces or locations of human infrastructures. In a civilian context, a CoI may be formed to search for missing people, rescue people from a derailed locomotive, or handle a fire in a high-rise building.

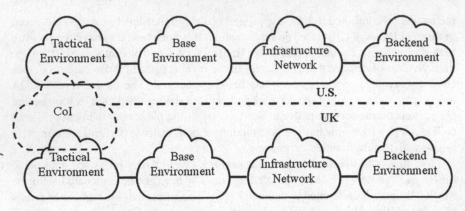

Fig. 11.8 Simplified model of a coalition network between the USA and the UK

A CoI brings together a set of assets, specific missions, and sets of policies that govern information security and sharing of information. The CoI environment would be built by combining assets from the tactical environments of multiple coalition partners, i.e., the dynamic CoI would take some assets from all of its partners in order to conduct its mission. One such sharing arrangement is shown in Fig. 11.8 where a dynamic CoI is formed between a US and UK coalition, e.g., when a joint patrol is formed to conduct surveillance in a specific area. In other cases, the CoI may also share assets from the base and other environments, including access to the back end.

When such a dynamic CoI is formed, assets from different partners may be shared. Each of the two nations may have policies limiting how the assets are shared, as well as how information from an asset may be shared with coalition partners.

11.6   Alternative Coalition SDN Architectures

In a coalition environment, we need to have a solution which brings together SDNC belonging to many different partners and have the resulting system work together seamlessly. Each partner in a coalition is likely to have a SDNC it operates and controls. In this section, we look at the various alternative options that can be used to coordinate different SDNC belonging to different partners.

For ease of notation, we are describing the coalition architecture as if there are two partners, the USA and the UK which are making a dynamic CoI. However, the architectures that are described here are applicable for a coalition of multiple partners (more than three) and may not include either of the two named countries. The two countries are just used as a short convenience for two coalition members.

Figure 11.9 shows one possible approach to support dynamic CoI in coalition SDN networks, which is to define a dynamic SDNC that is designated specifically for the CoI being supported. In this approach, if the USA and the UK need to form a

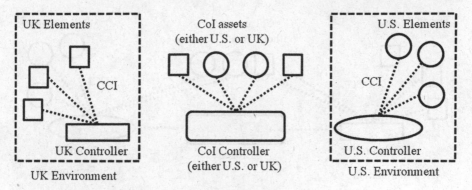

Fig. 11.9 Simplifying coalition CoI to a single organization CoI

tactical network with their assets, they designate one of their SDN controllers as the one to be used for the CoI. The different assets belonging to the coalition partners get configured and enabled by the CoI SDNC, as if they were part of the tactical environment for a single organization, as described in Sect. 11.2.2.

The advantage of this approach is that the operational logic and mechanics of the CoI is no different than that of the single organization network. The disadvantage of the approach is that it requires all nodes to interoperate with the SDNC. If the nodes from both countries use the same protocol, it is a nonissue. However, if the assets from different countries do not have the same protocol for communicating with the controller, the only viable solution is to use assets from only one country. Thus, the main decision in forming a CoI becomes which country/organization should be the one providing the assets. As a result, this approach does not enable efficient sharing of resources.

An alternative approach uses multi-domain multi-broker architecture in which the SDNCs retain their autonomy and communicate via a broker layer [6]. In such an architecture, an additional broker acts as the mechanism for enabling the decision making for SDNC from different countries, as shown in Fig. 11.10. In addition to the standard SDN controllers, a broker is introduced which acts as another layer providing the top-level hierarchy for coordinating SDN brokers. The layout of the broker and its relation to the SDNC of different coalition partners is illustrated in Fig. 11.10.

The advantage of this architecture is that each asset talks to the controller of their own organization, eliminating the challenges associated with interoperability. The broker provides the ability for the SDNC of each organization to work with each other, in effect, becoming a super controller. The main challenge with this approach is the issue associated with the operation of the broker. The coalition member operating the broker has a significant advantage in controlling the CoI compared to other partners. The issue of deciding which partner ought to run the broker can easily become very contentious.

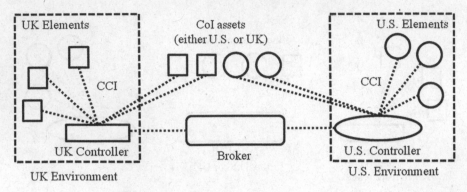

Fig. 11.10 Broker architecture for coalition SDN controllers

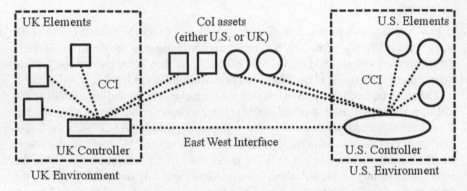

Fig. 11.11 Federated architecture for coalition SDN controllers

Another approach creates a distributed environment in which the broker is eliminated, while the equivalent functionality is provided by the collection of each country SDNC. This approach, illustrated in Fig. 11.11, avoids the tricky issue of control over the broker. In this approach, when a device requires direction for its DP actions, the controllers negotiate between themselves on an appropriate response that is forwarded to the device by the owning nation's SDNC. The distributed approach requires an east-west interface connecting different controllers and is operationally more secure since no additional elements are introduced which can act as a point of vulnerability.

These three solutions present alternative approaches for handling the issue of federation across different coalition controllers. The choice of the right solution depends on the level of trust among different partners and the degree of standardization between the nodes and SDNC. When SDNC and the nodes use the same interface, reducing the problem to a single organization system for the CoI would work. In other cases, the choice depends on the level of trust among coalition partners. When one partner is trusted to operate a broker, the broker-based approach will be most appropriate. When partners only trust each other partially, the distributed east-west approach is more suitable.

A comparison of the three different architectures is provided in [9]. The analysis performed there shows that the interoperability among different coalition environments is enhanced significantly by the federated and brokered architectures, as compared to the approach of simplifying the problem to a single organization architecture. Furthermore, from a complexity perspective, the simplification approach is the one with least amount of complexity. The broker approach is more complex, and the federated architecture is the most complex solution among the three. From a trust relationship perspective, the simplification approach and the broker approach require more trust in a single organization than the federated approach. From a standardization perspective, the simplification approach requires a higher degree of standards to be defined than the brokered or federated architectures.

11.6.1 Federated SDN-Based Cybersecurity for Coalitions

In a coalition environment, partners do not fully trust each other. As a result, the federated architecture described in Fig. 11.11 is the preferred solution for many coalition tactical environments. In these environments, each country network is likely to have their own SDNC, and all of the SDNCs need to be federated together to create a completely functional system for the overall network. As mentioned previously, that implies that the SDNC needs to be augmented with not just a north-south interface between the elements and the SDNC in individual country networks but with an east-west interface that is used to exchange information between the individual SDNCs. In this respect, the architecture we propose is similar in principle to coalition operations for ISR assets [7] and federation of military networks [8].

One way to define the east-west interface is to use a mechanism based on distributed systems such as Hyperledger [12]. Hyperledger is a system which allows tracking of transactions among different parties which all maintain a peer-to-peer relationship with each other and implements a distributed consensus protocol for all peers to determine whether or not a transaction has happened. An architecture for software defined coalitions based on Hyperledger is described in [13] and provides one of the ways in which the federated architecture described here can be implemented.

The architecture of a system with controllers from both the USA and the UK is shown in Fig. 11.12. In the figure, the oval and circular boxes represent assets belonging to the USA, while the square and rectangular boxes represent assets belonging to the UK. Each asset runs a device-level OODA loop, and let us assume that the network-level OODA loop is collocated with the controller in both countries. However, as mentioned earlier, such collocation is not strictly necessary.

The controllers in each of the individual networks are responsible for providing the policies, configurations, and parameters that drive the operation of each of their elements. The OODA loop implemented within the US elements and the UK elements could be quite different, with the use of different approaches in each of the individual country elements.

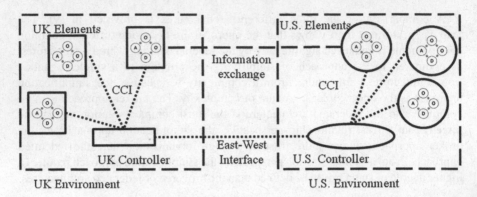

Fig. 11.12 OODA loop-based cybersecurity architecture using SDN for coalition networks

Devices in each of the two countries used the CCI interface to talk to their respective controllers. While the USA and the UK are not obligated to use the same protocol, a common protocol such as one based on a REST interface to harmonize policies and parameters of different elements is likely to be used in each nation. Nevertheless, the choice of specific names of variables and parameters, as well as policy format and specifications, are likely to be different in each nation. The east-west interface provides a mechanism for the controllers to work and interoperate with each other and to set up managed information exchange points between partner networks. This interface can be used to share policies or negotiate dynamic policies when CoI are formed dynamically.

Note that the east-west interface is used for control plane functions and to manage the data plane connections. In a coalition network, there may be multiple interconnections between the nodes for actual data exchange. Direct links may be established between US and UK nodes, if allowed by the applicable policies. The thin dashed line marked information exchange between the two nodes in Fig. 11.12 shows one such possible data path. Several of these data paths can be used in a coalition environment. As an example, if a UK node happens to be closer to several US nodes, it may choose to route packets using one or more of those US nodes instead of trying to connect only to the UK nodes. The control plane interconnection and data plane interconnections can be very different in these cases. This scenario is shown pictorially in Fig. 11.13, where the solid lines indicate the data flow used between the US and UK elements to implement an efficient routing mechanism (assuming that the same routing protocols are supported by both nations) and the dashed lines show the control flows, where each of the elements talks to the controller of their respective countries. Data flow may happen directly between the assets, but the control path information is provided by the controller of each of the two countries to their assets.

The federated coalition SDN architecture can be used to coordinate the security threat assessment and facilitate the sharing of information among different coalition partners. The information sharing can occur among the controllers (SDNC) of the

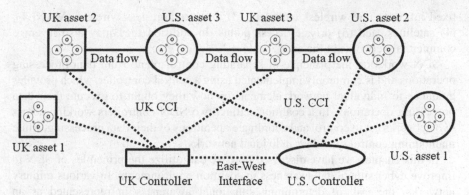

Fig. 11.13 Data path and control path flows in a coalition routing scenario

two countries, as well as directly between different nodes in the two countries. In the latter case, the SDNC would determine the policies that govern these direct exchanges but do not necessarily be on the path of actual data exchange.

As a very simple example, let us consider the case where a rogue terrorist is trying to launch an attack on the UAVs that are operated by coalition partners in a theatre of operation. Let us also assume that the terrorist has been able to determine the frequency at which commands are issued to the UAV and is trying to launch a scanning attack to determine if any communication port in the UAV is vulnerable. The USA may have detected the terrorist probes, and the US controller has installed a rule for orientation that maps more than three probes on illegal ports from a device to mark that device as unauthorized entity to be added to a blacklist. The UK detection module, however, may have ended up with a policy that locates the spatial region of the terrorist and in those regions disable all external communication and operate using a disconnected operation mode.

When a dynamic CoI is formed in which the USA and the UK both contribute UAVs for the operations, the controllers for both nations can share the policies they have formed with one another. This enables the UAVs for the CoI, which may have come from either country, to install the security policies which enable the joint insights from both nations to be used. The US UAVs can get insights about the vulnerability region in the theatre, while the UK UAVs get additional rules to learn the address of the device and block them dynamically even when exposed outside that region.

11.7 Conclusions

Coalition tactical networks are composed of different networks of two or more nations coming together for securing a mission in tactical arena. They may use heterogeneous networks using mixes of (1) handheld units, ISR devices, UAVs, (2) fixed infrastructure wireless (cellular), (3) infrastructure-less wireless (MANET), (4) satellites, and (5) private access points. In addition they may also leverage commercial networks in the area.

SDN works on the principle of separating control plane from data processing operations and is commonly implemented using a central controller, which provides guidance to individual network elements on how they ought to execute their data processing operations. In a coalition setting, two SDN controllers working across two networks act to control and coordinate operations of their data processing, while maintaining control over their individual networks.

In this chapter, we have discussed how we can utilize the principles of SDN to improve cyber situational awareness in coalition environments. In various military networks, the task of determining situational awareness in represented as an implementation of the OODA (observe-orient-decide-act) loop. In the context of security using SDN principles, we can draw an analogue of data plane and control plane in the context of cyber situational awareness. The data plane for situational awareness can be defined as comprising the set of elements that implement the actual OODA loop. The control plane for situational awareness can be defined as comprising the set of elements that provide the configuration, background knowledge, and configuration required by the data elements.

In this chapter, we have (a) introduced tactical coalition networks, (b) presented an architecture for applying SDN principles to address the task of cyber situational awareness for network security, (c) illustrated how the architecture can be used to understand the current situation for a cybersecurity threat, and (d) discussed alternative architectures for cooperation between different SDN controllers belonging to various coalition partners.

Review Questions

- What is a tactical environment?
- What are the key differences between a tactical environment and a backend environment like a data center?
- What are the different types of segments that make up a single organization network?
- What are the drawbacks of using the central controller approach for tactical environments?
- What are the different life-cycle stages for a node in a tactical environment?
- What unique issues are introduced by coalition networks in a tactical environment?
- What are the merits and demerits of collocating the network-level OODA loop data path functions and SDNC?
- What are the disadvantages in a coalition tactical network if all information exchange between partner environments is forced to go through their respective SDNC?

- Compare the benefits and drawbacks of the three approaches for coordination between the controllers of coalition partners?
- What are the typical control plane and data plane operations for a tactical environment node during its operational stage?

Acknowledgments This research was partially sponsored by the US Army Research Laboratory and the UK Ministry of Defence under Agreement Number W911NF-16-3-0001. The views and conclusions contained in this document are those of the authors and should not be interpreted as representing the official policies, either expressed or implied, of the US Army Research Laboratory, the US Government, the UK Ministry of Defence, or the UK Government. The US and UK Governments are authorized to reproduce and distribute reprints for government purposes notwithstanding any copyright notation hereon.

References

1. McKeown N et al (2008) OpenFlow: enabling innovation in campus networks. ACM SIG-COMM Comput Commun Rev 38(2):69–74
2. Willig A, Kubisch M, Hoene C, Wolisz A (2002) Measurements of a wireless link in an industrial environment using an IEEE 802.11-compliant physical layer. IEEE Trans Ind Electron 49(6):1265–1282
3. Brehmer B (2005) The dynamic OODA loop: amalgamating boyd's OODA loop and the cybernetic approach to command and control. In: Proceedings of the 10th international command and control research technology symposium
4. Ye F et al (2012) MECA: Mobile Edge Capture and Analysis middleware for social sensing applications. In: Proceedings of the 21st International Conference on World Wide Web. ACM
5. Verma D (2010) (ed) Network science for military coalition operations: Information Exchange and Interaction. IGI Global
6. Castro A et al (2016) Brokered orchestration for end-to-end service provisioning across heterogeneous multi-operator (multi-AS) optical networks. J Lightwave Technol 34(23)
7. Calo S et al (2009) Technologies for federation and interoperation of coalition networks. Information Fusion, 2009. FUSION'09. 12th international conference on. IEEE
8. Sørensen E (2014) SDN used for policy enforcement in a federated military network
9. Mishra V, Verma D, Williams C Marcus K (May 15–16, 2017) Comparing software defined architectures for coalition operations. In: Proceedings of the international conference on military communications and information systems, Oulu, Finland
10. Tsai C, Hsu Y, Lin C, Lin W (2009) Intrusion detection by machine learning: a review. Expert Syst Appl 36(10):11994–12000
11. Verma DC (2009) Principles of computer systems and network management. Springer, Heidelberg, Chapter 6, pp 143–155
12. Cachin C (2016) Architecture of the Hyperledger blockchain fabric. In: Proceedings of the workshop on distributed cryptocurrencies and consensus ledgers
13. Verma D, Desai N, Preece A, Taylor I A block chain based architecture for asset management in coalition operations. In: Proceedings of SPIE Defense + Commercial Sensing Symposium, Anaheim, CA, April 2017

Vinod K. Mishra received his PhD in Physics from the State University of New York (SUNY) at Stony Brook in 1983, with area of focus in theoretical nuclear physics. Earlier he got his Master of Science from Indian Institute of Technology, Kanpur (1977), and Bachelor of Science (Physics Honors) from Science College, Patna (1975). He was a postdoctoral researcher at various universities and research institutions before joining Lucent Technology Bell Labs, where he worked in many areas of optical and wireless networking. Later he came to Defense Information Systems Agency (DISA) and focused on advanced networking technologies. Currently he is a team leader at US Army Research Laboratory (ARL) conducting research in software-defined networking, dynamic optical networking, and quantum communication. He had published a book entitled *An Introduction to Quantum Communication* in 2016.

Dinesh C. Verma is an IBM fellow and manager of the Distributed Cognitive Systems area at IBM TJ Watson Research Center, Yorktown Heights, New York. In this role, he leads a research team creating new technologies that intersect the domain of cognitive computing, Internet of Things, and distributed systems and networks. He received his doctorate in Computer Science from University of California at Berkeley in 1992, Bachelors' in Computer Science from Indian Institute of Technology, Kanpur, India, in 1987, and Masters in Management of Technology from Polytechnic University, Brooklyn, NY, in 1998. He holds over 100 US patents and has authored over 100 papers and ten books in computer science. He is a fellow of the IEEE and a fellow of the UK Royal Academy of Engineering and has served in various program committees, IEEE technical committees, editorial boards, and managed international multi-institutional government programs.

Christopher Williams graduated from Oxford University with a first in engineering science and subsequently gained his PhD from Bristol University on the topic of chaotic waveforms for communications. Alongside periods in industry (research manager for Fujitsu) and academia (research fellow at Bristol University), much of his career has been in government defense research (Dstl and predecessors). His areas of expertise include novel waveforms, communications signal processing, modulation and coding, cognitive radio, and dynamic spectrum access.

An SDN and NFV Use Case: NDN Implementation and Security Monitoring

12

Théo Combe, Wissam Mallouli, Thibault Cholez, Guillaume Doyen, Bertrand Mathieu, and Edgardo Montes de Oca

12.1 Introduction

The development of software-defined networking (SDN) in the past few years and the more recent introduction of network functions virtualization (NFV) promise to simplify network management, with a significantly increased flexibility and real-time reconfiguration. The first application has been to apply this new SDN paradigm to existing networks, in order to simplify them. However one can go further in network softwarization, leveraging virtualization in both the control plane and the data plane, to build a fully virtualized network stack. Due to softwarization and standardization of hardware, development costs and times are shortened, and

T. Combe
Thales Services, La Défense, France
e-mail: theo.combe@thalesgroup.com

W. Mallouli (✉)
Montimage, Paris, France
e-mail: wissam.mallouli@montimage.com

T. Cholez
INRIA, Rocquencourt, France
e-mail: thibault.cholez@inria.fr

G. Doyen
UTT, Troyes, France
e-mail: guillaume.doyen@utt.fr

B. Mathieu
Orange, Paris, France
e-mail: bertrand2.mathieu@orange.com

E. Montes de Oca
Montimage, Paris, France
e-mail: edgardo.montesdeoca@montimage.com

© Springer International Publishing AG 2017
S.Y. Zhu et al. (eds.), *Guide to Security in SDN and NFV*, Computer Communications and Networks, DOI 10.1007/978-3-319-64653-4_12

the development of innovative network stacks from scratch is made possible. In this chapter, we present the DOCTOR architecture, which makes use of SDN and NFV to implement NDN, a networking paradigm in which routing is based on content names rather than host addresses. The goal of this paper is double: following a presentation of the NDN paradigm, we show how SDN and NFV can be used to provide an infrastructure layer on top of which the NDN stack can be deployed. In the context of DOCTOR, we aim at running this stack in a production network involving real users. We will detail the innovative aspects of the envisioned virtualized infrastructure, from the design of the architecture to its monitoring and interconnection with the IP World. We then focus on how to address security in this infrastructure. We perform a survey of the vulnerabilities introduced by NFV, SDN, and NDN and sort them in categories depending on the targeted components. For each attack we identify the target (SDN, NFV, or NDN), review possible remediations, and assess their feasibility. We finally propose a practical monitoring solution depending on NFV orchestration to collect information on network topology and on SDN to perform real-time remediation actions. This monitoring is performed by the CyberCAPTOR tool and Montimage Monitoring Tool (MMT) [1].

12.2   A Virtualized Architecture for the Deployment of Emergence Network Functions

Current networks generally consist of heterogeneous and vendor-locked hardware and software components, with little or no support for interoperability. This leads to complex network management. This vertical segmentation prevents telecom operators from rapidly deploying new services. Moreover, innovation cycles are often long, meaning that network operators are reluctant to introduce new paradigms or technology. New networking solutions require being fully designed (often including cumbersome standardization procedures), evaluated, monitored, and secured to ensure that they do not disturb existing services and can provide rapid return on investments. Faced with these limitations, telecom operators are adopting new approaches for building networks stemming from the wide adoption of virtualization techniques in data centers. Virtualization provides greater flexibility in sharing hardware resources, which result in cost reductions and faster service deployment. We are thus seeing the emergence of network softwarization consisting in building network functions virtualization components, which are treated as virtualized software instances deployed in virtual machines (VMs). In turn these virtual network functions (VNFs) can be chained and managed via software-defined networking controllers to create end-to-end communication services.

Our main objective in the DOCTOR project is to design a flexible and secure service-aware network architecture. The DOCTOR virtualized network architecture is designed with the NFV concept in mind to efficiently host network functions and services which can be performed at high throughput. Based on the SDN principles, the network control is separated from the data plane and is delegated to a controller. This controller allows configuring data routing, managing, and orchestrating network services. These services include network monitoring that makes it possible to secure the overall virtualized architecture for the detection of network anomalies and attacks.

12.2.1 Architecture Overview

Figure 12.1 shows an overview of the DOCTOR virtualized network infrastructure, including the functional blocks and their interactions. Note that the interactions or interfaces are numbered in the figure with different two colors (green and purple) to separate the SDN control plane for virtual network configuration from the NFV management plane, which concerns the virtualized functions.

We first designed a virtualized node to be able to deploy multiple network services as software instances or virtual network functions over a single physical host. Each deployed VNF thus runs on one or several virtual machines, depending on the design. As such, the DOCTOR virtualized node can be structured into three layers. The application layer contains the VNFs, deployed as virtual machines over a virtualization layer which provides an abstraction for the underlying hardware resources offered by the physical hosts. A virtual network based on programmable

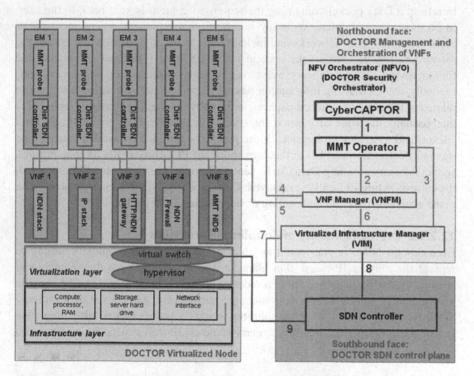

Fig. 12.1 Overview of the DOCTOR virtualized network infrastructure

virtual switches is then implemented to ensure end-to-end network connectivity between the virtualized machines but also to enable network automation at the control plane.

12.2.2 Deploying ICN-Based VNF: The DOCTOR Use Case

The flexibility of the DOCTOR virtualized infrastructure makes it possible to host existing or new network services. To demonstrate this, the deployment of both IP and NDN protocol stacks was undertaken. NDN [2] is a recent networking paradigm that proposes moving away from host-based communication networks toward content-based ones. The goal is to find a solution that is better suited for the massive diffusion of content in today's major Internet use cases, such as video delivery or social networks applications.

12.2.2.1 Named Data Networking Background
The novelty of NDN [2] relies on the key concept of naming content objects instead of naming hosts with IP addresses. NDN uses a hierarchical naming scheme for content objects, such as the Uniform Resource Identifier (URI). Communication in NDN is achieved using two types of packets: (1) Interest packets and (2) Data packets. A user issues a request for some content by sending an Interest packet. In return, a Data packet containing the requested content is sent back to the user. In NDN, a router implements many interfaces that represent a generalization of those provided by IP networks and include three main components that enable the forwarding process: firstly, the content store (CS) that is a local cache intended for improving content delivery by storing recently requested or popular content; secondly, the forwarding information base (FIB) that contains routing information related to the name of Interest packets; and finally, the pending interest table (PIT) that contains the state of emitted Interests with the purpose to route back Data packets and to aggregate requests. More precisely, for each forwarded Interest, the incoming interface is added to the corresponding PIT entry if not already present, so that the corresponding Data can be sent back to the user. For each Data received, the corresponding PIT entry is removed. Consequently, NDN defines a stateful data plane which enables efficient routing of Interest and Data packets.

12.2.2.2 On the Necessity of Coupling IP and NDN
Even though NDN is considered as a clean-slate approach eventually aiming to replace the current IP-based data plane, it appears that such a deployment will reasonably not occur in one shot. To address this, several studies [21–25] show to what extent IP and ICN (information-centric networking) can coexist by leveraging SDN. However, if each of these solutions brings a proof of feasibility, they also induce some limits (e.g., inability to carry standard IP traffic, need for an extension

of the OpenFlow protocol) due to the antagonist nature of these two networking paradigms. Consequently, a progressive deployment approach, standing for a serial combination of these protocol stacks, seems more realistic. This relies on the deployment of ICN islands inserted in the global IP network. Here, dedicated ICN/IP gateways are required to enable data transit through a boundary between heterogeneous domains. This solution can be of great value where ICN presents proven advantages when deployed on a particular topological location; and NFV appears as a promising means to enable such a deployment strategy.

The DOCTOR project advocates this type of deployment strategy that allows NDN to operate and to be assessed in real contexts without entailing high risks and costs. A typical use case could be the provision of a service (e.g., HTTP web traffic) consumed by real users generating real traffic patterns. From the perspective of users and the Internet, the deployment of NDN must be transparent, and the services must continue uninterrupted. To achieve this aim, dedicated gateways that convert the HTTP requests and responses, respectively, into Interest and Data packets have to be implemented and deployed. Figure 12.2 illustrates the operation of an NDN/HTTP gateway. Basically, an HTTP client sends an HTTP request (red arrow) to the ingress gateway which transforms it into Interest packets by mapping the initial URL to a name prefix. These are sent through the NDN via standard NDN routing to the egress gateway, thus benefiting from NDN mechanisms such as caching. The egress gateway collects the unresolved Interest packets, reconstructs the HTTP request, and sends them to the corresponding web server. The server then sends the Data in response to the egress gateway (green arrow) in the form of HTTP messages which, in a similar way, creates Data packets and sends them through the NDN to reach the HTTP client via the ingress gateway.

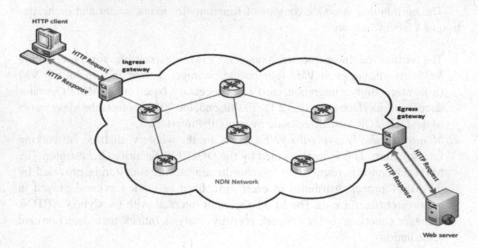

Fig. 12.2 NDN/HTTP gateway deployment

12.2.3 Managing the DOCTOR Architecture

Monitoring and managing the network is a critical task for network operators. It is necessary for guaranteeing the security and the performance of the network. It also provides valuable knowledge (e.g., network load, type of traffic, peak hours) useful for deploying and assessing new network services, such as the NDN protocol, or scaling existing services. To this end, specific virtualized functions were implemented for traffic monitoring and analysis, in particular for the detection and mitigation of network attacks specific to NDN. In this respect, each virtualized network service deployed in the application layer of the virtualized node is linked with an Element Manager (EM), which integrates a network monitoring function (provided by MMT (Montimage Monitoring Tool)), along with a distributed SDN Controller (dSDNC). These virtualized MMT probes and distributed SDN controller pairs allow to distribute the complexity of traffic monitoring over different virtual network functions in order to consolidate, intercorrelate, and aggregate monitored data (preprocessing) before sending them to the MMT Operator for deeper analysis in the context of unveiling network anomalies or attacks.

The DOCTOR virtualized network infrastructure also includes a framework providing dynamic configuration and management, as well as real-time security enforcement in the virtualized network. The proposed control and management plane (as represented on the right side in Fig. 12.1) consists in two function blocks:

- Infrastructure management and orchestration on the northbound interface
- Virtual network control on the southbound interface

The *northbound interface* consists of functions for management and orchestration of VNFs, which are:

1. The virtualized infrastructure manager (VIM), responsible for *provisioning hardware resources to VMs* (computing, storage, networking, including VM (re)configuration or migration, etc.) when necessary, based on the MMT Operator decisions (interface 3 in Fig. 12.1). To this end, the VIM controls the hypervisors of the DOCTOR virtualized node by using the interface 7.
2. *Monitoring and securing the VNFs*, to secure the whole virtualized networking infrastructure. This is implemented by the DOCTOR Security Orchestrator. The MMT Operator is responsible for coordinating traffic monitoring provided by the MMT probes distributed in each virtualized network service deployed in the project (interface 4). The MMT Operator interacts with the CyberCAPTOR manager (interface 1) for network security analysis (attack path detection and remediation).
3. *Management and configuration of the network functions* implemented with the VNFs. The MMT Operator obtains information from the CyberCAPTOR manager related to network security policies. It is thus able to apply remediations

or corrections on the virtualized network functions in response to network misuses (interface 2), through the VNF Manager using the interface 5. If needed, the VNF Manager can ask the VIM, via interface 6, to orchestrate (or allocate new) hardware resources for the VNFs.

The *southbound interface* of the DOCTOR control and management plane implements the *DOCTOR SDN control plane* which consists of an SDN controller interacting with virtual networks for dynamic configuration (interface 9). Following the SDN principles, the DOCTOR controller is mainly designed to acquire a global view of the network and enable centralized, intelligence-based network control. It actually interfaces with the DOCTOR Security Orchestrator (via the VIM using interface 8) to be notified of attacks or anomalies detected with the assistance of CyberCAPTOR, so as to correctly configure virtual networks to mitigate attacks. Its role includes, e.g., setting up the HTTP/NDN gateway to deliver traffic between heterogeneous network domains (i.e., IP and NDN), traffic load balancing, deploying rules in a firewall or an intrusion detection system/intrusion prevention system (IDS/IPS) service, adding/removing routes in NDN or IP router's forwarding tables, etc.

It is worth noting that the DOCTOR virtualized network infrastructure is designed respecting the recommendations from the ETSI NFV group, while leveraging the SDN principles for decoupling the control functions from the data plane. Thus, the application layer of the DOCTOR virtualized node consists of different VNFs which provide the suite of network services needed to deploy NDN; the virtualization and infrastructure layers of the node represent the NFV infrastructure (NFVI); and the northbound interface of the control and management plane in the DOCTOR virtualized infrastructure implements the NFV management and orchestration. The DOCTOR controller in the southbound interface is intended for making the virtualized network services programmable, allowing them to be managed and controlled by a central element. The SDN principles are thus implemented by the controller, enabling a clear separation between the control and forwarding planes and the centralization of network control to dynamically configure the network functions through well-defined interfaces.

12.3   Security Risks of SDN and NFV: DOCTOR Use Case

SDN and NFV facilitate security management but also introduce new threats. The flexibility they provide to network infrastructures allows their in-depth monitoring, with a central point gathering all needed information (the SDN controller and NFV orchestrator). However, these new features come with many new software elements and protocols, which increase the attack surface of the infrastructure. Moreover, some attacks specific to SDN and NFV have emerged. Consequently SDN and NFV have a bidirectional relationship with security: they both are security enablers and introduce vulnerabilities.

12.3.1 Security Issues Introduced by SDN and NFV

Network softwarization, in both control and data planes, generates a new attack surface that can be expressed as a set of vulnerabilities. These vulnerabilities target SDN control and data planes, NFV control plane, the virtualization layer, the accounting system, etc. In this section we propose a classification of the vulnerabilities related to SDN and NFV that need to be taken into account in a virtualized infrastructure.

In order to measure the risks faced by NFV and SDN, we adopt a practical point of view and survey the attacks. By attacks we mean any kind of malicious activity trying to collect, disrupt, deny, degrade, or destroy information or resources [3]] particularly targeting NFV and SDN. For this we identify the components that are likely targets and the possible attacks against them and propose ways to detect and mitigate attack occurrences. Although SDN and NFV are distinct technologies, they are complementary to form the infrastructure layer on top of which services are built. Therefore, threats on them can be assessed following the same taxonomy, i.e., the separation between control and data planes, which leads to a similar separation of threats.

12.3.1.1 Network Functions Virtualization Attacks
In a study [5], ETSI identifies the threat surface of NFV as the union of the threats to generic virtualization and networking. NFV being an implementation of cloud computing technologies for networking, we surveyed attacks that have been performed against cloud computing systems and hypervisors and analyzed the impact of such attacks on NFV.

Attacks on Virtual Network Functions
VNFs are software components providing network functions, so they are likely to be vulnerable to classic software flaws, such as denial of service (DoS), bypass of isolation, and arbitrary code execution using, e.g., buffer overflows. Denial of service is not a new threat, but in a virtualized environment, its scope changes since DoS attacks can have side effects and affect other services collocated with the target. Arbitrary code execution allows an attacker to take over a VM or a VNF component, potentially compromising the whole VNF and providing a machine to continue or launch attacks. The principle is the same as for classical software, and such vulnerabilities are widely described in the CVE (Common Vulnerabilities and Exposures) database.

Against these attacks, the proposed solutions consist in leveraging virtual machine introspection (VMI) which allows a monitor running on the host to check the integrity of the VMs. If a VM is taken over by an attacker (meaning that all detection mechanisms inside the VM are hence disabled or bypassed), the VMI can still detect and report the attack. An overview of VMIs is available in [6]. It provides a classification of VMIs that only report attacks and other ones that can take action against them. A detailed formalism is proposed in [7].

Attacks on Virtualization Layer

Several types of attacks can be performed on the virtualization layer, such as:

- *Code execution on the physical host*: Wojtczuk [6] presents several attacks against common hypervisors (QEMU-KVM, VirtualBox, Xen) that allow code execution on host from a compromised or malicious virtual machine. These attacks allow a malicious VM to escape isolation and execute code on the host. For instance, concerning the lightweight virtualization, older versions (e.g., <1.6.2) of Docker (used for implementing VNFs in DOCTOR) contain a vulnerability. It is identified by CVE-2014-9357 and allows uncompressing a Docker image to traverse the file system back to the root, permitting to override system binaries and leading to delayed arbitrary code execution. Another example, identified by CVE-2015-3630, shows how containers can modify shared resources to change host kernel parameters. This is possible when the isolation between hosts and containers is being assured by a blacklist of resources that cannot be accessed by containers, but the list is missing some elements that let containers access critical data on the host. For instance, some subdirectories like /proc and /sys are container-specific, and others are system wide.

- *Resource monopolization*: These attacks aim at overriding the hypervisor's resource limitations. Riddle and Chang [7] present attacks that steal resources. One, monopolization of CPU concerns VMs running over a Xen hypervisor that can use up to 98% of the physical host's CPU, hence denying the CPU to other VMs. This will provoke a DoS or abusive charging fees in a pay-per-cycle model. Another, determining whether two VMs are co-resident, can be the starting point of another attack such as a side-channel attack to steal data, taking advantage of Xen's credit scheduler.

  Yet another, I/O performance-based attacks, is based on knowing the scheduling of the hypervisor. This information can be used to overload I/O resources, resulting in slowing down co-resident VMs (or VNFs).

- *Data theft*: Data theft on the hypervisor can be performed by directly reading another VM's memory or disk by exploiting a vulnerability in the hypervisor or using a side-channel attack against cryptographic keys. Riddle and Chang [7] explain that if the target VM is co-resident with the attackers' malicious VM and is infected with malware, then the attacker can use memory bus or cache contention to stealthily steal data, e.g., keys, from the target VM [8], proposes a method to infer execution path in a co-resident VM from cache timing attacks. Containers are even more vulnerable than VMs. The vulnerability CVE-2015-3630 in Docker allows a malicious container to directly access information related to other containers. This is possible due to a shared file in the /proc directory. The kernel vulnerability CVE-2015-2925 allows to escape mount namespace (double-chroot-like) and can give a malicious container at least read access to another container's disk image.

- *VM monitoring evasion*: These attacks aim at evading VM monitoring. Riddle and Chang [7] present the VM rollback attack that is possible when the hypervisor is already compromised. The attacker may execute a VM from an older snapshot without the VM owner knowing of it, allowing to bypass security mechanisms. For example, if the attacker is brute forcing a password, causing the VM to raise a security alert, the compromised hypervisor can roll back to the previous snapshot so that the attacker can continue the attack. This allows avoiding internal VM monitoring.

Against all these attacks targeting the virtualization layer, a dedicated protection layer can be added by hardening the host to prevent the hypervisor process from accessing anything but the resources its associated VM can access (suited in the case of hypervisors running one or more processes per VM, as in the case of KVM or Docker). If an attacker manages to escape from a VM, it will have access only to the resources related to this VM on the host. Such hardening systems exist in Linux environments (e.g., SELinux and AppArmor). Moreover, attempts to access forbidden resources can be logged and reported (e.g., using auditd).

More generally, an intrusion detection system on the host (HIDS) can be used to detect VM evasion attacks (code execution and data theft on VM disks). For instance, in [9] the authors propose an architecture to automatically build AppArmor profiles that match the Docker containers' needs and trace their execution with an HIDS.

Orchestrator and/or VNF Manager

The orchestrator is in charge of placing the VMs on the nodes, triggering automatic scaling, chaining in the case of service chaining, reconfiguring the VNFs live (e.g., changing firewall rules in the case of a firewall VNF), etc. Thus, orchestrators are critical elements that centralize all configuration information. Attackers can target them either to disrupt services (DoS), to gain information on the infrastructure, or even to take control of the data path of the VNFs. For instance, the create_images_and_backing method in libvirt driver in OpenStack Compute (Nova), using KVM live block migration, does not properly create all the expected files. This allows attackers to obtain snapshot root disk contents of other users via ephemeral storage. In an NFV over OpenStack environment, this could be used to steal cryptographic keys from other VNFs, enabling further *eavesdropping*, data modification, or impersonation.

The orchestrator is subject to classical software vulnerabilities, so detection methods include hardening the machine on which it runs, logging all events and syscalls, or running the orchestrator inside a VM to benefit from virtual machine introspection. Since it is a single point of failure, redundancy is required to avoid DoS attacks.

Other Threats and Attacks

Apart from the abovementioned elements that are core components of an NFV architecture, security must also be ensured for the following miscellaneous elements:

Communications with and within NFV MANO (Management and Orchestration): Communications between the VNFs and NFV MANO are subject to classical network eavesdropping and tampering though man-in-the-middle (MITM) attacks.

However, authentication, encryption (TLS) of the communication, and the use of a dedicated control network can prevent this type of attacks.

* *Virtualized infrastructure manager*: The VIM is in charge of managing virtual resources and of directly controlling the hypervisor including VM images, snapshots, compute, RAM, and storage, located at the infrastructure operator domain. An attacker may breach the VIM to launch his own VNFs, modify VM images to add some code, exfiltrate data, etc. As we see here, the VMI is subject to classical software vulnerabilities, so detection methods are similar to those described in the previous subsection.

12.3.1.2 Software-Defined Networking Attacks

Decoupling the data plane from the control plane, SDN also suffers from threats on both of these two planes.

Packet Flooding

On the data plane, a known distributed DoS (DDoS) attack against SDN consists in flooding a switch by sending crafted packets with many different source addresses/ports. Each different source address leads to a flow miss, and the packet is forwarded to the controller. This results in the saturation of the link between the controller and the switch and of the controller's computing capacities.

Regarding the control plane, the following two topology poisoning attacks are unique to SDN and affect major SDN controllers such as Floodlight [10] and OpenDaylight [11]. They aim at deceiving the controller regarding the topology.

Host-Location Hijacking

This attack exploits the host tracking service of the controller that maintains a profile for each host in the network and updates it as the host migrates to impersonate a specific web server and phish users. To do so, the attacker first retrieves the target's identifier used by the controller to identify the host (here: the MAC address) and then injects fake packets in the name of the target host. As a result, users trying to access the genuine server are redirected to the malicious server.

The *host-location hijacking attack* could be tackled by adding an authentication mechanism on the packets, making sure received packets are issued by the legitimate host. However, this would require signature verification for each packet (with large overhead) and an additional public key infrastructure (PKI) for the hosts. Another proposed defense is to monitor preconditions and post-conditions surrounding a host migration. For instance, the precondition for a legitimate host migration is that the former location of the host and the corresponding switch port are not used anymore and that the controller has received a PORT_DOWN message. Similarly, a post-condition is that the host is unreachable at the previous location after migration. As a detection mechanism, the controller/switch could check these conditions when a migration occurs, and any migration that violates them (spoofed message from an attacker) could be detected and ignored in the host profile.

Link Fabrication

This attack consists in creating a fake link in the network either by injecting fake link layer discovery protocol (LLDP), a protocol used by the switches to automatically discover neighbors, packets, or via a relay fashion, i.e., without modifying the packets. This attack can be a first step for other attacks, such as a DoS attack, by taking advantage of the spanning tree algorithm used by OpenFlow controllers to incapacitate normal switch ports, or an MITM attack, by using the fact that once it detects that a new link is up, the controller recomputes the shortest route (Shin et al. [12 change]) and could redirect packets to a host controlled by the attacker.

The *link fabrication attack* could be detected by authenticating LLDP packets, introducing the same large overhead and PKI issues as for host-location hijacking. Another detection mechanism proposed is in the hypothesis that the attacker is not on an SDN switch but on a host linked to the network. In this case, SDN switches could tag all their ports as HOST or SWITCH, depending on whether they are connected to a host or another switch. Such identification is possible by detecting host-specific traffic (e.g., DNS, ARP) on the links. Since LLDP packets are only exchanged with other switches and the controller, any LLDP packet coming from a HOST-tagged port would be detected as an attack and dropped. To evade this detection, an attacker would have to stop all host-specific traffic on his machine. While this is possible on the attacker's own machine, it would disrupt normal service on a compromised host, leading to detection.

12.3.2 Security Threats in IP vs. NDN

NDN is designed to intrinsically prevent some types of threats that IP needs to solve using external mechanisms. In IP networks, an attacker can send altered data to end users, thus causing damage when content is delivered. To avoid this, IPsec or transport layer security (TLS) needs to be used to prevent any data alteration and avoid other security issues. On the other hand, NDN signatures are intrinsically computed and included in each NDN Data packet. The user receiving the Data packet can use the information to verify the signature, hence ensuring the authenticity of the content and avoid tampered data.

The caching technique also helps reduce the impact of denial of service attacks. In this type of attack, a targeted machine is flooded with superfluous requests in an attempt to overload systems and prevent legitimate requests from being fulfilled, but the caching mechanism intrinsically protects content servers from flooding attacks.

However, each NDN router keeps the incoming Interest packets in its PIT after forwarding them to enable the routing of related Data packets and also avoid the duplication of Interests. This exposes the PIT to an attack that consists of sending a large amount of Interest packets of nonexisting content in a short period of time. The consequence of this stateful routing mechanism is that the PIT can be overloaded and thus cannot process Interest packets from legitimate users. This type of attack is called interest flooding attack (IFA), and performing such attack is simple because NDN enables requesting content by name which can be easily crafted by attackers. It has been extensively studied [14–19], as in [20] that relies on a custom simulator component and provides guidelines for its design and implementation. A recent release of the NDN reference implementation (NDN Forwarding Daemon – NFD) partially solves this issue by implementing a NACK packet which enables the rapid removal of Interests for nonexisting content from the PIT. Nevertheless, there are still some attack patterns that are possible as indicated in [26].

For instance, if we consider the serial combination of IP and NDN domains, deployed into a virtualized infrastructure, one can easily understand that the stateful nature of NDN combined with in-network caching will exhibit different security properties as compared to the stateless nature of IP. To further understand the impact of this coupling on the overall security, we consider the IFA use case previously described but now implemented in a scenario in which NDN and IP are coupled to forward web traffic. In this case, an attacker, located in an IP domain who wants to reproduce an IFA in an intermediate NDN island by leveraging HTTP traffic, may try to flood the network with HTTP requests for nonexisting web content. However, as illustrated in Fig. 12.2, users are not directly connected to the NDN network but to the Ingress Gateway, thus moving the problem to this entry point that should be able to detect flooding attacks with regular DoS mitigation strategies for IP networks.

In order to successfully perform the IFA in a combination of NDN and IP domains, an attack must go beyond the basic IFA mechanism. A possible attack scenario consists in stretching the responding delay of any HTTP answers with the help of a malicious website (Fig. 12.3 IFA setup in an IP/NDN environment). The consequence of this scenario is that IP and NDN do not protect themselves, as before, but rather make the phenomenon harder to mitigate. From an IP perspective, the symmetric nature of the traffic, as well as its rate-limited nature, makes it an ideal candidate for the definition of detection rules that an intrusion detection system can implement. In IP domains, the attack traffic cannot be separated from the legitimate one. By contrast, in the NDN domain, the delay spent by Interest to get Data packets unavoidably fills the PIT and prevents the NACK from removing these illegitimate

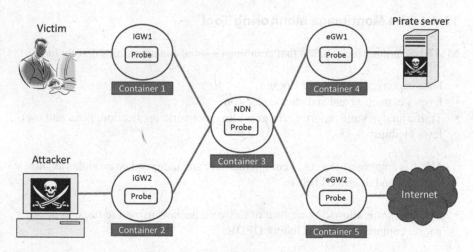

Fig. 12.3 IFA setup in an IP/NDN environment

entries. Decupling this pattern by endorsing a sufficient amount of partner websites can easily lead to PIT collapses in the NDN nodes.

To conclude, we have shown how the combination of networking domains can be easily deployed in a virtualized infrastructure. We have also shown that in the case of denial-of-service attacks, for instance, novel security mitigations are possible but new threats also exist and need to be addressed. The normal behavior in one domain may be considered as an abnormal in another due to the different protocols and network functions running. Furthermore, the security mechanisms are divided, and network operators in charge of a particular domain lack a global view of the threats that would allow them to better understand what is occurring in the network to be able to detect and mitigate attacks and malfunctions. The next section presents how practical tools can be used to defend against the aforementioned security threats.

12.4   CyberCAPTOR and MMT: A Set of Tools for a Secure Deployment of NDN as Virtual Network Functions

A major asset of SDN and NFV is to provide a high level of programmability to networks. This can be used to enforce complex security policies, detailed monitoring, and fast reaction on threat detection. In the DOCTOR project, collaboration between Thales and Montimage resulted in a cyber monitoring and reaction tool set that leverages SDN and NFV concepts and is adapted to the particular context of NDN. The Montimage Monitoring Tool provides network information on topology, metrics, and alerts of the NDN and NFV/SDN network to Thales' CyberCAPTOR tool, which relies on an analysis of attack graphs to assess possible attack paths and their level of risk. We describe these two components and their functionalities in this section.

12.4.1 The Montimage Monitoring Tool

MMT is a monitoring solution that combines a set of functionalities that include:

- Data capture, filtering, and storage
- Events extraction and statistics collection
- Traffic analysis and reporting for providing, network, application, flow, and user-level visibility

MMT is composed of a set of complementary and independent modules as shown in Fig. 12.4 and described below.

- *MMT Capture* allows the capture of network packets using the libpcap or other packet capture libraries including DPDK.

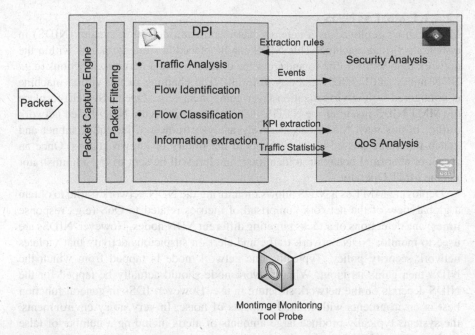

Fig. 12.4 MMT global architecture

- *MMT Filter* is a basic filtering tool that permits focusing on only some specific types of traffic depending on the usage of the network probe.
- *MMT DPI* is the core packet processing module. It is a C library that analyzes network traffic using deep packet and flow inspection (DPI/DFI) techniques in order to extract network and application-based events and measure network, per-application QoS/QoE parameters, and key performance indicators (KPIs). In the context of DOCTOR, a new plugin to monitor the NDN protocol stack has been developed to extract different NDN protocol field values and perform basis statistics. This extracted metadata is important for performing security analysis of the communications between different NDN nodes and detecting potential security flaws specific or not specific to NDN.
- *MMT Security* is a rule engine that analyses and correlates network and application events to detect performance, operational, and security incidents. The rules are written in XML and permit to aggregate detected events using logical (AND, OR, NOT) and temporal (BEFORE, AFTER) operators. It has self-learning capabilities to obtain network intelligence, perform dynamic threshold-based analysis, and identify possible denial-of-service attacks.
- *MMT QoS* allows providing visibility on the quality of the network in terms of different KPI, such as delays, jitter, response times, etc., that can also be used to help detect DoS attacks.
- *MMT Operator* is a JavaScript web application that allows visualizing reports and alarms generated by the probes.

12.4.1.1 MMT as NIDS

MMT can be deployed as a network-based intrusion detection system (NIDS) in a separate virtual machine. This NIDS can be placed at strategic points within the network to monitor traffic to and from the different virtual network functions (e.g., NDN nodes, HTTP/NDN gateway, firewall). The chaining of the virtual machine is configured by the virtualization layer component (e.g., Open vSwitch) to place the MMT NIDS just after the HTTP/NDN for intercepting the NDN-based network traffic. In this way, MMT can passively analyze traffic on the entire subnet and match the traffic passed on the subnets to the library of known attacks. Once an attack or abnormal behavior is identified, an alert will be sent to the administrator via the MMT Operator.

Deploying MMT as a NIDS allows monitoring the NDN network traffic to obtain a global view of the network comprised of metrics related to QoS (e.g., response times) and detections of attacks targeting different NDN nodes. However, NIDSs are used to monitor NDN network traffic and alert on suspicious activity that violates network security policy. Typically, one network node is tapped from which the NIDS then gains its input. What network node should actually be tapped for the NIDS depends on the network structure in use. However, IDSs in general function best in environments with limited amounts of noise. In very noisy environments, the systems typically produce large amounts of alerts including a number of false positives. Thus, NIDS needs to be placed at strategic points to monitor traffic to and from the different devices and virtual machines, and network policy will be enforced by the security rules defined and activated.

12.4.1.2 MMT Deployed Inside Each VNF

A lightweight version of MMT probes can be co-located with each VNF. This allows the analysis of metrics and security indicators related to the VNF. In this scenario, only parts of the parsing plugins in MMT DPI are needed to fulfill the list of protocols used by the VNF. Besides, the security analysis and intrusion detection needs only to target the risks and vulnerabilities identified for the given VNF application and differentiate abnormal activity from allowed activity. The security analysis methodology and properties of an NDN node are indeed different from the ones for a firewall or an HTTP/NDN gateway.

The performance impact of the monitoring probe can be reduced when it focuses only on part of the network traffic. Besides, the monitoring tool can analyze specific VNF security issues and apply advanced algorithms to detect pre-identified risks and attacks targeting the single VNF. It can be adapted to the specific requirements of NDN nodes to analyze NDN activity and detect any abnormal behavior. However, the monitoring tool installed in each VNF consumes part of the memory and CPU allocated for the VNF. This can have an impact on the network operation and can add delays in communications. Furthermore, the monitoring tool will have only local visibility of the VNF traffic which compromises the detection of collaborative attacks or attacks involving different network paths. This last limitation is addressed by the sharing of data between MMT probes (P2P cooperation) and by performing centralized analysis (done by the MMT Operator) in order to improve intrusion detection capability.

12.4.1.3 Collaborative Monitoring

The deployment of MMT probes inside VNFs or as NIDS and the collaboration between distributed probes, directly using P2P communications or through the centralized application, allow to dynamically build the network topology and even to detect at runtime any change that may occur during the network operation (e.g., adding or removing network nodes and functions).

This information, as well as the detection of network incidents including functional or nonfunctional incidents, allows providing valuable input to the CyberCAPTOR tool to assess the risk of such adaptive virtual network and propose relevant remediation to mitigate the impact of a vulnerability or stop an ongoing attack (e.g., malicious data exfiltration or scans). The remediation action to be taken needs to be selected at runtime (preferably in an automated way) and then orchestrated by the VNF manager and/or SDN controller to ensure the security of the NFV-/SDN-based environment.

12.4.2 CyberCAPTOR

CyberCAPTOR is a security monitoring tool based on an attack graph model. Initially developed for physical networks, it was later adapted to virtualized networks and eventually NDN in the particular context of the DOCTOR project. It is composed of four main modules forming a data pipeline and a graphical visualization interface. These modules are attack graph generation, attack paths extraction, attack path scoring, and remediation. The first three modules are automatically chained (with parameters given by the operator), while the remediation module requires manual validation to commit a remediation proposal.

CyberCAPTOR's inputs are the network topology, vulnerability scans of the machines, fixed and variable costs for applying elementary remediation, operational costs for the infection of a given machine or denial of service, and an up-to-date vulnerability database (the NVD database [13]). Its outputs are the complete attack graph, all the extracted attack paths, their scores, and a list of remedies (i.e., list of actions to perform) for a given attack path.

12.4.2.1 Attack Graph Generation

The attack graph approach allows a defender to enumerate all possible attack paths for an attacker, given a network topology (i.e., network and software configuration, VM placement, and domain dependencies). It relies on an up-to-date vulnerability database and a global knowledge of the network. CyberCAPTOR depends on the MulVAL attack graph engine [4]. It is an engine that uses generic rules and vulnerability information from the system to produce attack graphs. A few dozen

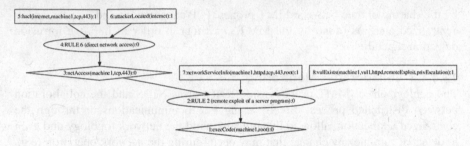

Fig. 12.5 Simple attack graph

rules are enough to model most attack steps. System topology and vulnerability information are used as parameters for the generic rules, thus forming attack steps. These attack steps have several inputs, called preconditions, and an output, called post-condition. MulVAL then produces an AND-OR graph, composed of three types of nodes: AND nodes, OR nodes, and LEAF nodes.

An attack step needs all its preconditions to be true to satisfy its post-condition. For this, "AND" logical nodes are used. On the other hand, "OR" nodes represent different ways for an attacker to gain some level of privileges on the network (e.g., different attack steps that lead to the same post-condition). LEAF nodes are nodes without preconditions. They correspond to elementary preconditions or "facts," i.e., information given as input. These facts are the conditions that can further be remediated. In the example shown by Fig. 12.5, there are four leaves, two AND nodes, and two OR nodes.

12.4.2.2 Attack Path Extraction
The complete attack graph for a company network is very large (potentially millions of edges for a few hundred machines), so that it is not relevant to present it to an operator. Due to the complexity of many information systems, focusing interest on particular subgraphs of the attack graph is necessary. A noticeable subgraph category is attack paths.

An attack path is a subgraph of an attack graph corresponding to all graph nodes an attacker can cross to reach a certain objective (generally execute code on a given machine). It is a directed acyclic graph (DAG) rooted on the target machine. Its LEAF nodes are all facts of the topology that can be used to attack a particular target. Attack paths consequently show the subset of facts that can be changed in order to thwart the attack (Fig. 12.6).

12.4.2.3 Scoring
Attack paths are scored according to various metrics, in order to automatically present the most relevant paths to an operator. This is done by assessing the criticality of each attack path or the likelihood of their occurrence. Attack path scores have two components: impact score and risk score.

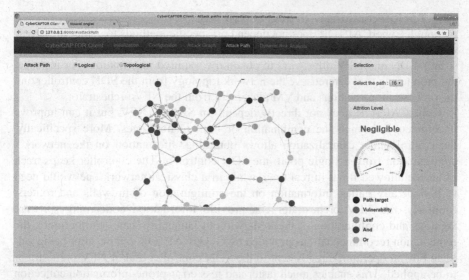

Fig. 12.6 Attack path extraction with CyberCAPTOR

The impact score is defined as the sum of local impacts for all vertices of the attack graph. The local impact for each vertex is defined by the user, often motivated by operational aspects. By default, each rule (e.g., vulnerability exploitation, network access) has a constant local impact.

Risk scores model the likelihood of the realization of an attack path. It is computed from the LEAF nodes of the attack path to its root: each LEAF represents a fact, with a default risk (depending on the fact), and each AND and OR nodes has a risk depending on the corresponding fact or rule and the number of ingoing and outgoing vertices of the node.

Each attack path is given a score, which are then normalized between 0 and 1 and sorted.

12.4.2.4 Remediation

CyberCAPTOR provides information on possible remediation actions to prevent the exploitation of identified attack paths. This corresponds to a list of actions that need to be carried out on the network topology that will disable the attack path. A remediation action is an elementary change in the topology. Each remediation action roughly corresponds to a different precondition. For instance, a patch remediates a vulnerability, a firewall rule remediates a network access, and moving a VM protects it from security incidents on a particular host.

Since multiple-action combinations can be applied, all combinations are proposed so that the operator can choose the best one according to functional/business needs. Once a remediation has been chosen, the attack paths are recomputed to take into account the topology changes.

12.4.2.5 Interactions with SDN and NFV

Although CyberCAPTOR does not depend on specific methods to gather the necessary knowledge (e.g., network scans, static configuration file analysis, vulnerability scans), SDN and NFV offer ways to obtain the required information. For instance, the monitoring tool can retrieve the network topology from the SDN controller and the orchestration relations and VM placement from the NFV orchestrator.

CyberCAPTOR does not directly depend on SDN or NFV, but it can improve its efficiency through the combination of both technologies. More specifically, the control plane centralization allows obtaining information on the network's configuration from a single point: the SDN controller. The controller keeps track of all the allowed flows in real time, while in a classical network one would need to periodically gather information on the configuration of firewalls and routers. Similarly, the NFV orchestrator can provide information concerning software versions and configuration of the VMs without launching scans. Furthermore, the remediation recommendations provided by CyberCAPTOR can be, after being validated by an operator, directly sent to the SDN controller and/or NFV orchestrator to be applied. This enables much faster and less error-prone information collection and remediation enforcement than can be achieved manually.

MMT and CyberCAPTOR are therefore fully complementary: the first can provide from its deep monitoring the detailed states of the virtualized architecture to CyberCAPTOR, which can in turn give back the critical attack paths to be monitored and the remediations to perform, leading to a very efficient architecture to secure the deployment of NDN as virtual network functions.

12.5 Conclusion

SDN and NFV promise a greater flexibility in networks, by the means of a separation between the control and data planes, a centralization of management via controllers and orchestrators, and the massive use of virtualization for the data plane, at the expanse of an increasing complexity of the infrastructure. We showed through the architecture of the DOCTOR project how these emerging technologies allow deploying novel network stacks such as NDN that can coexist with IP thanks to network slicing while bringing new services like optimizing content distribution at the network level.

Moreover SDN and NFV allow improved security monitoring, permitting faster and more accurate knowledge of the network through a centralized control plane. However the added complexity, both in SDN/NFV and in the NDN stack, brings a large attack surface, which we tried to assess, in order to thwart the most likely attacks. For each technology, we presented the main known attacks and ways to detect and mitigate them.

Our prototype is monitored and secured thanks to a proactive approach with CyberCAPTOR and a reactive approach thanks to Montimage Monitoring Tool, both tools being complementary and needed to secure such a complex and innovative architecture.

The natural following of this research work is to assess the whole infrastructure while processing real user traffic while facing attacks in the same time. Therefore, we plan to involve soon real users thanks to the HTTP/NDN gateway.

Exercises

- What is NDN? Is it secure? How to detect an NDN attack?
- Which network use cases are addressed by NDN?
- What are some practical applications of SDN and NFV?
- How do SDN and NFV make NDN implementation possible? Are they necessary?
- What risks and vulnerabilities are brought by SDN and NFV?
- How to use SDN and NFV as levers to secure an information system?

References

1. Montimage website. Available: http://www.montimage.com/products.html
2. NDN. Available: https://named-data.net
3. CNSS, National Information Assurance Glossary. Available: http://www.ncsc.gov/nittf/docs/CNSSI-4009_National_Information_Assurance.pdf
4. MulVAL Project at Kansas University. Available: http://people.cs.ksu.edu/ xou/mulval/
5. ETSI-ISG-NFV, Network Functions Virtualisation (NFV); NFV Security; Problem Statement, 2014. Available: http://www.etsi.org/deliver/etsi_gs/NFVSEC/001_099/001/01.01.01_60/gs_NFVSEC001v010101p.pdf
6. Wojtczuk R (2014) Poacher turned gamekeeper: lessons learned from eight years of breaking hypervisors. In: Black Hat USA, 2014
7. Riddle ARCASM (2015) A survey on the security of hypervisors in cloud computing. In: IEEE 35th International conference on distributed computing systems workshops, 2015
8. Wang G, Estrada ZJ, Pham C, Kalbarczyk Z, Iyer ARK (2015) Hypervisor introspection: a technique for evading passive virtual machine monitoring. In: WOOT, 2015
9. Kreutz D, Ramos FMV, Verissimo AP (2013) Towards secure and dependable software-defined networks. In: HotSDN, 2013
10. Floodlight OpenFlow Controller. Available: http://www.projectfloodlight.org/floodlight/
11. The OpenDaylight Platform. Available: https://www.opendaylight.org/
12. Shin S (2014) Rosemary: a robust, secure, and high-performance network operating system. In: CCS, 2014
13. National Vulnerability Database. Available: https://nvd.nist.gov/download.cfm
14. Gasti P et al (2013) DoS and DDoS in named data networking. In: Conference on Computer Communications and Networks (ICCCN). IEEE, 2013, pp 1–7
15. Dai H et al (2013) Mitigate DDoD attacks in NDN by Interest traceback. In: Proceedings of IEEE INFOCOM NOMEN Workshop, 2013
16. Compagno A et al (2013) Poseidon: mitigating interest flooding DDoS attacks in named data networking. In: International conference on Local Computer Networks (LCN). IEEE, 2013, pp 630–638
17. Afanasyev A et al (2013) Interest flooding attack and countermeasures in named data networking. In: IFIP networking conference. IEEE. 2013, pp 1–9
18. Nguyen T, Cogranne R, Doyen G (2015) An optimal statistical test for robust detection against Interest flooding attacks in CCN. In: FIP/IEEE international symposium on Integrated Network Management (IM), I. 2015, pp 252–260

19. Nguyen TN et al. (2015) Detection of Interest flooding attacks in named data networking using hypothesis testing. In: IEEE international Workshop on Information Forensics and Security (WIFS), . 2015, pp 1–6
20. Virgilio M., Marchetto G., Sisto R (2013) PIT overload analysis in content centric networks. In: Proceedings of 3rd ACM SIGCOMM workshop on Information-centric networking. ACM. 2013, pp 67–72
21. Vahlenkamp M, Schneider F, Kutscher D, Seedorf J (2013) Enabling information centric networking in IP networks using SDN. In: IEEE SDN for Future Networks and Services (SDN4FNS), 2013, Trento, pp 1–6
22. Salsano S., Blefari-Melazzi N., Detti A., Morabito G., Veltri L. (2013) In: Information centric networking over SDN and OpenFlow: Architectural aspects and experiments on the OFELIA testbed, Computer Networks, 57(16), 13 Nov 2013, pp 3207–.3221, ISSN 1389-1286
23. van Adrichem NLM, Kuipers FA (2015) NDNFlow: software-defined named data networking. In: 2015 1st IEEE conference on Network Softwarization (NetSoft), London, 2015, pp 1–5
24. Nguyen XN, Saucez D, Turletti T (2013) Efficient caching in content-centric networks using OpenFlow. INFOCOM, Proceedings IEEE, Turin, 2013, pp 1–2
25. TalebiFard P, Ravindran R, Chakraborti A, Pan J, Mercian A, Wang G, Leung VCM (2015) An information centric networking approach towards contextualized edge service. In: 12th Annual IEEE Consumer Communications and Networking Conference (CCNC), Las Vegas, 2015, pp 250–255
26. Mai HL , Nguyen NT, Doyen G, Ploix A, Cogranne R (2016) On the readiness of NDN for a secure deployment: the case of pending interest table. In: proceedings of the 10th IFIP WG 6.6 International Conference on Autonomous Infrastructure, Management, and Security, AIMS 2016. pp 98–110. Lecture Notes in Computer Science 9701. Springer International Publishing, 2016

Théo Combe is a research engineer at Thales Services. He graduated from the Ecole Polytechnique, France, and followed a double degree at Télécom ParisTech, where he studied networks and cybersecurity. In 2014, he had a 4-month internship at the National Cybersecurity Agency (ANSSI, Paris, France) on side-channel attacks against asymmetric cryptography. In 2015, he worked at Thales Communications and Security in the SDN-NFV research group, as a part-time project along with his studies.

Dr. Wissam Mallouli is currently a research and development project manager at Montimage, France. He received his PhD in computer science from Telecom and Management SudParis (France) in 2008. His topics of interest cover formal testing and monitoring of functional, performance, and security aspects of networks and cloud-based systems. He is working on several European and French research projects. He also participates to the program/organizing committees of numerous national and international conferences. He published more than 30 papers in conference proceedings, books, and journals.

Thibault Cholez is an associate professor at the University of Lorraine. He teaches at TELECOM Nancy, an engineering school in computer science, and undertakes his research activities within the laboratory Loria/Inria Nancy-Grand Est. He previously got a PhD degree in Computer Science from Henri-Poincare University. His research interests concern data network monitoring and analytics, with a particular focus on content diffusion protocols and their security.

Guillaume Doyen is an associate professor in University of Technology of Troyes (UTT), France, since 2006. He is affiliated to the Charles Delaunay Institute (ICD – UMR CNRS 6281) where he is the cochair of the cybersecurity transversal research project. His current research interest focuses on the design of autonomous management and control solutions applied to the performance and security of content distribution and cloud computing. He has published more than 40 papers in the network and service management community. As an active member, he is a TPC member of high-venue conferences (e.g., IEEE/IFIP CNSM, IEEE/IFIP IM and NOMS, IFIP AIMS) and a regular reviewer for the top-related journals (e.g., IEEE CommMag, IEEE TNSM, Springer JNSM, Wiley IJNM) and has been a cochair of several events (e.g., ManSDN/NFV, IFIP AIMS). He has been involved in several research projects (e.g., ANR-Doctor, IA-Request, ANR BBNet).

Dr. Bertrand Mathieu joined France Telecom, Orange Labs, in 1994. He received a Diploma of Engineering in Toulon, the MSc degree from the University of Marseille, and the PhD degree from the University Pierre et Marie Curie in Paris. Until 1999, he worked on network management including interfaces, protocols, and platforms. Since 1999, he is working on distributed computing, programmable networks, and he is currently focusing his research activity on dynamic overlay networks, P2P networks, and information-centric networking. He contributed to several national and European projects (Corsica, Safari, FAIN, Ambient Networks, OneLab, P2Pim@ges, Envision, eCousin, Doctor). He published more than 50 papers in international conferences, journals, or books. He is member of several conferences of Technical Program Committee and an IEEE and SEE senior member.

Edgardo Montes de Oca graduated as engineer in 1985 from Paris XI University, Orsay, and DEA from Paris VI, Paris. He has worked as research engineer in the Alcatel Corporate Research Center in Marcoussis, France, and in Ericsson's research center in Massy, France. In 2004 he founded Montimage and is currently its CEO. Montimage specializes in the development of network and application monitoring tools for performance and security analysis. His main interests are designing state-of-the-art tools to test and monitor applications and telecommunication protocol exchanges and the development of software solutions with strong performance and security requirements. He has participated in many research collaboration and product development projects for Alcatel, Ericsson, and Montimage (e.g., Diamonds-Itea2, SIGMONA-CelticPlus, SENDATE-CelticPlus, SISSDEN-H2020, DOCTOR-ANR). He is member of NetWorld2020 and has published many papers and book chapters on SDN/SVN, testing, network monitoring, and network security and performance.

Index

A

Acceptable use policy (AUP), 154
Access control lists (ACLs), 152
Administrative Function (ADMF), 58–59
Advanced persistent threats (APT), 216
Analytic Hierarchy Process, 208
Apache Spark-based analytics, 217–218
Application-level attacks, 174
Application Programming Interface (APIs),
        205
Attestation identity keys (AIKs), 106
Authentication, authorization, and accounting
        (AAA), 49–50, 133

B

Bandwidth depletion attacks, 174
Batch data processing, 220
Big data analytics
    alerts, 218
    analytics engines processes, 217–218
    APT, 216
    configuration, 220–222
    data processing pipelines, 217
    end-to-end security approach, 218
    machine learning, 218–220
    SIEM and logging systems, 215
    vNSFs role, 216–217
Botnets, 176
Broadband Network Gateway (BNG), 130
Broadband remote access server (BRAS), 130
Business support system/operations support
        system (BSS/OSS), 130

C

Certification authorities (CAs), 133
Cinder, 25, 65
Client Policy Handler, 160
Client Table Handler, 160

Cloud computing
    alternative IT infrastructure, 6
    NIST, 7–8
    provisioning services, 6–7
    security challenges, 13–14
    security requirements, 10–11
Cloud service provider (CSP), 175
Coalition tactical networks (CTN)
    situational awareness
        cybersecurity, 290–291
        OODA loop (*See* Observe, Orient,
            Decide and Act (OODA) loop)
        operational states, 285–286
        orientation phase, 289
    tactical environments
        autonomous vehicles, 277
        CoI, 291–292
        military and civilian contexts, 277
        satellite network, 277
        security, 278–279
        segments, 277–278
Cognitive data analysis engine, 206
Common Gateway Interface (CGI) module,
        161
Common Vulnerabilities and Exposures (CVE)
        database, 308
Community of interest (CoI), 291–292
Control plane (CP), 276, 286–288
Core Root of Trust for Measurement (CRTM),
        56
Cross-site scripting (XSS), 131
CyberCAPTOR
    attack graph approach, 317–318
    attack path, 318–319
    impact score and risk score, 318–319
    interactions, 320
    remediation, 319
    vulnerability scans, 317
Cybercrime techniques, 199–201
Cybersecurity, 208–209

© Springer International Publishing AG 2017
S.Y. Zhu et al. (eds.), *Guide to Security in SDN and NFV*, Computer
Communications and Networks, DOI 10.1007/978-3-319-64653-4

D
Data analysis and remediation engine (DARE)
    dashboard, 207
    data analytics engines, 206
    remediation engine, 206
Data plane (DP), 276, 286–288
Data Processor, 161
Deep packet inspection (DPI), 177, 213
Denial of service (DoS), 173
Directed acyclic graph (DAG), 318–319
Disrupt services (DoS), 310
Distributed denial of service (DDoS) attacks,
        311
    aggregated services, 175
    application-level attacks, 174
    bandwidth depletion, 174
    botnets, 176
    cloud services, 174–175
    cloud's on-demand resource, 176
    definition, 173–174
    detection and remediation
        fat-tree network topology, 188
        impact of DDoS attack, 188–190
        module deployment, 190–191
    isolation, 175
    large-scale availability, 175
    legacy defence systems
        deployment challenges, 177–179
        network functions virtualisation,
            181–182
        software-defined networking, 179–180
    prevalence, 175–176
    resource depletion, 174
    SDNFV-based security framework
        challenges, 186–187
        characteristics, 183–186
        high-level architecture, 182, 183
Distributed SDN Controller (dSDNC), 306
Docker virtual containers
    architecture, 114
    Deutsche Telekom, 113
    integrity verification, 113
    performance analysis, 115
DOCTOR virtualized infrastructure
    ICN, 304–305
    monitoring and managing, 303, 306–307
    NDN, 304–305
    security risks
        communications, 310–311
        features, 307
        host-location hijacking, 311
        IP and NDN domains, 312–314
        link fabrication, 312

    orchestrator, 310
    packet flooding, 311
    VIM, 311
    virtualization layer, 309–310
    VNFs, 308
Domain Name System (DNS), 188
Dynamic Host Configuration Protocol (DHCP)
        Server, 130
Dyn disrupted services, 176

E
Economic denial of service or sustainability
        (EDoS), 174
Elasticsearch, 176
Element management systems (EMS), 130
Element Manager (EM), 306
Endorsement key (EK), 106
ETSI Network Functions Virtualization (NFV),
        262–263
European Telecommunications Standards
        Institute (ETSI), 78
Event Handler, 159

F
Finite-state machine (FSM), 156
5G
    multi-operator orchestration, 256–258, 271
    SDN and NFV, 256
Fraudulent resource consumption (FRC), 174

G
Generic Routing Encapsulation (GRE), 130

H
Hardware security module (HSM), 46–47
Home gateway (HGW)
    home network LAN attacks
        historical reasons, 137–138
        layer 2 protocols, 138
        network functionalities, 138–139
        security problems, 139
        user session management, 139
    replacement ratio, 128
    vulnerabilities, 135–137
Hosted Communications Provider model, 40
Hosted Network Operator model, 40
HPE Virtual Application Networks (VAN), 117
HTTP/S events, 217
Hyperledger, 295

I

IaaS cloud platform
  overview of, 22–23
  security challenges, 22–24
  security solution recommendation, 24–25
ICMP packet, 161–162, 165–166
Identity and access management (IAM), 20–22
Incident Object Description Exchange Format
      (IODEF), 240
Industrial control system (ICS) security, 245
Industrial operating system (IOS), 245
Industry 4.0 security
  architectural scenario, 236–237
  attack scenario, 238–239
  communication data, traffic samples, 240
  engineering sources, 240
  enterprise management sources, 240
  event management, 240
  IDS, 241–242
  IUNO, 232
  machine-controlling software, 239
  ONF, 232, 233
  pre-Industry 4.0 production, 234–236
  relevance, 248
  remote maintenance
      dynamic firewalls, 245
      Netbiter communication gateways,
          243–245
      OPEX, 243
      vs. remote desktop, 243, 244
      requirements, 245–246
      SDN-based security architecture,
          246–248
      standards, 245
      VNC, 243
  vulnerable systems, 239
Information-centric networking (ICN),
      304–305
Infrastructure as a service (IaaS), 7
Infrastructure service provider (ISP), 18
Integrity measurement architecture (IMA),
      107–108, 118–119
Intelligence, surveillance, and reconnaissance
      (ISR) devices, 277
Interceptrelated information (IRI), 57
Interface to Network Security Functions
      (I2NSF) working group, 120
Internet Protocol (IP)-based communication,
      291
Internet Protocol Security (IPSec), 267–268
Intrusion detection and prevention (IDP), 182
Intrusion detection and prevention system
      (IDPS), 201

Intrusion Detection Message Exchange Format
      (IDMEF), 240
Intrusion detection system (IDS), 241–242
Intrusion detection system/intrusion prevention
      system (IDS/IPS) service, 307
Intrusion Prevention Systems (IPS), 214
IP Front End (IPFE), 130
ITU-T X.805 standard
  access control, 260–261
  authentication, data integrity, and
      non-repudiation, 260
  availability, 261–262
  control plane, 258, 259
  data confidentiality and privacy, 261
  (End-)user plane, 258, 259
  management plane, 258, 259

K

Kernel-based Virtual Machine (KVM), 140
Keystone, 23–24, 66, 68

L

Latent Dirichlet allocation (LDA), 221
Lawful interception (LI)
  ADMF, 58–59
  content of communication, 57
  cryptographic algorithms, 61
  HBRT, 60–61
  IRI, 57
  LI virtual machine, 58, 59
  operations and management systems, 62
  POI, 57, 58, 60
  reference points, 59, 60
  requirements, 57–58
  run-time techniques, 61
  system-hardening and logging techniques,
      61
  trombone effect, 59
Legacy defence systems
  deployment challenges
      cost and inefficient management, 178
      customised services, 179
      detection, 177
      lack of deployment flexibility, 178
      limited functionality, 179
      mitigation techniques, 177
      prevention, 177
      vendor lock-in, 178–179
  network functions virtualisation,
      181–182
  software-defined networking, 179–180

Levels of assurance (LOAs), 56, 120
Link layer discovery protocol (LLDP), 312
Locality, 112–113

M
Machine learning, 217–220, 241–242
Managed Network Service on Customer
        Premises Equipment, 40
Managed Network Service on Customer
        Premises model, 40
Management and orchestration (MANO)
    infrastructure integrity, 121
    I2NSF working group, 120
    NFV, 6
    SDOs, 119
    standardisation, 120
    TCG, 120
    trustworthiness, 119–120
mGuard Tele Service, 245
Mobile ad hoc network (MANET), 277–278
Monolithic Operator, 39
Montimage Monitoring Tool (MMT), 306
    collaboration, 317
    complementary and independent modules,
        314–315
    functionalities, 314
    NIDS, 316
    VNF, 316–317
Multi-administrator isolation, 51, 52

N
Naive Bayes classification, 206
Named Data Networking (NDN)
    CyberCAPTOR
        attack graph approach, 317–318
        attack path, 318–319
        impact score and risk score, 318–319
        interactions, 320
        remediation, 319
        vulnerability scans, 317
    MMT
        collaboration, 317
        complementary and independent
            modules, 314–315
        functionalities, 314
        NIDS, 316
        VNF, 316–317
    virtualization
        components, 302
        DOCTOR (*See* DOCTOR virtualized
            infrastructure)
        network control, 302–303

overview of, 303–304
National Institute of Standards and Technology
        (NIST), 7–8
Netbiter QuickConnect software, 244
Netflow events, 217
Network access control (NAC), 155
Network Address Port Translation (NAPT),
        130
Network address translation (NAT), 165,
        235–236
Network appliances and functionality (VNFs),
        212
Network-based intrusion detection system
        (NIDS), 316
Network functions virtualization (NFV),
        211–212
    access control, 92
        authorization, 96
        characteristics, 93
        example, 94–95
        operating systems, 93–94
        operations, 96
        policies, 95
        resources, 95–96
        trusted parties, 93
        users, 96
    analysis, 88–91
    architecture of, 6–7
    bootstrapping trust
        assurance level, 53
        certification authority, 53
        chain of trust, 56
        CRTM, 56
        hypervisor, 55
        life cycle, 53
        LOAs, 56
        lowest plane, 51, 53
        platform's integrity information, 55
        remote attestation, 55
        run-time attestation, 57
        secure boot and measured boot, 55
        secure wipe and verified destruction, 53
        trustworthy boot, 55
        virtual network appliances, 53
    centralized security management, 38
    challenges, 38
    classification, 39
    cloud environment, 38–39
    decomposition, 36
    deploying security updates, 38
    end-to-end connectivity, 36
    ETSI security problem
        Application Providers, 40
        authenticated time service, 50

customer premises equipment, 40
customer premises model, 40
Hosted Communications Provider, 40
Hosted Network Operator, 40
management infrastructure, 44–45
Monolithic Operator, 39
multi-administrator isolation, 51, 52
Operator Hosting Virtual Network
    Operators, 40
performance isolation, 48–49
private keys, 50
reverse engineering and side-channel
    attacks, 41
secure crash, 47–48
secured boot, 45–47
technical and contractual position, 41
topology validation and enforcement,
    42–44
user/AAA, 49–50
virtualized test andmonitoring
    functions, 50–51
hypervisor introspection, 38
incident response, 38
infrastructure transitions, 36
integrated architecture, 78–80
introspection, 37
lawful interception (*See* Lawful interception
    (LI))
legacy defence systems, 181–182
limitation, 35
limitations, 91–92
MANO, 6
NDN (*See* Named Data Networking
    (NDN))
ONF, 36
OpenStack security
    catalog service, 69
    compute agent, 66
    controller node, 66–67
    Keystone project, 66, 68
    Message Queue Server, 67
    physical network isolation, 67
    PKI infrastructure, 68
    scheduler, 67
    SuperTel, 69
    telemetry agents, 66
    UUID, 69
orchestration andmanagement, 80–82
platform security
    access control guarantees, 86
    accountability, 87
    compromised components, 86
    deployment, 83, 86
    enforcement, 87

type of network, 83–85
    validation, 88
resource distribution, 97
security challenges, 11–12
security management and monitoring,
    62–64
security requirements, 10–11
service chain, 75, 78
service orchestration, 77–78
switching elements, 6
Telco cloud, 34
TPM (*See* Trusted Platform Module
    (TPM))
vHGW device (*See* Virtualization of the
    home gateway (vHGW) device)
virtualization technologies, 5–6
VNFs, 78
Network Time Protocol (NTP), 133, 188
Next-generation firewalls (NGFW), 178
NFV security management functional block
    (NSM-FB), 63
Northbound interface (NBI), 5, 28, 276
Nova, 24

O
Observe, Orient, Decide and Act (OODA) loop
    control and data plane components, 282,
        286–288
    example, 286
    phases, 285–287
OpenAttestation (OAT) framework, 118
Open Cloud Integrity Technology, 209
OpenFlow protocol, 242
Open Networking Foundation (ONF), 4–5, 78,
    232, 233
Open Platform for NFV (OPNFV), 78, 80
Open-source TC Linux-based platform (Open
    TC), 211
OpenStack security
    catalog service, 69
    challenges, 22–24
    compute agent, 66
    compute node, 66
    controller node, 66–67
    deployment, 66
    documentation, 65
    HTTP server, 65
    Keystone project, 66, 68
    Message Queue Server, 67
    Neutron project, 65
    overview of, 22–23
    physical network isolation, 67
    PKI infrastructure, 68

OpenStack security (*cont.*)
  PKI token structure, 69–70
  scheduler, 67
  security solution recommendation, 24–25
  SuperTel, 69
  Swift and Cinder, 65
  telemetry agents, 66
  UUID, 69
Operational expenses (OPEX) savings, 128
Operation and management (OAM)
         verification, 121
Operator Hosting Virtual Network Operators,
         40

P
Path Computation Element (PCE)
         confidentiality, 269–270
Pattern-based analytics, 217
"Pay-as-you-Go" pricing model, 175
Personal Computer over Internet Protocol
         (PCoIP), 243
Platform as a service (PaaS), 7
Platform Configuration Registers (PCRs)
  benefits, 106
  digital signature, 106–107
  extend, 106
  service measurement, 107–108
  storing measurements, 105
  trusted boot, 107
  verification, 108–109
Point of interception (POI), 57, 58
Policy Enforcer, 159
Policy Table, 159, 160
Privacy certification authority (PrivacyCA),
         106
Programmatic incident investigation, 242
Protocol data units, 276
Public-key infrastructure (PKI), 133, 269

R
Real-time data processing, 220
Remediation engine, 206, 221–222
Remote Authentication Dial-In User Service
         (RADIUS) authentication, 130
Remote Framebuffer Protocol (RFP), 243
Resource depletion attacks, 174
Revocation Table, 160
Root of Trust for Measurement (RTM), 56
Rule-based anomaly detection, 241
Ryuretic controller
  Event Handler, 159
  packet object, 157, 158

Policy Enforcer, 159
Policy Table, 159, 160

S
SDN controller (SDNC), 276
  alternative coalition
      advantage of, 293
      broker architecture, 293–295
      cybersecurity, 295–297
      dynamic CoI, 292–293
      federated architecture, 293–295
  bandwidth constraints, 280
  challenges, 281–282
  disruptions and failures, 280
  life cycle, 282–283
  short lifetime, 280
  tactical network nodes, 283–285
SDNFV-based security framework
  challenges, 186–187
  characteristics, 183–186
  high-level architecture, 182, 183
Secure and trusted channel (STC), 210
Secure crash, 47–48
Secured boot, 45–47
Security-as-a-service (SecaaS), 208
Security data analysis engine, 206
Security incident and event management
         (SIEM) systems, 215
Security policy transition
  acceptable use policy, 154
  ACLs, 152, 153
  communication channel, 161–162
  finite-state machine, 156
  FlowNAC, 156
  ICMP packet notifications, 165–166
  NAC, 155, 167
  NAT, 165
  network operator sets, 153, 154, 168
  operational expenses, 153
  patch compliance, 153
  PolicyCop, 156
  Ryuretic controller, 157–159
      Event Handler, 159
      packet object, 157, 158
      Policy Enforcer, 159
      Policy Table, 159, 160
  spoofed ARP packets, 163–164
  TCG, 169
  test environment, 162–163
  traffic redirect, 166–167
  Trusted Agent, 154, 159–161
  validation authority, 154
Security requirements

ETSI NFV, 262–263
ITU-T X.805 standard
    access control, 260–261
    authentication, data integrity, and
        non-repudiation, 260
    availability, 261–262
    control plane, 258, 259
    data confidentiality and privacy, 261
    management plane, 258, 259
    (End-)user plane, 258, 259
SHIELD project
    big data
        alerts, 218
        analytics engines processes, 217–218
        APT, 216
        configuration, 220–222
        data processing pipelines, 217
        end-to-end security approach, 218
        machine learning, 218–220
        SIEM and logging systems, 215
        vNSFs role, 216–217
    cybercrime techniques, 199–201
    DARE layer, 206–207
    deployment network, 203–204
    detection and protection, 202–203
    functioning, 203
    global cybersecurity, 208–209
    high-level architecture, 202
    infrastructure verification
        attestation result, 210
        ETSI NFV standardisation group, 211
        MACsec/IPsec, 210
        node attestation, 210
        Open TC, TClouds, and SECURED,
            211
        periodic attestation, 211
        SDN-fashioned architecture, 211
        secure channel, 210
        STC, 210
        TPM, 209
        trusted computing, 209
        vNSF attestation, 210
    ISPs, 208
    remediation and recovery, 221–222
    SecaaS, 208
    vNSFs
        components, 202
        IDPS, 201–202
        monitoring, 212–213
        orchestrator, 205, 214–215
        policy enforcement, 204
        reacting security services, 213–214
        SMEs, 201
        store, 205

        traffic monitoring, 204
        types, 204–205
Small and medium enterprises (SMEs), 200,
    201
Software as a service (SaaS), 7
Software-defined networking (SDN)
    access control, 92
        authorization, 96
        characteristics, 93
        example, 94–95
        operating systems, 93–94
        operations, 96
        policies, 95
        resources, 95–96
        trusted parties, 93
        users, 96
    alternative coalition
        advantage of, 293
        broker architecture, 293–295
        cybersecurity, 295–297
        dynamic CoI, 292–293
        federated architecture, 293–295
    analysis, 88–91
    Industry 4.0 security (See Industry 4.0
        security)
    infrastructure layer, 4–5
    integrated architecture, 78–80
    legacy defence systems, 179–180
    limitations, 91–92
    NDN (See Named Data Networking
        (NDN))
    ONF, 4–5
    OpenFlow, 5
    orchestration andmanagement, 80–82
    platform security
        access control guarantees, 86
        accountability, 87
        compromised components, 86
        deployment, 83, 86
        enforcement, 87
        type of network, 83–85
        validation, 88
    resource distribution, 97
    security challenges, 12–13
    security policy transition framework (See
        Security policy transition)
    security requirements, 10–11
    service chain, 75, 78
    service orchestration, 77–78
    tactical environments
        bandwidth constraints, 280
        challenges, 281–282
        disruptions and failures, 280
        life cycle, 282–283

Software-defined networking (SDN) (*cont.*)
  short lifetime, 280
    tactical network nodes, 283–285
  TPM (*See* Trusted Platform Module
      (TPM))
  VNFs, 78
Software-defined security (SDSec)
  Catbird, 26
  combat security attacks, 25
  design of, 25
  orchestration, 25
  SDS$_2$, 26–29
  vArmour, 26
  vShield, 26
Software-defined security service (SDS$_2$)
  architecture of, 26–27
  controller, 27–28
  data center security, 28–29
  NBI, 28
  SBI, 28
  VSF, 28
Southbound interface (SBI), 5, 28, 232–233,
    276
Standards Developing Organisations (SDOs),
    119
Stored Measurement Log (SML), 107–108
Supervised learning, 219
Support vector machine (SVM), 206

T
TC-based cloud computing platform
    (TClouds), 211
Threat analysis method, 264
  configuration issues, 266–267
  destruction of information, 266
  disclosure of information, 266–267
  flooding, DDoS, and interruption of
      services, 267
  gaps
    PCE confidentiality, 269–270
    privacy, 270, 271
    trust, 269
  multi-provider scenario, 264, 265
  orchestrator hijacking and service
      interruption, 266
  privacy issues, 266
  SDN controller hijacking, 266
  SDN/NFV domain, 264–265
  security schemes, 267–269
Transmission Control Protocol (TCP), 291
Trusted Agent, 157, 159–160

Client and Revocation Tables, 160
Client Policy Handler, 160
Client Table Handler, 160
Data Processor, 161
testing requirements, 167
web servers, 161
Trusted boot, 45–47
Trusted computing (TC), 209–211
Trusted computing base (TCB), 61, 117
Trusted Computing Group (TCG), 105, 169
Trusted Platform Module (TPM), 209
  integrity verification
    controller and switches, 116
    dynamic configurations, 115
    legacy networking, 116
    OpenFlow, 117
    operations, 117
    synchroni-sation, 116
    trusted computing techniques, 117
    VAN, 117
  MANO components
    infrastructure integrity, 121
    I2NSF working group, 120
    SDOs, 119
    standardisation, 120
    TCG, 120
    trustworthiness, 119–120
  remote attestation
    AIKs, 106
    analysis customisation, 118
    chain of trust, 105
    EK, 106
    incremental reporting, 118–119
    PCRs, 105–106
    periodic attestation, 119
    PrivacyCA, 106
    process, 106–107
    quote, 106
    root of trust for measurement, 105
    service measurement, 107–108
    trusted boot, 107
    verification, 108–109
  virtualisation
    Docker virtual containers (*See* Docker
        virtual containers)
    services, 109
    software entity, 109
    virtualised instances, 109
    vTPM (*see* Virtual Trusted Platform
        Module (vTPM))
Trust Monitor (TM), 210–211
Trustworthy boot process, 55

U

Unified Extensible Firmware Interface (UEFI), 46

Unmanned aerial vehicles (UAVs), 180, 277, 298

Unsupervised learning, 219

V

vCPE-NAT, 130

Virtual intrusion detection VNF (vIDS), 146

Virtualised security appliances
  monitoring vNSFs, 212–213
  NVF, 212
  reacting vNSFs, 213–214
  vNSF orchestrator, 214–215

Virtualization
  data centers storage, 9–10
  elastic and scalable resource, 9
  IAM, 20–22
  isolation
    example, 17–18
    ISP, 18
    standard security solutions, 20
    types, 18–19
  multiplexing, aggregation/emulation, 8–9
  security issues, 15–16
  solutions and guidance, 16–17
  virtual machines, 9

Virtualization of the home gateway (vHGW) device
  architecture design, 128–130
  design solutions
    COTS Server OS, 142
    diagnostic process, 141
    larger-scale disruption, 142
    management interfaces, 141
    patching and upgrading processes, 142
    performance isolation, 143
    power cord, 142
    regulatory compliance, 141
  diagnostic tool, 146
  inherent risks
    home LAN extensibility, 143–144
    security, 144
    user sessions, 144
  IPFE, 144
  local functionalities, 128
  OPEX savings, 128
  security architecture, 140
  security framework
    challenges, 130
    ETSI NFV ISG security, 132–134
    network architectures, 131–132

    residential broadband Internet access service (*See* Home gateway (HGW))
    risk analysis, 134–135
    security KPIs, 145
    third-party security tools, 146
    vIDS, 146
    VSP, 129, 145

Virtualized infrastructure manager (VIM), 311

Virtualized network func-tions (VNFs), 132–133

Virtual LAN (VLAN), 131

Virtual machine (VM). *See* Virtual Trusted Platform Module (vTPM)

Virtual machine introspection (VMI), 308

Virtual machine manager (VMM). *See* Virtual Trusted Platform Module (vTPM)

Virtual Network Computation (VNC), 243

Virtual network functions (VNFs)
  components, 302
  DOCTOR (*See* DOCTOR virtualized infrastructure)
  MMT, 316–317
  network control, 302–303
  overview of, 303–304

Virtual network security functions (vNSFs)
  components, 202
  IDPS, 201–202
  monitoring, 212–213
  orchestrator, 205, 214–215
  policy enforcement, 204
  reacting security services, 213–214
  SMEs, 201
  store, 205
  traffic monitoring, 204
  types, 204–205

Virtual private network (VPN), 131

Virtual security functions (VSFs), 26–28

Virtual Trusted Platform Module (vTPM)
  architecture, 110–111
  components, 110
  limitations, 112–113
  performance analysis, 111–112

VNF layer security function (VSF), 63

vNSF orchestrator (vNSFO), 205

W

Web servers, 161

X

Xen hypervisor. *See* Virtual Trusted Platform Module (vTPM)

Printed in the United States
By Bookmasters